CULTURE, TRADITION AND SOCIETY IN THE WEST AFRICAN NOVEL

AFRICAN STUDIES SERIES

The African Studies Series is a collection of monographs and general studies which reflect the interdisciplinary interests of the African Studies Centre at Cambridge. Volumes to date have combined historical, anthropological, economic, political and other perspectives. Each contribution has assumed that such broad approaches can contribute much to our understanding of Africa, and that this may in turn be of advantage to specific disciplines.

BOOKS IN THIS SERIES

1 *City Politics: A Study of Léopoldville, 1962–63*
   J. S. La Fontaine

2 *Studies in Rural Capitalism in West Africa*
   Polly Hill

3 *Land Policy in Buganda*
   Henry W. West

4 *The Nigerian Military: A Sociological Analysis of Authority and
   Revolt 1960–67*
   Robin Luckham

5 *The Ghanaian Factory Worker: Industrial Man in Africa*
   Margaret Peil

7 *The Price of Liberty: Personality and Politics in Colonial Nigeria*
   Kenneth W. J. Post and George D. Jenkins

8 *Subsistence to Commercial Farming in Present-day Buganda: An
   Economic and Anthropological Survey*
   Audrey I. Richards, Ford Sturrock and Jean M. Fortt (eds.)

9 *Dependence and Opportunity: Political Change in Ahafo*
   John Dunn and A. F. Robertson

10 *African Railwaymen: Solidarity and Opposition in an East African
    Labour Force*
    R. D. Grillo

11 *Islam and Tribal Art in West Africa*
    René A. Bravmann

12 *Modern and Traditional Elites in the Politics of Lagos*
    P. D. Cole

13 *Asante in the Nineteenth Century: The Structure and Evolution of a
    Political Order*
    Ivor Wilks

14 *Culture, Tradition and Society in the West African Novel*
    Emmanuel Obiechina

15 *Saints and Politicians: Essays in the Organisation of a Senegalese
    Peasant Society*
    Donal B. Cruise O'Brien

CULTURE, TRADITION AND
SOCIETY IN THE
WEST AFRICAN NOVEL

EMMANUEL OBIECHINA

Lecturer in English, University of Nigeria, Nsukka

CAMBRIDGE UNIVERSITY PRESS

CAMBRIDGE

LONDON · NEW YORK · MELBOURNE

Published by the Syndics of the Cambridge University Press
The Pitt Building, Trumpington Street, Cambridge CB2 1RP
Bentley House, 200 Euston Road, London NW1 2DB
32 East 57th Street, New York, NY 10022, USA
296 Beaconsfield Parade, Middle Park, Melbourne 3206, Australia

Library of Congress Catalogue Card Number: 74-80358

ISBNs:
0 521 20525 5 hard covers
0 521 09876 9 paperback

First published 1975

Typesetting by Linocomp Ltd, Marcham, Oxon.

Printed in Great Britain
at the University Printing House, Cambridge
(Euan Phillips, University Printer)

The extracts from *Things Fall Apart* by Chinua Achebe © 1959 are
reprinted by permission of Astor-Honor Inc., New York, N.Y. 10017, and
William Heinemann Ltd; the extracts Copyright © 1964 by Chinua Achebe
are reprinted from *Arrow of God* by Chinua Achebe by permission of
The John Day Company Inc., an Intext publisher, and William Heinemann
Ltd; the extracts from Nkem Nwankwo's novel, *Danda*, and Gabriel Okara's
novel, *The Voice*, are reprinted by permission of André Deutsch Ltd; the
extracts from Elechi Amadi's novel, *The Concubine*, are reprinted by
permission of Heinemann Educational Books Ltd.

Contents

Acknowledgements   vii

Part I: Introduction

1   Background to the West African novel   3
     Literacy and the broadening of consciousness   3
     The spread of mass media   7
     The literate middle class and the rise of the novel   8
     Cultural nationalism   14
     Foreign novelists on West Africa   17
     Oral tradition   25

Part II: Domestication of the novel in West Africa

2   Oral and literary traditions in West Africa   31
3   Nature, music and art   42
4   Characterization   82
5   Space and time   122
6   Setting   140
7   Language   155

Part III: The changing scene

8   Culture contact and culture conflict   201
9   Conclusion   260

     Notes and references   267

     Bibliography   279

     Index   285

Acknowledgements

In its original form this work was submitted to the University of Cambridge as a dissertation for the degree of Doctor of Philosophy. Considerable structural changes have however been made in the book.

The novels themselves provide most of the background material for the discussion. Where necessary, I have gladly gone to the specialists – to sociologists and anthropologists especially, but also to the historians, theologians, etc. – for the evidence with which I have attempted to elucidate the subject. I have acknowledged my various indebtedness to these different sources in the accompanying notes.

I wish to thank the following people for the encouragement, advice, and suggestions which I have received from them during the course of the investigation leading to the preparation of the book: Lord Ashby, Master of Clare College, Cambridge; Professor J. R. Northam, former Senior Tutor, Clare College; Dr John Newton, Fellow of Clare College; Professor Edward Shils of King's College, Cambridge, and the University of Chicago; Professor Molly Mahood, former Professor of English, University of Ibadan; Professor K. Onwuka Dike, former Vice-Chancellor of the University of Ibadan; and Mr John Ramsaran, former Senior Lecturer in the Department of English, University of Ibadan. I am also very grateful to my supervisor, Professor Jack Goody, Fellow of St John's College, Cambridge and formerly Director of the Cambridge Institute of African Studies; Dr Tony Tanner of King's College and the Department of English, Cambridge; and Dr Godfrey Lienhardt of Oxford University, who gave me invaluable advice about the organization of my material. I am indebted to several friends, especially Dr Ikenna Nzimiro of the Department of Social Anthropology, University of Nigeria, Nsukka; and Cristian Huneeus of Centro de Estudios Humanisticos, Universidad de Chile, with whom I discussed aspects of the subject. I wish also to thank the Ford Foundation for making a research grant available to me, Clare College, Cambridge, for the generous help and sympathetic attention which it accorded me during the period of the research and the Cambridge University African Studies Centre for allowing me facilities for this work. I am also grateful to my friend Goddy Nwili Okoli, Sub-Librarian, University of Nigeria, Nsukka, for the indexing of the work. Above all, I am much indebted to my wife, Maria, without whose constant support and encouragement it would have been difficult to do the work.

November 1974   E.N.O.

Our women made black patterns on their bodies with the juice of the *uli* tree. It was beautiful, but it soon faded. If it lasted two market weeks it lasted a long time. But sometimes our elders spoke about *uli* that never faded, although no one had ever seen it. We see it today in the writing of the white man. If you go to the native court and look at the books which clerks wrote twenty years ago or more, they are still as they wrote them. They do not say one thing today and another tomorrow, or one thing this year and another next year. Okoye in the book today cannot become Okonkwo tomorrow. In the Bible Pilate said: "What is written is written." It is *uli* that never fades.

Isaac Okonkwo in *No Longer at Ease*

Each generation must, out of relative obscurity, discover its mission, fulfil it, or betray it.

Fanon

I INTRODUCTION

I

Background to the West African novel

The process of modernization powerfully transforms individual lifeways.
The move from the familiar and deeply personal life of a family farm
in an isolated village to the strange impersonality of a "job" in a busy
city crowded with unknown persons is one such transformation.
Daniel Lerner in *The Passing of Traditional Society*

The relationship between literature and society has long been recognized;
but it has not always been fully appreciated how far a particular society
both influences the themes and subject matter of its representative literary
types and also profoundly affects their formal development. Though most
commentators on West African fiction are quick to point out its main
peculiarities, they sometimes fail to see that these are clearly determined
by the West African cultural tradition and environment. The result is that
such commentators tend to expect West African writers to write like
writers with different cultural and environmental compulsions.

This study is an attempt to establish the determining background factors of the West African novel. It relates the writing to their cultural and
environmental situation; it aims to show that the changing cultural and
social situation in West Africa both gave rise to the novel there, and in
far-reaching and crucial ways conditioned the West African novels' content, themes and texture.

Literacy and the broadening of consciousness

The most important single factor is the introduction of literacy into West
Africa where, before, the dominant cultural tradition had been based on
the spoken word.[1] Literacy is crucial to the emergence of the novel, because the novel is meant to be read by the individual in quiet isolation,
and complex narrative is more easily sustained and followed by reading it
than by hearing it.[2] Moreover the achievement of literacy produces psychological and social capacities in the individual which facilitate the growth
of the novel.

The spread of literacy has been, obviously, a major source of change in
human life and society. Richard Hoggart's *The Uses of Literacy* describes
how the establishment of mass literacy introduced far-reaching changes
in the culture and social habits of the British working class. The introduc-

tion of literacy into the predominantly non-literate West African societies brought about an even more profound social change. And this, in turn, registers unmistakably in the history and content of the novel in West Africa.

The novel demands both from the novelist and from the reader a gift of empathy, the ability to slip imaginatively into circumstances and conditions of life beyond their immediate milieu. Writing or reading a novel implies this widening of the imaginative capability of writer and audience, so that the one can manage a faithful portrayal of social reality and the other an adequate reception of the vicarious experience. The situation implies a fundamental rapport between novelist and reader. Literacy mediates between the novelist and the reader and makes the rapport possible.

Both the novelist and reader are themselves products of a literary tradition which gives the capacity and training that the mind requires to absorb facts, realities and experiences which may not be part of the immediate milieu. Literacy increases the mobility of the individual mind by widening the individual's experience and his imaginative capacity to enter into new situations, or at least to envisage them with a fair degree of certainty. The introduction of literacy into West Africa therefore necessarily involved a profound change both in the traditional mode of acculturation and in the psychological outlook of the people. As David Riesman observed in *The Lonely Crowd*, literacy and written literature are potent factors in the shift from tradition-direction to inner-direction in the education of the individual . . . and in the shaping of individual attitudes and values.[3] Literacy increases individual awareness of separateness from the collectivity and increases the power to enter imaginatively into other individualities in a way not possible within the oral culture.

Before the introduction of Western literary education, African children were inducted into the traditional way of life in two ways: by formal teaching in initiation ceremonies, and by informal teaching in seeing and following the examples of grown-ups – through "watching and imitating" as Phoebe and Simon Ottenberg have called it. By participating in the everyday life of the community they came to know the rights and duties of the individual, the values, beliefs and mores of the community, the sanctions and etiquette of social behaviour; and in the same way they acquired a knowledge of the material repertoire of the culture. Cultural content and cultural behaviour were transmitted to the individual by contact and deliberate induction. Experience outside the immediate cultural environment was beyond individual apprehension because it was inaccessible to the individual through traditional education. The individual therefore tended to see the world in terms of his own circumscribed milieu, and to apprehend only those experiences which had been culturally determined for him. The chief effect of the introduction of Western education was to break the psychic insularity of traditional education and limited physical mobility, and to substitute for it a cosmopolitan and mobile psyche.

Through the introduction of literacy, the corpus of Western, indeed world civilization, its institutions and values, arts and sciences, philosophies and theology, its aesthetic values, and the artefacts of its material culture were made available to people in West Africa and, as James Coleman says, "awakened new aspirations, quickened the urge toward new emulation and provided the notions". Moreover, the use of a cosmopolitan language like English as a medium of instruction provides a vital link for West African peoples who speak different mother-tongues: this encourages greater physical mobility and consequently the broadening of their social as well as psychological outlook.

The introduction of Western education, the creation of Westernized urban settlements (as distinct from traditional urban settlements), and the establishment of a cash economy and modern industries opened new opportunities to the individual, and drew together people from different ethnic areas into urban aggregations. To fit into the economic scheme the individual had to acquire literacy, and through literacy some specialized skill or profession. The result was that he removed himself from a community where status and social hierarchy had determined the individual's place in society and where the individual counted in terms of the group to which he belonged, and entered a situation in which he was free to assert, if only in a limited way, his individuality. He thus predisposed himself to play a range of roles which did not exist in the traditional setting – roles depending on his level of education and professional training.

More important still, especially from the point of view of the novel, was that while following one skill or vocation the individual's broadened contact and multifarious attachments to others in different walks of life made him capable of envisaging himself imaginatively in any of the roles attached to the other professions and vocations. The school-teacher who can imagine himself as a daring leader of the underworld can, if he turns his mind to novel-writing and if he has the gifts of the novelist, be expected to explore the life of his hero with a reasonable degree of conviction; and his readers can be expected, if he has done his job competently and if they are sufficiently imaginative, to enter into the life and circumstances of the hero.

The significance of the development of greater physical and imaginative mobility for the emergence of the novel in West Africa can be seen

5

by reference to the novelists themselves. We can take Achebe as an example. His first three novels deal with the impact of Western civilization on the traditional culture of Africa, seen in the life of two essentially traditional characters, Okonkwo (in *Things Fall Apart*) and Ezeulu (in *Arrow of God*), and the disintegrative forces of tradition and modernism on the character of a Western-educated Nigerian (*No Longer at Ease*). For all his middle-class educational background and upper-middle-class job, Achebe is able to enter imaginatively into the lives of his traditional characters and to explore the strains to which they are exposed as a result of the disruptive effect of a foreign culture on the relatively stable and self-sufficient culture they grew up in. His rural upbringing is an advantage in developing his peculiarly lucid insight into the predicament of his traditional characters, but he has never himself experienced the actual circumstances of Okonkwo or Ezeulu. His ability to portray them and their predicament convincingly shows his capability, extended by his literary education, which equips him to imagine people and circumstances in a historic setting, though the outline of that setting remains still visible. His Obi Okonkwo, though a graduate like himself, and a man of his own generation, is no self-portrait. Almost every point in Obi's life differs from Achebe's; that both of them have teacher–evangelist fathers is a coincidence. In the fourth novel, *A Man of the People*, we find a complex picture in which the point of view shifts rapidly between identification and dissociation, between the author's seeing things through the eye of the major character–narrator and standing aside to take a critical look at the narrator, a feat made possible by the author's imaginative nimbleness in moving between moral positions. For that reason the novel is a tribute to the kind of imaginative awareness which is the point and product of literary education. It follows the course of events so doggedly and intelligently in accordance with the truths of human and social behaviour that its fictional world and the world of conventional reality merge; the military *coup d'état* predicted in the novel actually happened while the novel was with the printers.

The multiplicity of imaginative detail, the social variety of the characters involved, the complexity and variety of personality involved, and the numerous hiatuses that have to be imaginatively overleaped between what is available in immediate experience and what must be anticipated, assumed or made up by the author, all these would have been too much to demand from the traditional imagination subsisting largely on the limited powers of the unaided memory and conditioned as it was by the orally transmitted knowledge of the group.

The spread of mass media

The broadening of empathetic power is also a function of mass communication. The media – newspapers, radio, television, cinema – also advance the process of modernization.

Through them the West African is made aware of "an infinite vicarious universe",[4] of diversity of peoples, climates and costumes, customs and manners, morals and values; diversity in all the things which compose a way of life. These media affect people in different ways according to the mode of appeal of each.

The function of the press in moulding opinion is too obvious to require comment. Access to the content of newspapers requires literacy. Apart from specialized articles, most of the content of newspapers is available to literate West Africans who have completed primary education. For those not literate in English there are vernacular newspapers. So the acquisition of literacy opens up for the individual this new way of absorbing ideas and of broadening his mind. He is exposed to a battery of fresh ideas through leading articles, readers' opinions and editorial comment. He is called upon to balance points of view, to sift evidence, to accept or reject opinions – in short to train his imagination to cope with situations within and sometimes outside his milieu, and to be involved in the lives and situations of other people. He is also introduced directly through advertising to the material repertoire of world industrial civilization.

The cinema, radio and, in recent times, television are accessible both to the literate and to the illiterate. Through suggestion they tend to affect the life-ways of traditional people and broaden their experience by introducing them to other ways of life. In West Africa, the mass media have disrupted the old social order and accelerated social change. They have rapidly expanded their audiences, and so their capacity for spreading new cultural influences is growing. Millions of people read English-language and vernacular newspapers, go to cinemas, listen to the radio and watch television; this is in stark contrast with the hundreds or the few thousands who once listened to the harangue of the "crier", or the smaller numbers in the country areas who spread "information" face to face. By extending cultural influence, especially by familiarizing the individual with different situations of life, by increasing his store of knowledge of material culture through their pictorial representation and by acquainting him with changes in the society in which he lives and the world outside it, the mass media have increased the individual's perceptive power, and could be said to have prepared the ground for the emergence of the novel.

The actual relationship between people working in the mass media and their audiences is not often direct or physical, but obviously the first group, by the very nature of their calling, must be interested in the lives and situations of their audience and are sometimes overwhelmingly tempted to explore them in a more intimate way through the medium of the novel. It is no coincidence that nearly all the West African novelists have at some time been involved in mass communications. Achebe was in broadcasting between 1954 and 1966, Ekwensi moved from broadcasting to the information service, Nwankwo was in *Drum* magazine before taking up radio work and later turned to newspaper work, Nzekwu was first a teacher and then went over to journalism, Gabriel Okara has been in the information service for the greater part of his working life, and Ayi Kwei Armah spent some time as a scriptwriter on Ghana Television.

The movement from mass communications to novel-writing is a natural one. The journalist, radio scriptwriter or announcer, film or television producer, in addition to his other functions, is an agent of change in the social system and in the personalities of his audience. As novelist he would be expected to explore characters in relation to social life. Having helped to direct change through the mass media and having an interest in human beings and social situations, the media man may find the novel suitable for a more direct and personal imaginative effort.

Ian Watt observes of Defoe and Richardson and their connection with the mass media of their time: "By virtue of their multifarious contacts with printing, bookselling and journalism, . . . they were in very direct contact with the new interests of the reading public."[5] Equally, the development of mass media in West Africa has helped to produce the kind of society in which the novel can subsist, and it had also provided the first group of West Africans whose contact with contemporary culture and people of different walks of life has qualified them to engage their creative energies in the exploration of character and society. Even novelists not directly concerned with mass communications are in touch with a cross-section of society or involved in the modernization process, and so they can feel the pulse of social and cultural movements among the population. Soyinka's work in the theatre and Amadi's and Conton's school-teaching gave them insight into cultural and human dispositions in the unfolding West African scene. In that regard, they are also exposed to the impulses that find creative outlet in the novel.

The literate middle class and the rise of the novel

Given the effect of literacy and the mass media in preparing the ground, psychologically and socially, for the emergence of the novel, it remains that the actual writing of novels tends to be confined to those who add a fairly high level of education to the basic intellectual sophistication needed to be able to cope with its technical demands. Just as the oral story-telling technique is acquired by constant attendance at story-telling sessions, that of the novel is likely to be achieved by a wide reading of novels and an understanding of the intricacies of characterization, plot, language, and social and psychological insight. The serious reading of novels in West Africa does not begin before the grammar school, so it follows that exposure to the novel takes place at that level of education, as is clearly borne out by the educational backgrounds of the novelists. Of the ten novelists whose works are studied here, all but two are university graduates, and those two have had full grammar school education or its equivalent. It is also no coincidence that all but one of the novelists were educated in the government colleges of Ibadan, Umuahia and Ughelli in Nigeria and Achimota in Ghana and at Fourah Bay College in Sierra Leone. These were the best secondary schools in English-speaking West Africa and provided the best education. They offered the best opportunities to the talented among them, preparing them for higher education and for their subsequent careers as writers. In other words the novelists belong to the cream of the modern educated West African middle class, the class that pioneered the novel in the other parts of the world. The story of the training of the literate middle class in West Africa can only be touched on here; but a few sentences are necessary to show the educational background and social circumstances which gave rise to the novel in West Africa.

Formal literary education was introduced in West Africa by the Christian missionaries, and was an offshoot of the evangelical and pietistic movement of late eighteenth- and early nineteenth-century Protestant Britain. The English philanthropists and abolitionists who between 1787 and 1800 encouraged the establishment of Freetown for freed African slaves also made sure that education and evangelization were focal points of the policy of those who ran the new settlement. From the first decade of the nineteenth century, elementary and grammar schools were set up in Freetown by various missionary bodies, and from the mid-nineteenth century elementary and grammar schools were established in such main coastal towns as Bathurst, Cape Coast, Accra and Lagos, as well as in Freetown. Wealthy education-conscious Africans in these coastal towns sent their children to school both locally and overseas, and these towns became centres of a small educated African elite of wealthy businessmen, lawyers, doctors, teachers, ministers of religion, architects and so on. Fourah Bay College, established in 1827, played an important role in the development of education both in Sierra Leone and all over West Africa.[6]

Education was utilitarian from the beginning. The spread of the Christian religion, the introduction of modern institutions and the running

9

of modern government required a cadre of literate men and women. Education was therefore geared towards producing clerks, teachers, evangelists and artisans – personnel for the lower ranks of the civil service and commercial enterprises and for teaching and missionary work. The Sierra Leoneans and the Ghanaians, because they had an early start over the Nigerians, were recruited into Nigeria and became known as "native foreigners". Some of them rose to prominent posts in the colonial administration.

West African education was based on the educational system in English schools. Especially in Sierra Leone, where the Creoles were distinctly affected by the evangelical Christianity of their Methodist and Church Missionary Society emancipators and teachers, it was old-fashioned, classical and theological rather than practical and scientific. The Victorian partiality for black-coated callings – clerkships and teaching – and the professions dominated the aspirations of the early middle-class coastal elite. (They were called "Black Victorians" and "Black Englishmen" by West Africans of later generations.)

Between the second half of the nineteenth century and the 1930s, the literate middle class grew gradually and was constantly being reinforced by immigrants from the West Indies and Brazil. Its members formed a sub-cultural group who entertained one another in newspapers and in journals, pamphlets and public addresses couched in elaborate Victorian prose. They also staged operas and plays which they reviewed by stringent European standards. Evidence from the journals and newspapers shows that the Black Victorians, like their counterparts in the metropolis, were interested in culture as the expression of the people's historical and contemporary experience and as a scale for the evaluation of human achievement, an unfortunate extension of scientific Darwinism into human institutions and cultures. Influenced by the climate of the time, some of the Black Victorians felt their traditional culture was of a lower order than the European culture and so strove to uphold the European and to show hostility towards the traditional culture. Others stood for African "authenticity" and preached the rehabilitation of African traditional culture in education and in creative art and literature.

Prominent among the supporters of the traditional culture were Dr Edward Wilmot Blyden, author of *Christianity, Islam and the Negro Race* (1888) and other polemical treatises against the anti-Negro philosophers of the nineteenth century, Dr Africanus Horton of Sierra Leone, an M.D. of Edinburgh University, who wrote *West African Countries and Peoples* (1868) and John Casely Hayford of Ghana who wrote *Gold Coast Native Institutions* and *Ethiopia Unbound: Studies in Race Emancipation* (1911). These were the pioneers of West Africa's cultural nationalism who spent their learning and intellectual energies in defence of the native heritage.

Below the highly educated gentlemen were the masses of less well-educated teachers, clerks and artisans, who could not share their elite culture and even satirized their Victorian tendencies by setting up anti-theatres like the Lagos "Melo Dramatic Society" which staged such plays as *Don't Use Big Words*. This was obviously a retaliation against the anti-traditional snobbery of the elite, some of whose members referred to vernacular plays as "low forms of heathenism",[7] and to national costume as "a recurrence of primitive quasi-nudity".[8]

Some West Africans in the latter group began, with the active collaboration of the missionaries, to record local history and the customs of their peoples, to write grammars and dictionaries of the indigenous languages, and to record the oral tradition, sometimes in the vernacular and sometimes in English. The missionaries, as in Europe after the fall of the Roman Empire, had earlier converted the vernaculars into writing. There is a parallel between the entry of European literary forms into West Africa and the introduction of Graeco-Roman models into Anglo-Saxon Britain by Augustine and his missionaries fourteen centuries before.

It is natural to ask why the novel did not develop in West Africa until the mid-twentieth century, even though there had been this educated middle-class elite from the mid-nineteenth century. There may be many reasons: the most important only need be mentioned here. First, despite their knowledge of Tennyson, Milton and Aristotle (they quoted from them in their essays and polemics), the coastal intellectual elite were essentially cultural parasites, despised by the British, whose culture they were assiduously cultivating; in their turn they despised African culture, which they regarded as uncivilized. "Couriferism" – an uncritical imitation of Western customs[9] – was not conducive to creative confidence. Status-consciousness, another aspect of their Victorian outlook, also inhibited literary creativity. The Black Victorians were keenly attached to the sedate and "respectable" professions, such as medicine, law and the Christian ministry; so far as literary interests were concerned, they shared the puritan suspicion of fiction as ineffectual, frivolous, even morally subversive. They never went beyond genteel literary activities such as writing journals, newspapers, diaries, polemical pamphlets and amateur anthropological monographs. At the lower level, "passing my Cantab" and the pressure to work for a certificate, a necessary passport to good employment, narrowed the scope of reading too much to allow for adequate cultivation of a distinct literary taste, one obvious prerequisite for the cultivation of the creative habit. Finally, the educated middle class was too small to offer a would-be novelist a large enough

11

potential audience. All in all, the social, psychological, cultural and educational conditions for the novel did not exist until the 1950s, but events were beginning to move towards it in the thirties.

The cultural watershed was the return of overseas-trained graduates with their roots in the hinterland. Most of these, like Azikiwe and Ojike of Nigeria, were graduates of American universities whose egalitarian philosophy inspired them to challenge the class and status assumptions of the old British-educated coastal elite. It was not so much the numbers of this new type of graduate which made their impact on the society so strong but the zest and enthusiasm they brought into national life. Ojike stirred his country by preaching a return to the traditional modes of life (his motto, "boycott the boycottable", fired the popular imagination). Azikiwe set up a chain of newspapers of which *The Pilot* (1938) was the most important, and which threw open its pages to the growing number of grammar school and elementary school leavers.[10] The pages of these papers were full of letters to the editor written by those who could never have been published by the earlier newspapers. The popular press thus set up gave the literate common man his first apprenticeship at literary expression in print. Others had put their literacy to use in private correspondence, by writing letters for themselves and their illiterate relations and neighbours; it was different to see oneself in print for everyone to see and read.

The major creative achievement came at the end of the Second World War, with the upsurge of popular pamphlet literature in the market town of Onitsha in eastern Nigeria. The first pamphlets appeared in 1947, the work of the new literates. School-teachers, low-level clerks, artisans, provincial correspondents of daily newspapers, railwaymen, literate farmers and even secondary school students now dealt with the problems and experiences of ordinary men and women and their efforts to cope with such matters as love and marriage, life in the town and especially how to earn and save money. For the first time, the common man's awareness of the new forces actively forming around him and shaping his consciousness and his destiny reached creative expression. For the first time, written literature became a medium for clarifying the issues of everyday life and experience, for seeking and proffering answers to social problems and for celebrating the realities of the changes sweeping over the land.

Among the factors which gave rise to the popular pamphlet literature in Onitsha were the location of the town and its market (the largest in West Africa), the post-war growth of the number of literate people there, the growth of the urban population, the spread of locally owned and operated printing presses, and the diversion of much post-war energy and wealth into commercial, industrial and technological development in and

around the Onitsha Market.[11] The pamphlets were aimed at an exclusively local audience, but offered an apprenticeship to the first prominent West African novelist, Cyprian Ekwensi. His short romance *When
Love Whispers* and a collection of Igbo folk-tales called *Ikolo the Wrestler
and Other Igbo Tales* were issued by a local publisher, Tabansi Bookshop,
in 1947. These were soon followed by other pamphlets, so that when
Ekwensi's first novel, *People of the City*, appeared in 1954, the pamphlet
literature had already become a flourishing phenomenon in Onitsha.

There is a direct connection between this popular writing and the novel,
going beyond their being written by the same person, a coincidence that
recalls the connection between Defoe and Grub Street pamphleteering and
the rise of the English novel. For the social conditions in which the popular
literature emerged were also auspicious to the novel; the cultural impulses
which led to the popular literature were in the end to drive the more
formally educated towards the novel; both forms show the same burgeon-
ing of a democratic social awareness, the same heightened sense of
individual identity, and the same urge to criticize and clarify the values
of society, to interpret and make sense of the changing world. The conditions which crystallized in Onitsha to give rise to the popular literature
were already widely diffused in West Africa, but once the Onitsha
phenomenon became recognized for what it represented in the cultural
history of the region, it was only a matter of time before the more sophisticated and intelligent authors went further.

Two books which appeared in Ghana before the popular literature
of Onitsha deserve notice. The first is John Casely Hayford's *Ethiopia
Unbound* (1911). Though it was presented as fiction, its interest was
fundamentally factual; it is fair to say that the fictional technique merely
subserves an argument, and that its concern with concepts such as African
colonial politics, native institutions, racial relationships, nationalism, the
problem of culture and allied questions far outweighs the interest in
human experience and action. The work also lacks the formal structure of
the novel. In fact, its sub-title, *Studies in Race Emancipation*, makes it
clear that Hayford is using the fictional element as a mere crutch. The
work belongs more to the tradition of Johnson's *Rasselas* than to that of a
true novel. Its urbane humour and unhurried prose look back also to the
eighteenth-century essayists.

The second prose work, R. E. Obeng's *Eighteenpence* (1943), in spite
of a brilliant literary commentary supplied by Dr J. B. Danquah, is a
thinly fictionalized didactic treatise on the theme of rags to riches. Obeng-
Akrofi, a poor man with determination, buys a matchet for eighteen pence
and uses it to attain prosperity. The fable is too simple, almost simplistic,
to be regarded as a novel. Indeed, it is more like a popular moral tale than

a novel. These early Ghanaian efforts indicate promise rather than actual fruition. The stage was not ready for the emergence of the novel because the social, psychological and cultural moment was yet to come.

In the 1940s, while popular authors were producing the pamphlet literature, the new elite was almost wholly absorbed in nationalist politics; but politics itself advanced the cause of creative writing by generating new intellectual movements and catering through popular newspapers for the rapidly growing literate class. It created mass enthusiasm for the nationalist movement and for the first time drew millions of urban and rural people into an active national commitment, which had the effect of broadening their social awareness.

The 1950s saw the beginning of important creative writing, including the novel, and a reaping of the harvest of the previous decade of educational expansion, urban growth and social changes. Political independence was on the way. The literate class had grown tremendously.[12] In Nigeria, for example, the number of native graduates was only 30 in the 1920s; in the 1950s it had grown to 1,000 with 3,800 in the process of becoming graduates. The number of secondary school graduate students in the 1920s was 200; in the 1950s it had rocketed to 31,000 with 31,500 in secondary schools. Where the total number of pupils in 1926 was 143,459, in the 1950s it had grown to 1,100,000.

Moreover, the university colleges of Ibadan and Ghana, which were founded in 1948, were in the fifties turning out graduates who had grown up under the influence of the new intellectual elite. The older generation among the elite had been totally taken up with nationalist politics, but the new educated middle class found employment in the government, administration and commercial bureaucracies. The more forcefully imaginative of them also directed their energies into creative writing, a situation of which the novel was a major beneficiary.

Cultural nationalism

The impulse towards the novel at this time bears testimony to the recovery of a creative confidence all but lost during the period of colonialism. But the fact that this creative phenomenon coincided with the period of great nationalist assertion has left its mark on the texture of the West African novel. The novelists were driven in the direction of cultural affirmation, towards expressing and affirming the past of the ex-colonial people, validating their autochthonous values (especially so far as these survive into the present), often at the expense of the received new values. The novels have, in other words, a strong impulse of cultural nationalism in them.

14

The close correspondence between political nationalism and literary nationalism is not an accident but a result of the nature of the colonial relationship. It is a well-known sociological fact that when the political relationship between two people is changed, all other types of relationships are adjusted to reflect the change, and myths and images are re-interpreted to justify and sustain the changed political situation. The matter is well illustrated by the history of European colonialism and even in pre-colonial "domination" states in Africa.

A direct result of the European colonization of Africa was the stereotyped image of Africa and Africans in the popular European imagination. The imposition of political control also involved a conscious or unconscious devaluation of the African culture. Loss of political freedom was inevitably attended by loss of cultural confidence by the Africans themselves. Furthermore, African "primitiveness", essentially a product of political domination, received, in the second part of the nineteenth century an almost authoritative stamp from anthropological Darwinism, which in the evolutionary scheme of cultural hierarchy placed African culture at the bottom and Western culture at the top of the scale. The popular image of Africa in the European mind was a place with primitive institutions, inhabited by primitive, irrational people on whom the civilizing will of Europe needed to be imposed.

Nationalist movements oriented towards the ending of colonial domination in Africa were understandably attended by cultural nationalism. Like similar movements in Latin America, Ireland and the dependent states of nineteenth-century Europe, African cultural nationalism took the form of the rehabilitation of the old cultural tradition and its values, including a reawakening of interest in the folklore, arts, music and cultural habits of the local people which most distinguish them from the metropolitan culture.[13]

In West Africa, cultural nationalism found expression in different ways. It was expressed in its most explicit conceptual terms in the Négritude movement in French-speaking Africa; and in English-speaking West Africa in the psycho-political concept of the African personality.

Négritude is the more coherent, because more ideological, of the two concepts. The movement took root among Negro African intellectuals of French expression whose French intellectual background with its "ideological orientation, neat intellectual habits and quality of elegance" equipped them to erect an ideological framework to meet a situation which African writers of English expression are content to treat in a more pragmatic manner. The word "Négritude" was invented in 1932 by Aimé Césaire, the coloured poet–politician from Martinique in his well-known poem "Cahier d'un retour au pays natal", but its ideology has been

15

defined by the Senegalese poet–politician, Léopold Sédar Senghor.[14] Its significance can be seen against the background of all nativistic ideologies. It repudiates certain intrinsic values of European civilization, such as its machine technology, its materialism, its success-orientation, its contractual determination of social relationship, and its slavish belief in the scientific planning of every detail of life. On the other hand, it extols the African's close attachment to the soil and to nature, the warmth of his humanity in personal relationships and his vitality and zest for life, which are not circumscribed by too much planning.

No such clear ideology has yet emerged in the writers of English expression; they would assent to Négritude in its insistence on the special qualities of the African, but their concept of the African personality differs from Négritude because it applies to the continental African alone whereas Négritude embraces all people of African origin including Afro-Americans. W. E. Abraham in *The Mind of Africa* sees the concept of the African personality as providing the framework for the reconstruction of post-independence Africa.[15]

Abraham's approach to cultural nationalism is pragmatic, as is the approach of most English-speaking West Africans. The French African writer, often a product of the French intellectual tradition, residing in Paris, which has been a centre of philosophical primitivism ever since the Rousseauist phantom *le sauvage noble*, may not see the danger of glamorizing his African heritage and so calling its authenticity in question. The English-speaking African with his background of British education and his pragmatic outlook, sidesteps the pitfall. He regards his cultural heritage as needing no apology, and no idealization. All that he wishes is that his traditional life and culture should be portrayed with fidelity. Thus, nineteenth-century African scholars like Blyden and Horton campaigned for the establishment of a West African university in which African culture would be studied and restored to dignity to counteract the despotic Europeanizing influences which warped and crushed the Negro mind.[16] The next generation devoted themselves practically to writing the histories of their people and recording their customs and oral tradition. Later still, with the beginning of creative writing, the writers prove decisively that African culture and life are worth writing about, and that there is no more valid way to write than to write about them. Whether in the work of the musicologist and ethnologist Kwabena Nketia of Ghana recording and interpreting the funeral dirges of the Akan, or of the Sierra Leone novelist William Conton invoking the beauty of the country life in Sierra Leone, or of Achebe reconstructing Igbo traditional culture in its dignity and autonomy before the colonial impact undermined it, or of Tutuola assembling and embellishing Yoruba folk-tales, or of young people and playwrights drawing elaborately from traditional themes and motifs and also from the mythology and symbolisms of the West African traditional culture, the traditional elements stand out and give the literature a characteristically West African flavour.

This literature has no recognizable and overtly formulated ideology such as Négritude. Rather it arises out of certain cultural compulsions which are both natural and induced by a recent colonial past. As Middleton Murry observes, "At a certain level of general culture, with certain combinations of economic and social conditions . . . certain artistic and literary forms impose themselves."[17] The writers treat African life because it is the life they know. That they do so implies their recovery of the creative impulse emasculated by colonialism.

Achebe outlines the case for cultural nationalism in a lecture called "The Role of the Writer in the New Nation",[18] in which he stresses the writer's duty to infuse the present generation of Africans with a sense of pride in their traditional life and culture. Ekwensi, another novelist, defines African writing as "writing which reveals the psychology of the African".[19]

As a result of their cultural commitment the West African writers tend to show a strong didacticism in their works. This has been deprecated by some English and American readers including Professor Martin Tucker, who wants African writers to worry less about the immediacy of their fictional milieu.[20] From the polemical replies to Professor Tucker's article from the writers, it is obvious that they reject any attempt to "impose a pattern" on them. The pressure of cultural nationalism operating on them is stronger than any narrow dogmatic consideration.

Foreign novelists on West Africa

One essential factor shaping West African novels by indigenous writers was the fact that they appeared after the novels on Africa written by non-West Africans. Until 1952 when Faber and Faber published Amos Tutuola's *The Palm-Wine Drinkard*, almost all prose fiction on West Africa written in English was by non-West Africans, chiefly Europeans. Even now that indigenous West Africans have "captured" the field, the fictional works by non-West Africans are still a considerable portion of the entire body of creative fiction on West Africa.[21] That alone would justify their mention in a book on West African novels. But, more importantly, the foreign novels embody elements which indigenous writers had to react against when they set out to write.

The position, stated bluntly, is this: foreign writers on West Africa express in their writing prejudices and preconceptions which distort their

17

picture of West African life. Sometimes the writer is aware of these distorting elements and boldly works them into the technique and texture of his narrative; in other circumstances they may operate on him as an unconscious projection of his reaction to something strange and disturbing. In either case, the result is different from the view of West African life held by West African writers who see it from the inside. The contrast is so clear that West African writing by the natives cannot help reacting (coming later in time) to works by the non-natives. This is why novels by foreigners are a factor operating on the indigenous writer and impelling him, consciously or unconsciously, to counter through his own writing the outsiders' view.

Early European awareness of Africa grew out of the writings of Arab geographer-explorers and Portuguese historians, an awareness which comprehends not only geographical facts but what the Arabs called "il m'ajá 'ib al-Buldān", the science of the marvels of countries. Between the fifteenth century and the end of the nineteenth century this awareness was reinforced by the writings and memoirs of European explorers, merchants and missionaries who visited or lived in Africa, and also through the slave trade and colonial contact. It is not surprising that Africa finds a place in popular European imagination and that this should be reflected in European literature. In English literature we begin to find allusions to Africa in Elizabethan and Jacobean writing. Most of these indicate that what Leonard Schapiro called "the popular mythology of Africa" had already begun to take root.

By the eighteenth century, with the growth of the conventional novel, Africa began to be used as a setting and to be given thematic treatment in narrative. Defoe, with his journalist's instinct for discovering the sensational, saw the immense potential of Africa (with its connotation of mystery, barbarism and inexhaustible wealth) as an exotic setting. Accordingly, Captain Singleton, one of his Puritan individualist adventurers, is made to stride across the continent amassing wealth and surmounting impossible difficulties. *The Life, Adventures and Piracies of the Famous Captain Singleton* (1720) contains a mass of circumstantial detail drawn by Defoe from travel journals and the geography books of his day; in addition it also embodies most of the stereotypes which were to characterize later European writing on Africa – the irrationality and gullibility of the African, who would barter food, cattle and other necessities for a few pieces of European iron and silver frippery; the poverty of Africa's material culture (often equated with the absence of a civilization); the fabulous wealth of the continent waiting to be exploited by the resourceful Europeans; the fear of the white man's might (usually the fear of his gun), all this supporting that unbridled paternalism, the

18

sense of the "civilizing mission" of the white man, which reached its full development during the Victorian age.

By the late nineteenth and early twentieth century, the peak period of European colonial adventurism in Africa, English writers like Rider Haggard, Edgar Wallace and Evelyn Waugh were exploiting the popular European image of Africa and the interest generated by the Empire to weave elaborate and exotic romances set in Africa for the amusement of the masses of the English urban industrial populations, cut off from their own popular culture and incapable of digesting serious literature – the kind of cheap popular entertainment and fantasy spinning analysed by Q. D. Leavis in *Fiction and the Reading Public* and by F. R. Leavis and Denys Thompson in *Culture and Environment*. In these African romances, which descend from Rider Haggard's *She, King Solomon's Mines* and *Allan Quartermain* to Wallace's Sanders of the River series, there is a decreasing interest in truth, which is sacrificed to the steadily cruder extravagances of the imagination. In a book about the sociology of one literature, a point about the sociology of literature in general can be made. Rider Haggard, in his romantic bookish way, made one important point. He saw the analogy between the pastoral warrior peoples of southern and eastern Africa – the Zulu and the Masai – and the Homeric Greeks and the heroic Norsemen, whose literature so enthralled the classically educated English of public school and ancient university. In *King Solomon's Mines* there is an awestruck regard for the Zulu fighting man, and Haggard's hero Sir Henry Curtis, a reincarnate Norseman, naturally finds his place fighting beside them and with them. Haggard's African hero, the chief Umslopogaas, is a Homeric warrior figure, treated with dignity. In other words, the spectacles of an English literary education, where the taste of Arnold for the Greek epic is linked to the taste of Morris for the Norse epic, gave the reader a romantic but not inappropriate view of one kind of African society. If he had lived long enough, Rider Haggard might have been thrilled by the recovery of African heroic literature (only now being published) and would have felt a kind of justification: a pastoral people naturally produces a heroic literature, and some of the African praise songs and narratives take their place beside Homer and the Norse sagas.

But as Mrs Leavis points out, the development of the English popular literature is mostly a degeneration. If we turn to the descendant of Rider Haggard in the 1920s and 1930s, we have Edgar Wallace. His Sanders of the River is as much less of a real gentleman as his Bosambo (a betraying crudity: the Black Sambo of American racialism is given a thinly Africanized name) is less of a real chief. Against the childish irrationality of stereotyped African savages is set the superhuman resourcefulness of the European colonial adventurer. There are hair-raising adventures described against the background of witchcraft, magic and sinister mysticism which is identified with Africa. There are senseless orgies of cruel massacre, human sacrifice (*The Green Crocodile*, a short story by Edgar Wallace in which human sacrifice is made to a sacred crocodile has provided for this species of European writers the sobriquet the "crocodile writers") and of course hidden treasure hoarded by men who regard gold and diamonds as ritual objects.

From the 1930s onward this kind of fantasy-spinning gave way to an attempt at realistic exploration of African themes. In West Africa, this took the form of exploring the problem of Westernization and its impact on Africans and the African traditional culture. Some of the novelists concerned also began to explore the personal and psychological factors of colonization, especially in the European colonial officials carrying the "white man's burden".

I distinguish these realistic European writers on West Africa under two headings. First, there are the non-West African writers who had either not been to West Africa at all or had paid brief visits to acquaint themselves with the physical setting and who consequently may be supposed to be drawing in their novels from personal impressions, material based on travellers' tales, historical and anthropological records or the popular European image of Africa. The most important of these is Graham Greene, who visited West Africa a number of times either on a quasi-intelligence mission or to familiarize himself with the physical setting of a projected novel. His West African writings include *Journey without Maps* (1936), an account of his tour of Liberia through Sierra Leone; *Convoy to West Africa*, based on a visit to Sierra Leone and Lagos in 1941–3; *In Search of a Character* (1959) based on a visit to the Belgian Congo; and two novels – *The Heart of the Matter* (1948), set in Freetown, and *A Burnt-Out Case* (1960), set in the Belgian Congo. His novels essentially have little to do with Africa or Africans, except that he indicates that the African heat speeds the disintegration of some of his European characters. He is in the main preoccupied with psychological and religious issues of action and motive, guilt and expiation, religious conscience and human nature, and he uses the few African characters merely as background.

Other foreign writers worth mentioning here are Elspeth Huxley, a white Kenyan now living in the United Kingdom whose novel *The Walled City* (1948) – the material of which owes much to Margery Perham's studies of indirect rule in northern Nigeria and the life of Lord Lugard – deals with the contact between European culture and the Muslim culture of northern Nigeria, and whose *Four Guineas* (1954), is a highly journalistic travelogue based on a tour of Gambia, Sierra Leone, Gold Coast (now Ghana) and Nigeria; and Peter Abrahams, a coloured South African immigrant formerly settled in England but currently living in Jamaica, whose novel *A Wreath for Udomo* (1956), set in London and Ghana, is based on a brief visit to Ghana. One might also include in this group Joseph Conrad, whose brief sojourn in the former Belgian Congo as a steamship captain (May 1890–February 1891) produced the two terrifying short stories, *An Outpost of Progress* and *Heart of Darkness*, which reveal an insight into the seamy side of Belgian colonialism and the so-called *mission civilisatrice*.

The second group of foreign writers are those who have lived for some time in West Africa and who draw the material of their novels from first-hand experience. Prominent among these is Joyce Cary, a former administrative officer in the Borgu emirate of northern Nigeria (from 1913 to 1920), whose novels *Aissa Saved* (1923), *An American Visitor* (1933), *The African Witch* (1936), *Castle Corner* (1938) and *Mister Johnson* (1938) – one-third of his published creative work – were based on notes and jottings made in Nigeria.[22] Cary also wrote political and historical tracts on Africa, the chief of which are *Case for African Freedom* (1944) and *Britain and West Africa* (1946). Another non-native West African novelist, less well known and of imaginative calibre inferior to either Conrad or Cary, is William Loader, a former classics lecturer in the University College of Ghana and author of two novels, *No Joy of Africa* (1955) and *The Guinea Stamp* (1956), both of which are set in pre-independence Ghana. There is also Margaret Field, the well-known ethnologist and author of, among other works, *Search for Security: An Ethno-Psychiatric Study of Rural Ghana* and *Religion and Medicine of the Ga People*. Under the pseudonym Mark Freshfield she published *Stormy Dawn* (1946), a short but interesting novel. One must not forget novels by West Indians set in West Africa, as for example O. R. Dathorne's *The Scholar Man* (1964). The writers identify more with Africa than Europeans and, coming much later than the others, escape many of the pitfalls of the European novelists.

It is impossible to discuss these authors in detail here, but a few general statements about their works can be made. First, most of the writers merely use West Africa as an exotic setting. This is particularly true of the "crocodile writers", who sensationalize the unfamiliar in the African way of life; but it is also true of Graham Greene, who uses West Africa as background to the exploration of issues which have not much directly to do with Africa. It was also true of Conrad, for whom the mysteriousness of the Congo (the heart of Africa) provides a symbolic setting for the exploration of the more sombre aspects of the European mind or the

21

human mind generally. The theme of Africa as a primitive scene where impulses which in the European have been bottled up and contained by centuries of "civilization" and rationalized behaviour can burst open like a sewer is particularly attractive to European writers, especially since Freud. There is in *Heart of Darkness*, for example, more than a hint that the barbarity which engulfs Kurtz is not altogether externally induced. He responds to evil because the evil in him provides an answering chord to the dark suggestions of the mysterious heart of Africa. In other words, writers like Greene and Conrad use Africa as an allegorical setting within which they can explore European characters and issues pertinent to European civilization. That is, they write as if their Africa is a backdrop; in the foreground are the Europeans agonizing; a few inconsequential Africans performing peripheral functions appear as servants and go-betweens.

Second, European writers on West Africa who treat authentic local themes are handicapped by their ignorance of African culture and their lack of understanding of the African psyche. When they write about Europeans in West Africa they are on sure ground, and they explore their predicament with confidence, but as soon as they begin to explore Africans, whether traditional Africans or those affected by Western education and culture, they are out of their depth.

There are many reasons for this, but three deserve to be mentioned. The first is that the European writer can only see the African culture from the outside unless he has undergone a severe discipline of dissociating himself from his own cultural presuppositions. The second is that as a result of the premise of inequality in the colonial relationship the European creative writer on West Africa lacked the necessary humility and serious concern for truth normally expected in the imaginative exploration of characters and situations in a foreign milieu. A colonial administrator like Joyce Cary, socially removed by colonial protocol from the generality of his African subjects, could hardly be expected to understand the African way of life and the mind of the African. It is not surprising that he thought that his Nigerian subjects were "still little advanced from the Stone Age",[23] a conclusion which he generously confessed to be wrong in his *Case for African Freedom*. The third reason is that what is called "the popular mythology of Africa" has permeated European imagination so deeply and for so long that European writers, even when they mean to explore an African theme from an objective viewpoint, sooner or later fall into projecting a version of African life which will fit into the image of Africa in the popular European imagination. So we find tribal and communal violence constantly cropping up in West African novels written by Europeans. Joyce Cary's African novels (with the exception of *Mister Johnson*), no matter how peacefully begun, are sooner or later engulfed in violence – dynastic violence (*The African Witch*), religious violence (*Aissa Saved*), inter-tribal violence (*An American Visitor*). In fact Cary is aware of, and complacent about, this quality of violence in his African novels. "The African setting," he writes in the prefatory essay to the Carfax edition of *The African Witch*, ". . . just because it is dramatic, demands a certain kind of story, a certain violence and coarseness of detail, almost a fabulous treatment, to keep it in its place." A little earlier he writes about the religious wars which abound in his novels: "The attraction of Africa is that it shows these wars of belief, and the powerful often sub-conscious motives which underlie them, in the greatest variety and also in very simple forms. Basic obsessions which in Europe hide themselves under all sorts of decorous scientific or theological or political uniforms are there seen naked in bold and dramatic action."[24]

These writers are not interested in reality and authenticity. They are ex-ploring the Africa of the European imagination – an Africa of tribal and communal violence, as in Cary's novels, Elspeth Huxley's *The Walled City*, Peter Abrahams' *A Wreath for Udomo*, and William Loader's *The Guinea Stamp* (which perversely suggests that violence is in the nature of the African and of the African environment rather than being a pro-duct of a certain kind of social and cultural situation); the Africa of religious hysteria and ritual murder (as in Cary's *Aissa Saved* and *The African Witch* and Elspeth Huxley's *The Walled City*), of witchcraft, magic and mumbo-jumbo (as in Cary's *An American Visitor* and Huxley's *The Walled City*).

Third, European writers sometimes use their novels to put forward an attitude, a sociological theory or a psychological statement. They are often fascinated by the problem of change arising from the impact of Western culture (which they know about) on the traditional African culture (which they know very little about). They end by distorting the situation or making facile statements about it.

In *The Walled City*, Miss Huxley treats the theme through a series of debates between characters upholding two different schools of thought: those standing for a laissez-faire or "tourist" attitude which advocates the preservation of everything African because it is different and has met the needs of Africans, and progressives who advocate change as a means of liberating the African from the evils of fear, superstition and material poverty. The debate is inconclusive, but the failure of her Benjamin Morris to live up to the ideal of Western relationships and ethical be-haviour – especially his easily succumbing to the wiles of the lingam – may be taken as the symbolic defeat of the progressive school. Joyce Cary's African novels are largely preoccupied with the same debate. His

23

administrative officers are either conservatives or progressives. He also introduces virtuous but zealously misguided missionaries and – to confuse the situation further – anarchistic sentimentalists obsessed with the Rousseauist idealism of the unspoiled children of nature.

The view implicit in both Cary's and Miss Huxley's discussion of the religious situation – that Christianity liberates its adherents and binds them by love, whereas the traditional religion enslaves through fear and superstition – shows that they are able to see one side of the problem but not the other. Traditional religion presents itself to them in the form of ritual murder, superstition and the uncritical acquiescence of a weak-minded people. It is interesting to compare their treatment of religion in Africa's changing culture with the same theme in indigenous West African writers like Achebe and Nzekwu.

Stormy Dawn alone escapes these criticisms. Margaret Field has two assets which most of the other writers lack. First, as an ethnologist who lived for many years in intimate association with the Ga people of Ghana, she has an intimate understanding of African life. Secondly, as a psychiatrist, her understanding of African life is strengthened by her understanding of human behaviour. She is also a writer of considerable merit, with a comic style which prises open the most secret thoughts and motives of her characters. Her Africans are real people with virtues and vices, desires and obsessions, faith and illusions, loves and hates, hopes and despondencies. She succeeds in giving them flesh and blood by avoiding racial myth-making and those generalized inanities which the other foreigners inflict on their readers.

Her young hero, Folu Dinkuna, is no stereotyped évolué who comes to grief because he gets lost between two conflicting cultures. His tragedy is largely implicit in his character-weakness. Having worked hard to achieve academic success, he plunges, while within easy grasp of it, into despair and suicide because he has in him the stuff of which potential suicides are made: a temperamental, flighty nature which relies on external stimuli, especially the esteem of the world, to sustain it. His less intelligent brother succeeds where he fails, because he has a more stable temperament and knows what he wants out of life.

What is even more interesting about this novel is its intelligent insight into the social background of the characters. Miss Field neither romanticizes nor patronizes African life. She sees it realistically as neither wholly perfect nor wholly imperfect but one in which people aspire to normal self-fulfilment and ambition. Her sympathetic understanding of African religion is only comparable to that of another expatriate, Denys Craig (real name Dennis Gray Stoll), in an equally short but evocotive novel, *Man in Ebony*.

Margaret Field is aware of the harm which some writing by foreigners, especially the "crocodile writers", had done to the African image in the past, and she satirizes them through her District Commissioner who came out to Africa with a mind brim-full of the stereotyped European ideas of the continent:

> He had come out to West Africa twenty-five years before, prepared for many thrills – the thrill of suppressing hideous, bloody fetishes, of amassing a smoke-room repertoire of Edgar Wallace stories tinged with the fear and sinister mystery of darkest Africa, of establishing the flag of beneficent justice amidst grateful and respectful people. But it had not been a bit like that. The office work was heavy and dull and the administrative ritual was soul-destroying. The people were not grateful and respectful. The mind of the African did not work in that quaint, primitive way that makes the native of the travel book so endearing: most of the African minds that he had to deal with were preoccupied with sordid and complex intrigues about money and politics.[25]

These novels have helped to determine the direction of West African novels by indigenous authors. It should be obvious that the documentary nature of most West African novels is the result of the young African writers' eagerness to explain African traditional life both to non-Africans and to those Africans who have, by reading non-indigenous writing disparaging this life, begun unconsciously to be influenced in their attitudes by such reading. In other words, the African writer has to correct the false impressions of African life contained in foreign writing on Africa. Achebe, the finest English-speaking novelist in West Africa, said that he began writing his classic novel *Things Fall Apart* as a reaction to Cary's *Mister Johnson*. Even the most cursory reading of the two novels will reveal that the world of Cary's novel is largely created out of the fabric of Cary's own imagination, whereas that of Achebe's novel represents an objective world lit up and given full significance through the resources of art.

Oral tradition

The most noticeable difference between novels by native West Africans and those by non-natives using the West African setting, is the important position which the representation of oral tradition is given by the first, and its almost complete absence in the second. This is a statement of fact rather than a criticism of non-West African writers, few of whom understand West African vernaculars. If, for example, we compare Joyce Cary's Nigerian villagers and Chinua Achebe's villagers, we notice that

Cary's peasants speak in straightforward English prose – with the exception of Mr Johnson, who speaks and writes "babu" English. Cary's Nigerian peasants speak like Cary himself, whereas Achebe's Nigerian villagers weave into the fabric of their everyday conversations allusions from folk-tales, legends and myths, and back their opinions and attitudes with appropriately chosen proverbs, traditional maxims and cryptic anecdotes. In other words, whereas the nationality of Cary's peasants cannot be guessed at from the way they speak, Achebe's villagers' speech shows them unmistakably people who are closer to an oral than a literary tradition.

The other West African writers with whom this book has to deal also show themselves aware of the significance of oral tradition as an integral part of West African culture. By incorporating the oral tradition of West Africa into their writing they have largely succeeded in giving an air of authenticity to their writing and established a consciousness which is characteristically West African.

Commentators on West African literature have almost ignored the significance of oral tradition as one of its major impulses. As John Ramsaran of the University of Ibadan puts it: "No aspect of the developing literature of West Africa is so much neglected as the folk tale which is still a most vigorous form of expression in the cultural life of the people. Perhaps because of its very popularity and age-old association with a largely non-literate society the folk tale tends to be forgotten or is deliberately by-passed by sophisticated writers and readers who equate modernity with excellence."[26]

African writers themselves are not deceived into striking an exclusively modernist pose, ignoring the surviving elements of the traditional culture. The essential reality of contemporary West African culture is that within its oral tradition continues to exist side by side with the encroaching literary traditions. It is sufficiently vigorous to be incorporated by West African writers into the various literary forms which have been developed there. Whether in the tales of Amos Tutuola, in the novels of Achebe, in the plays of Clark and Soyinka or in the poems of Okigbo, we are aware that the writers are drawing on West African folklore, traditional symbols and images, and traditional turns of speech to invest their writing with a truly West African sensibility and flavour.

This attempt to take the West African oral tradition into their writing is not a literary fad or an attempt to exoticize West African literature. The truth is that oral tradition has survived in West Africa in spite of the introduction of Western writing and the foreign tradition which it bears.

There are good reasons why West African oral tradition should survive, despite the changes induced by the introduction of a literary tradition from Europe. First, by far the largest number of West Africans are still illiterate. If we take Nigeria as an example, the literacy rates in the English language according to the 1952–3 census (about the time of the appearance of Tutuola's *The Palm-Wine Drinkard*) were 33·7 per cent for Lagos, 0·9 per cent for the Northern Region, 9·5 per cent for the Western Region, 10·6 per cent for the Eastern Region and 6 per cent for the country as a whole. Each percentage is raised (especially in northern Nigeria) if we add the number of those who at this time were literate in the vernaculars only, but from a purely statistical point of view, a preponderant part of the West African populations continue to subsist largely within an oral rather than literary culture, and to express a consciousness which is more typical of the oral than of the literary tradition.

Secondly, at least three out of every four West Africans live in traditional village communities or traditional urban settlements which enjoy relative cultural homogeneity, a common historical outlook and a unified linguistic development, all of which contribute to the existence of an oral tradition.

Thirdly, even those who are increasingly influenced by literary culture never lose touch with their oral culture. Literate people in urban areas which are centres of the literate cultural influence often visit their relations in the villages, and are thus also exposed to the influence of the oral culture which predominates in the villages and traditional towns. Western-educated West Africans are familiar with their own folklore, have a comprehensive knowledge of the popular proverbs and other traditional speech forms, and can speak their vernaculars competently. They also share the values, attitudes and structures of feeling (to use Raymond Williams' convenient phrase)[27] which are implicit within their oral culture.

A fourth factor has contributed to the continued vitality of oral tradition in West Africa, the factor of cultural inertia. Social anthropologists tell us that certain areas of a changing culture always tend to be more resistant to the pressures of change than others. One such area has to do with the value aspect of a culture. In contrast to the material aspect, the value aspect tends to persist longest. A purely oral culture, such as the West African culture obviously was before the introduction of the Roman and Arabic scripts, embodied its values and attitudes in its proverbs and fossilized saying, its beliefs in its myths and religion, and its consciousness of its historical life, collective outlook and ethics, in its legends, folk-tales and other forms of oral literature. All those have been embedded in the consciousness of the West African peoples as cultural groups; even the introduction of elements of the Western literary culture has merely modified traditional oral culture but has not destroyed the consciousness deriving from its tradition. So long as the relation between the town and the village remains complementary, and so long as a large number of people live in the villages, and those who live in the towns also live in the villages part of the time, so long will oral tradition continue to inform the consciousness and determine the sensibility of most West Africans.

West African writers who attempt to recreate West African cultural life in fiction (either in its contemporary or historical setting) have chosen to do so through the oral tradition of West Africa, because it best expresses the West African consciousness and sensibility. Even while they are writing, for the benefit of the reader, in what may be regarded by the superficial observer as an authentic Queen's English, the sensibility they express is purely West African. In other words, the writers are involved in transporting the oral tradition of West Africa into the literary tradition of Europe. The result is new, and exhilarating in its novelty.

How crucial oral tradition is in the definition of West African creative literature is clear from the following conclusion from a conference of teachers of English held in the Institute of Education and the Department of English, University of Ibadan, between 26 April and 1 May 1965: "The traditional material of folk tale, myth and legend is so intimately connected with the life of Africa, that some knowledge of it is necessary to an intelligent understanding of certain areas of African creative writing" and that "quite a few of the writers of today must be influenced consciously or otherwise by the work of traditional artists like story-tellers and praise-singers."[28]

II DOMESTICATION OF THE NOVEL IN WEST AFRICA

2

Oral and literary traditions in West Africa

The way the writer arranges his subject matter and the ideas and concepts which he presents to his readers, the social habits and customs and the modes of thought and action which he takes for granted in his writings all give a distinctive quality and tone to his work which can be related to the culture to which the author belongs. Leslie Stephen puts the point in his discussion of Pope's translation of the *Iliad*:

> Will the epic poem which was the product of certain remote social and intellectual conditions, serve to express the thoughts and emotions of a totally different age? Considering the differences between Achilles and Marlborough, or the bards of the heroic age and the wits who frequented clubs and coffee-houses under Queen Anne it was at least important to ask whether Homer or Pope – taking them to be alike in genius – would not find it necessary to adopt radically different forms.[1]

The point is incontestable. The *Iliad* belongs essentially to an oral tradition,[2] whereas Pope and his contemporaries are fully immersed in a literary tradition. The characteristics of both traditions are relevant to an understanding of the quality and tone of African creative fiction; for here we find literature which has to carry several different epochs rolled into one, to bear the experiences peculiar to the oral and the literary traditions and to express the sensibilities peculiar to worlds as different as Homer's and Pope's, but existing side by side.

"Tradition" is used here in two senses: first in the sense in which the *Shorter Oxford English Dictionary* defines it, as "transmission of statements, beliefs, rules, customs, or the like, especially by word of mouth, or by practice without writing"; and second in the sense in which T. S. Eliot uses it, to comprehend "all those habitual actions, habits and customs, from the most significant religious rite to our conventional way of greeting a stranger".[3] When I speak about oral and literary traditions, I am using the word in the second sense, but when I speak about the "traditional culture" or "traditional beliefs and practices", the first sense of the word is uppermost. "Oral tradition" therefore implies a situation in which cultural transmission is carried on by word of mouth through direct contact between individuals depending largely on memory and habits of thought, action and speech for cultural continuity. Within a literary tradition on the other hand, cultural transmission is also carried on through writing and the existence of written records.

Each tradition has its own peculiarities, but every human society, including those with a long-standing literate tradition, has gone through an oral phase and retains a residue of the oral quality of its early beginnings. Goody and Watt have observed of Europe that in spite of the alphabetic script, printing and universal free education, which make for a highly developed literary culture, the transmission of values and attitudes in face-to-face contact remains "the primary mode of cultural orientations".[4] But the association of writing with the large-scale organization of society, with scientific progress and the development of modern industrial and professional skills, and as a means of transforming ideas and social attitudes, has made the literate tradition the vehicle of a world civilization based on technological progress and the institutions which sustain it. This world technological civilization is the goal towards which developing countries strive, sometimes with considerable obstruction from their local, oral, traditional culture. The superimposition of the literary tradition on the oral tradition in Africa, Asia and elsewhere, with the inevitable changes involved, can be seen as "the clash of world civilization with individual cultures".[5]

Oral cultures are relatively more homogeneous than literate cultures because oral transmission depends on face-to-face contact and ensures common customs, beliefs, techniques, sentiments and general outlook. Individuals tend to share moral attitudes and concepts of the good life and of the rights and obligations of individuals to the community and vice versa. Family ties and social solidarity are closer and stronger. These characteristics have been established by ethnologists studying West African peoples and their oral cultures, both segmentary folk communities like the Tiv, the Tallensi and the Igbo and the centralized semi-urbanized societies of Yorubaland, Ashanti and non-Islamic northern Nigeria.

Literacy makes face-to-face contact as a mode of cultural transmission irrelevant. The international transfer of cultural elements through the written record has made the development of a world civilization possible. Where the oral tradition ensured relative stability in the living conditions and customs of non-literate people, the introduction of literacy has brought new cultural elements, new beliefs and moral values, new attitudes, new technological skills, new aspirations, new ideologies and new outlooks, which upset the equilibrium of the old indigenous cultures.

In West Africa the introduction of literacy made it possible for European colonial administrations to bring together various West African peoples into single national frameworks governed by a modern bureaucracy; to introduce large-scale public works and social services such as roads, railways, air- and water-transport; to organize scientific medicine, modern technology and the extensive use of machinery; and to cultivate new organs of mass communication and new forms of art, literature and leisure.

The differences in cultural transmission between the two traditions produce different modes of preserving continuity between past and present. The oral tradition relies largely on human memory for the preservation and transmission of the cultural repertoire, and so develops elaborate mechanisms for helping the human memory. These include a high degree of ritualization of belief, actions and concepts, of symbolization as a means of concretizing experience, and of routinization of everyday actions, fostered no doubt by the homogeneous nature of beliefs, sentiments and attitudes. The literate tradition, because it relies on written records, is more elaborative, exploratory and experimental than the oral tradition and leads to greater diversity of beliefs, sentiments and attitudes. It tends to produce greater scepticism than the oral tradition and is the basis of modern scientific progress.

The supernatural has a stronger hold on the oral tradition than on the literate tradition. Belief in magic, witchcraft and the gods tends to be in inverse proportion to scientific progress and control of the environment. Godfrey and Monica Wilson connect economic complexity and control of the material environment, non-magicality, impersonality and mobility to the changes which take place when small-scale indigenous societies are welded into larger units and brought under the direct influence of world technological culture. But all these factors, interrelated as they are, are mediated through the existence of an alphabetic literacy which aids the documentation of cumulative scientific knowledge; where this knowledge is developed men are not so ready to attribute their misfortunes to mystic agencies.

The modes of apprehending reality within the two traditions therefore differ in important respects. In all societies knowledge is apprehended through the senses, some of men's daily actions must derive from direct learning from events and situations as they occur, and a certain degree of experiment, building on previous experience, is necessary if the community is to go on living. In other words, some simple empiricism is important for survival. But, because writing provides a basic facility for experiment and the documentation of results, the literary tradition tends to foster a scientific outlook. Within the oral tradition, on the other hand, the absence of this facility tends to inhibit the scientific outlook and to leave the people more at the mercy of environmental factors. They therefore attempt to explain their problems, as well as all mysterious phenomena, through recourse to a theory of supernatural or mystical causality. Thus where the basic science of the oral culture fails to provide an answer, one is found through magical, mystical or supernatural theory.

We may say that reality is apprehended scientifically within the literate tradition and mystically or metaphysically within the oral tradition. These are terms of convenience only, because belief in supernatural causality is strong even in highly developed literate societies, while scientific empiricism is present in the thoughts of even the most underdeveloped, non-literate peoples.

All this is important to the development of the novel in West Africa and to its quality and tone. Since the fifteenth century, contact between the literate culture of Europe and the oral culture of West Africa has caused changes in the aboriginal cultures. These changes were at first peripheral, affecting only a few miles of the Atlantic coastal region. By the mid-nineteenth century, with the establishment of European colonies in West Africa, radical changes began to take place and have gone on since. These changes have been largely induced by the development of literacy and by the establishment of new territorial frameworks and new institutions, as well as by the introduction of new consumer goods and a new system of exchange based on the cash nexus. All these have caused changes not only in the original oral societies but also in the people themselves, in their whole attitude to life. But considerable areas of the old oral culture still remain side by side with the elements that came with the new literate culture: the new urban settlement exists alongside the traditional village, the tractor with the hand hoe, the psychiatrist with the diviner, belief in science with belief in magic and witchcraft.

West African literature therefore reflects features which appertain to the oral tradition and to the literary tradition but which have been juxtaposed by the peculiar circumstances of the meeting of Europe with Africa; this has largely determined its texture. The blending of impulses from the oral and the literary traditions gives the West African novel its distinctive local colour.

The novel is the only major literary genre which has no strict equivalent in the oral tradition of West Africa, partly because it is a product of literacy, but also because the social factors which determine its rise and define it as a distinct literary form are also the factors which marked the change in the West itself from the old traditional culture to the modern industrial culture. In West Africa however, the form has been borrowed and assimilated to a new cultural reality, in which the old indigenous culture and the new technological culture have been and still are being painfully married. Like every other item of cultural borrowing, the novel is, in West Africa, still undergoing a process of "domestication", and even though one can now regard it as fully assimilated much in the same way as one regards the motor car and hire-purchase as assimilated into modern West Africa, it has peculiarities of its own deriving from the West African cultural situation. One could go further and say that to understand the experiences conveyed by the West African novel we need some background understanding of this cultural situation.

One may begin by asking whether one can speak of a "West African" novel in the same way as people speak about an English novel, an American novel or a Russian novel. There are reasons why one can rightly speak of a West African novel. One thing not implied by the term is a "school" of West African novel-writing. No such school exists, since all the novelists are as different from one another as any group of writers can be within one literary form.

Five reasons can be given for speaking of the "West African" novel:

1. Obviously enough, the West African novel is a novel written in West Africa about West African life.

2. More specifically it is a genuinely regional novel. The novelists draw largely from the local environment to give local colour to their stories. They represent local speech habits, beliefs, customs and mores in order to give a distinct quality to life and action which reflects West African realities.

3. It has an essentially sociological emphasis. Because the West African novel has risen at a time when large-scale social and economic changes are taking place, the writers show an almost obsessive preoccupation with the influence of these conditions. This is the condition of life; these are the ways in which people feel its pressure; these pressures demand expression.

4. It is explicitly or implicitly didactic, even propagandist. The West African novelist functions, among other things, as teacher and social reformer. He uses his writing to explore the problems of society and to indicate, through the aspects of contemporary West African life he is criticizing, the social reforms which he wishes to see. The West African novel is a true example of *la littérature engagée*.

5. Finally, the West African novel reflects the peculiar cultural situation of West Africa, where elements of the oral kinship-oriented culture of old Africa exist side by side with elements of the world technological

35

contract-oriented culture. This generates tensions, conflicts, contradictions and ambivalences in the lives of individuals. Moreover, and this is an important distinction, the West African novel tends to show individual characters not through their private psychological experiences, but through community or social life, and activities of a collective or general nature, with individual sentiments and actions deriving force and logic from those of the community.

The West African novel necessarily derived from Western models and is, up to the present, written in English. But it has been so adapted to local life and culture that it has acquired a personality of its own. In this respect it is like other regional novels – the Indian, West Indian, Australian for example – which reflect local settings, local themes and local impulses.

In describing the qualities which give the West African novel its character, there is one difficulty which arises from the difference in nature and intensity of the process of culture-change between the village and the urban area. Culture-contact is likely to have least effect on the villager and most on the townsman: the villager tends to be more traditionalist than the urban dweller. This is not to establish any polarity between town and village – on the contrary, there is a traffic between them, with the village influence flowing into the town and the town influence flowing into the village – but to emphasize what is obvious: in purely statistical terms, traditional elements predominate over non-traditional elements in the village, and the position is reversed in an urban setting. Less than 20 per cent of the people of West Africa live in the urban areas, and more than 80 per cent of them live in the villages and traditional towns. Hence in spite of the rapidity of social change (necessarily fastest in the urban centres and slower in the villages) the traditional still outweighs non-traditional cultural elements.

So the best way to describe the domestication of the novel in West Africa is to recognize the disparities between rural and urban West Africa in novels, and the factors which help to determine these disparities. The peculiarities of thought, action and feeling in rural novels will approximate to the patterns of traditional thought, action, and feeling; those in the urban novels will approximate to the patterns of the industrial urban situation.

Influences do constantly flow from town to country and back again. Urban dwellers try to create for themselves a rural, tradition-oriented life by setting up "Improvement" and "Patriotic" societies which provide them with something of a traditional framework and as much of the old security of the rural community as can be mustered within the town. Thus, in comparison with the New Yorker or Londoner, the average town-dweller in West Africa (except perhaps for the Sierra Leone Creoles and a few members of the old Brazilian and former West Indian families of the southern towns with a tradition of Western education going back to the early nineteenth century) is still a peasant at heart, with a thin layer of modernist sophistication concealing the deep centre of traditional beliefs and feelings. Even the intellectuals of West Africa, who are most exposed to world intellectual traditions and the world urban–technologist culture, are equally at home in their local traditional cultures. What Professor Edward Shils observed of Indian intellectuals applies with equal validity to the African intellectuals: "Most of the Indian intellectuals I have met in person, or encountered through their writings, seem to be quite firmly rooted in India, in its past and present. By 'rooted' I mean possessing within themselves, and accepting, important elements of its traditions and its present life."[6] The West African intellectual is in the same position. And if this is true of the "cosmopolitanized" intellectual it is even more so of the locally oriented non-intellectual.

Despite this qualification the distinction between town and country is fundamental, especially as the novels themselves lend logical support to it. The scheme helps to reveal the dichotomy in the lives of most West Africans, who have to step from the traditional village to the town and vice versa, and the consequent social and mental adjustments involved.

The scheme allows the village to be used to define the traditional setting and the town to define the modern setting. Finally, it throws some biographical light on the novels themselves. Here a close correspondence has been established. West African writers like Achebe, Nzekwu, Okara, Nwankwo and Amadi, who have lived in both the traditional and the urban environments, tend to set their novels within either or both. Their narratives flow from one to the other without strain. Those who have not had both experiences, like William Conton and to some extent Aluko, are often unsuccessful in their effort to describe the social background of their novels. On the other hand, those who have grown up in the urban setting alone, as Ekwensi did, tend to avoid a sustained exploration of traditional village life. The identification of the writer with his setting is significant in the West African novel because it ensures close familiarity with the externals of life, habits, customs and attitudes; with social institutions and the inner stresses in these institutions which affect individuals in their day-to-day relationships. As a result the novels have a social authenticity which is impossible in vicarious reporting. The absence of rapport between writer and setting is the obvious weakness of West African novels by non-indigenous writers.

The representation of reality within the rural novels takes account of the traditional world view. This does not divide the universe rigidly into the

37

spiritual and the non-spiritual, the celestial and the mundane, the cosmic and the terrestrial, as with a modern scientific world view. It recognizes a supreme and creative deity who lives in the sky, and a hierarchy of lesser gods who inherit cosmic and natural phenomena. There is also a belief in minor spirits who inhabit the forests, air and streams, and in the ancestors between whom and the living there exists a mystical bond and charter for the continuity of society. The whole creation has an occult vitality which can be reinforced or diminished by the proper kind of magical invocation. Man is at the centre of the traditional universe, not because he is most powerful but because he is able to regulate his relationship with the gods and the ancestors and to manipulate the immanent occult vitality of nature.

Traditional habits of thinking are compounded of empiricism and metaphysics. A large part of daily life is determined by actions to which the principles of empirico-rational behaviour are germane – actions such as cooking meals, eating and drinking, making love, farming and storing grain, building houses, making clothes, hygiene and so on. Here reality is perceived by the individual largely through the senses. But, because the traditional world view embraces both the physical and the unseen universe, the traditional mind's perception of reality transcends the sensory and such levels of experience as could be regarded as empirical, rationalist and realistic; it perceives reality also at a super-sensory level of consciousness, mainly as a hierarchy of forces operating within the universe.

Father Placide Tempels has worked out a useful scheme displaying this hierarchy of forces. According to him, the hierarchy comprises divine force, celestial and terrestrial forces, human forces, animal forces, vegetable forces and material and mineral forces.[7] The hierarchy corresponds to a hierarchical concept of being which has God, the Creator, at the top of the pyramid and materials and minerals at the base. Human force is situated in the middle, with divine, celestial and terrestrial forces above it. The forces above the human force can act on it without being correspondingly acted upon by it. Man has therefore to placate and expiate those forces and generally sweeten their disposition through sacrifices and religious rites. On the other hand, human force can act on the lower forces without being acted upon by them. Man manipulates them to his advantage as a way of reinforcing his own vital force or diminishing potential hostile mystic influence. In other words, religion provides an operative basis for regulating the relationship between man, the gods and the ancestors, while magic provides the answer to the threats of the harmful mystical forces that beset man in this world. Within the traditional setting, therefore, reality is apprehended empirically and rationally as a sensory phenomenon and metaphysically as an invisible force which operates in the universe. Thus, apart from the areas of action which can be regarded as truly empirical, there are others which can only be subsumed under religious or magical manifestation. The world of traditional West African village life depends on the constant interplay of these two aspects – the physical, seen world and the unseen world of the gods, ancestors, spirits, witches and magicians.

Magic is even more central to the characteristic literature of the oral culture, the folk-tale – but we must distinguish between the place of magic in the folk-tale world and in the conventional West African novel. In the folk-tale, magic is all-pervasive and is espoused actively in pursuit of ends which are essentially fantastic and sensational. In the novel, magic, inseparable from the general outlook of the traditional mind and the structure of human relationships, is present (but not necessarily accepted) in its functional aspect. Here lies the difference between D. O. Fagunwa's Yoruba tales, Tutuola's writing after him, and the novels of Achebe, Soyinka and others. Whereas Fagunwa's and Tutuola's heroes with the aid of magic carry out their quests from the world of the living to the world of the dead across a largely anthropomorphized intermediate universe, no such fantasy is admissible in the conventional reality embodied in the novels.

In the novels, ordinary daily experiences far outweigh the areas of experience determined by belief in magic. In fact, magical influence is peripheral to the day-to-day experience even of the traditional African people. But it is an integral part of belief, and therefore an essential factor in plot development in the novels. In *Wand of Noble Wood*, for example, the tragic culmination of the action depends on the absence of the "vital" white stone which renders null the expiatory ceremony. Again, the picaresque nature of *Burning Grass* is very much determined by the protagonist's having a wandering disease "put on him" by his enemies; this induces him to set out on his futile quest and away from the normal transhumant route followed by the members of his family. In *The Concubine*, the entire plot turns on the fact that, without knowing it, the heroine is a watermaid and wife of a jealous Sea King. Like the mermaid in Arnold's "The Forsaken Merman" Amadi's watermaid has left her husband to join the human species. The affronted and vengeful husband allows the flighty wife her whim, provided she never marries any human; the only status allowed her is that of concubine. Her other-worldly beauty makes her highly desirable to young men in need of wives, and, like the femme fatale of the European imagination, she brings tragedy and death to her eager suitors. The cult of the watermaid is strongly held in the Niger delta where Amadi's story is set. So the story maintains a high

39

degree of imaginative credibility in spite of its heavy magical and super-natural assumptions.

An important fact about traditional life is its collective nature. Every aspect of human experience – actions, beliefs, thoughts, ideas, ideals and human behaviour – derives its realistic authority from past usage, handed down from generation to generation. This is the real basis of traditionalism – all human knowledge is supposed to have been developed and perfected in the remote past of the people's history, during its golden age, and then handed down intact by every generation to its successor. The traditional individual's apprehension of reality is therefore the collectively shared vision of reality certified by custom. This is linked to the ancestors, who are regarded as the custodians of the traditional. Collective tradition as the basis of the expression of human experience is only possible in a situation such as that which obtains in traditional societies, where there are community life and permanent face-to-face social relationships among those who share a common historical and ancestral background within a limited area. That cultural transmission is carried on orally tends to foster this collective tradition.

The representation of reality in the urban novels is influenced by the composite nature of modern urban culture. Modern towns are inhabited by an aggregation of people drawn from different traditional areas. As a result they lack the historical identification, social homogeneity and collective outlook of the traditional community. Western cultural impact is greatest here, and so is the scientific outlook on life. Individual experience as opposed to collective tradition tends to form the basis of the apprehension of reality. In other words, there is no collective world view and no collectively defined reality as it impinges on each particular consciousness. But because most urban settlers bring with them a background of traditional experience, they tend to have in them residual traditional elements. Thus, for instance, the metaphysical outlook of the traditional individual becomes the superstitious outlook of the city-dweller, the difference being that the metaphysical apprehension of reality in the former is an essential aspect of the "logically" conceived world-order, but is in the latter a mere fragmentary phenomenon unrelated to the general "realistic" outlook, which is scientific. Belief in magic within the traditional environment is an aspect of the collective cultural equipment and plays an important part in social relations, whereas within the modern setting, it is a private reality. The individual may only have recourse to it in pursuit of private gain or private vengeance.

Furthermore, townsmen show greater scepticism and impiety than traditional people as a result of their exposure to the literary tradition and the absence of collective tradition within the urban setting. Still, it would be unwise to overemphasize this scepticism; for, even among middle-class professionals and university-educated West Africans who have been most intensely subjected to Western acculturation, a large body of traditional thinking still survives, though it is often glossed over with a thin layer of sophistication. Moreover, supernaturalism is an aspect of the Christian religion which is a major modern influence and an important aspect of the social reality of contemporary West Africa.

3

Nature, music and art

The treatment of nature, music and art brings out in broadest outline the points so far made about traditional and modern approaches to the representation of reality in the West African novel. Those three topics are important because they are those through which people express their individualities as well as their interrelatedness and a sense of responses shared with others.

The traditional world view has an important bearing on attitudes to nature and this in turn is reflected in the novels. It implies a mystical yet utilitarian outlook on nature instead of an externalized appreciation of it in forms like fine landscapes, beautiful flowers, cascading waters or the colours of the rainbow. In this tradition the beauty of the particular tree comes to be inseparable from its "vital" property, demonstrable in pharmaceutical or magical efficacy or the shade it provides from the heat of the sun. The uniqueness of a particular stream or wooded landscape resides in some supernatural manifestation, either as the abode of a communal deity or a local spirit identifiable with the destiny of the community. The rainbow is apprehended first and foremost as an externalization of an internal force portending good or ill for an entire community. Nature is not "other" as in the industrialized and urbanized West, but is apprehended by the traditional West African as an integral part of his world order.

Speaking of England, Leslie Stephen says that the divorce between London life and country life not only deprived English people from the seventeenth century onwards of closeness to nature or integration into their setting but also led them to contemplate nature as an independent phenomenon with an aesthetic or religious or philosophic reality.[1] In traditional West Africa, the attitude to nature is like that of pre-industrial Europe. And the rural novels provide a testimony to this. The absence of scenic description is related to the integrative attitude to nature. Nature is so inextricably woven into the social, economic and metaphysical realities that it cannot be satisfactorily portrayed as if it has an independent existence.

In rural West Africa, one is acutely aware how closely human life is integrated with physical nature. The people are farmers, constantly in contact with the earth. They till the soil and sow their crops in it. They have to clear the forests and the bush to make room for the crops. They depend on rain for success, and, since they sometimes go far to set up farms, they cross streams and brooks and forests and woodlands daily. Since many of the villagers do not have pipe-borne water, they have to go to the local stream daily. They see birds and animals of all sorts and recognize them as part of the environment, to be put to human use or in some cases treated with reverence and religious awe. They recognize bird-songs and build them into the consciousness as a way of telling the time or interpreting reality, since the songs of some birds are ominous.

Agriculture forces rural people to be interested in different types of terrain. In the search for good farmland they scan the hills and high grounds, valleys and plains. Sunshine, rainfall, clouds, forests, bushes, trees, streams, brooks, winds, rocks, hills, mountains, valleys, plains are part of the perennial human quest for livelihood, economic survival and, in some cases, religious and mystical security.

But in the traditional imagination, physical nature is not dead. It is imbued with immanent vitality and spirit force. Behind nature there is supernature, the spirit which animates it and infuses it with occult potency. Everything in nature is either a manifestation of matter, tangible, physical and responsible to sensual perception, or supernature, that which is nature's hidden power and life. The perfect combination of the two aspects ensures the harmony and ordered progress of the traditional world, which means that the earth will go on yielding its bounties, that the sky will continue to let down its showers, that the sun will bless and vitalize the earth in perpetuity, and that the streams and brooks will perennially provide the fluid of life as well as life-sustaining food. Since nature is so intimately woven into the traditional consciousness, it is an ever-present reality constantly within view. Understandably, it is more an object of veneration than of aesthetic appreciation.

The novelists reflect this integrative and functional perception of nature. They often refer to the nature gods who dominate the lives of the villagers, such as Ala (Ani) the Igbo earth goddess, Idemili (the god of water), Amadioha (the Igbo god of thunder) and Shango (the Yoruba equivalent). Then there are numerous nature spirits associated with groves, streams, markets and trees who sometimes prove decisive in the shaping of the destiny of people and defining the movement of events.

The importance of these nature gods and spirits is linked with their function. In *Arrow of God*, the priest of Idemili describes the significance of his deity as follows:

> Idemili means Pillar of Water. As the pillar of this house holds the roof so does Idemili hold up the Rain-cloud in the sky so that it does not fall down.[2]

The explanation is couched in mythological terms, but more realistically it shows the importance of rain to an agricultural community and explains why the Sacred Python, the totemic "emanation of the god of water"[3] is treated with high ritual reverence. The association of rain and thunder and lightning also gives the gods of those natural phenomena an important place in the pantheon. In both Yoruba and Igbo mythologies, the god of thunder and lightning has a role in the ordering of the traditional societies, and its priests are important religious functionaries. In *The Concubine* Amadi emphasizes this:

> The god of thunder was connected with rain, so Nwokekoro [the priest of Amadioha] was also the chief rain maker. Everyone in the village knew that he kept a mysterious white smooth stone which, when immersed in water, caused rain to fall even in the dry season. Nwokekoro could also dispel heavy rain-bearing clouds by merely waving a short mystic broom black with age and soot.[4]

In Aluko's *One Man One Wife*, Shango is both the manifester of thunder and lightning and the chief security officer and executioner of undetected and menacing criminals, as illustrated in the death of Elder Joshua.[5]

As a vital element in life, flowing water is deeply revered. It is invested with divine and spiritual essence, which is in turn woven into the myths and the archetypal images of the traditional mind. Thus the little stream Mini Wekwu in *The Concubine* is an important economic, geographical and religious factor as well as a mystical border between the people of two villages:

> Mini Wekwu, a stream with a powerful god, formed the boundary between the two villages [Omokachi and Chiolu]. The worship of Mini Wekwu often coincided with the clearing of the path [joining the villages]. Worshippers from the two villages would meet and offer their sacrifices jointly. It established goodwill and the god ensured that no evil crossed from one village to the other. For instance, no wizard from Chiolu would dare cross to Omokachi to make havoc. Mini Wekwu would certainly liquidate him.[6]

In its physical and metaphysical manifestations, nature provides men with vital sustenance and security from harmful mystical forces. And the

44

more striking the natural object is, the more mystically relevant it is in the service of man's material, emotional and psychological need. Such are the caves described by Achebe in *Things Fall Apart* which contain the shrine of Agbala and its oracle, the Oracle of the Hills and Caves, whose voice is powerful in resolving the crises of life because it is the spokesman of the all-powerful earth-mother goddess:

> People came from far and near to consult it. They came when misfortune dogged their steps or when they had a dispute with their neighbours. They came to discover what the future held for them or to consult the spirits of their departed fathers.[7]

The significance of the Caves as the abode of an all-seeing spirit becomes clear when the physical setting is described:

> The way into the shrine was a round hole at the side of a hill, just a little bigger than the round opening into a hen-house. Worshippers and those who came to seek knowledge from the god crawled on their belly through the hole and found themselves in a dark, endless space in the presence of Agbala. No one had ever beheld Agbala, except his priestess. But no one who had ever crawled into his awful shrine had come out without the fear of his power. His priestess stood by the sacred fire which she built in the heart of the cave and proclaimed the will of the god. The fire did not burn with a flame. The glowing logs only served to light up vaguely the dark figure of the priestess.[8]

It is not difficult to see, and readers of E. M. Forster's *A Passage to India* never fail to see, why caves express aspects of the deeply embedded levels of the human unconscious. In the traditional imagination, it is not necessary to delve deep to discover the mystical significance of such caves. The significance of the Caves, the Oracle which resides there and the priestess who mediates between the Oracle and people who consult it are well expressed in *Things Fall Apart*, which conveys a view of life intimately woven from the physical environment, metaphysical realities and the social and economic needs of individuals and the community. Sacred caves like the one described in *Things Fall Apart* actually exist in Ogbunike, some nine miles from Onitsha, and close to the setting of the novel. They have had religious and mystical significance for the local people from time immemorial.

Mystical association with nature is well illustrated by the large number of trees sacred to minor gods and spirits. Almost all the novels set in traditional villages mention sacred or mystically charged trees which are objects of worship, veneration and awe. In *Things Fall Apart*, the bicycle

45

belonging to the white man murdered "riding the iron horse" is tied up on a sacred silk-cotton tree,[9] and elsewhere we learn that the field at which wrestling matches are held in Umuofia has a "big and ancient silk-cotton tree which was sacred"[10] and before which the drummers sit. We learn incidentally that this tree is connected with fertility: "Spirits of good children lived in that tree waiting to be born. On ordinary days young women who desired children came to sit under its shade."[11] In *Arrow Of God*, it is the *udala* tree in the village square which is sacred to the ancestors[12] while in *The Concubine*, as in *Things Fall Apart*, it is the silk-cotton tree which is sacred.[13]

Physical nature is so intimately integrated into the lives and experiences of rural Africans that the conscious and subconscious levels of their minds are saturated with it. Their folklore and mythology are full of symbols and images drawn from the natural world. And these are realistically lived through in nightmare situations or at time when the conscious mind is overridden by fantasy – as when a character is suffering from serious illness which disrupts the conscious process of the mind. Such is the state of Araba's mind as it wanders through a sort of mythopoeic geography while he is comatose with a dangerous fever:

> The road to spirit-land passes seven lands, seven seas, seven plains, seven deserts. The stopping places include where the sun was born and where it was bathed with blood, the home of the maimed who had lost their lives by violence, and finally led to the home of the old woman who gave the travellers spirit food which sets the mark of no return on their foreheads. Araba reached the old spirit's hut but there stopped his ears, bound his head with akwala string and refused to eat the food. He would not cross the line that divided spirits from men for if he did that Nwokeke would triumph.[14]

Nature is not always conceived of as beneficent. In the traditional imagination, it is also full of threatening possibilities. The forest is full of mystery. In Igbo village life, the terror of the evil forest is a living reality, as Achebe explains in *Things Fall Apart*:

> Every clan and village had its "evil forest". In it were buried all those who died of the really evil diseases, like leprosy and smallpox. It was also the dumping ground for the potent fetishes of great medicine-men when they died. An "evil forest" was, therefore, alive with sinister forces and powers of darkness.[15]

But even ordinary forests contain possibilities of mystery, evil and danger, like that in which Ikemefuna is murdered, again in *Things Fall Apart*:

46

The footway had now become a narrow line in the heart of the forest. The short trees and sparse undergrowth which surrounded the men's village began to give way to giant trees and climbers which perhaps had stood from the beginning of things, untouched by the axe and the bush-fire. The sun breaking through their leaves and branches threw a pattern of light and shade on the sandy footway.[16]

Even denser and more mysterious is the forest enfolding the shrine of Amadioha in *The Concubine*:

Rank trees bordered the dark path. Some climbers were so thick they looked like ordinary trees. At the shrine absolute stillness reigned and it was quite cold as the high majestic roof of thick foliage, like a black rain cloud, cut off the sun completely. Even the wind could only play meekly among the undergrowth.[17]

The feeling in these descriptions is aesthetic only in a very particular sense. The grandeur of the virgin forest is a terrible kind of beauty, but beauty all the same; for, in the traditional imagination, power is an aspect of beauty, and so is mystery. Power is the expression of vitality mixed with mystery. The forest manifests power, natural and supernatural power, with its unlimited scope for mystery. The feeling it inspires is awe tempered with fear.

This feeling is often extended to cosmic nature. The sun and the moon are perceived in their powerful, vital, and therefore beneficent or harmful aspects. They are approached with a mixture of feelings, as in the welcoming of the new moon by the people in Ezeulu's compound in *Arrow of God*:

The little children in Ezeulu's compound joined the rest in welcoming the moon. Obiageli's shrill voice stood out like a small *ogene* among drums and flutes. The Chief Priest could also make out the voice of his youngest son, Nwafo. The women too were in the open, talking.

"Moon," said the senior wife, Matefi, "may your face meeting mine bring good fortune."

"Where is it?" asked Ugoye, the younger wife. "I don't see it. Or am I blind?"

"Don't you see beyond the top of the ukwa tree? Not there. Follow my finger."

"Oho, I see it. Moon, may your face meeting mine bring good fortune. But how is it sitting? I don't like its posture."

"Why?" asked Matefi.

"I think it sits awkwardly – like an evil moon."

47

"No," said Matefi. "A bad moon does not leave anyone in doubt. Like the one under which Okuata died. Its legs were up in the air."[18]

Occasionally the moon can become an object of aesthetic feeling, especially when it is full and sheds its luminous beams on the village carnivals and moon dancers (egwu-ọnwa). On such occasions, the Igbo say, cripples begin to hunger for a walk. But the moon is also associated with abnormal psychic conditions and lunatics and those possessed of "agwu" or mystically caused eccentricity respond to the moon's phases.

The sun is also regarded with mixed feelings, since it can be the source of life as well as of death, beneficent as well as malevolent. In the rural novels, the sun is closely observed and related to the rhythm of planting, propagation and harvesting of crops, especially in so far as it is also associated with rain. One of the unforgettable pictures in *Things Fall Apart* is of the sun pouring down its rays upon the earth, unrelieved by any cloud cover, and ruining the year's crop:

> The blazing sun returned, more fierce than it had ever been known, and scorched all the green that had appeared with the rains. The earth burned like hot coals and roasted all the yams that had been sown.[19]

Given the disasters which fall upon rural communities through natural agencies, it is not surprising that the traditional attitude to nature is not romantic or one of aesthetic enjoyment. Nature is so overpowering and intimately connected with basic survival that it has to be seen largely in terms of metaphysical forces to be conciliated and coaxed to extend their beneficent influences to man. Religious and mystical attitudes are more appropriate. The vast potential occult energy of nature is also exploited by man for his own ends in his struggle for survival. But in all these, the practical interest far outweighs the purely aesthetic consideration.

Where there is little scientific knowledge it is not surprising that natural phenomena should seem to have divine and metaphysical powers: are they not throbbing with life, and in adverse circumstances, do they not cause sudden and devastating death and destruction? Life and death, creation and annihilation, are these not the qualities that reveal divine presence and action? It is not suggested that man in the traditional setting is a total victim of natural forces, or impotent to deal with threats to his survival. On the contrary, man is resourceful enough to survive by manipulating nature. He extracts from nature some of its vital properties for his own use, to fight inimical natural and mystical forces. For example, when Okonkwo's favourite daughter, Ezinma, is sick with malaria he goes into the bush and procures "a large bundle of grasses and leaves, roots and barks of medicinal trees and shrubs"[20] with which he cures the fever. In *The Concubine* with its magical and religious perception of life, the dibias Anyika and Agwoturumbe rely to a large degree on the curative quality of herbs and trees empirically proved efficacious, including the precious "rats' ears" and mbelekuleku leaves.[21] In spite of the ritual invocations, the solid empirical basis of traditional medicine remains incontestable. The ritual formula is not a substitute for empirical efficacy but is meant to reinforce the vital force already present, and to fend off inimical outside mystical influence that might prevent the medicine from taking effect. The pharmaceutical and metaphysical forces in trees are exploited for the benefit of man; but if this fails recourse can always be had to religion and magic.

Traditional people have their own sense of beauty; they have a highly developed aesthetic sense but, because it is differently oriented from that of industrial man, it perceives beauty, harmony and formal perfection differently. The experience of Europe shows that the subjective, independent aesthetic enjoyment of nature belongs to a period of social development after increasing industrial and urban pressures had separated European man from his rural roots, nature thereafter becoming "other" to him and open to individual, subjective appreciation. The traditional Africans with whom the rural novels deal have not undergone this industrial and urban separation from the primal, integrated life of the village and of agricultural man. It is fair to say that the taste for horticulture of all sorts, landscape gardening, ornamental gardening, the development of garden parks, zoos and so on widely noticeable in the environmental and architectural history of the past few centuries in Europe, especially since the eighteenth century, represents modern man's attempt to re-establish some kind of contact with a domesticated nature to replace the relationship which he has all but lost through industrialization and urbanization. Natural woods and forests are replaced with cultivated gardens and parks, natural animals by those in the zoos, natural streams and brooks by ponds, moats and canals. Natural darkness is negated by electricity. The moon is obliterated by the street lights in built-up urban centres.

Urban West Africans are living through this shift. As urban centres spring up and push out into the forests and woods, as roads and railways criss-cross hills, valleys and plains, and bridges span rivers and streams, as factories and office blocks supplant farmsteads, man in the urban centres of West Africa establishes his dominance, and wild nature hastily recedes. And with this recession go many of the traditional attitudes held by West Africans towards nature, especially religious and mystical attitudes.

49

But the separation of man from nature has not gone as far in West Africa as it has in industrialized Europe. The modern West African town, often an outgrowth of a previous traditional village or "town" has not always wiped away all the natural features of its rural beginnings. Indeed, some of those rural features give the urban phenomenon in West Africa its uniqueness. One still encounters in the heart of sophisticated Lagos (or any other urban centre) a rambling procession of Shango-worshippers, or the rites of the harvest season in a town like Onitsha, or the masked celebration of one of the numerous nature gods of Africa in any of the sparkling new townships. Again, old streams and rivers continue to be worshipped by some people even after they have been absorbed in the new urban settlements. Since the urban phenomenon is new in West Africa and many of the settlements are still quite small, the West African new town is never too far from rural surroundings. The forests and rivers, the sacred woods and enchanted hills are never beyond walking distance. And most of the so-called urbanized West Africans are living only part of their lives in the towns and the other part in their ancestral villages, so shifts in attitudes to nature among urbanized West Africans have not gone as far as in the highly industrialized societies of Europe and America. The people still share in some measure the concepts of nature and the supernatural central to the world view of their rural relatives.

But considerable changes have taken place. The townships of West Africa contain their parks and ornamental gardens. Private houses inhabited by the new African elites are planted with gardens. The streets are lined with trees. Areas which in the colonial days were little outposts of Europe have retained their garden city bloom even now that they are largely inhabited by the black elites. The universities and schools are decorated with ornamental trees and gardens. Churches and public places are decorated with flowerpots.

Nature is being recreated in the urban settlements as it is in the industrialized parts of the world; and individuals, especially the educated middle class, are beginning to develop modern aesthetic attitudes towards nature and modern concepts of it. The Western aesthetic outlook tends to affect to an increasing degree Africans who live in the urban environment or who have been brought up on Western literature. Thus, Kisimi Kamara's excursion to the Lake District and his rapturous interest in the English countryside[22] are eloquent tributes to his English literature teachers who have so Westernized his aesthetic outlook that he has begun to develop an individual taste for nature. Thus also, urban characters like Jagua (in *Jagua Nana*) and Yaniya and Wilson Iyari (in *Beautiful Feathers*) find welcome reprieve from the neurosis of the hectic life of Lagos, Jagua in the rural serenity of Ogabu where life is well integrated against a background of "the palm trees and the Iroko, the rivulets and the fertile earth"[23] and Wilson and his wife in the Arcadian outpost of the Ol' Man Forest.

In *The Beautyful Ones Are Not Yet Born*, the new black politicians and professionals who have supplanted the colonial elite are distinguished by their attachment to flowers, gardens and lawns. In the prestigious Upper Residential Area where the partyman Koomson lives, the houses are surrounded by high hedges. Koomson's house has a big garden in front of it, as well as a vast expanse of "lush grass", a lawn cared for by a professional gardener.[24]

Soyinka has a certain scorn for the intellectual taste for flowers and cultivated nature. He sees it as a symptom of bourgeois snobbery and as deadly in its artificiality, like being in love with frozen postcard images. Sagoe the journalist has that type of artificiality in mind as he walks across Carter Bridge over Lagos lagoon and contrasts the natural condition with the retouched tourist pictures: "Not today the postcard lagoon and hair-oiled Nat-King-greasy-Cole hair ripples, not today the petrified palm trees and the glazed shore. The lagoon was a trough of shea-butter churning, and cockroach huts of ako stalks circled the water edge in uncertain nibbles."[25] Soyinka has an undisguised disdain for the bourgeois attempt to organize and systematize nature for show. With so much that is authentic all around, he sees in the effort an uncritical absorption of foreign tastes and aesthetic values which betrays the inauthenticity of the elite. Ikoyi suburb, with its gardens and ornamental trees is "dead".[26] (Compare Achebe's observation that "For all its luxurious bungalows and flats and its extensive greenery Ikoyi was like a graveyard".[27]) But for Soyinka, the real limit of artificiality is the attachment to flowers, especially the "gory carnations" with which they bury their members,[28] the vulgar plastic flowers with which they decorate their houses. For instance, Sagoe shows marked repugnance for his fiancée Dehinwa's wardrobe, with its handle of petrified flowers.[29] But Professor Oguazor's "petrified forest" of decorative plastic fruits draws the fiercest of Soyinka's satiric attacks:

> From the ceiling hung citrous clusters on invisible wires. A glaze for the warmth of life and succulence told the story, they were the same as the artificial apples. There were fancy beach-hat flowerpots on the wall, ivy clung from these along a picture rail, all plastic, and the ceiling was covered in plastic lichen. Sagoe had passed, he now noticed, under a special exhibition group of one orange, two pears, and a fan of bananas straight from European wax-works.[30]

In sober truth plastic flowers, fruit and even trees for internal decoration have gained acceptance among the elite of West Africa in their effort to keep the life-style absorbed from the West. Soyinka seems to say that there is no need to turn to artificial nature where true nature is a living fact of the environment. For his "interpreters", nature is very much alive and still integral to life's experiences. They feel the power of natural forces in their lives by refusing to cut themselves off from active experiences. For them, the mystery of the creeks and lagoons, the terror of the sky as Shango unleashes his thunderbolts and electrical flares in a storm, the immanent occult vitality of sacred rocks and streams, all are living experiences which sharpen their awareness of the environment and quicken their responses to the environment. Most of them are artists or of artistic temperament, and this may explain this sensitivity.

But even for these people, the perception of nature differs conspicuously from that of traditional people. Nature principally affects them through its healing power, which means that they, his characters, are not so different from the other middle-class characters who escape to nature in moments of crisis, strain or emotional upheavals. The best example of this flight is Egbo's "pilgrimage" to Ogun River in search of renewal after the night of his sexual initiation:

> Some balance in his life was upset and he boarded the train that Sunday afternoon feeling distinctly hollowed out, weak, nervous and apprehensive. Someone must know, someone must have born witness to his night of fantasy, when the sorceress Simi took him by the hand and led him into paths and byways of the most excruciating ecstacy.[31]

And now in search of restoration he repairs to the river. He needs spiritual regeneration and turns to the healing balm of immense powers and mysteries:

> Egbo never ceased to thrill to the dark rumble of the wheels as the train passed through the bridge at Olokemeji, and to look out at the rocks overrun by Ogun River at its most aloof. The bridge spanned the Ogun where the boulders appeared like those rugged Egba ancients in conclave. They were far-flung toes of the unyielding god, Olumo black of Egba. Always for Egbo, the god expanded through the forest from his seat at Ikereku, his colossal feet thrust through the soft underbelly of earth, for he had come to rest and his tired foot submitted to the soothing run of the waters of Ogun. Egbo deserted the train at Olokemeji, the sweet and heavy dark liqueur smell of coal smoke had turned him drowsy, and Lagos was far and the offices stale and unplaced in these new proportions of life.[32]

His swim in the river revives him with a power that renews his flagging

52

spirit. In the terror of the night and in the heart of its mystery – the dark waters and deeper grain of night, without stars and glow-worms – Egbo undergoes another, more profound, initiation through fear into manhood:

> So now, for the first time since his childhood ascent into the gods' domain, Egbo knew and acknowledged fear, stood stark before his new intrusion. For this was no human habitation, and what was he but a hardly ripened fruit of the species, lately celebrated the freeing of the man.[33]

Thereafter, we are told, Egbo made this spot "a place of pilgrimage", for he has established contact here with the deeper levels of his own nature through communication with nature and the supernatural. In a sense, Egbo's night experience by the Ogun is a pilgrimage into the traditional soul and a discovery at once of nature's secrets and the secrets of integrated being:

> He left with a gift that he could not define upon his body, for what traveller beards the gods in their den and departs without a divine boon. Knowledge he called it, a power for beauty often, an awareness that led him dangerously towards a rocksalt psyche, a predator on Nature.[34]

The uniqueness of Soyinka's approach to nature in this novel derives from acute psychological observation which he brings to bear on his characters. The other novelists are aware that their urban characters tend to fly to the natural setting of the countryside in moments of stress, but none of them has traced this tendency with the same insight.

Art in the traditional environment is decidedly collective and utilitarian. There is no strict differentiation between pure and applied art and there is always an underlying rapport between the artist and the community, except in the rare cases of the esoteric music and symbolic pictography of secret cults, where the artist appeals to a coterie. The traditional artist is a specialist, but his work is inspired by a collectively shared aesthetic vision from which he derives his motifs, symbolisms and functional framework. There are numerous instances in the West African novels where we see this collective aesthetic determinism at work; but the point can best be made by reference to music and art alone. I shall begin with music.

Music serves as entertainment, as an accompaniment to the dance, and for religious or ritual purposes. It also features in many different settings within traditional society: palm-wine drinking, hunting, games and sports, harvesting and other aspects of agricultural work, death, funeral, burial and second burial, marriage and so on. West African novels show the immense importance of music, song and dance in the community life of traditional society, and how they express its predominantly collective emotion at any particular time. Whether it is sorrow, fear, suspense, exaltation, happiness, anger or reverence, the community expresses its inner tensions and exuberances in rhythm and melody.

Indeed the novels show that traditional societies might reasonably be called musical communities. Everyone, man, woman or child, sings, dances and produces rhythm at some point or other in the action. Though there are specialist musicians, vocalists, instrumentalists and dancers, everyone is moved by the musical impulse to express himself in some musically defined way. The novelists take trouble to identify their characters in terms of this general attachment to the musical atmosphere of the traditional life.

In *Things Fall Apart,* several characters are musically identified. Okonkwo's father, Unoka, is a musician. Achebe says of him: "He was very good on his flute, and his happiest moments were the two or three moons after the harvest when the village musicians brought down their instruments, hung above the fireplace. Unoka would play with them, his face beaming with blessedness and peace."[35] Okoye, Unoka's creditor, is also a musician, who plays on the ogene.[36] Even the gruff warrior himself is moved by music, as when he hears the drums beat the wrestling rhythm: "Okonkwo cleared his throat and moved his feet to the beat of the drums. It filled him with fire as it had always done from his youth. He trembled with the desire to conquer and subdue. It was like the desire for woman."[37] The murder squad on its way to execute the boy-hostage cannot resist the temptation to discuss the ozo music whose sound is wafted towards them from some neighbouring village.[38]

Danda and *The Concubine* have musicians and dancers for their chief characters as well as audiences who appreciate song and rhythm. In them life is almost one long expression of rhythm, song and dance, and though solemn and serious affairs, including some perplexing and some tragic, obtrude from time to time, it is the light-hearted, musical spontaneity and its accompanying laughter and gaiety which prove the dominant mood. Danda is the embodiment of this spirit of musical spontaneity. Wherever he goes, his little wooden flute, the oja, goes with him, and with its music he always transforms the atmosphere by injecting into it irresistible gaiety and vitality. His audiences also never fail to respond to his musical enthusiasm with appreciative shouts and gestures and by doing impromptu dances. As in the other rural novels, everyone in *Danda* expresses himself most spontaneously through dance and song. Even Danda's austere and patriarchal father, Araba, responds to music now and again, as for example on the eve of his second son's return to his urban base, Araba is seen to stagger "winefully" into his hut at the end of the celebrations, "crooning a masquerade song".[39]

Most of the characters in *The Concubine* are competent musically. Ihuoma, the heroine of the novel, is the best woman dancer in the village; her fiancé, Ekwueme, is a great alto singer and says of himself: "Singing is my life."[40] The members of the village musical troupe include Wodu Wakiri the wag, who is the best soloist and a fine dancer, Adiele the oduma beater (xylophonist) and Mman the drummer, whose fingers have been made crooked by his constant drumming. These and other characters are shown on numerous occasions composing new songs and new tunes, singing or dancing on formal or informal occasions.

Even in the caricatured village of Isolo in *One Man One Wife*, music has a place. Both the traditionalists and the newly converted Christians express themselves in song, music and dance, and if the boundary separating orthodox Christian hymn-singing from the rhythmic celebration of the rites of Yoruba nature gods is not always clearly marked in the mixed-up village of Isolo, it is because in musical appreciation a rigid division on the lines of strict doctrinal orthodoxy is unnecessary. The important thing is that everyone dances to the drums during festive occasions, including the grave elders of the church and the mighty teacher Royasin himself. As Aluko reminds us in his mocking Aristophanean style, "the virus of conviviality was no respecter of persons and personalities".[41]

Music and dance feature in the nightmare world of *The Voice* though there is no singing. Music and dance appear as an expression of moral evil. They are the music and dance of "possession". The men and women are described as dancing frenziedly, "like ants round a lamp hung on a pole".[42]

The novelists naturally associate music with specific periods of the agricultural year. People like music at other times, but the season defines the time of the most concentrated musical activities of the groups and communities. The most favourable musical period is the lax season between the last rains of the passing agricultural year and the beginning of the new one. Nkem Nwanko describes the setting of this season in that section of *Danda* suffused with musical gaiety and festivities: "The scorch season was dying. The happiest time of the year, the season for feasts, when men and women laughed with all their teeth and little boys, their mouths oily oily, ran about the lanes blowing the crops of chickens to make balloons."[43] And Nzekwu also notes the significance of this season as he traces the progress of his hero through Christianity into the realities of an active and living traditional culture of Ado. Patrick's return sets the scene: "Patrick returned to Ado in September, which was the

55

beginning of the festival season and the season for the harvesting of farm crops, particularly yams. It was also the season of masquerade displays."[44]

The major festivals in the rural novels are located within this period: the New Yam Festival in *Things Fall Apart* (pp. 31–3), the Feast of the Pumpkin Leaves in *Arrow of God* (pp. 82–90), the Feast of the Founding Ancestor's Day in *Danda* (pp. 17–26), the masquerade festivals and sports in *Blade Among the Boys* (pp. 54–66, 68–74, 93–8), the "outing" of women's dances in *Danda* (pp. 40–4) and the second burial ceremony of *Arrow of God* (pp. 271–2). Two things, the end of the year's agricultural work and the reaping of plenty from the year's harvests, combine to make this the ideal time for festivities, communal rejoicing and musical entertainment, with music underscoring the dominant mood. This season of music, song and festivities remained an essential reality of rural life in West Africa even after the introduction of Christianity, because the major Christian festivals fall within the same period. Christmas and Easter, and of course the secular New Year's Day, provide opportunities for musical festivities in the villages. Both the traditionalists and Christians of the West African villages regard these as occasions for music, song and dance, and there is often considerable intermingling of the two groups.

Three types of musical situations are clearly discernible in the rural novels. The first is the impromptu situation in which an individual or a group of people suddenly burst into song or dance or improvise a rhythm under the immediate impulse of an overwhelming emotion, usually elation, happiness or triumph. In that situation music, song and dance cease to be objective realities and become modes of responding, instinctive externalization of an internal state. Very often, the musical response is dictated by the situation.

A few examples can be given here. Impromptu musical expression is a marked feature of *The Concubine*. In one incident, three drinking companions gradually transform a palm-wine celebration, with no actual musical instruments, into a musical session:

> In the reception hall they drank and joked. Later, Wakiri started a familiar tune. Ekwueme supplied the second part while Nuadi [the host] joined them hesitantly. Nnadi would rather have listened to the other two than sing himself. But he knew this would not make for good companionship. So he sang on like a man who had eaten maize. At times . . . he broke through with a fine, harmonious . . . tenor part. As the singing warmed Ekwueme looked around for a short drum stick. He found one and, with it, converted one limb of

a three-legged chair into a percussion instrument. Inside the kitchen Ihuoma unconsciously ground her pepper to their rhythm and her clear igele voice floated into the reception hall. Wakiri could no longer contain himself. He got up and seizing one edge of his trailing wrapper danced very gracefully either because or in spite of his knock-kneed legs.

One song followed another and the wine gradually disappeared as the shadows began to grow.[45]

On another occasion, Ihuoma and her two grown children do an impromptu dance to the sound of drumming coming from a neighbouring village.[46] A casual visit of one musician to another develops into a full-scale musical session with the assembled audience participating.[47]

The musical interest of *The Concubine*, especially the spontaneity and easy expression of rhythm in song and dance, is an aspect of the novel's idyllic nature. In *Danda* the same musical mood is noticeable. Danda is the focus of musical interest, but the spontaneity of others and the dramatized responses which the audiences give express the same spontaneity, create the same idyllic setting, since they are also an expression of communal well-being and social peace and integration. The arrival of the first motor car to be owned by a local man in Aniocha illustrates this musical spontaneity and the audience response to it. Danda, like every Aniocha villager, is impressed by the importance of the occasion, and having had a drink or two of brandy to loosen his tongue, he strikes up a song. He sings, we are told, "in a husky-sweet voice shaking his head from side to side and occasionally stopping to bawl: 'Ewe ewe ewe! that's the way we do it!'" Then he moves from singing to fluting, stirring up his audience by calling individuals by their pet and praise names. The audience responds; one man jumps to his feet and does a running dance, shouting "ewe ewe ewe!" while the owner of the house and the motor-car brings out his double-barrelled gun and crying, "That's how it is, flute man, . . . I hear you!" lets off "two volleys into the heavens".[48]

The point is that the occasion creates its own music, given the presence of a musical improviser like Danda. There is no set music for the celebration of motor cars, but a talented musician can make up a tune and a theme to suit the occasion. This gift for musical improvisation means that every event can be celebrated in song and rhythm and every situation can be rapidly transformed into a musical situation.

Most contexts of musical expression in the rural novels are formal occasions which fit into well-defined and recurrent patterns of the agricultural year, including the chief festivals, games and sports, birth, marriage, death and other key moments in the lives of individuals. The musical range is

57

very wide, from the children's lullaby to highly ritualistic sacred music. Two functional categories can be clearly defined: the first involves the use of music for aesthetic entertainment, and the second its use for ritual or religious purpose. The distinction is not rigid, and there is a good deal of overlapping. The distinction however separates the largely secular function of traditional music from the purely sacred and the ritualistic. Certainly, the musical accompaniment to pure entertainments like wrestling matches is itself musical entertainment pure and simple, while that associated with religious rites, such as the Feast of the Pumpkin Leaves, is truly ritual or religious music. Borderline cases, such as the "outing" of masquerades like that of the Otakagu age-group in *Arrow of God* and the numerous masquerade groups in *Danda* and *Blade Among the Boys*, have an element of aesthetic entertainment as well as of ritual significance, since masquerades, whether for entertainment or as services in religious functions, still represent the cult of the ancestral mystery. Even the hobbledehoy, sporting masquerades described by Nzekwu in *Blade Among the Boys* still enjoy the prestige of ancestral authority. Funeral music, such as that composed in honour of Emenike in *The Concubine*, partakes of the two aspects of music, aesthetic entertainment and ritual and religious significance.

Whether the musical situation is meant to provide entertainment or is created for ritual and religious purpose, the ultimate effect seems to be the same: to bring the community together, to forge a social, aesthetic or mystical link among its members and to unite emotional responses around defined rhythmic waves and melodies. Music, dance and song become for the community an instrument for creating social, emotional and aesthetic solidarity.

Most of the dance situations make for group participation. In addition to the instrumentalists and vocalists, there is often a troupe of dancers who perform in groups. Unlike "individualistic" modern ball-room dancing, traditional dancing almost always assumes a group of people dancing together as well as periodic solo performances. But even the solos are integrated into the structure of group performance. The group is always at hand to offer support by clapping or humming, or swaying or making encouraging and approving sounds. Amadi captures the rhythm of group dancing in this passage from *The Concubine*:

> Young men and women moved round and round the instrumentalists singing in response to the soloists. The wrappers of the men and the married women swept the arena, but the maidens wore theirs up to knee level and also had beads above the calves, at the ankles and around their waists.

58

For a time they moved round and round swaying to the rhythm in a half-stoop. Suddenly the soloist stopped and the instruments took over completely.

No one talked, not even the old men who sat around the arena on their three-legged chairs. This was the time to know the top dancers. Everyone bent low. Faces were as rigid as masks. The men moved their backs and shoulders but the women moved only their waists and every bit of their energy seemed to be concentrated there. The vibrations were extremely rapid. It was admirable how they maintained the rhythm at such high speeds. For several seconds tension was at fever pitch. Then one by one the men straightened out and watched the women admiringly.[49]

Similarly, Nwankwo described a poignant little scene of solo dancing with group collaboration at the outing for the Uwadiegwu dance:

The Uwadiegwa umunna had gathered at the ogwe, a wooden stand rising in tiers, consisting of wooden benches placed on forked stakes. The men sat on the benches and snuffed. The women had formed a circle in an open square adjacent to the stands and were singing and clapping vigorously. A girl stood in the middle dancing the warrior dance and cutting through the air with the right hand in imitation of the slash of the matchet.

"Obulu nimalu aja.
Gbuo nu mma ndi Agbaja
Iye-e-e eiye eye."

There was some colourful quality in the refrain which dispelled the spirit of darkness. For the night, even with the moon shining, has a heavy pressure that subdues the heart. But the song made the heart light and the eyes shine.

"Iye-e-e eiye eye
Gbuo nu mma ndi Agbaja
Iye–"[50]

The traditional audience at a musical session is always a participant. Often its members react rhythmically by doing some of the steps outside the group or by presenting gifts to the dancers, singers and instrumentalists. Appreciation may take the form of unconscious body movements such as shaking the head, twitching or limb movement in rhythm with the dancers. This rapport between the audience and the performers is re-created in the rural novels; it reflects two characters of the rural environment and its musical tradition. First, the traditional village being a small community, everyone sooner or later comes to know what is happening in

59

musical circles and to participate in them. Secondly, much traditional music is rhythmic and dance-oriented and therefore directly appeals to the sense of rhythm of the whole people. Most of the rhythmic patterns within the musical tradition are so generally familiar to the members of the particular society that even when a new dance is being exhibited by the professional group, the existence in the new music of identifiable dance rhythms easily permits the audience to become an active participant. That is not to say that traditional music lacks complexity or that it cannot be intriguing in its novelty, but the ear trained to distinguish the logic of traditional music rhythms will easily pick out the key rhythmic patterns, which are often determined by the key instrument, or the vocal line built around the "rhythm of dance". With these in firm possession, an audience can take part by beating or clapping time, shaking the head or performing other voluntary or involuntary acts of participation. It can afford, for a start at any rate, to overlook the polyphonic or polyrhythmic elaborations of the new dance which merely provide a background support to the central rhythm.

This peculiarity of traditional music, dominated by the central rhythm of dance, explains a number of details recorded in rural West African novels. For example, on numerous occasions we find Danda appearing at a musical scene and, unrehearsed, joining a musical performance already in full session. This is only possible where the rhythmic structure of a piece of music is sufficiently flexible not to be upset by the introduction of a few more notes. Again, because of the structural peculiarity mentioned above, it is possible for the practised ear to pick out the different rhythmic units of an elaborate musical ensemble, as Achebe informs us in *Things Fall Apart*:

> He [Unoka] could hear in his mind's ear the blood-stirring and intricate rhythms of the *ekwe* and the *udu* and the *ogene*, and he could hear his own flute weaving in and out of them, decorating them with a colourful and plaintive tune. The total effect was gay and brisk, but if one picked out the flute as it went up and down and then broke up into short snatches, one saw that there was sorrow and grief there.[51]

The justness of Achebe's and Nwankwo's observation concerning the flexibility of the *oja* in a musical ensemble is well supported by an independent specialized view. In an article called "Rhythm of Dance in Igbo Music" the author makes the following comment:

> In the Atilogwu dance music, the two instruments which determine the rhythm of dance are a short vertical flute with a melodic range

of a sixth called *oja* and a bass gong called *alo*. During the opening or the transitional intermission between one structural dance move-ment and the next, the next dance movements are called on this flute. At the end of this call, the bass group player and the dancer work in close co-ordination. The rhythm of the bass gong . . . synchronizes with the rhythm of the dance steps.[52]

The nature of traditional music makes it a music par excellence of mass participation and of massive improvisations. But in this popular manifesta-tion lies its significance as an index of the emotional movements in the lives of traditional people, for it underlines the structures of feeling which flow from melodic and rhythmic strands of a given musical exhibition. Nkem Nwankwo is again nearest to establishing the psychological and emotional basis of musical communication within the traditional society when he sums up the great musical carnival that celebrates the founding of the clan of Aniocha:

> You have probably heard that music: the nervous agony of the ekwe, the poignant melancholy of the oja, the clamorous swell of the drums and the plaintiveness of the ogene; all combining to bring down the sky with lusty pulsation, to create the rhythm that some say was brought back from the land of the spirits by the great Ojadili: he who wrestled with the ten-headed king of the spirits and made the monarch's back kiss mother earth; the music that for ages has led Aniocha men to rage in riotous abandon, that takes a small drop of the day and inflates it into a tempestuous sea in which the men and women drowned, that snatches from time one small moment and gives it the vastness of eternity.
>
> "Cle-tum cle-tum cle-tum!" And the world was annihilated. Our dance too is like our music, obstreperous; it does not suggest or insinuate; it states boldly, crudely. And what it has to say is very much after our hearts.[53]

Nwankwo has put his finger on the complex process involved in musical appreciation within the traditional society: the multiple-layered inter-action between patterns of sound and the surface interpretations placed on them and the underlying feelings which develop from the further deepen-ing of appreciation of both sound and interpretation by having them seen against the wider, all-embracing picture of the world – the generalizing of the particular and the eternalizing of the temporal. It is when sounds and their symbols are seen through this universalizing and internalizing tele-scope that they assume a sharp focus which falls emphatically on the emo-tions and registers most strongly on the imagination. There is an area of

61

the traditional psyche where the physical and the metaphysical, the natural and the supernatural meet and there create new being and a new aware-ness, an area of artistic upheaval where the most significant and profound feelings and emotional responses take shape, where the scattered frag-ments of waking reality combine with mythopoeic images as ground matrix in the traditional memory to produce a synthesis of ordered ex-perience. Nkem Nwankwo associates the reality of musical melody and rhythmic patterns with an underlying mythopoeic substratum to produce a unified musical experience, for it is in the marriage of the two levels and their active integration as a method of knowing and feeling that the traditional imagination arrives at its precise definition of reality. The effect of musicality which traditional music produces arises first from a sense of regular harmony and its variations, but more than that, from the fact that the sound itself is either symptomatic or suggestive of something bigger than the music itself, that the music opens a door of knowledge into the deep folds of human consciousness and communion with the wider mystical universe. This process of making contact with the universal essence is neither boldly nor crudely brought about; it insinuates and filters through all the coarseness of externality to reach, largely through suggestion, the appreciative soul. The assumption of this occult, com-munally defined sector of artistic (including musical) experience, is at the base of artistic appreciation in the traditional society. Achebe expresses this corporate, mystical basis of musical appreciation when he describes the effect of the drumming on the villagers of Umuofia before the wrestling matches are due to begin:

> The drums were still beating, persistent and unchanging. Their sound was no longer a separate thing from the living village. It was like the pulsation of its heart. It throbbed in the air, in the sunshine, and even in the trees and filled the village with excitement.[54]

Soyinka makes the same point when he says about Yoruba tragic music that it functions "from archetypal essences whose language derives not from the plane of physical reality or ancestral memory (the ancestor is no more than agent or medium) but from the numinous territory of transition into which the artist obtains fleeting glimpses by ritual, sacrifices and a patient submission of rational awareness to the moment when his fingers and voice relate the symbolic language of the cosmos".[55] The cosmic illumination of the musical structure is shared by both artist and audience; both need it to keep alive the rapport without which mutual intelligibility would cease. The artist, being in possession of a greatly heightened sensi-tivity, only catches at these realities more quickly than his audience.

This raises the question of the nature of musical creativity within traditional society, and the relationship of the musical artist to his audience. All the evidence indicates that the traditional musician, like other traditional creative artists, is a specialist, but that his performance is determined by collective sentiment and receives its inspiration from the traditionally transmitted mode of expression of a particular musical type. Thus the official drummer or singer whose function it is to remind the community of its collective solidarity acts as the keeper of the communal memory by reiterating on special occasions the entire history of the people from the time of the founding father to the present day, recounting the community's glories and triumphs, calamities and disasters.[56]

Achebe and the Guinean writer Camara Laye give two good studies of traditional musicians and their intimate relationship with their societies and their collective tradition. Achebe's Obiozo Ezikolo (King of the Drum) is a typical drummer, and we are shown him working in his highly rhetorical and evocative style through the history of Umuaro and finally settling on the great deity, Ulu, whose festivity is being celebrated:

> Soon after, the great Ikolo sounded. It called the six villages of Umuaro one by one in their ancient order: Umunneora, Umuagu, Umuezeani, Umuogwugwu, Umuisiuzo and Umuachala. As it called each village an enormous shout went up in the market place. It went through the number again but this time starting from the youngest. People began to hurry through their drinking before the arrival of the Chief Priest.
>
> The Ikolo now beat unceasingly; sometimes it called names of important people of Umuaro, like Nwaka, Nwosisi, Igboneme and Uduezue. But most of the time it called the villages and their deities. Finally it settled down to saluting Ulu, the deity of all Umuaro.[57]

A comparison of this sort of account with Nketia's interpretation of the drum speech of the Akan shows why the drum holds a central place in the collective imagination of African people. Its style is epic and it builds its effects by arousing visions of grandeur, heroism and power which though rising subjectively within the individual imagination of the musician are soon objectified as the collective image of the people's history. The *griot* (praise-singer) in Laye's *L'Enfant Noir* is obviously a private practitioner, but his performance is closely informed by a sense of history; while deploying his personal inventiveness to embellish his eulogy of Laye's illustrious ancestry, his freedom is considerably restricted by historical truth. As Camara Laye says, it is the griot's duty as communal historian to preserve traditional truth.[58]

Musicians on other occasions have to make their idiom and tone accord with the aesthetic requirements of the particular genre as determined by

63

tradition. Thus Danda, the Aniocha poet-cum-musician-cum-parasite, brings tears to the eyes of his audience when with the lyrical lilt of his flute he sings the tragedy of the Aniocha warrior caught in an ambush and done to death by the enemy. The language is poetic, but it acquires force by touching the chords of communal legend and the image of fallen manhood – "He fell to them but not until a dozen warriors had been sent to the land of the spirits."[59] Danda's musical talent is more fully explored in his swan song, his last poetical splash before his father's ill-advised attempt to make him into a man of title.[60] The passage is too long to be quoted here but *Danda* draws so deeply from collective traditional lore that it never fails to touch the imagination of those who have lived in the West African village and been brought up in the poetic tradition.

Or to take another example, from *The Concubine*, the death of Emenike is an important occasion for the music-makers of his village. The members of the village band set feverishly to work to produce appropriate music. It is a businesslike, deliberate affair with every stage of the musical detail planned well beforehand. The essential objectifying factor is "Emenike's death provided the theme", but "the tune and the arrangement of words presented the problem" – the musicians have to draw on their creative resources for that. We feel the effort involved. "At first Ekwueme's sister chuckled with restrained laughter as the two friends rambled uncertainly through the scale hunting for a tune. But as the tune grew, she hummed unconsciously with them. The villagers were about to stir from their first sleep when the songsters finally satisfied themselves."[61] At the display itself, these vocalists set up the tune which dictates the rhythm of dance that gives the cue to both the instrumentalists and the dancers. The same individual composition within the corporate framework is evident in the making of satirical songs against the unlucky woman, Aleruchi Oji, who knocked down her husband during a fight,[62] and a man in Chiolu who tried to make love to a woman on the farm.[63] In each of these musical situations, there is evidence of a distinctive creative musical hand, even though the creativity takes place within the existing musical tradition and satisfies the expectations of particular musical genres.

Art is one of the key realities in West African rural novels. West African societies are artistic communities. Within them art is integral to the functional culture. It is not only that in West Africa religious and ritual activities draw from artistic symbolisms and find concrete expression in masks and statuettes, but also that artistic perception is part of the humanity of all the people and finds outlet in their immense desire to paint, mould, carve and decorate, to alter the natural state and beautify it. Virtually everything that has a surface is subject to the decorative effort of man in this part of the world. The better-known artistic master-pieces of West Africa such as the bronzes of Ife and Benin, the terra-cottas of the Nok civilization, and the richly ornamental art treasures of Igbo-Ukwu discovered recently by Professor Thurstan Shaw tend to obscure the fact that art has a manifestly democratic appeal in West Africa, that in addition to its aristocratic representation in the bronze heads of kings and queens and members of the aristocracy, its religious and ritual representation through the numberless sculptures and figurines in the iconographic galleries and medicine houses of the great, art is widely diffused among the population and is put to such common domestic uses as wall- and floor-decoration, door-carving, pottery, decoration of household utensils and everyday implements, and body-painting.

Art represents basic realities and social truths. For example, the reli-gion of traditional society is concretely symbolized. The gods and spirits which embody mystic powers are given concrete form as sculptured figures. Every family medicine-house or shrine is a store-house of icons which represent the gods and spirits, departed ancestors and personal spirits. William Fagg suggests that at least 80 per cent of African tradi-tional art has religious or spiritual significance.[64] The cult of ancestral spirits provides much scope for the creation of masks which symbolize the hidden powers and mystery of the ancestors. Among the Igbo, for ex-ample, the love of art and the perception of religion through art meet in the creation of Mbari art-houses sacred to the earth-mother goddess who is also the patroness of art and creativity. Each Mbari-house represents the attempt by the community of artists to represent a whole world, from the gods to the most up-to-date social realities.[65]

But apart from the formal and specialized art-tradition, life itself is a continuous celebration of the beauty and joy of artistic creation through the incessant effort to improve and decorate nature. In many West African villages, the outside walls of the houses and the insides of living rooms are painted, and the main entrance doors are elaborately carved with decorative and illustrative pictures and patterns. Most of the motifs are taken from nature (including trees, animals and birds) and from fables and legends, as well as from abstract symbols. Virtually every object in daily use – things like water pots and cooking pots, wooden utensils, carving boards, mortars, vats, ladles, knife-handles, combs, walking-sticks, stools, handbags – is decorated, even if the decoration is as rudimentary as burnt-in dots on the surface forming a simple pattern. The idea is always to improve natural appearance by adding a dimension of decorative design. Even the human body is decorated.

65

Women go in for body-painting, intricate hairdos and teeth-filing; men, face-carving or cicatrization and sometimes teeth-filing also.

The importance of these decorative arts in the lives of female characters is often brought out in the novels, especially during the crucial periods of puberty and marriage, and the associated rites of passage. The ritual and social preparations are matched by a corresponding aesthetic heightening of the personality. Among the Igbo, for example, the bride is painted with *uli* and other decorative colours, has a special coiffure and sometimes has her teeth carved. In those of Achebe's novels set in Igboland, the young brides are elaborately made up, as is Obika's wife Okuata in *Arrow of God*: "She wore a . . . coiffure befitting her imminent transition to full womanhood – a plait rather than regular patterns made with a razor . . . Her hair was done in the new *otimili* fashion. There were eight closely woven ridges of hair running in perfect lines from the nape to the front of the head and ending in short upright tufts like a garland of thick bristles worn on the hair-line from ear to ear."[66] The bride in *Things Fall Apart* is even more elaborately beautified. "She wore a coiffure which was done up into a crest in the middle of the head. Cam wood was rubbed lightly into her skin, and all over her body were black patterns drawn with *uli*."[67] In *The Concubine*, Ahurole, the young bride, has her body painted with a "beautiful indigo design" and her hair built into the *ojongo* hair style.[68] She would have had her teeth carved but for her fear of pain.

Not only brides but virtually everyone and everything is beautiful and artistically prepared during great festivals, like the New Year Festival described in *Things Fall Apart*:

> The festival was now only three days away. Okonkwo's wives had scrubbed the walls and the huts with red earth until they reflected light. They had then drawn patterns on them in white, yellow and dark green. They then set about painting themselves with cam wood and drawing beautiful black patterns on their stomachs and on their backs. The children were also decorated, especially their hair, which was shaved in beautiful patterns.[69]

Painting and pattern-making have a meaning. Distinct motifs – human, vegetable and animal motifs as well as those taken from folklore and legends – are identifiable. The patterns are generally recognized and named. The most frequently used elements are dots, line, curvilinears, triangles and rectangles (isinwoji), circles (oloma, onwa), crescents, concentric coils (agwolagwo) derived from the snake, double triangles, (mbo-agu-leopard's claw).[70] These and other shapes constitute a body of symbols and signs on which artists draw in all forms of decorative art, including painting, sculpture, etching and engraving.

The most significant use to which art is put in the rural novels is in religious and ritual situations. But even here the decorative intention is never absent. As William Fagg has said, "While 80% of African art has a ritual function, i.e. is connected with some religious or magical cult, in nearly all tribes the ritual objects are, or may be embellished in response to what clearly are aesthetic impulses."[71] In *Arrow of God*, for example, the ritual and decorative intentions meet in the making of the great sacred drum of Umuaro:

> The Ikolo was fashioned in the olden days from a giant iroko tree at the very spot where it was felled. The Ikolo was as old as Ulu himself at whose order the tree was cut down and its trunk hollowed out into a drum. Since those days it had lain on the same spot in the sun and in the rain. Its body was carved with men and pythons and little steps were cut on one side; without these the drummer could not climb to the top to beat it.[72]

The novelists refer in passing to the iconographic collections in the "medicine-houses" or religious groves without providing detailed descriptions. So, after painstakingly describing the physical surroundings of the shrine of Amadioha in *The Concubine*, Amadi merely refers to the sacred statuettes of Amadioha as "two carved figures clothed in blood and feathers".[73] Achebe's interest in the matter in *Things Fall Apart* is purely functional: "Near the barn was a small house, the 'medicine house' or shrine where Okonkwo kept the wooden symbols of his personal god and of his ancestral spirits. He worshipped them with sacrifices of kola nut, food and palm-wine, and offered prayers to them on behalf of himself, his three wives and eight children."[74] In *Arrow of God*, the rash Akukalia is said to have taken out an adversary's ikenga "from his shrine" and split it into two.[75] When Danda's father, Araba, receives a conciliatory cock from his oldest wife as an atonement for hitting him on the head, he cuts its throat with a small knife and pours the blood on his ikenga.[76] There is a noticeable reticence and lack of elaboration in this, which is unusual in the West African novels. One may well speculate that this is because the writers do not wish to pry too deeply into the mysteries of the traditional religion, for no religion can be stripped down too closely without losing some of its spiritual force.

But there is ethnological comment in plenty elsewhere. For example, the ikenga, which features so frequently in rural novels, is a key factor in the structure of the Igboman's religious and philosophical beliefs. It stands for good fortune, and is symbolized by a man sitting upon a stool, carrying a knife in the right hand and a skull in the left. The man's head is surmounted by two ram's horns. Each unit of the sculpture is clearly symbolical: the right hand is the means of human achievement, the hand with which a man wields his farming implements. The matchet represents all farming tools, and hence economic labour, and is an index of strength and achievement in farming, hunting, fishing, trapping, trading and warfare; the skull represents the end to which the man has applied his genius, his actual achievements in all those enterprises, not only in warfare. The ram's horns represent physical strength and drive, and reinforce the power motif which is already strongly suggested in the other parts of the figure.[77] The ikenga is so strongly identified with the individual's fortune that whenever he intends to undertake an important or a dangerous enterprise or to make a dangerous journey, he has to make a sacrifice to it, and when he emerges successful he has to congratulate his ikenga. He can also discard an ikenga that has failed him persistently and make himself another. When he dies, one of the last rites is the splitting of his ikenga into two to show the cessation of the present phase of his life. One-half of the ikenga is buried with him and the other half is thrown away. Obviously, Achebe is laughing at the ignorance of the British District Commissioner in *Arrow of God* who describes the ikenga as "the most important fetish in the Ibo man's arsenal . . . [which] represents his ancestors to whom he must make daily sacrifice".[78] It represents the man's aspirations rather than his ancestors.

If the writers are sparing in their discussion of the artistic representation of traditional religion they are quite lavish, almost exuberant, in their description of the cult of the ancestral spirits. Most novels set in the Igbo villages give space to this semi-religious and semi-ritual cult activity. I suspect that in this area the writers stand somewhat away from the core of traditional religion and so can write with less inhibition. The masquerade may be officially regarded as an ancestral spirit come back to earth, but the form of this return makes the cult-interest more dramatic than religious in the strict sense. It can be seen of course that the masquerade cult is taken very seriously as part of the political and judicial institutions of traditional society. But the aspect of the mask activities which appeals to the writers is the decorative and artistic one, the masks seen as symbolic representations of diverse personality types, and not only as part of the costumes, dance and drama in which they are used.

The range of the carved ancestral masks depicted in the different novels is wide, and reflects the diversity of personality types perceivable by traditional people. There are the delicate and the gentle, the beautiful

and the graceful, the fierce and the aggressive, the splendid and the powerful, the sinister and the grotesque. These personality types are widely
represented in the novels. In *Danda*, for example, Nwankwo describes
with endearing meticulousness some of these masquerade personalities.
The Ijele is a magnificent mask, referred to variably as "the pride of
Aniocha" and "the king of the spirits". He is described in all his artistic
splendour:

> As ornaments he carried with him complete worlds. The first
> which belted him round the waist was the human world of beauti-
> ful men and women, lions, birds, which did not look so much carved
> out of wood as real. Then there was the world of dead heroes, war-
> riors, men who rode on horses, carried bows and arrows, hunted
> the stick-legged deer. The enormous chest was circled by a world
> of mirrors which flashed blindingly as the king swayed to the
> rhythm of the drums.[79]

The Ijele was of such gigantic proportions and artistic lavishness that it
was reputed to appear only once in a generation, and to constitute, whenever it did, the high point of artistic celebration in the masquerade festivals. In contrast the Agaba mask such as that staged by the Otakagu
age-group in *Arrow of God* is a fierce and powerful spirit: "The face
held power and terror; each exposed tooth was the size of a big man's
thumb, the eyes were large sockets as big as a fist, two gnarled horns
pointed upwards and inwards above its head nearly touching at the
top." It is described as "not a Mask of songs and dance. It stood for the
power and aggressiveness of youth."[80]

Totally different from the fierce and powerful masks is the maiden
spirit or Agboghommo who is the embodiment of feminine beauty
and is distinguished by its gentleness and grace. The contrast is clearly
brought out by Achebe in his description of Edogo's sacred art work-
shop, where he carves the masks. Of the masks surrounding him Achebe
writes: "Most of [them] were for fierce, aggressive spirits with horns
and teeth the size of fingers. But four of them belonged to maiden-spirits
and were delicately beautiful."[81] The maiden spirit has the head of a
maiden decorated with arch-shaped coiffure, carved combs and mirrors,
the *uli* body-painting motifs. Its costume, in an exciting variety of
colours, is intricately patterned with organic motifs. Its music is melodic
and designed for delicate dance steps. In *Danda*, for example, the
Agboghommo is "ushered in by gaily-dressed drummers. Their music
was tender and ritualistic. The Agbogho Mmonwu did not dance but
merely walked the ebe spraying the crowd with maize ears for fertility."[82]

The significance and force of mask art in the novels is in the opportunity it presents to the writers to express the aesthetic conceptions of traditional society. The structure of the mask itself draws on a number of different but coherent artistic activities. The carving of the mask requires the services of a sculptor and of a painter. The costumery calls for a different skill. Then the actual performance of the mask requires the skills and supporting accompaniment of music and dance and often poetry. The mask celebration is therefore a perfect combination and consolidation of all the major traditional artistic genres – sculpture, painting, costume, music, poetry, dance and drama. As a dance drama in which the transformed performer enacts a role, dramatizes an idea or celebrates an event, the mask festival gives the writer dealing with the traditional setting the best scope for exploring his subject aesthetically without dropping into abstractions. And the mask festivals are integrated into the agricultural year and the rhythm of work and rest, so the writers also express a social reality when they devote their efforts and space to the subject.

Traditional art is not merely social or the expression of the collective consciousness. It can relate the individual to cosmic forces. Laye's smithy in *L'Enfant Noir* is conducted under the influence of the black totemic snake, "the guiding spirit of our race", as he calls it; when Edogo carves the mask of the ancestral spirit he does it in a dark room away from the profane gaze of women and children. The implication is that the artist is in a sacred state while producing religious or ritual art and, it may be surmised, in a profane state while working on a secular subject, as for instance when Edogo carves his main-gate door.

Ritual and magical significance also attach to aesthetic expression in the traditional dance, because apart from the need to acquire the skills and the movements of a particular dance, the soloists (like Laye doing the Douga) or groups of performers (as in the case of the Otakagu age-group "outing" their mask) are attempting to protect themselves magically against the envy and malevolence of enemies. Two incidents show how the possibility of magical intervention may threaten the success of a musical display. In the outing of the Otakagu Agaba the presence of a notorious medicine man nearly wrecks the show: "From what was known of him and by the way he sat away from other people it was clear he had not come merely to watch a new Mask. An occasion such as this was often used by wicked men to try out the potency of their magic or to match their power against that of others. There were stories of Masks which had come out unprepared and been transfixed to a spot for days or even felled to the ground."[83] The situation is saved when Obika, one of the two attendants to the mask, sends the menacing dibia packing in spite of the risk. In *Danda* the presence of another medicine man is dramatically handled by Nwankwo. The Izaga, a masquerade that dances on high stilts, feels so threatened by this medicine man that the severe crisis which develops almost becomes a catastrophe. "The izaga dance is a perilous one," he informs us, "perilous for the dancer. For there are always among the spectators some malevolent dibias who would want to try out the power of a new ogwu by pulling the izaga down. To counter the nsi the izaga needed to be as strong as dried wood." But Nwankwo's izaga is afraid, in spite of his own medicines: " 'Get out!' he shrieked. 'Get out!' he waved his fan nervously . . . 'Get back home. This is no place for you – . . . You cannot harm me! . . . I have never offended you. The whole of Aniocha will stand behind me. You cannot take sand from my footprints –' "[84] Being appealed to, the crowd rally to the poor izaga and menace the dibia until he quits the scene. To dance on public occasions or to perform the music on such occasions not only requires the acquisition and perfection of technique but also permits the reinforcing of the *force vitale* through magic. In other words, the aesthetic state is not merely social and capable of rationalization; it is also a metaphysical state. The two elements together give a rounded picture of life within the traditional society.

In the representation of traditional art in the novels we are made aware of the collective aesthetic outlook of the traditional culture. The novels convey shared views of what constitutes the beautiful, the decorous and the sublime. They reflect the peculiar combination of empiricism and magicality, the constant interplay of the sacred with the profane. The arts are functional, religious and decorative as well as recreational, but in all these aspects, they derive their necessity from a collective vision of the universe and the place of the arts within it.

The representation of art or music in the rural novels recognizes this collective aesthetic outlook as well as individual creativity. The individual artist and his talent stand to the artistic sense of the community in the same relationship as the medieval European artist, drawing his inspiration from the unified world picture of his time. He gives cohesion to the concept of the universe by harnessing art, music and drama to ritual and liturgical observance as well as to entertainment and didactic purpose.[85]

A sense of the significance and social value of art in modern urban society, on the other hand, is decisively affected by urban social change, the heterogeneous nature of the urban population aggregations, and the impact of Western artistic philosophy and increased occupational specialization, all of which operating simultaneously have made impossible that unified social and cultural outlook essential to aesthetic collectiveness. Atelier art of a secular nature, nurtured in Western-type schools and expressing an essentially individual vision, subsists within the modern urban centres, and with it, a separation of art from common culture and the growth of coterie audiences. There have been exhibitions of the works of individual artists sponsored by governments and drawing audiences made up largely of Europeans and Africans whose artistic outlook has been influenced by their Western education.

West African artists working in the modern idiom attempt from time to time to derive their motifs from traditional folklore and artistic forms.[86] A spate of "tourist" art modelled on classical African artistic forms is also produced for the benefit of foreign curio-hunters, but again, these works produced outside the cultural matrix of the true traditional art seem utterly lifeless and vulgar. As Fagg says, "to associate tribal and post-tribal art in a single exhibition could be in the nature of a confrontation rather than a demonstration of unity".[87] Despite the growth of art schools sponsored by government and missionary bodies, and the proliferation of art studios and workshops more or less involved in keeping traditional artistic expression alive, art as an integral part of a functioning culture seems to be receding with increased urbanization and specialization.

This situation is often deplored by West African intellectuals and writers, who would prefer to see the traditional artistic values preserved in spite of the encroaching social changes. In his latest novel, *A Dream of Africa*, Camara Laye, one of the writers most deeply committed to the values of the past, handles this question of shifting artistic values. His hero's father explains why the works of contemporary African artists appear inferior to those of bygone artists whose works are now mostly preserved in museums. According to him, contemporary art is impoverished by the lack of a spiritual basis. Traditional art belonged to "an epoch when the hind, emerging slowly from the wood under the tongue of the adze, served the cause of magic, served a cult. It was a time when the blacksmith-sculptor was a magician, was a wizard, was a priest, when he practised more than a mere craft – but advanced with his art higher goals of tradition by modelling the images of the ancestors, the totem, masks for ritual dances and cult objects. But now, the "mystery" and the "power" of traditional art are "beginning to fade away under the influence of modern ideas" and art objects produced outside the religious and mystical matrix "will never be anything more than an ornament, a decoration".[88]

The attitude, though understandable, is unrealistic. It is hard to see how artistic homogeneity can be preserved in a rapidly fragmenting cultural situation, how the sacred and religious basis of art can be sustained in a secularizing society. The more realistic attitude is to accept the inevitability of change, given the realities of Africa's recent history, and the realities of historical movement on a global scale. Changes are not absolute, but embody in their mainstream significant continuities. For it is a salutary fact of ordered social change that there is never a total break with the past: elements of the past are constantly brought forward in modified forms.

The mask art tradition remains vigorously alive today, even though the aura of mystery is no longer as strong as in the past. Some of it is still to be observed in the villages, but in the towns masks are purely objects of artistic entertainment rather than of religious and ritual reverence. English-speaking West African novelists tend, like their French counterparts, to regret the change and portray it as a part of the wholesale vulgarization of life. Nzekwu, for example, contrasts the masquerade displays in the urban centre of Kafanchan and in the traditional setting of Ado in *Blade Among the Boys* and regrets that "the masquerade displays at Kafanchan, compared with those at Ado, were mere child's play. There, masquerades were men and boys dressed in strange costumes at Christmas and Easter, singing and dancing from house to house, collecting presents. Here, they were spirits from the other world on a visit to mankind."[89] Even less traditionalist are those comically grotesque masquerades described by Achebe in *A Man of the People* who feature in Christian festive entertainment and conduct their singing in pidgin English.[90] What these writers do not notice is that the masquerade performance in the urban setting still embodies a number of features of the traditional situation – the group participation is there, the aesthetic elements already described in the traditional setting are there too, and so are the drama, the colour and the excitement. Some broadening of attitudes towards and sympathies with one's urban neighbours may result from the participation in mask performances of people from different ethnic areas. In other words, even though the mystical elements may be missing the social gains may be considerable.

The essential feature of art in the modern setting, offsetting its secular nature and lack of relatedness to a collective tradition, is its positive inspiration by an individual impulse. Where the traditional artist works in intimate association with society, taking from it his themes, functional relevance and his symbols, and rewarding the society by sharing with it his vision in the interpretation of public realities, the modern artist is an individual who draws his artistic impulse from his own imagination and makes his creation available to society for its own edification. He is not commissioned by the community to produce his work, as his traditional counterpart would have been, and the community is under no obligation to patronize his product. He may take some of his motifs from the culture but these are used in a way which only his personal imagination will define. The result is often a breakdown in artistic collaboration between artist and society, a collaboration which was implicit in the traditional aesthetic. Artistic individualism is an aspect, and indeed a symptom, of cultural fragmentation. Here, the artist is to a large extent a creator not integrative of but often in confrontation with society. His individualism is constantly drawing him in directions which may be tangential to and disruptive of existing social and artistic order.

The Interpreters illustrates both the way artistic values have shifted as between the past and the present and the significant continuities. Of the two artists who feature in the novel, Sekoni is an amateur sculptor and Kola a lecturer in art. Their artistic background is modern in that they have learnt artistic skill in a formal school. Kola has taken his artistic training up to university level, and is teaching students who are going to become art graduates themselves. Their style of work also distinguishes them from traditional artists. Sekoni's masterpiece, *The Wrestler,* is an individualistically conceived work. The inspiration is a fight he had watched several years before between Egbo and a hectoring barman in a club. The experience left a lasting impression on Sekoni's mind and became a powerful image to be subsequently transferred into a sculptured figure and used, as a metaphor, for exploring a character who excites him. The intensity of conception and felicity of execution combine to make *The Wrestler* a great work. Soyinka tells us how Sekoni produced it.

> He had not asked Bandele or anyone to sit for him, but the face and the form of the central figure, a protagonist in pilgrim's robes, was unmistakably Bandele. Taut sinews, nearly agonising in excess tension, a bunched python caught at the instant of easing out, the balance of strangulation before release, it was all elasticity and strain. . . . Only Bandele's unique figure could have come to such pliant physical connivance with the form.[91]

Kola's artistry is of a more conventional kind. He is painting the Yoruba pantheon and using friends and acquaintances whose characters or features match those of the different gods as his models. The correspondence is closely established and deliberately pursued. Of Joe Golder's suitability as model, for instance, we are told that "Kola, even before he began his canvas on the Pantheon, had remarked how well he would translate into one of the gods; when he at last began the mammoth task, Golder fell in place as Erinle only less obviously than Egbo as Ogun. And now, with the frizzled skin all peeling on his face, frizzled in little loops and curls with a few clean patches of arid land, Joe Golder had assumed an after-sacrifice fierceness, bits of slaughtered feather sticking to his face."[92]

As in traditional art, the religious motif is strong here. It is significant that for his masterpiece, Sekoni received the final imaginative urge while a pilgrim in Mecca. The infusion into the statue of a force approaching mystical vitality is derivative from traditional artistic practice; what is really absent is a close association with some culturally defined function. *The Wrestler* is acclaimed as a work of genius in that it captures a moment of artistic truth, but because this truth is not harnessed to any corporate interest, the work is destined for a private collection or a gallery where the new elite will come to admire it. In fact, both *The Wrestler* and Kola's Pantheon are for an artistic exhibition which in the context of the novel is a moment of resolution, a drawing together of the numerous strands of the complex plot. Significantly, this resolution is a matter of every man for himself. Art is catharsis and a means of consolidating and organizing emotions, but the element of individualism is dominant: the exhibition holds different messages for the different participants. For Egbo, who is a "primitive" among sophisticates, the exhibition is a means of straightening out the mystical current of his life. He makes contact with a reality that had baffled and eluded him up till now: that beyond the violence of emotional vitality exists a calm beckoning to be recognized, that the chance encounter with an unknown girl-student whose voice in Shelley's words "was like the voice of his own soul", holds the door open to him for emotional salvation from his storm-tossed life:

> The act of the slaughter, and the taste of wine on the pungent smell of roast flesh reached backwards again for Egbo and plucked forth the single, isolated act, the first companion to his sanctuary by the river, and Egbo knew he could not hold her merely as an idyllic fantasy, for the day rose large enough and he was again overwhelmed by her power of will . . . [93]

For Bandele, the exhibition reinforces his moral austerity, his emotional integrity and purity of heart:

> Bandele held himself unyielding, like the staff of Ogboni, rigid in single casting. And it seemed he was asking of the outwardly composed figure on the stage, what have you brought us to witness? Some deceit of expurgation? Bandele sat like a timeless image brooding over lesser beings.[94]

And for Kola the artist there is no resolution; his artistic imagination absorbs the disparate impressions without ever integrating them, because the artist's commitment to others, to past and present, as well as to

75

posterity, conspires to rob him of the composure which comes from reconciling oneself to the realities of each given moment:

> Kola looked at Bandele and he thought, if only we were, if only we were and we felt nothing of the enslaving cords, to drop from impersonal holes in the void and owe neither dead nor living nothing of our selves, and we should grow towards this, neither acknowledging nor weakening our will by understanding, so that when the present breaks over our heads we quickly find a new law for living.[95]

Joe Golder, the half-caste black American homosexual, finds his emotional fragility and total isolation confirmed:

> Outwards from the black edges of the moveable proscenium which framed him, an archaic figure disowned from a family album, Joe Golder sought the world in hope, the faceless, unfathomed world, a total blank for the man whose every note tore him outward. Joe Golder bared his soul, mangled, spun in murky fountains of grief which cradled him, the long-lost child, but would not fling him clear . . .[96]

As for the Oguazors and the philistine "patrons" of the arts who also come to the exhibition, they are lost beyond recall. Not even art with its power to redeem and illuminate can touch them. Once hoisted on the artificial hangers of false gentility, they need only the merest stir of the wind to collapse back into insensitivity and complacency: "they left quickly as a housefly or two were seen arriving on the heady trail of palm wine".[97]

This exhibition, like the works exhibited, holds a mixture of traditional and modern interests. First, it is not an ordinary exhibition but one meant to be an occasion also to honour the dead Sekoni. And this transforms the occasion from a drab and arid arty affair into something of a communion. The slaughter of a black ram gives it the element of a sacrifice. The effect of communion and sacrifice is reinforced by the availability of palm-wine, indispensable at all sacrificial and festive occasions. Then the combination of different artistic interests (Sekoni's sculpture, Kola's pantheon and Joe Golder's musical concert) gives the composite effect of a typical traditional artistic festival. Something in this mélange of traditional and modern elements must strike the culturally fastidious as odd and irreverent. It is no wonder that Professor Oguazor and his train feel it is an assault on their bourgeois susceptibilities. For Soyinka, however, art is a communal concern and a means for establishing a rapport among kindred spirits, even if in the end what the individual takes from the artistic experience must strictly accord to his predispositions and individual sensibilities.

The exhibition symbolizes the broad cultural cleavage between the modern educated class and the rest of society, the separation of the artistic culture of the elite from that of the common people. Those attracted to this exhibition have in common that their taste has been formed in Western-type schools, whereas in the traditional society artistic education, like other forms of education, was derived from the broad flow of cultural life. Its members participated in this common culture and absorbed its artistic tradition by seeing and doing and experiencing. Art was to the individual part of his social experience and shared with everyone. Even in hierarchically organized traditional societies with a high degree of role differentiation and functional specialization, including artistic specialization, the artist's world and functional interests are determined for him by the common culture and social practice.

In a rapidly changing cultural environment with its enormous pressures on the individual, artistic individualism may be the essential outlet for preserving individual integrity. Where a society becomes oppressive and predatory, as in the dictatorial world of *The Voice*, artistic individualism becomes a safety device keeping alive the hope of freedom and ultimate salvation. In this novel where the autocrats have taken over and emasculated the collective will, artistic individualism represents one of the few surviving outlets for keeping alive the individual spirit of man. Okolo, wandering in "the think-nothing stream" through the streets of Sologa, is pleasantly surprised to stumble on an oasis of creativity in the desert of barren and blighted lives. He encounters an artist "creating heads out of created wood" and recognizes him as an ally in the resistance to the forces of darkness. Like Okolo the moral reformer, the artist has got *it* and "his inside is sweeter than sweetness".[98] He is a collaborator in creative freedom. Art, in the world of dictatorship as in the bourgeois world, becomes an affirmation, a way of answering corruption and of preserving purity. The liberating effect of art is thus anchored in individualism, in its being able to express the inner states and the subjectively defined reality of the artist, rather than in a collectively determined view of life and experience. For this reason, it is easier for the artist to preserve the integrity of his vision from authoritarian corruption. So the artist preserves independence and becomes a focus of resistance. This revolutionary potential of art is well recognized and has often marked artists out in times of social and moral decay as the vanguard of the fight for freedom and social regeneration. Okara does not develop the full implications of the artist's presence in Sologa except to contrast him, as a symbol of light and creative hope, with the rest of the "think-nothing" multitude trapped in the corruption of dictatorship.

*   *   *

77

Between traditional art and the art of the elite there exists a flourishing popular art which has grown up in the towns. It is centred on markets, private shops, tradesmen's workshops, art studios and workshops. Like modern elitist art, this popular art is rooted in individualism, but unlike it, and very much like traditional art, it is functional, often harnessed to some practical purposes. It is extensive because it covers the vast area of modern urban activities. It covers sign-writing, poster-painting, stamp-making, painting of hair styles for barbers' signs and notices advertising wares, tradesmen's notices, paper flowers, papier-mâché objects, landscape painting of conventionalized pictures, murals in public houses and hotels, and the carving of masks, walking- and swagger-sticks and human, plant and animal figures. This popular art is produced by people with little or no artistic training in the modern sense but who would have done well in a traditional setting by lending their personal gift to the conventional forms. As it is, in the modern setting, they become artistic pirates and iconoclasts, with little or no respect for the canons of the modern art school. With a mixture of natural talent and an audacity made desperate by poverty and the pressures of the cash nexus, these "pop" artists flood the towns with their works and eke out a precarious livelihood. Luckily, they hardly ever depend entirely on their art for a living.

The outstanding qualities of their work are spontaneity, gaudiness, exuberance of colour and design, simplicity, and immediacy of impact. They communicate all they have to communicate without complication. In traditional art, much is conveyed in the language of symbols. There is often a shift from the concrete to the abstract; natural forms are reduced to pictographs, and conversely, concrete realities are made abstract to convey the metaphysical qualities of functions and virtues. This constant shifting from the real and concrete to the abstract and ideal means that to appreciate traditional art one must be familiar with its assumptions and symbolic language. Equally, because it demands interpretive skill and a sense of technique, modern art assumes in the audience a certain degree of artistic training. This is not necessary to enjoy popular art. The pop artist is a surface-texture artist who takes the shortest routes between his artistic means and his communicative ends. The audience absorbs the import with very little expenditure of intellectual and imaginative effort.

This popular art is best represented in popular West African writing, like the pamphlets from Onitsha Market. There are pop cover designs and illustrative sketches meant to enliven the writing. But the serious novels show hardly any trace of this art. This is not surprising – since the novelists, with the exception of Ekwensi, tend to ignore that section of the urban population appealed to by the works of pop artists. Even when the novelists write about this emerging urban working class, they do not seem to notice the artistic realities of the life. When the novelists describe hotel and pub scenes, they ignore the gaudy, scintillating wall paintings, the work of pop artists, which are an inescapable aspect of the background of these scenes.

Popular music receives better treatment. "High life" has become the music of the urban populations of English-speaking West Africa just as Latin American rhythms (originally deriving from African traditional rhythms) have become the music of French-speaking West Africa and the Congo. The "high life" is a product par excellence of cultural and social change and Afro-European musical syncretism. The rhythm is largely traditional, but the instrumentation is largely Western (traditional drums with Western brass instruments). A certain degree of specialization is necessary, since a good "high life" band is a regulated commercial concern with an entrepreneur who provides the capital outlay for the instruments and who pays the troupe of instrumentalists and vocalists. It derives its existence partly from the pressures of the cultural situation and partly from modern economic rationalization.[99]

"High life" is essentially a democratically oriented music. Urban West Africans are "high lifers" all. In a crowded "high life" dance hall, one is likely to find the entire spectrum of the urban population, from ministers of state (in the old civilian political days) down to the office messenger and the artisan. Of course, people choose their tables carefully and sit in little groups of friends and colleagues, but once the band strikes up, the floor is open to all and is likely to be covered by a "levelled" democratic concourse of dancers. The lack of a rigid formal dance tempo reinforces this general, popular appeal of "high life". Achebe describes this informality of "high life" dance in *No Longer at Ease*:

> There were as many ways of dancing the high-life as there were people on the floor. But, broadly speaking, three main patterns could be discerned. There were four or five Europeans whose dancing reminded one of the early motion pictures. They moved like triangles in an alien dance that was ordained for circles. There were others who made very little real movement. They held their women close, breast to breast and groin to groin, so that the dance could flow uninterrupted from one to the other and back again. The last group were the ecstatic ones. They danced apart, spinning, swaying or doing intricate syncopations with their feet and waist.[100]

The "high life" song, like the "high life" dance, is also a simple affair. The sentiments are trite or satirical, but often contain some observation on modern urban life, like the song in *No Longer at Ease* which advises a young man to buy his girl-friend a nylon dress if he means to make her happy. (The song was composed at a time when nylon had just reached West Africa and was greatly in demand. Many of the "high life" lyrics are an invaluable source of social history in West Africa.)

Music in the towns is also provided by the radio and record player, so that musical appreciation is no longer necessarily a community affair. It is more often a private and individual experience. Music as a romantic background has become a feature in the urban novels. Musical taste has been made cosmopolitan by the immense varieties of choice, from classical music through popular Euro-American, Indian and oriental music to acculturated and traditional African music. The compartmentalization of the arts has begun, and may lead to an ever-increasing separation of music (like art) from the common culture, or at least to the unhealthy categorization of music into pop and serious following on specialization, and the growth of minority cultures.

In the novels set in the towns, the life of the arts, with the sole exception of "high life" music and art in *The Interpreters*, is very thin. Townsfolk are so taken up with social and economic pursuits that their aesthetic awareness is limited to the enjoyment of "high life" music, which reflects the desperate gaiety of urban life and is sometimes regarded as escapist musical entertainment, much like jazz in South Africa and the blues and the spirituals in the United States. The fragmentation of cultural vision in the towns, especially the splitting of experience into secular and the spiritual, with the former given all the attention and the latter none, has led to artistic impoverishment. The art which furthers collective awareness and community life within the traditional society is pushed to the periphery of individual and semi-group activities in the urban situation.

The novelists interpret traditional reality with much objective sympathy. We do not gather whether the novelists themselves share the vision of the traditional world contained in their novels. Apart from Aluko, in whose *One Man One Wife* the religious aspect of traditional life is ridiculed, all West African novelists dealing with the traditional environment show a detached impartiality in their portrayal of characters and situations which an empirically oriented intellectual outlook would have predisposed them to regard as unrealistic. They are concerned to portray the traditional way of life, as an authentic and logically organized way of life. Because supernaturalism and magicality play an important functional part in this way of life, the novelists, treating these things as part of the day-to-day experiences of their characters, merely reflect the facts of the societies they are dealing with.

They have sought above all to establish the collective outlook of traditional society. All reality within it receives its legitimating authority from custom and common usage. They see this, as they see everything else about the society, from inside.

In the modern urban setting to which the novelists now belong, they have established individual experience as the basis for determining what is real and what is not; the result is that the metaphysical aspects which were an essential aspect of the collective world view of traditional society have paled into insignificance.

Individual experience as the measure of reality is a product of Western acculturation, and an accelerator of social change. Because the writers are emotionally involved in the modern social situation, they have not always managed the degree of objective impartiality which they have shown towards social reality within the traditional culture. They have been critical of tendencies towards individualism, and the assertion of the autonomy and integrity of individual experience as opposed to collective tradition. The modern individual, outside the immediate pressures operating within the traditional social structure, is more likely to see his own individual experience as his arbiter of reality, but since he has little or no guidance from a collectively conceived moral or sociocultural universe, he becomes a victim of the social, economic and political forces which operate in a rapidly changing society. By showing their scepticism about the values of urban culture, the writers are reflecting the deep conservatism of intellectuals through the ages, who regard any far-reaching changes in culture, especially the change from a folk community to an urban industrial one, as a disaster. This is a tendency which they share with all those anti-industrialist European writers since the early nineteenth century who have diagnosed the ills of urban civilization. There is of course more to it than just an intellectual resistance to urban culture. City life is open to justifiable criticism, especially in a place like West Africa where the modern city is a relatively new phenomenon.

4

Characterization

The process of the novel's domestication in West Africa becomes more clear when examined against a background of the inherited characteristics of the novel form – characterization, temporal and spatial setting, and language.

I will first consider how each of these characteristics is handled in novels set in the traditional culture and then those set in the urban situation. I take characterization first.

As well as physical characteristics, each individual within the traditional setting bears a proper name. The name has an ontological significance in the thinking of traditional Africans. The name is the man and the man is the name.[1] They are not divisible. This tendency of the name to be identified with the essence of its object is the fundamental assumption of what E. Cassirer calls "the myth-making consciousness". The novelists show this in different ways. When Achebe makes Obi's mother admonish her daughter to call a child by name before waking him up,[2] or when Ekwefi answers, "Is that me?" to a call coming from the outside instead of, "yes," for fear it might be an evil spirit calling her,[3] they are responding to the traditional belief that the proper name and the person who bears it are one. This has the implication that a man might be harmed through his proper name. A child born under the tutelary influence of an ancestor often bears the ancestor's name, the inference being that the influence is thus reinforced.[4]

Apart from proper names which strictly express the individual personality, there are praise-names which people acquire for social purposes. Praise-names sometimes describe the temperament of their bearers, so that Thunder implies a tempestuous temperament, or Rain (which is Danda's praise-name) a phlegmatic temperament, and so on. Gabriel Okara in *The Voice* pokes fun at the absurd high-sounding praise-names which the tyrant chief, Izongo, and his stooge councillors heap on themselves.[5] Often praise-names represent a kind of wish-fulfilment in their owners. Under Western impact, villagers who do not speak English pick up praise-names like "governor" and "Hitila" (after the German dictator) which they may have heard mentioned by their more sophisticated neighbours. Names are also used to express status in those areas of West Africa where society is status-stratified. This is certainly true of the Igbo, about whom many of the novels are written. As soon as a man is initiated into the ozo title-cult, he chooses a title-name by which he is known thereafter. The novels set fully or partly in the village illustrate these different ways of establishing the identity of the characters.

Though in the traditional culture the individual, apart from his physical characteristics, is also distinguishable by his proper name and praise-name, title-name and perhaps some aliases as well, it must be observed that he is less an autonomous individual than in the Western sense. In his social capacity his individuality is largely predetermined by social institutions, his social status and his specific position within the social hierarchy as defined by the society. He is born into a clan already bearing an ancestral stamp, for he is supposed to be under the tutelary influence of one of his ancestors whose name he bears. He will, if he lives long enough, beget children who will continue the life of the clan. He is therefore not solely an autonomous individual but has mystic bonds with the dead and the living of the clan. He is born into institutions which have been perfected and sanctioned by checks and balances. He cannot change those institutions because they derive their charter from past usage and the authority of the ancestors. Change, when it occurs at all, is collectively determined, as Achebe clearly illustrates in his account of the introduction of a new deity in Umuaro to combat external aggression.[6] The individual has a real existence only in terms of the general social framework of the community.

A man's individuality within the traditional society is further determined by a series of ritual inductions from one status to another, and within each status his general behaviour is determined by the behavioural expectations attached to the particular status. Thus at birth he becomes a new member of his clan, at his naming ceremony he acquires a personal identity and a personality, at initiation he ceases to be a child and becomes a social adult, at marriage he begins his own nuclear family and acquires a higher responsibility for protecting his descendants and guarding the mores and traditions of the clan. There is also a clear distinction between men and women in economic, political and especially magico-religious activities. Within the traditional society the individual's personality as defined through his or her actions will depend on whether he or she is father, mother, sister, brother, spouse, man, woman or child, young or old, priest or layman, noble or commoner.[7]

83

The roles attached to any such status have been determined by customary usage and protected by social, jural and supernatural sanctions.

In addition to achieved or ascribed social status there are inherited disabilities such as the status of the osu or cult slaves among the Igbo of eastern Nigeria and, to some extent, of ordinary domestic slaves all over West Africa.[8] Among the Igbo, the individual whose ancestors were osu is osu for that reason, and his successors will be osu. Now an osu is an outcast of society, an abominable human who cannot have normal intercourse with non-osu and who has no political or civic rights. An osu therefore inherits all the disabilities that belong to the status in spite of his intrinsic personal qualities. In fact, it is doubtful if an osu can actually develop a personality within the traditional setting since personality is a thing one can cultivate only in intimate social intercourse with other people and there is very little room for this intercourse between the osu and the non-osu.

The hold of kinship on the development of the individual personality is also crucial. A man's actions, especially if they are blameworthy, are regarded as a reflection on his kinship group. For this reason, the group exerts pressure on its members to ensure social conformity and this in turn helps to curb the development of an adventurous spirit without which true individuality cannot emerge.

These various factors inhibit the development of autonomous individuality or the existence of a mobile self. The individual cannot see himself outside the status which he holds in society; the others cannot see him independently of this status – the extent of deviation from the expected norms is therefore very limited.

Obviously, temperamental differences occur and allowances are made for them. Ruth Benedict observed about individual temperaments and cultural integration: "No culture yet observed has been able to eradicate the differences in the temperaments of the persons who compose it. It is always a give and take. The problem of the individual is not clarified by stressing the antagonism between culture and the individual, but by stressing their mutual reinforcement. Thus their relation to individual psychology."[9]

The novelists are constantly aware of this psychological factor in their works. For example, Danda has the prerogative, as the Aniocha village Akalogholi (nonconformist and good-for-nothing), of getting away with petty offences for which the more "respectable" members of his village would have been pilloried, though this tolerance for the poet and social misfit always implied a definite demarcation between levity which may be innocuous and crime which may injure the moral and social health of the community. Okonkwo's temperamental weakness of short temper and his impatience of laziness and social failure are recognized and borne with, but when they drive him to break certain religious and social taboos, he is made to feel the full rigour of the community's repression.

The social and political institutions of the traditional society have perfected the art of exacting conformity from the individual and discouraging deviations and subversion of the common will. In all their workings, these institutions emphasize the primacy of the group over the individuals who compose it. The careers of important characters like Okonkwo (*Things Fall Apart*), Ezeulu (*Arrow of God*), and Araba (*Danda*) illustrate this primacy of the society over the individual. All of them are shown to be powerful in their communities, but in their conflicts with their communities the primacy of the latter is soon established. In the cases of Ezeulu and Araba, it is shown that the individual cannot find fulfilment outside the protective wing of his community. Ostracism is the most dreaded, because the most effective, of all penal sanctions of the traditional society.

Social homogeneity and conformism are so strong within the traditional society that the sort of characterization needed by the novel might seem impossible, for characterization depends on individual mobility, mental and physical, which in turn produces conflict between individual drives and aspirations and the collective sentiment of society. By making provision for resolving potential conflicts, traditional society considerably limited the scope of human experience which the novel might explore. Powerful characters like Okonkwo and Ezeulu would have lived and died peacefully within traditional society but for the impact of European culture. Once the equilibrium of the traditional culture is upset by this impact, conflicts arise which the traditional framework is unable to cope with, at least at the initial stage. The conflicts take shape when traditional characters thus acquire an extra dimension of dynamism. They become the champions of tradition against innovation. So Okonkwo and Ezeulu attain full individual stature in the confrontation between the traditional and Western cultures. They show individual foresight and mental independence. Okonkwo is one of the first people in Umuofia to realize with clarity the nature of the threat which faces the traditional way of life as a result of the establishment of the missionary outpost in the village. His defeat and tragedy are inevitable because as a result of his still relatively limited psychic and physical adaptability he does not understand the immensity of the power he is up against, a power which at that time maintained an empire larger than the world had ever known. Ezeulu's tragedy also derives from his inadequate understanding of the white man's ways. His sending one of his children to the mission school as an observer in the enemy camp is a sagacious move which unfortunately contains the seed of its own defeat. The important thing however is that, faced with a totally new challenge, the traditional character becomes dynamic, adaptable and resourceful. He retains the background of beliefs and values which are commonly held, but he strikes out in his own way, in defence of the collective heritage. He attains growth and liberation even though he ends by being defeated.

Characterization in the rural novels therefore recognizes the corporate nature of the social environment and its conditioning influence on the traditional, and therefore corporate, individual. Every level of the community is represented. At domestic level we find idyllic situations in which parents exercise judicious care over their children in scenes of genuine tenderness. The children are happy because their domestic environment is secure and stable, and they celebrate this happiness in the large store of folk-tales with which they entertain one another and their mothers at night. The most movingly portrayed domestic scene in all the West African novels is that given to us by Achebe in *Things Fall Apart* showing Ezinma's relationship with her mother, Ekwefi. The reader is all the time aware of the current of sympathy which flows between mother and daughter, the mother's anxiety for the health and well-being of an only child and the daughter's reciprocity in unforced affection and blitheness of temperament.

Fathers as disciplinarians are apt to be severe, but under a surface of sternness there is a reservoir of affection and solicitude for the family. Despite his external fearful mien, Okonkwo loves Ezinma; Ezeulu, for all his austere sacerdotal bearing and detachment, is at heart a loving father and husband, and, even the tartar, Araba, loves his children (including the gadabout Danda) and his wives (especially his senior wife, with whom he has achieved a condition of absolute understanding). Even in the serious occupations of politics and religion, which are restricted to men, especially in their capacity as heads of their households, we find that the aspirations and destinies of individuals affect in a far-reaching way those around them. We see that Okonkwo's arrest after the burning of the Umuofia mission house brings down a blanket of sorrow over his family, and that the fate of Ezeulu and Araba after they have been ostracized by their clan is shared by the members of their families. The exploration of both the domestic and external aspects of life through characters interacting with a cross-section of the local population is a distinguishing feature of novels set in the traditional environment.

In the main the characters chosen are defined by whether the author's view of rural life is tragic, idyllic, comical or satirical. But in all cases there is an effort to differentiate the characters, to distinguish their physical peculiarities, temperamental variations and sometimes psychological distinctiveness. In *Danda*, there is a gallery of characters touched in with a dab of Nwankwo's comic brush. Danda, the hero of the tale, is described as a lithe, thin man draped in a blue cloak lined with small bronze bells which tinkle wherever he goes.[10] His father, Araba, is a short, stocky man of title, with restless eyes and disproportionately large head.[11] Ebenebe is a little gnome of a man with small, sharp eyes, a dry parched face and a thin leathery neck bent "sideways so that he walked like a crab".[12] Okoli Mbe (like the tortoise from whom he takes his name) is short with narrow head and sharp cunning eyes.[13] Akomma Nwego is a giant with a goatee and bright, lazy eyes. He is always smoking a long, slightly charred pipe.[14] Nnoli Nwego, his brother, is also a giant with huge shoulders and a small head.[15] The old chieftain of Aniocha is a peevish-looking man whose small leathery face sprouts wisps of white hair, while his son Nwokeke is an impressive figure, light in complexion and massive.[16]

These are characters humorous in the sense in which the Elizabethans used the word. They are comical for the most part, but they are also temperamentally defined. Their physical peculiarities tend to suggest underlying moral characteristics. For example, the description of Araba as "short" and "stocky" with "restless eyes" and a "disproportionately large head" conjures up, without the need to use the word "truculent", the picture of a stubborn, wilful and intransigent man, while his son's lithe, thin figure suggests a kind of artist, the cloak of bells necessarily defining his line of artistry. We notice also that Achebe describes Okonkwo's father, Unoka, a considerable artist in his own right and a kind of social misfit like Danda, as "tall but very thin". The humorous quality is suggested by giving the characters some broad temperamental trait which is typified by a peculiar physical trait. Eyes for Nwankwo are a way of giving a sense of character. Araba has "restless eyes" and is said by his clansmen to be irascible, authoritarian and stubborn; Akumma Nwego's "bright, lazy eyes" are those of "the most notorious loafer in the whole umunna" and of "a wily rogue . . . too clever ever to be caught"; Ebenebe's "small, sharp eyes" are those of a crypto-capitalist, a wealthy man with a large flock of sheep and goats and heavily yielding fruit trees, a man covered all over with rumoured scandals, such as that earlier in life he had murdered his father and sold a virgin into slavery. Okoli Mbe's "sharp, cunning eyes" are those of a trickster, of a human tortoise. We are told of him that "just as the tortoise was always the centre of all fables so Okoli Mbe knew of all the alus [abominations] that were perpetrated in Aniocha".

Nwankwo's schematic use of physical peculiarities shows how different the individuals are from one another. But the differences are not explored in detail because his interest is concentrated on Danda and the situations through which his personal qualities are revealed. The rest of the characters play a supplementary role and merely help to set him off. Danda is conceived essentially as a picaresque rogue, artist and popular entertainer. He is a simple, happy-go-lucky village poet and social misfit who spreads mirth and confusion all about his village. He lacks high seriousness, has a chaotic, near-anarchic attitude to life and is indifferent to things on which others lavish care and concern. But through his flute he becomes a virtuoso performer, a magician, whose poetry and mellifluous tunes transform life into a delightful fairy-tale. His presence in private homes, in market places and at public ceremonies transforms the atmosphere, injecting it with animation and infectious gaiety.

Danda's life and activities illustrate a comic vision of village life, just as Achebe's characters illustrate a tragic vision. Nor is this mere chance. Comedy is a strong element of traditional life, since within the traditional societies there is a highly developed sense of the laughable, the ridiculous and the absurd. The tendency to label characters through physical features that distinguish them from others derives from the same comic impulse; the trait that is selected is likely to show a character in an unflattering light. Anyone who has lived within the traditional setting and observed the methods adopted by satirical masquerades or satirical ballad singers will understand why a writer like Nwankwo in an effort to project a comic view of the village and its people adopts this satirical capsule characterization and labelling.

The same comic impulse is at work in Aluko's *One Man One Wife*, but where Nwankwo is realistically comical, Aluko moves towards exaggeration and caricature. His short novel is teeming with these caricatures and grotesque characters who seem to derive more from a Dickensian sense of the comically grotesque than from the traditional sense of comedy. Pastor David is a Dickensian grotesque, a one-eyed giant "with a big head that was bald in the front and fringed with a horse-shoe formation of hair – a mixture of black and white in a ratio that left age a mystery.[17] Royasin's mother is described as having a "mountainous bosom".[18] Chief Loton is a toothless old man with a wrinkled nose; Bible Jeremiah suffers from tuberculosis and is tormented by a permanent rasping cough which tends to neutralize his biblical enthusiasm and thunderous denunciation of the heathen. Most of the characters, including the Asolo of Isolo and Bada, the priest of the god of smallpox, are in various stages of decay and senility. Aluko's use of age and disease for satirical comment inverts the traditional taste, which respects age and hardly ever regards illness as a laughing matter.

But the strongest satire is reserved for the verbal mannerisms of the characters, through which Aluko expresses his attitudes to the characters. Grandma Gbemi's only reaction to a disconcerting experience is to cry out weakly, "not in my house, not in my house"; Bible Jeremiah's stock responses are: "That is the way of Christ" or "That is not the way of Christ," while the teacher – catechist-turned-letter-writer, J. Ade Royanson Esq., Public Letter Writer and Notary, Friend of the Illiterate and Advocate of the Oppressed, expresses himself in elaborately woven diads and triads, his letter-writer's art being gobbledegookery.

There are numerous characters with potential for development who fizzle out somewhere between their promising beginnings and the overwhelming pressures of the author's desire to caricature and distort. Such are Dele, the bright young son of Joshua; the young girl Toro, betrothed in infancy to Elder Joshua; and Joshua's son Jacob. These characters, like Toro's fiery mother, Ma Sheyi, are inadequately explored. Elder Joshua himself is hardly developed before he is capriciously removed by being killed by lightning.

Satire is only incidental in *The Concubine*. Amadi's concern in the novel is the projection of an idyllic vision of traditional society. Life flows at an even tenor. The villagers of Omokachi are peaceful, kind and generous-minded people. There is only one thoroughly nasty character, Madume, the stocky, axe-headed land-grabber, the only discordant note in the otherwise sweet, smooth progress of life. Some of the village people are described in physical terms, others through their behaviour, all in their social relationships. The ones who feature prominently in the action of the novel are described in their physical aspect. Thus Emenike, the good and noble villager, is contrasted with the bad villager Madume, both in physical appearance and character: "Emenike was slight of build but well proportioned, and he ranked as an average wrestler. Madume had a narrow square head (axe-headed according to villagers) and an iroko trunk. Worse still, he had a temper as bad as that of a man with whitlows on his ten fingers."[19]

The contrast is made in other terms as well. Madume is disliked by most villagers for being covetous (big-eyed) and never being satisfied with his own share of any good thing; he would always start a quarrel over land, palm-wine trees, plantain trees and other property, whereas Emenike is cited by the elders as an ideal young man, good-looking and well-behaved. He is a favourite among the girls. Other characters, like those in *Danda*, are cryptically labelled. Wodu Wakiri, the village wag, is a comic figure, stunted, knock-kneed and large-eyed but with an inexhaustible store of jokes and quips. Nwokekoro the priest of Amadioha is short, fat and white-headed; Ahurole is tall, slim and dark-complexioned, with a beautiful face and unmarked white teeth. But more important than the physical descriptions of the characters are their social or professional definitions. A character is no sooner mentioned than his or her position in the network of social relationships or his professional role is immediately established. Thus, when the dibia Anyika is mentioned, Amadi describes his progression at the same time: "To the villagers, he was just a medicine man and a mediator between them and the spirit world.[20] He is not a local man, so there is no need to place him within the structure of kinship relationships. When Nwokekoro is first mentioned, the information is added that he is "the priest of Amadioha the god of thunder and the skies".[21] Married women are often defined by their husbands and children by their parents, as for example when a reference to Wolu is often followed with the information that she is "Madume's wife" or to Mgbachi as "Nnadi's wife" or to Ogbuji as "Ihuoma's father". Wives of a polygamous household are defined in their order of seniority both in this and other novels.

These methods of defining characters are based on the traditional view of social identification. A wife's identification in terms of her husband is an acknowledgement of the patrilineal basis of family organization in the villages with which the novels deal, whereas the identification of children through their parents, and vice versa, indicates the social significance of these relationships. Grown-up sons of a man tend to be given considerable autonomy of identity because, as the proverb goes, when a man is so big that people no longer ask whose son he is, they will begin to ask whose father he is. Indeed, Ezeulu phrases the matter precisely in a moment of disappointment with Obika, his second son, who is about to get married: "When strangers see him they will no longer ask *Whose son is he?* but *Who is he?* Of his wife they will no longer say *Whose daughter?* but *Whose wife?*"[22] Characters like Ekwueme, Wodu Wakiri, Mmam, Adiele, etc. are not immediately described in terms of their parentage because they are supposed to have attained their majority and therefore have a measure of individual autonomy.

Characterization in the novels which are comic, satiric or idyllic tends to remain on the surface, whereas some effort is made to see characters in full if they are tragic characters. The light, comic, idyllic characters tend to be carried away by situations and to be defined by those situations, whereas tragic characters are widely and deeply explored in all their tragic force: through their physical aspect, behaviour, temperament and psychological responses. And what is more, they tend to be more closely related to the social, cultural and psychological realities of traditional life. These characters – Okonkwo in *Things Fall Apart*, Ezeulu in *Arrow of God* and Ihuoma in *The Concubine* – require closer attention since they illustrate so well the traditional impulses behind characterization in West African novels.

In *Things Fall Apart* the character of the hero is drawn with great vividness:

> He [Okonkwo] was tall and huge, and his bushy eyebrows and wide nose gave him a very severe look. He breathed heavily, and it was said that, when he slept, his wives and children in their out-houses could hear him breathe. When he walked, his heels hardly touched the ground and he seemed to walk on springs, as if he was going to pounce on somebody. And he did pounce on people quite often. He had a slight stammer and whenever he was angry and could not get his words out quickly enough, he would use his fists. He had no patience with unsuccessful men. He had no patience with his father.[23]

A big, fierce man of title, a stammerer with a fiery temper, impetuous, impulsive and impatient of weakness and failure, Okonkwo is well symbolized by the mask of the Ndichie which has "a huge wooden face painted white except for the round hollow eyes and the charred teeth that were as big as a man's fingers" and which carries "two powerful horns" on his head.[24] The picture of a powerful, high-strung character is well conveyed even in the transmuting symbolism of the ancestral mask. The psychological roots of his character are also revealed:

> His whole life was dominated by fear, the fear of failure and of weakness. It was deeper and more intimate than the fear of evil and capricious gods and of magic, the fear of the forest, and of the forces of nature, malevolent, red in tooth and claw.[25]

But this same psychological factor is rooted in another personality, his father, who is everything that Okonkwo is not: or to put it more correctly, Okonkwo is everything he is because of what his father was:

> In his day he was lazy and improvident and was quite incapable of thinking about tomorrow. If any money came his way, and it seldom did, he immediately bought gourds of palm-wine, called round his neighbours and made merry . . . Unoka was, of course, a debtor, and he owed every neighbour some money, from a few cowries to quite substantial amounts.
>
> He was tall but very thin and had a slight stoop. He wore a haggard and mournful look except when he was drinking or playing on his flute.[26]

In other words, Unoka is a musician and a poet as well as a procrastinator and an improvident spender. Being a musician is no discredit in itself (in fact one of his creditors, Okoye, is described as "also a musician"[27] and even though his neighbours deprecate his habitually borrowing money from them and swear to lend him no more, "Unoka was such a man that he always succeeded in borrowing more, and piling up his debts."[28] Dr Obumselu is therefore doing less than justice to the people of Umuofia and Achebe when he suggests that Unoka is ill-used because the Igbo are a gloomy people who "contemn the arts".[29] All the evidence points to the contrary. Unoka is treated with indulgence, since his neighbours continue to lend him money in spite of his failure to pay back. As to their being a gloomy people who contemn the arts, the last chapter shows that the Igbo think highly of the arts and that the rhythm of their life comprehends a vast area of artistic experience. It is a mistake to regard Okonkwo as a representative figure whose likes and dislikes represent those of the race. He hates everything his father stands for, including his gentleness, which he regards as weakness. This attitude is different from that of another Igbo with a flute-playing indolent relation. Araba is just as distressed by his son Danda's indolence as Okonkwo is by his father's, but he makes it clear that what he deplores is not his son's flute-playing but his idleness. " 'He flutes!' shouted Araba. 'He flutes from the cry of the cock to the time the chickens return to roost. . . . I don't say he shouldn't make music. In my time I sang with the flute and beat the drums. No man could dance the Ogwulu-gwu dance better. But a man cannot sing all day. A man should stand below the sun, should not bow down before the rain –' "[30] Okonkwo's alienation from his father results from his father's failure to provide for his family, which meant that Okonkwo knew want and deprivation from the very beginning and had to work harder than most people to make up for those things which other fathers gave their children. We are told explicitly that

> With a father like Unoka, Okonkwo did not have the start in life which many young men had. He neither inherited a barn nor a title, nor even a young wife. But in spite of these disadvantages, he had begun even in his father's lifetime to lay the foundations of a prosperous future. It was slow and painful. But he threw himself into it like one possessed. And indeed he was possessed by the fear of his father's contemptible life and shameful death.[31]

But Okonkwo's success is dearly bought; it leaves a psychological scar and sours his whole personality. This psychological factor is emphasized time and time again in *Things Fall Apart* because it provides the key to the understanding of Okonkwo's character. We understand Okonkwo's reactions as those of a highly strung individual with weaknesses that would drive it into serious difficulties, but it is also necessary to see the part played by social pressures in the making of those reactions. Okonkwo's sensitiveness about his father's failure is exacerbated by the fact that the failing of parents, in this traditional society, reflect on their offspring. Even so, individuals can, by their own efforts, redeem themselves from the failings of their parents. "Among these people a man was judged according to his worth and not according to the worth of his father."[32] Herein lies the psychological dilemma which causes the extreme aspects of Okonkwo's character. His father's record has been a dismal one and this casts a shadow over his life, but he also has the ability to redeem himself and the family honour and restore his house to renown and respectability. This imposes pressure on him to go several steps better than others. The neurotic streak in his character carries him beyond the limits of common standards, but it is doubtful whether the pressure on him to redeem himself and his family would have been so strong if he had lived in a society in which individuals were less closely tied to the fortunes of their families.

Here, therefore, is evidence of Achebe's grasp of the true nature of the relationship of the individual to society. It is significant in the drawing of characters that even after the individual identity has been established, the definition of his individuality is often deeply influenced by factors outside himself, factors which are lodged in society and the history of the character.

The same concern with personal character and its social determination is noticeable in *Arrow of God*. Deciding how much of the character of Ezeulu is due to purely personal development and how much is a result of his response to the demands of his high office as Chief Priest is crucial to a proper assessment of his character and actions. Like Okonkwo, his physical distinctiveness is well established. He is a handsome, imposing figure. Winterbottom, the hard-edged British District Commissioner, is struck by the man's presence at their first encounter and describes him as "a most impressive figure of a man. He was very light in complexion, almost red."[33] But for a full apprehension of his physical appearance, one has to go to his second son, Obika, who is described as a carbon copy of the Chief Priest. Achebe describes him thus: "Obika was one of the handsomest young men in Umuaro and all the surrounding districts. His face was very finely cut and his nose stood *gem*, like the note of a gong. His skin was, like his father's, the colour of terracotta."[34]

That Ezeulu could be described through his favourite male son is not itself surprising, since the nature of the society, especially the close identification of parents and children, makes this plausible. In *Things Fall Apart* the absence of such an identification supplies the major psychological tension. In this case the identification goes deep and underlines the strong sympathetic relationship between Ezeulu and Obika. Even though Ezeulu feels anxiety about Obika's wild nature, at the deepest level of mutual contact their relationship is stronger than that between Ezeulu and any other of his children. This is why during the Chief Priest's most dangerous period in his confrontation with Umuaro Obika is about the only person who understands his position and deepest feelings. It is Obika's death that brings home to Ezeulu the fact of his defeat.

Ezeulu is not a simple character, in the sense that one may regard Okonkwo as a simple character. His motives are always mixed, and spring from numerous, often conflicting interests dictated in part by his personal drives and in part by the demands of his sacerdotal office. The result is that he appears in different ways to different people. To his eldest son, Edogo, he is a quintessential paternalist. Edogo complains that "He must go on treating his grown children like little boys, and if they ever said no there was a big quarrel. This was why the older his children grew the more he seemed to dislike them."[35] To Ogbuefi Akuebue, his best friend, he is a proud and stubborn man but at the same time a model of integrity. Akuebue defends his integrity to the rest of the elders over the New Year Feast controversy, when it is suggested that he is starving the community out of his capricious will and not in obedience to the will of Ulu. " 'He is a proud man and the most stubborn person you know is only his messenger' [says Akuebue]; 'but he would not falsify the decision of Ulu.' "[36] His enemies, especially Nwaka of Umunneora and the Priest of Idemili, see him as a power-monger who delights in imposing his will on others. " 'He is a man of ambition; he wants to be king, priest, diviner, all. His father, they said, was like that. But Umuaro showed him that Igbo people knew no kings'."[37] Captain Winterbottom sees him also as a man of integrity who could stand up for truth against a whole clan during the land dispute between Umuaro and Okperi, but attributes this integrity to the man's religious scruples; "he must have had some pretty fierce tabu working on him,"[38] he said.

One central fact is clear however: Ezeulu the man cannot easily be separated from Ezeulu the Chief Priest of Ulu – though it is possible to see when the factor of personal character is dominant, as in Ezeulu's dealings with the members of his family, and when the priestly character takes over, as in the consideration of serious affairs of politics and religion. But one must not overemphasize the separation of these aspects and the roles attaching to them. Even in his private relationships, the priest is often not far away from the man. Ogbuefi Akuebue sums up the composite nature of Ezeulu's personality when he says to him: "Half of you is man and the other half spirit",[39] a fact symbolically represented when half his body (the spirit side) is painted over with white chalk on religious and ritual occasions. We are also told that "half of the things he ever did were done by this spirit side".[40] And herein lies the essentially tragic nature of Ezeulu's character, with the divine essence in him always straining to assert its integrity in the face of distracting interference from his human essence, Ezeulu cannot separate the two essences in him. His personal pride and stubbornness find immense reinforcement when he feels he is acting with the weight of his sacerdotal authority behind him, as when he twice defies the elders and takes up his position against them in their conflicts with outsiders. But the same pride and stubbornness might lead him astray or drive him to misjudge the will of his deity at crucial moments. There are times when he makes such inflated claims for himself that the impression gains ground that his obsession with personal power is an obstacle which will bring him down, as it does in the end, when he overreaches himself and refuses to call the Feast of the New Year.

The element of traditional religion in the delineation of characters in *Arrow of God* is also noticeable in Ogbuefi Nwaka of Umunneora. His unprecedented and successful defiance of Ulu and its Chief Priest is said to be due to Nwaka's being backed by Idemili, his kindred deity, and its priest, Ezidemili.[41] In addition, Nwaka is said to have found favour with Eru, the Magnificent, the One that gives wealth to those who find favour with him.[42] Nwaka is aware of this favoured position. He is not a priest, so he directs his advantage not towards religious and ritual ends but towards secular ones, towards politics, oratory and demagogy: "Nwaka was known for speaking his mind; he never paused to bite his words."[43] He was a spell-binder and called "Owner of Words by his friends".[44] Again, "He was one of the three people in all the six villages who had taken the highest title in the land, Eru, which was called after the lord of wealth himself. Nwaka came from a long line of prosperous men and from a village which called itself first in Umuaro."[45] Physically, he is well favoured. Like Ezeulu, Nwaka was "tall and of a light skin" in contrast to Ezidemili his friend and mentor who is "very small and black as charcoal".[46] But Nwaka is a very different kind of man from Ezeulu. He lacks the self-assurance of the latter and is always dependent on Ezidemili. He is a flamboyant man of broad gestures like his garish, boastful mask called Ogalanya or Man of Riches, which is "bedecked with mirrors and rich cloths of many colours".[47] His flamboyance he seems to owe to the popular image of the god from whom he derives his wealth. Earlier in the novel, Ezeulu has described how on dark stormy nights people might catch a glimpse of Eru, always dressed like a wealthy man carrying a big elephant tusk across his shoulder and wearing the red cap of the titled elder, surmounted by an eagle feather. Nwaka's character therefore cannot be fully assessed without some attention to the common image of Eru on whom he has patterned his exterior bearing.

Ihuoma's character in *The Concubine* draws on religion and popular myth. She is not conceived as an ordinary human but as a watermaid turned human, wife of the dreaded Sea King. This is not made clear until the very end of the story so that it does not stand in the way of a conventional realistic appreciation of the novel. But one has a suspicion from the beginning that she is too good to be altogether true. She is physically very attractive:

> She was a pretty woman: perhaps that was why she married so early. Her three children looked more like her brothers and sisters . . . Ihuoma's complexion was that of the ant-hill [the complexion Achebe describes as the colour of terracotta]. Her features were smoothly rounded and looking at her no one could doubt that she was "enjoying her husband's wealth" . . . [Her] smiles were disarming. Perhaps the narrow gap in the upper row of her white regular teeth did the trick. At that time a gap in the teeth was fashionable. Any girl who was not favoured with one employed the services of carvers who could create them.[48]

And not only in physical appearance is she attractive. She has the best reputation of any woman in the village, full of good breeding and good sense and with a gentle sympathetic nature.

A series of strange events leads to the truth of her background. First her husband dies after a fight with a neighbour. Then that same neighbour quarrels with Ihuoma and is blinded by a spitting cobra and later hangs himself. The village of Omokachi is understandably disturbed by such grave losses and even Ihuoma herself muses that "It was bad for Omokachi village to lose two young men in two years. At that rate there would be too few left to organize village activities."[49] The culminating point involves a third young man, the most eligible in the neighbourhood, who falls under her charm even though he is already engaged to a young and attractive woman. The dibia Anyika is called in and confirms rather late in the day what he suspected before, that Ihuoma is a mermaid in human form, wife of the Sea King. He reveals that the two deaths had something to do with the Sea King's vengeance and that the intended marriage must be abandoned to avert more deaths. Another dibia is called in to perform sacrifices to "bind" the Sea King's anger.

While hunting for lizards for this sacrifice, Ihuoma's eldest child pierces the would-be bridegroom with an arrow and the Sea King claims his third victim on the eve of Ihuoma's second marriage.

Even when all is clarified through the mediation of diviners and the assumption of spiritual intervention, *The Concubine* still poses a problem for the reader. For example, how appropriate is the title itself when it is known that Ihuoma's first husband had been married to her for six years before he met his death, that is, before the Sea King began to exert his revenge? How can we reconcile the long forbearance of the Sea King with the underlying scheme of the novel? Is Ihuoma a concubine or just an unlucky wife whose life is spoilt for her by capricious chance? There is one possible way to answer these questions and it lies in the recognition of the different phases in the character of the heroine. Given the two aspects of Ihuoma's nature, the spirit and the human aspects – it is necessary to establish when the one aspect is dominant and the other underplayed and what effect the changes have on the general action. In the early Ihuoma, the spirit aspect is dominant. She is a solid block of perfection, almost cold and inhuman in her perfection. Amadi describes this stage of her life vividly:

> That she was beautiful she had no doubt, but that did not make her arrogant. She was sympathetic, gentle, and reserved. It was her husband's boast that in their six years of marriage she had never had any serious quarrel with another woman. She was not good at invectives and other women talked much faster than she did. The fact that she would be outdone in a verbal exchange perhaps partly restrained her from coming into open verbal conflict with her neighbours. Gradually she acquired the capacity to bear a neighbour's stinging remarks without a repartee. In this way her prestige among the womenfolk grew until even the most garrulous among them was reluctant to be unpleasant to her. She found herself settling quarrels and offering advice to older women.[50]

This Ihuoma is hardly human. She is a spirit feeling its way towards a human identity. As long as her spirit essence is dominant and the human element has not entered into her in a way to disrupt her spirit nature, the Sea King recognizes the situation as a concubinage between a spirit queen and a human lover. But the situation alters radically after Emenike's injury sustained in a fight with Madume. The event shakes Ihuoma out of her spirit composure. She begins to develop positive human feelings. Emenike's sufferings fill her with unhappiness and concern, his recovery fills her with joy and excitement. We next see her admiring herself in the mirror and doing impromptu dances with her first two children and being admired by her husband. The scene is full of tenderness as husband embraces his wife and "honours" her dancing with a gift. A new Ihuoma is emerging, full of warmth and affection, playful with her husband almost to the point of being kittenish. The process of her humanization has begun, and that is what the Sea King will not bear: a state of technical concubinage is becoming a real marriage. Even though Emenike is already up and about, he wilts suddenly and dies from what the people diagnose as locked chest. What locked his chest is only revealed much later in the tale. Ihuoma's humanization goes on in the rest of the story and at times she feels the burden and oppressiveness of the spiritual essence because living it down brings its own problems and retards the pace of her assumption of total humanity. Her best friend recapitulates her human predicament as a result of the intruding spirit essence at the time of Ekwueme's whirlwind courtship of her:

> As her prestige mounted its maintenance became more trying. She became more sensitive to criticism and would go to any lengths to avoid it. The women adored her. Men were awestruck before her. She was becoming something of a phenomenon. But she alone knew her internal struggles. She knew she was not better than anyone else. She thought her virtues were the products of chance. As the days went by she began to loathe her so-called good manners. She became less delighted when people praised her. It was as if they were confining her to an ever-narrowing prison.[51]

Towards the end of the novel she shakes off even this residual constraint and affirms her full humanity by publicly acknowledging her love for Ekwueme. The change that comes over her is worth noting in detail:

> She carried herself proudly and gracefully and a new radiant form of beauty suffused her face. With Ekwueme near her she experienced an inner peace and security that had eluded her for a long time. She encouraged him to stroll with her on occasions through the village and did much to dispel his feelings of shame and humiliation over past events. He was amazed at her boldness. Here was an Ihuoma he had never known, a new Ihuoma – confident without being brazen, self-respecting yet approachable, sweet but sensible.[52]

The effect is to madden the Sea King and he cuts down Ekwueme before the marriage can be celebrated.

Ihuoma's character illustrates a peculiarity already observed in the West African novels in the traditional environment. That is that the boundary between human beings, gods and spirits tends to become blurred and the characters tend to be affected by this blurring or are actually designed to reflect such a blurring. This peculiarity is best developed in the rural novels but characterization in the urban novels does not altogether escape this reality of the West African world.

The Concubine also contains the first truly neurotic character in the rural novels. This is the character of Ahurole, the young wife of Ekwueme whose marriage proves a total disaster because of her neurosis which is defined by sudden changes of moods and a tearful disposition. Her state is described as follows:

> Ahurole had unconsciously been looking for a chance to cry. For the past year or so her frequent unprovoked sobbing had disturbed her mother. When asked why she cried, she either sobbed the more or tried to quarrel with everybody at once. She was otherwise very intelligent and dutiful. Between her weeping sessions she was cheerful, even boisterous, and her practical jokes were a bane on the lives of her friends, particularly Titi. But though intelligent, Ahurole could sometimes take alarmingly irrational lines of argument and refuse to listen to any contrary views, at least for a time. From all this her parents easily guessed that she was being unduly influenced by agwu, her personal spirit. Anyika did his best but of course the influence of agwu could not be nullified overnight.[53]

Ahurole's symptoms would be identified by modern psychiatry as a manifestation of some form of manic depressive neurosis, but in the traditional setting the abnormal psychological state is interpreted in mystical terms. She is said to be possessed by *agwu*, a minor Igbo spirit which takes possession of those marked out for ritual, religious or artistic roles. *Agwu* is a form of visionary madness, of the kind the Greeks associated with poets and great artists, priests and diviners. When it takes over a person who does not fulfil any of these defined roles, it gives rise to unpredictable, unconventional behaviour and is recognized by the society as a form of sickness. And this calls for the services of a medicine man (the traditional equivalent of the psychiatrist) who would attempt to exorcise the harmful spirit. In Ahurole's case, the therapeutic efforts fail and so her marriage ends almost in a tragedy when the medicine she procures to arrest her husband's flagging interest causes his temporary insanity.

Possession by *agwu* is a wide concept in Igbo character-definition (Amadi is wrong to translate the word as "personal spirit" – everyone has a personal spirit or *chi* but not everyone is possessed by *agwu*). It creates a broad framework for categorizing abnormal behaviour as well as providing a rationale for such behaviour. The result is that the individuals so defined cannot be held entirely responsible for all their actions since the hand of the spirit is in many of their deviations from normal behaviour. This recognition of diminished individual responsibility in turn justifies the greater tolerance shown by the community in its treatment of some non-conformists, errant characters and social misfits. Danda, for instance, whose father sometimes accuses him of having *agwu* in his head and sometimes of acting with all his senses correct, certainly escapes the consequences of some of his actions because he is regarded as not altogether responsible for his weakness. He luxuriates in the immunity conferred on him by the reputation of being possessed by *agwu* and says of himself on one occasion: "Some people say that Danda is a tortoise, others that he is mad. I am not mad, people of our land, but I am not so sure that I am sane."[54] *Agwu* can be a creative as well as disruptive factor in character-formation. Thus, Danda is not only an akalogholi, he is also a poet, musician, popular entertainer and ironsmith. The effect of *agwu* of course neutralizes some of the gains of his creativity. For example, he scarcely gets adequate payment for the knives and hoes he produces, especially when he sells them to women. He considers himself quite well paid when the women smile on him and pretend they have no money to pay with; as he confesses he cannot run away from the smile of a woman.

But the tolerance shown to the psychologically abnormal is not extended to seriously individualistic, ethically revolutionary or intellectually non-conforming characters. The social misfit, the satirical gadfly and wag, or the neurotic do not threaten anyone, at least not seriously, and surely they do not threaten the stability of established order. The same thing cannot be said of intellectually precocious individualists who may also manifest disconcerting tendencies towards non-conformity. Such people can overturn society and are therefore often feared and distrusted, especially by those in authority. In traditional society, they are again categorized, except that in this case they are shown to be a danger to society. In places where there is no belief in witchcraft, such people are easily accused of being witches and are thus avoided or persecuted by the community. The danger of persecution is often limited by the fear in which such characters are held. Often they are more likely to be avoided by the community than oppressed. The practice is well documented by Benjamin Akiga in *Akiga's Story* where he describes how a number of coincidences and the fact of his being a precocious child earned him the reputation of possessing *tsav*, the witchcraft substance. At first he was persecuted by members of his family and the neighbours but gradually he was feared and held in awe by his village. He did everything to enhance his new reputation, which gave him virtual immunity from persecution.[55] In the West African novel the best example of this

100

attack on individuality and non-conformism in the traditional setting is Tuere in *The Voice*. She was branded as a witch by a society that was afraid of her potential for exposing the moral bankruptcy of the leaders. Explaining her situation to Okolo she says:

> I was put out of the way by the Elders like a tree that has fallen across a path. I put a strong fear into their insides because they thought I was going to turn the insides of the people against them. So they got rid of me and felt they held the whole world in their hands.[56]

Like Akiga, Tuere recognizes the advantage of her position and uses it against her persecutors:

> They now feel that I really am a witch, so I put fear into their insides. That sweetened my inside because I had wanted to remain a witch in their eyes so that I could do something against them.[57]

Tuere, naturally recognizing a certain affinity with Okolo (an affinity forged in resistance to authoritarianism and backed by moral austerity and visionary venturesomeness), makes common cause with him and in the end shares in his martyrdom.

Characterization in the rural novels can be seen to partake of the special nature of the traditional culture, especially the status and professional definition of individuals, the organic nature of family and community relationships, the religious and mystical interpretation of character traits through such phenomena as relationship with tutelary deities, possession by a deity or spirit and the imputations to particular people of witchcraft and extraordinary psychic powers. It is necessary to distinguish between these factors, which provide material for the understanding of the minds and emotions of the characters, and the realistic social behaviour of the characters themselves. A knowledge of the influences and how they affect the behaviour of the characters is essential to understanding, but should not become a substitute for seeing the characters as real human beings within realistic structures of personal and social relationships. In other words, these characters must be seen first and foremost as persons living in society with other persons affecting them and being affected by them. It is when we probe deeper and seek underlying explanations for their actions that the cultural and environmental factors provide insights. And in this, the writers have left the signposts needed to help the reader to penetrate the minds and feelings of their characters. Where the modern Western novelist might derive his signposts from Freudian psychology, Marxian dialectics or existentialist philosophy, the African novelist finds his cues in traditional beliefs and values which determine the psychological responses of characters born and bred within traditional society.

Characters in the modern urban setting tend to be marked by their extreme individualism. They appear as single and often isolated individuals. The absence of a unified cultural ethos leaves them with an immense degree of individual initiative and they are much freer in their thinking. The chances thrown up by great social and economic change encourage them to be physically and mentally mobile. A combination of all these factors produces a prototype urban individual. He is not so much intelligent as clever and shrewd in a worldly kind of way. He is adaptable because the wider scope of his experiences in the city prepares him to step into different roles. His lack of a unified vision of cultural (including moral) values leaves him free to indulge his instincts, drives and appetites. He is therefore likely to be free about sex, to drink and smoke too much, to lie and cheat in such a way that he gets all the advantages out of life without giving anything back in return – in short, to have a code of behaviour based on unmitigated egotism. Obviously, not all the urban characters conform closely to this prototype but it is a convenient point from which to start the discussion of urban characterization since most of the urban characters in the novels are fundamentally of this kind. We are most aware of these characters first as urban types – with the emphasis on "urban" – before being aware of them as individuals.

This is certainly most true of the characters in Ekwensi's *People of the City*. Amusa Sango, the hero, is a typical urban character. He is physically and mentally mobile. He is a newspaper reporter for the *West African Sensation* as well as a band-leader at the All Language Club. He exudes vitality, chasing after crime news with as much determination as he chases after his women, whom he uses with ruthless cynicism and then discards. In him we see the transforming effect of the city on its inhabitants. He comes to the city from an eastern Nigerian village, full of hope and with a heart responsive to filial loyalty and affection, but he is soon sucked into the miasma of urban corruption, coarsened by the overwhelming materialism of the city and toughened by the constant struggle for survival.

Like him, many of the urban characters in the West African novels are drawn to the city by the lure of the lights and are thereafter swallowed by the city much as a corn-mill swallows corn, grinds it fine and reissues its peculiar end-product. As a result they largely represent the pervasive corruption, restless vitality, insatiable greed and shameless superficiality of the city. Sango represents its restless individualism, the landlord Lajide and the Syrian Zamil (they are both fat, grotesque and unprepossessing) its avarice and sensuality, Beatrice the First and Aina its sordidness and degradation. Except for Jagua herself, Ekwensi's second novel, *Jagua Nana*, also contains a gallery of flat characters bearing the unmistakable stamp of the city.

All these characters are individualistic, but they are hardly realized individuals. They are mere urban types. We are not shown anything of their inner personal experiences, those little points of individual character which are revealed informally through intimate personal relationship (when the character is least self-conscious) and which provide an insight into the true self of a character as opposed to his manufactured self, his professional self, his night-club self, his Casanova self, and his many other selves without the one genuine self that confers humanity on his individuality. We can pick out each of these superficial selves from the milling crowds that fill the narrow streets of Lagos, throng the night-clubs or overcrowd the dingy slums but we would not know them as persons. The city seems to drain away their individual humanity.

Other West African novelists who write about the townspeople and their situations tend, like Ekwensi, to prefer "type" characters to "round" ones. This is true of Achebe's characters in *No Longer at Ease*. Obi Okonkwo, the hero, is just one more innocent newcomer to Lagos with the best of intentions, who strives briefly to resist the pressures of the city and its corrupting influence but is ultimately overwhelmed and pushed under like the rest. Even his ill-fated relationship with Clara, the poor osu girl, does not reveal anything of his intimate self to the reader. We only get a glimpse of this intimate self when in the serenity of his family home in the village of Umuofia we see him in a teasing and joking relationship with his sisters and his mother. This reveals an underlying harmony of relationship which can only exist between those who share sympathy and affection, and seems to show that the development of individual character or its expression depends to a large extent on the atmosphere within which the individual subsists. An integrated environment such as that represented by a harmonious household is more apt to show individuals in their most intimate personal individuality than the vast urban environment within which they vanish into profound anonymity.

In the midst of these urban individualists and egotists, it is a pleasant shock to come across the character of Jagua (in *Jagua Nana*). She has the initial handicap of being a prostitute, but Defoe showed in *Moll Flanders* (and Brecht in *The Good Woman of Setzwan*) that prostitutes can be good material. In Jagua, Ekwensi gives us one of the few truly indi-

103

viduated characters in the West African urban novel. She is as much a product of the city as any of the others and like them she has been drawn to Lagos by the lure of adventure, freedom, prosperity and, above all, the shield of anonymity which it holds out to the dissatisfied (she came to Lagos to escape from the deadness of a childless and incompatible marriage) and to the adventurous provincial. She too has to fight hard to keep afloat in a place where anyone who is weak is soon pushed under. Being a prostitute and therefore socially handicapped, she has to fight even harder to survive. Being middle-aged in a profession in which the youthfulness of the competitors as well as professional legerdemain play an important part, she has to rely on the latter factor and use it with a persistence that betrays her desperation. And yet in all her struggles for survival in the city, in her attempt to procure for herself a young educated husband as a kind of old-age insurance, in her relationships with all manner of people including parvenu politicians, men of the underworld, the feuding patriarchs of Bagana, with her young perfidious lover and with her fellow prostitutes, she fascinates the reader by her warmth of feeling and vitality, her underlying good nature and charitableness in the midst of so much greed and egotism.

I cannot agree with Professor Echeruo's criticism of Ekwensi's delineation of the character of Jagua.[58] It seems pure distortion to compare her as Professor Echeruo does with Zola's Nana, "a brutal fille without a conscience or a soul". Ekwensi's *Jagua Nana* probably owes its origin to Zola's *Nana* but where Zola is using the conventional French conception of realism in the novel as a mode of expressing low life for its own sake (which embodies a glorification of tough cynicism and carnal extremism), Ekwensi's writing has no such dogmatic bearing but is preoccupied with exploring, through individuals like Jagua, contemporary urban manifestations like obsessive materialism, crime, violence and prostitution, which are essentially products of a particular changing social scene. It is to Ekwensi's credit that Jagua's personality shines through the vicissitudes and corruptions of the city. She is an authentic individual not because she is a prostitute (there is a generous collection of them in the novel) but because, in spite of being one, she is able to win and retain our respect to the end.

In discussing characterization in the urban novel, one has to consider the flat symbolic characters which abound in such works as Gabriel Okara's *The Voice* and Ayi Kwei Armah's *The Beautyful Ones Are Not Yet Born*, themselves parabolic explorations of the themes of materialism and political corruption; the two novels have characters which represent aspects of the moral issue being discussed. Some of the characters do not even have proper names or real identity. No one knows what the Big One (*The Voice*) looks like, but he stands for an insidious force of political repression, and his equally faceless informants are as sinister and threatening as himself, because as inscrutable. In *The Beautyful Ones Are Not Yet Born*, Armah also employs a gallery of flat, parabolic characters some of whom, like the Man and the Naked Man, also do not have proper names. Among these, we can identify the good man clinging precariously to his moral integrity in a corrupting world, the disillusioned and bitterly cynical outsider, the corrupt politician, the disappointed and contemptuous wife, the hate-filled mother-in-law. These are among the numerous cardboard characters used by Armah to explore social corruption in post-independence Ghana. Parabolic characterization is suited to that type of fiction in which a preoccupation with the moral state of society is more important than the exploration of individual psychology. There is no serious attempt to see the characters except as aspects of the black and white moral environment; they are either good or bad, and represent virtue or vice.

Okolo is a Christ-like advocate of moral revolution in a world darkened by political corruption and materialism. He is a voice calling for decency, sobriety and humanity, but he is hardly an authenticated, individualized person. His name means "The Voice" and is probably selected for its parabolic significance. We are not given many authenticating details of his personal history. What was Okolo's background like? Who were his parents? What were the childhood experiences that formed his moral and social outlook? How did he prepare himself for his messianic campaign? What does he look like? Is he tall or short, heavily built or spare, handsome or ugly? What is his age? What are his likes and dislikes? These details are not given because the interest is more in the moral force he represents than in his inner qualities and the details of his personal life. He is introduced with the minimal expenditure of descriptive detail and largely in terms of his moral campaign and of public attitudes to him: "Some of the townsmen said Okolo's eyes were not right, his head was not correct. This they said was the result of his knowing too much book, walking too much in the bush, and others said it was due to his staying too long alone by the river. So the town of Amatu talked and whispered; so the world talked and whispered. Okolo had no chest, they said. His chest was not strong and he had no shadow. Everything in this world that spoiled a man's name they said of him, all because he dared to search for *it*. He was in search of *it* with all his inside and with all his shadow."[59] The only personal detail we are given is that Okolo has been educated abroad and on coming back discovers that things have changed so much for the worse that he feels called upon to mount a cleansing campaign. From fragments of information

105

dropped during the narrative, it is possible to gather that Okolo's education has not gone beyond the secondary school. But such snippets of information are related more to the development of the theme than to the building-up of a full picture of the character.

In the same way, other characters are broadly categorized. Chief Izongo is a brutal autocrat and consistently remains so throughout the novel. Councillor Abadi, M.A., Ph.D., who is proud of being educated in England, America and Germany, is said to be Izongo's adviser but he is more of an opportunist and puppet than an adviser. The elders of Amatu are also puppets, and in compensation for their lack of substance vest one another with fanciful names like "One Man One Face", "Water", "Fire", "Pepper", "Bad Waterside", "Ant". Most of the names indicate the wish to hurt others so strong among the people. A rigid line separates the assortment of bad characters in the novel from the good characters; Okolo himself, Tuere "the Witch" and Ukule the Cripple. Each of the characters is defined mainly in terms of the position he or she occupies in the moral scheme of the novel: there is no close particularization of them.

In *The Beautyful Ones Are Not Yet Born* there is a similar polarization of characters. There are the idealists who hoped for much from political freedom but who have since reaped disillusionment. They include the Man, the Naked Man, Mannan and Kofi Billy. Then there are the beneficiaries of the corrupt status quo Koomson and his wife Estella and then there is the Man's wife Oyo and her mother who would benefit if they could. They are presented rather in terms of the moral attitudes they live by than by their overt personality traits. There is of course greater particularization here than in *The Voice*. We know for instance that the Man has a domestic life, that his wife thinks him weak for his moral scruples and that his mother-in-law hates him, that he is intelligent and would have gone to the university but for his prematurely taking up family responsibility, and that he is a railway clerk. We know also that he lives in the working-class quarter of Accra and struggles incessantly to live within his income and not enrich himself corruptly. All these details are there but they do not enhance our understanding of the Man, the inner springs of his life, the intricacies of his personal relations and the tensions that necessarily arise from them. We are most aware of him as a moral watcher, a sensitive observer of the slightest nuances of the general decay and social corruption and not as active social agent. Koomson is the opposite of the Man, morally insensitive, active in pursuit of easy gain and achievement at all costs, and grown fat with the spoils of office. And yet he never really moves out from the general backcloth of corruption to assume full autonomy. He remains to the end a figure from a morality tale, an impersonation of certain specific ideas of corruption without becoming fully autonomous as a person. The crucial fact is that these characters are morally defined and therefore best seen in their moral attitudes rather than in the revelation of their psychological development. In fact they undergo no growth at all because they are lacking in psychological depth. As soon as the moral attitudes are established, it becomes easy to follow the characters through the windings and turnings of the tale. For example, the Man is quite different from the Naked Man in the sense that he has not withdrawn from participation in social life even though he shares with the latter a deep pessimism about the present state of things. The Koomsons on the other hand are so deep in corruption that they do not recognize how bad things have become until they are engulfed.

It may be asked why this parabolic approach to characterization is so noticeable in West African novels. (A recent novel by Kofi Awoonor called *This Earth, My Brother* has also followed the parabolic approach.) Two reasons suggest themselves. First, the moral determination of parabolic characterization suits West African novels with their overwhelming preoccupation with social morality, and more specifically with social corruption in the new states. In the second place, one must see this as a "back accretion", or reversion, to the method of characterization familiar in traditional narrative. Particularized characterization is often beyond the scope of oral story-telling. Even though the novel as a literary form provides greater scope for elaboration and particularization, the earlier narrative methods of the oral traditions persist. In the folk-tale – the kind of oral narrative with which it is most profitable to compare the novel – characters are generalized rather than particularized; they are deployed as fixed moral traits rather than explored for their psychological complexities. The approach yields stock characters morally defined, like the trickster, the villain, the sage or soothsayer, the picaresque hero and the anti-hero. Such characters neither grow nor change. For example, Tortoise the trickster is consistently a person who lives by his wits, Leopard is always projected as a bully, and so on. When this method of characterization is transferred to the novel, it gives rise to parabolic generalization, with men and women defined strictly by their moral positions. Nor should we be surprised that the novelists should assimilate oral narrative elements to a form as profoundly literary as the novel since this is part of the avowed intention of the West African writers; they are always attempting to marry elements from the foreign to native tradition and vice versa. And the exercise is self-validated when theme and subject matter suit the form adopted, as is the case with the parabolic approach.

107

One important element of characterization in the West African novel is that much of it also receives its impulse from the Bible and the Christian religion. I suggested in the introduction that Christianity is an important factor of social change in West Africa and that it helps to condition the consciousness of educated West Africans. Images and symbols drawn from the Bible account for much in the shaping of the African literature. In popular West African writing, as in that of the Onitsha Market, this effect is overt and stands out clearly for all to see.[60] In the novels and other works of more sophisticated African writers, the effect is subtle and so well assimilated that it is not always obvious. The Passion story is the focal point of the fascination which Christianity exercises. The life of Christ provides an irresistible analogy. Parabolic novels especially yield to this patterning on the Christ story: *The Voice* even more than *The Beautyful Ones Are Not Yet Born*.

Okolo, the hero, is a Christ-like figure and many of the incidents in his life are analogous to those in the life of Christ. F. W. Dillistone in his study *The Novelist and the Passion Story* writes about novels patterned on the Christ story:

> The . . . possibility open to the novelist is to write about his contemporary world openly and frankly but with the essential pattern of the Passion narrative forming the inner framework of his own story. It is, of course, impossible for him to do this unless he believes that the successive stages in the recorded life of Jesus do correspond to the general sequence of events which may be traced in the career of every heroic figure who carries out a mission of redemption for his fellow men. Such a mission may be performed by an individual seeking consciously to follow in the steps of the Christ and to fashion his life after the pattern displayed in the Gospels. But not necessarily so. In dedicating himself to the service of his fellows he may almost unconsciously find himself caught up into a sequence of temporary acceptance, growing opposition, rejection, suffering, dereliction, vindication, strangely similar to that which marked the career of Jesus of Nazareth himself.[61]

Though *The Voice* is not patterned on Christ's life as consciously as Kazantzakis' *Christ Recrucified*, there is enough of the Passion story in it, especially in the character of the hero, to deserve attention.

Okolo, like Christ, carries on his moral campaign from a position of moral superiority – he possesses *it* while the people whom he sets out to convert do not possess *it*. He is single-mindedly devoted to his mission in spite of the personal risks. His commitment to his messianic mission contrasts with the different kind of commitment evident in the artist who "puts his shadow into creating faces out of wood" – a kind of creative virtue commendable in itself but too subjective to have a cleansing impact on the moral environment. Okolo, like Christ, is the man who cares, where everyone else is content to let things slide. In a world in which everyone is a comedian (to use Graham Greene's famous differentiation) he is the only tragedian. He sees the moral ruin which has overtaken his society and he is prepared to risk life and security to assault the forces of darkness. One of Okolo's main targets of attack, like Christ's is the establishment which is not only corrupt in itself but corrupts the rest of the people. Chief Izongo and the Elders of Amatu are like the Scribes and Pharisees; the white colonialist in charge of the Big One's security service who imprisons Okolo in Sologa is like Pontius Pilate. We even have a Nicodemus-figure in the Elder Tebeowei who comes to Okolo at night, not to learn more about his message but to persuade him of the futility of his effort. Okolo's collaborators and converts, the outcast Tuere and the cripple Ukule, could be likened to Christ's humble disciples. Most of the evils denounced by Christ are also deplored by Okolo in the village of Amatu and the corrupt town Sologa of the Big One.

All the main stages in the Passion story are followed in Okolo's life – the actual drama of Okolo's moral campaign is very brief. As in the story of Christ, the formative period of the hero's life remains shrouded in obscurity. Like Christ, Okolo goes through the stages identified by Dillistone – temporary acceptance (when people begin to listen to his moral promptings, the autocrats have to move quickly against him); suffering (Okolo has a good deal of this both in the village and in the town); dereliction (the very limit is marked by Okolo's death by drowning, tied up with the unfortunate Tuere in a rudderless canoe which drifts from one bank of the river to another like "debris carried by the current" until drawn into a whirlpool); and vindication: there is more than a hint that Okolo's mission will triumph over the forces of human tyranny. Ukule the cripple assures Okolo before he is led away that "Your spoken words will not die" but even before this, a convert to Okolo's viewpoint has said with emphasis: "Nobody withstands the power of the spoken word. Okolo has spoken. I will speak when the time is correct and others will follow and our spoken words will gather power like the power of a hurricane and Izongo will sway and fall like sugarcane."[62]

There is no doubt that Okara conceives Okolo as a Christ-figure rather than a Promethean revolutionary, as a man who appeals to the soul and the deeper faculties rather than one who channels emotions into revolutionary violence. In this too he goes further than Ayi Kwei Armah whose characters the Man and the Naked Man have only the beginnings of Christ-like awareness. Where the Naked Man takes refuge in with-

109

drawal and the Man in tortured passivity, Okolo commits himself to moral agitation and pins his hope on the power of the spoken word to redeem erring man.

In its preoccupation with social corruption *The Interpreters*, like other urban novels, shows a tendency to see characters solely in terms of the moral positions which they occupy in the scheme of its actions. Broadly, there are three groups of characters: at the one extreme, there are the morally and socially corrupt characters; at the other, those who criticize them; and in between, the neutrals who fill the gaps and help to set off the two main groups. In the first group are the corrupt politicians and public servants and pretentious and snobbish academics; the second group consists of young professionals critical of the state of society who constitute the "interpreters" of the modern scene. The third group includes all other characters. Some members of the first and third groups are described largely in strokes of caricatures and grotesquery, but coarseness is avoided by poeticization. Professor Oguazor, the chief comic butt, is a snob and a hypocrite and ridiculously obsessed with "merals" and ferreting out those guilty of "meral turpitude"; Chief Winsala is fat and ungainly, a vulgarian and buffoon; Sir Derinola is nicknamed "the Morgue" for carrying about the graveyard countenance he has cultivated as a judge, and he is always covered with the *abetiaja* cloth-cap; the sad, black American, Joe Golder, "had big teeth and his lips slid apart in a near snarl" when he laughed; Sibi is "the goddess of serenity", the "Queen Bee, with the skin of light pastel earth, Kano soil from the air" – she is "Simi of the slow eyelids". In his portrayal of the second group, the interpreters, Soyinka is most realistic. Its member are individuals with distinctive virtues and faults. They are often critical of one another and are in turn criticized and interpreted by the author.

From the point of view of character-differentiation, *The Interpreters* is very much a conventional novel. Each of the main characters is clearly distinguished in physical appearance, personal history, temperament, profession and idiosyncrasies. Of the group of interpreters, for example, Egbo is a run-away prince, a fiery, superstitious, pugnacious man and a sensualist; Sekoni is conscientious, saintly, philosophical, full of subdued, immense inner perception, and a stammerer; Kola is a conventional artist, listless, tortured by the chaos of whirling imaginative stimuli, uncertain and disorganized in his responses, a mixture of the compassionate angel and the mischievous imp, lacking the strong inner deliberate energy to achieve an abiding goodness or a devastating wickedness; Sagoe is an honest, compassionate man, easily irritated by cant, hypocrisy and humbug, an embryonic revolutionary with a partiality for the bottle; Bandele is hefty, level-headed, benign and a stabilizing influence in the lives of the other interpreters and the world around him. Lasunwon, the lawyer–politician, is a man of few words, cautious (perhaps over-cautious) and not altogether at ease with the other interpreters. He is described by Egbo as "an eternal garbage can for . . . sporadic splurges".[63] The differences between them are conveyed by their different attitudes to identical situations, as for example their reactions to Lazarus' ritual at his Lagoon church and the different ways each reacts to Sekoni's sudden death. Sometimes these differences are conveyed more emphatically by their verbal responses to a common event or experience. Thus, after the storm which occurs at the beginning of the novel has demolished a house in a Lagos slum, Sekoni is worried by the thought of those made home-less by the misfortune: "The-th-they will b-b-be homeless to . . .n-night. P-p-p-perhaps we should stop there and see if wwwe can h-h-h-help," was his response, while for Egbo, "The sky-line has lost a tooth from its long rotted gums."[64]

The women equivalents of the interpreters, like Dehinwa, the secre-tary and Sagoe's fiancée; the English girl, Monica, married to the un-worthy social-climber Faseyi; Faseyi's progressive-minded mother; and the young, unnamed girl student who becomes pregnant by Egbo are well individuated and positively explored in the novel. They all have an inner life, those complex springs which condition human actions and responses, as they interact with one another. They are carefully observed in their work and recreational situations, in their loves and hates, private triumphs and secret defeats. The society and its affairs are a background and a conditioning factor but in the end the interpreters stand or fall by their own designs, their individual will and imaginative adjustment to society and its numerous pressures.

One aspect of Soyinka's character-portrayal which places the novel squarely in the mainstream of West African writing is his subtle absorp-tion of traditional cultural matter into the essentially modern framework of his novel. More specifically, Soyinka draws on Yoruba religion and mythology for material with which he elaborates and elucidates his modern characters. We have noticed that one of the narrative strands in *The Interpreters* is Kola's effort to paint into a huge canvas the figures of the Yoruba pantheon. In this endeavour, he uses his friends and others as models. But it soon becomes clear that the artist is not just looking for general surface resemblances or mere representational figures but is searching for deeper levels of correspondence. Those chosen must show demonstrable qualities that agree with those of the gods and goddesses they represent. The effort underlines two ideas which have been consis-tently pursued by Soyinka in his plays.

First, modern man is not a product of an isolated modern situation but

111

of a long and continual process of human evolution which has had to accommodate the common heritage of religion, mythology and culture. The effort to interpret men through the gods and represent the gods through men is thus a way of stating concretely this perception of the universe as a continuum, a flowing of consciousness from the beginning of existence to the present. Secondly, this approach to characterization emphasizes the fact that human nature is ever old and ever new, always the same. This theme is well developed in the play *A Dance of the Forests* in which Soyinka debunks the attempts by some Africans to romanticize the past, by showing that the past like the present, contained bad men and women. Given the weaknesses of human nature and the anthropomorphic nature of religion and myth, it is at least conceivable that gods and men have virtues as well as vices and that the traditional world of spirits, gods and ancestors is not so very different from that in which modern man finds himself.

Wole Soyinka's interest in Yoruba religion and mythology was sharpened by his study of Yoruba sacred drama, which showed him how very like humans the gods are, and suggested the possibilities of translating this knowledge into an active narrative principle in *The Interpreters*. His article "The Fourth Stage", in which he discusses the Yoruba concept of tragedy as developed in the Ogun and Obatala Mysteries, throws some light on his use of the pantheon as a device of characterization in *The Interpreters*. In this article, the significance of Ogun and Obatala is explored in some detail. Ogun, god of creativity, guardian of the road, god of metallic lore and artistry, explorer, hunter, god of war, custodian of the sacred oath, is described as the "essence of suffering and as combative will within the cosmic embrace of the transitional gulf".[65] In contrast to Ogun, Obatala as god of purity and creation is a suffering spirit. His drama is composed of captivity, suffering and redemption: he is "symbolically captured, confined and ransomed. At every stage he is the embodiment of the suffering spirit of man, uncomplaining, agonized, full of the redemptive qualities of the spirit of endurance and martyrdom. The music that accompanies the rites of Obatala is all clear tone and winnowed lyric, of order and harmony, stately and saintly."[66]

If we look closely at Soyinka's characterization in *The Interpreters*, it is obvious that the Ogun and Obatala principles are very heavily drawn upon, not just in the superficial surface impressions of graphic representation but in the structuring of the inner qualities and psychological details of character-portrayal. Egbo is the model for Ogun on Kola's canvas just as Sekoni, the patient, the long-suffering martyr to the evil world of corrupt and venal bureaucracy and politics, is the human equivalent of Obatala. Egbo is constantly contrasted to Sekoni. He is impulsive and impetuous where Sekoni is full of patient understanding and saintliness. Sekoni is playfully nicknamed "Sheikh" by his friends but everyone understands the justness of the nickname, whereas Egbo's "Ogun" volatility is recognized by all: "In fact it was the point of Egbo battling with the world that experience led him to his spoken acceptances, and he formulated nothing before."[67]

In the article referred to, Obatala is described as a creator god and a mighty force for harmony and reconciliation, but his work really begins and is sublimated after Ogun has performed his own task of cosmic will which embodies a large measure of destruction. This Obatala–Ogun relationship is symbolized in *The Interpreters* in Sekoni's masterpiece, *The Wrestler*. The impulse for the work was Egbo's fight at a club, an act of will as well as of destruction. The impression is translated by Sekoni into a great sculptured figure. The use of the myth can be traced deeper into the plot and structure of *The Interpreters*. The position of Obatala is central and therefore critical in the understanding of Yoruba mythology and metaphysics. This is how Soyinka represents it:

> What impulse ... do we discover in the drama of Obatala, representative though it is of the first disintegration experienced by godhead? We are further back to the origin, but in the fragmentation of Orisa-nla, the primal deity, from whom the entire Yoruba pantheon was born. Myth informs us that a jealous slave rolled a stone down the back of the first and only deity and shattered him in a thousand and sixty-four fragments. From this first act of revolution was born the Yoruba pantheon.
>
> The drama that stems from this is not the drama of acting man but that of the suffering spirit, the drama of Obatala. Yoruba myth equates Obatala, god of purity, god also of creation with the first deity Orisa-nla.[68]

This myth is absorbed into the fabric of *The Interpreters*. If, as one imagines, Soyinka casts Sekoni in the personality of Obatala (and by extension to that of Orisa-nla), then Sekoni's destiny would be expected to have a far-reaching effect on the lives of the closely related group of interpreters. And this is what actually happens in the novel. The death of Sekoni constitutes a watershed in the evolution of the characters of the interpreters. Everyone is sobered by the event and undergoes a sudden transformation. Each plunges more meaningfully into a serious search for self-knowledge. The shallow flippancy, facile scepticism, logic-chopping and purposeless bantering of the earlier period are replaced by a deep delving into the mysteries of life and death, accompanied by a refining of the qualities of personal relationship. The crowning exemplification of the new change in the lives of these preeminently rationalistic men and women is their having to sit patiently through the ritualistic orgies in the church of Lazarus. That would have been unlikely before the death of Sekoni.

It ought to be recognized that Soyinka is a very complex artist and quite unlikely, once he has set up a framework, to be totally imprisoned in this framework without any attempt to diversify or alter it in some way. Even though it is quite easy to identify Egbo with Ogun and Sekoni with Obatala, there is a complication in that some of the attributes peculiar to these gods are distributed further among the rest of the interpreters. Thus Sagoe, and to a lesser extent Kola, share the Ogun principle with Egbo. The Sagoe who begins tossing plastic fruits out of the "artificial" reception room of Professor Oguazor is really a Sagoe of Ogun's revolutionary outrage. In the same way, the Obatala principle is not monopolized by Sekoni but is shared by Bandele, who is the major force for harmony among the interpreters. He is the keeper of the collective conscience of the group, a fact to which Soyinka attests when Bandele batters the self-righteous, hypocritical dons at the end of the narrative. Soyinka reaches out to the oriki to find the poetry to celebrate Bandele's moral integrity: "Bandele, old and immutable as the royal mothers of Benin throne, old and cruel as the *ogboni* in conclave pronouncing the Word."[69]

It is hard to appreciate Soyinka's characterization in this novel without bringing to bear on it the realities of Yoruba mythology which form an active matrix that holds the action together. Even though the characters have an autonomy of their own, it should be obvious that they are conceived in terms much larger than themselves, in terms of a higher totality that comprehends traditional myths and metaphysics. It has been relatively easy to identify such peculiarities in the discussion of characters in the rural novels, but not in a work as modern in its external feaures as *The Interpreters*. For example, it is quite easy to discern in *Arrow of God* that the personal and public conflicts which bedevil the life of Umuaro are related to the opposing personalities of the deities from whom the rivals draw their support and inspiration, that Ihuoma's character in *The Concubine* is closely patterned on the Owu-worshippers' expectations of the behaviour of a mermaid queen in human form, and that Ahurole being under the influence of *agwu*, the Igbo spirit of divination, magic and possession, suffers in her life from neuroses that would make her a disaster as a housewife. That kind of overt reference to traditional beliefs is not readily made in *The Interpreters* because of its modern setting and because its action is enveloped in language of a sophistication that nearly obscures the traditionalist strands. But unless these strands are unearthed, much useful insight is lost to the reader and much remains obscure. For example, the attraction of Simi to Egbo cannot altogether be explained at the surface level of sexual attraction; it has deep roots in a certain mystical contact which the true creek man makes with a true water-sprite. Egbo's deltaic origin and Simi's association with the watermaid provide the credible link. Very early in Egbo's life when as a college boy the spell of Simi first fell upon him, the incident was playfully seen by his friends as like a Sea King being fascinated by a would-be Sea Queen: "Simi, at the immortal period of her life, sat in the midst of a gathering which he was to know quite familiarly, dispensing her favours on none. Her table reeled with laughter, with much emptiness it was true, but Simi seemed untouched by it. She has the eyes of a fish, Egbo murmured, and the boys said, Oh, the creek man has found his Mammy Watta" (a pidgin name for a watermaid).[70] Subsequently, the fascination of terror develops into an abiding attraction, for even though Egbo is greatly drawn to the student the spell of Simi is never broken and this makes Egbo's "a choice of a man drowning".[71] For in spite of his deep sense of obligation to the girl he has made pregnant, he cannot easily wave away an association formed on the mystical and imaginative planes as well as on the purely emotional level.

The complexity of Soyinka's characters derives from two qualities. First, the characters are conceived and patterned on well-known traditional and folk myths and metaphysical assumptions, and secondly, they exhibit, in larger measure than in any other West African fiction, the qualities usually associated with modernism. Compared with them, urban characters like Obi Okonkwo, Peter Obiesie, and Odili Samalu look remarkably like peasants turned out in three-piece suits. The essential distinguishing factor of Soyinka's characters is what sociologists refer to as the quality of inner-direction, a quality of intellectual, emotional and psychological self-reliance and independence. This is the basis of true individualism, that is, individualism with responsibility. It is a quality which Soyinka's interpreters share with Okara's Okolo and Armah's the Man. The point will be elaborated later.

Literary criticism is bound to reveal that the approach to characterization differs from writer to writer. This is as it should be. It would be surprising if Ekwensi, a panoramic novelist who set out to paint a broad canvas of modern urban corruption, were to use the same type of character as Achebe, an essentially analytical novelist whose intention is to show how the drama that takes place in society is paralleled by the drama that takes place within individuals. Nor could one expect a poetic novelist like Okara, who sees people and the world they inhabit, poetically, "through symbols and sustained metaphors", to utilize characters like

115

Nwankwo's, who subsist entirely on the surface of the quaint, anarchic world of the gown-and-bells clown, or those who inhabit the world of those veritable pedagogues Nzekwu and Conton, who set out to instruct the reader about the excellences or the uniqueness of "the African way of life". Nor indeed, is any of these likely to find caricature adequate to his purpose as Aluko does in his attempt to portray the "idiocy" of traditional village life. None of these could altogether adopt the same strategies of characterization used in the highly complex, many-faceted fiction of Soyinka, the dense parabolically defined characters of *The Beautyful Ones Are Not Yet Born* or the idyllicized peasants of Amadi's *The Concubine*.

In spite of the various approaches which the novelists adopt, one general statement can be made about character in the West African novel: the cultural situation in West Africa influences the creation of character within the novels. In a great majority of cases, especially in the novels appearing before 1965, characters do not seem to have an inner psychological existence apart from their public or surface life and ordinary everyday relationships. Their awareness of the self as an autonomous unit with a distinct moral and personal responsibility is only very vaguely realized, and that only in one or two of the novels. Elsewhere the characters exist mainly on the level of surface experiences and public and social interaction. One case in which there is something approaching self-awareness is in Ekwensi's *Beautiful Feathers,* in which the main character, Wilson Iyari, gradually comes to realize in a process of inner illumination that he has been driven by his misguided idealism to destroy not only his peace and security but also the happiness of his wife and children. In the rest of the novels, the characters never attain this inner awareness but are dominated by public pressures to which they make public concessions or gestures of dissent.

One might seek for the explanation of this phenomenon in the nature of the West African cultural situation. Within the traditional setting, collective tradition tends to inhabit that development of individuality which nurtures an awareness of the self as a distinct entity with aspirations and ambitions and a destiny independent of the group to which the individual belongs, and which would have been a source of psychological conflicts and moral tensions. Within the urban situation, on the other hand, the disorganization of social life, especially the disintegration of traditional values before there has been time for them to be replaced by new values, has left people at the mercy of social and economic forces. Again, as a result of the sociological emphasis of the West African novels, characterization is strongly conditioned by the writers' tendency to use characters as vehicles for sociological statements. Thus, individuals, instead of standing for themselves, may represent aspects of social reality as seen by the writers. We tend therefore to find two types of character, which correspond to the rural and urban social and cultural realities described earlier: the traditional character whose life is very much socialized and whose actions derive largely from the collectively defined modes of behaviour within the particular traditional community, and the urban character who is an individualist and whose actions derive largely from unrestrained personal response to the social and economic factors which impinge on his consciousness. Yet these types are similar in detail, since they tend to be dominated by environmental factors.

The reasons influencing character-creation in West Africa are not unique in themselves, but could be shown to exist in other parts of the world, and to give rise to similar results. Two literary discussions – D. H. Lawrence's preface to his translation of Giovanni Verga's *Mastro don Gesualdo*[72] and Thomas Uzzell's discussion of John Dos Passos' *Manhattan Transfer*[73] – throw some light on the matter.

In his preface, Lawrence attempts to develop the concept of soul in his discussion of Verga's characterization. According to this concept, the character with a soul is one with "subjective consciousness", a self-awareness, and "the soulful idea" of himself. Now Sicilian peasants, in Lawrence's view, have no souls. This fact Lawrence attributes to the peasant community outlook and the Roman Catholicism of the Sicilians; these submerge the individual in the collective consciousness of the community, a tendency which inhibits the development of individual self-awareness. He compares the Sicilian peasants' lack of subjective consciousness to the same lack among the classical Greeks and medieval Europeans. Were he alive today to witness the great upsurge of literary creativity in West Africa, his acute sense of the basic unity or likeness in things apparently dissimilar would have led him to see the underlying affinity between Verga's Sicilian peasants, the classical Greeks and the medieval Europeans on the one hand, and the West African traditional villagers portrayed in the novels of Achebe, Nwanko, Amadi and Nzekwu on the other. He would have categorized them as soulless characters since they all lack fully developed individual awareness and are largely conditioned by traditional sanctions and taboos, especially by those of the traditional religion. He would have been interested in the principle of *chi*, which is central to the traditional West African's concept of self and its position in the universe – it is a complex concept which embodies belief in the personal god, destiny and luck – but it does not embody any clearly developed idea of guilt and sin in the way that this is understood in modern Western society. But he would have been able to make more of the resemblances than many of his less perceptive countrymen.

In Thomas Uzzell's discussion of Dos Passos' novel, we come face to face with a completely different situation from that with which Lawrence deals. Here is Manhattan, the hub of New York's megalopolitan life, a city within a city, whose life is marked, according to the author, by unutterable wickedness, sin and decay. The novelist contemplates this city with horror and sets about creating characters which embody the worst aspects of its life. We see in Dos Passos' techniques something similar to Ekwensi's technique in his Lagos novels. The significant thing about this novel is that its characters are not subjectively aware individuals but personifications of the writer's perception of the moral decay which he associates with the general life of the city. As in the Lagos of West African urban novels, the characters in *Manhattan Transfer* have no subjective consciousness because the pressures of urban living, especially economic and social pressures, tend to control them so completely as to negate their individuality. Thus we see that for quite different reasons, traditional village society and corrupt urban society tend to produce similar flat characters.

The position thus stated is slightly falsifying because it tends to exaggerate whatever truth there is in it. Traditional characters have greater freedom of action than the novelists tend to give them credit for, and there must be greater disharmonies within traditional societies than most commentators are usually aware of. Of course social control in a small-scale oral society, in which people maintain face-to-face contact, interact on a purely personal level and observe the same customs and beliefs, is bound to be much better developed than in the towns, where people tend to be self-reliant or determined by the workings of new institutions whose spirit may be altogether foreign to them. And yet one may also see in the so-called lack of individual control in the town an obvious exaggeration which students of West African urbanization know to be far from completely true. For there the establishment of clan and "town" unions, also known as "Improvement" and "Patriotic" unions, tends to exercise considerable moral and social influence on their members. Also many people carry with them to the towns habits formed in the villages, and vice versa. In this sense the impression given in the novels that urban characters are highly individualistic and uncontrolled is true only in contrast with the more rigid traditional situation. These so-called individualists would look like peasants in their response to traditional life when compared in real situations with the inhabitants of Manhattan or any other big Western city. The problem of the characters in the urban novels is really that their creators think of them as if they were New

Yorkers or Londoners, while at heart they know that they are really controlled by the taboos and prohibitions of the old traditional culture.

One of the interesting things about character-creation in the urban novels is that characters who wear sophistication on their sleeves discover with something of a shock how very close they still are to their less sophisticated kinsmen in the villages, how their prejudices are the old prejudices, how their reflexes are the old reflexes, how their attitudes are the old attitudes. The writers also tend to share this shock of discovery which they stumble upon when they are most preoccupied with proving the contrary. Thus characters like Obi Okonkwo and Peter Obiesie, who attempt to assert their modern individuality, never really make it, because their inner convictions accept the traditional values which outwardly they profess to disavow.

The writers of course enjoy the prerogative of creative artists to set up myths where and when they find them useful to their imaginative effort. And anyway, the implication of E. M. Forster's distinction between homo fictus and Homo sapiens[74] seems to allow the novelists slightly more flexible manipulation of social truth in the interest of their fiction. Urban atomism and individualism may thus be exaggerated where this aids artistic truth. And so of course the theme of traditional innocence versus urban sinfulness is in reality an over-dramatization of a partial social fact.

A number of novels which have appeared since 1965, including *The Voice, The Interpreters, A Man of the People* and *The Beautyful Ones Are Not Yet Born*, contain characters who display considerable self-awareness, at least to a degree unknown in the earlier novels. They constantly plunge into themselves and seek from themselves the inner inspiration and strength with which to surmount the pressures of the outside world. Their awareness of the self as an entity, separate and apart from the collectivity, is better developed than in the earlier characters. And because they can disentangle themselves from the collective consciousness and establish the autonomy of their individual consciousnesses, they are able to see with greater clarity the problems that bedevil individual lives in society and (which is even more important) to project solutions based on this perception. Whenever they do this, their detachment and intellectual independence make them a reliable guide in social criticism. For this reason, these characters tend to become the mouthpieces of the authors, with whom they share a common background and ideas. This common background contains the features which define self-aware, inner-directed characters, including a good formal literary education, professional training, economic independence from familial control, and social rather than community relationships. Above all, these characters are capable of formulating distinct and radical views of man, the environment and society, and of consolidating those views around certain bodies of ideas firmly rooted in modernity.

These inner-directed, intellectually oriented characters have been exposed to considerable formal and humanistic education. Unlike the rural characters, they have been exposed to a world literary education inculcated through the arts, literature and history, and the natural and social sciences, and giving rise to scientific, rationalistic and humanistic views of man and society. Every one of these characters has had at least a full grammar school education; indeed, with the exception of Okolo and the Man, they are all university graduates. A good many of them have not only been educated locally but also outside the locality, in Europe and America. So they have been exposed to a battery of new ideas inculcated through formal education and also to new ways of life in other places, new attitudes, outlooks and assumptions. With their intellectual training, they are equipped to put all the mass of knowledge through the selective and organizational sieve of the mind to provide matter for comparison and contrast with the present state of life. Moreover, these characters are fully established in some profession or occupation from which each earns a living. Even though they cannot be described as rich, they are at least sufficiently well paid to remain respectably independent, and thus to resist some of the financial and moral pressures of the social system. Even the Man, who is only a clerk, is not totally indigent. The pressure operating against him is more moral than economic, in the sense that he is able to manage on his earnings. The real crisis is how to convince his family that it is best for people to live modestly than to succumb to easy and corrupting materialism or to attempt economic success at all costs.

For these reasons, these subjectively aware characters are filled with self-confidence and depend on the inner dictates of their own minds rather than acting according to externally induced pressures; and because they are constantly drawing from within, they are always self-questioning and undergoing inner conflicts and crises in their attempts to vindicate every decision by the integrity of the inner judgement. Thus Okolo is always asking himself questions as to the nature of his perception of his mission, whether this mission itself is not an illusion, and indeed whether there is any better way open to him than his frontal assault on social and moral corruption. His greatest temptation is the seduction of conformism, the abjurement of his messianic vision, to buy the peace and cheap security of "the think-nothing stream".[75] This challenge of creative individualism also faces Armah's the Man, Soyinka's interpreters, and Achebe's Odili. These characters survive the seductions as well as the brutalities of conformist degeneracy by drawing upon the inner qualities of individual courage, integrity and moral austerity. The degree of their resistance, which in extremity involves serious physical danger and death, becomes, in the final analysis, a measure of their vindication of their individualities.

5

Space and time

The novel is unlike oral literature in its insistence on the "precise spatial and temporal location of individual experience".[1] The folk-tale (the nearest thing in the West African oral literature to the novel) begins with "Once upon a time" and then tells a story set in a never-never land where fantastic things happen. The novel, insisting on a life-like adherence to the details of human action, would have it set in a particular place and for a certain duration of time. The novelist can only make sense of individual lives by placing events and incidents connected with them within temporal and spatial dimensions. Within the folk-tale, the essential factors are the moral lessons conveyed by the particular story and its entertainment value; where and when the story takes place is not important. Instead of the novel's interest in particular characters, the folk-tale is interested in morally defined character-types like Anansi (the Ghanaian trickster figure), heroes and villains of all kinds.

The West African novelists adopt the formal requirements of the novel in respect of time and place, but have taken account of the different ways in which they are apprehended in the traditional and urban environments of West Africa. This in itself tends to add local colour and determine rhythm. I shall begin by examining the concepts of place and time in the traditional environment and then the urban environment, and show their implications for the domestication of the novel in West Africa.

Some consciousness of time and space is essential in the shaping of experience in traditional society. Actions and incidents acquire meaning only when placed within a setting. But like other aspects of traditional life, time and space are collectively determined.

The important landmarks in and around the community are well known to its members. The village square is a social, political, judicial and religious centre; it is the communal meeting ground for sports and games, political discussions and communal tribunals and is also, because the tutelary deity of the clan often has a shrine there, the centre of communal religious worship and sacrificial feasting.

Certain large or exceptional trees, houses of prominent clansmen, wayside shrines and spots with local historical association become in the mind of the community the chief landmarks which are used to measure distance, so substituting a concrete image for an abstract one. A speaker can illustrate the distance between two places unknown to his hearer by a comparison with the distance between places well known to him. Unknown time-duration is conveyed by reference to known time-duration. Thus a man can describe the time it took him to get to his new farm by comparing the approximate time-distance between two generally known places – for example, that it took him five times the time it takes to go from the market to the local stream. This concretization of space–time distance by the use of a familiar situation is part of the mental habit characteristic of the traditional mode of conveying experience; unnecessary abstractions, especially in the empirical sector of everyday life, are eliminated. This is an inbuilt mechanism for aiding the human memory in societies in which anything worth knowing has to be converted to memory.

Time and space are also socialized. Thus time, apart from being reckoned by such events as the first and second cock-crow, sunrise, sunset, overhead sun, or the length of shadows, is also reckoned by meal-times, wine-tapping times, time of return from the farm and so on. These factors are not arbitrary. For instance, the use of meal-periods does not imply that all eat their meals at exactly the same time, but that everyone has a reasonably accurate idea what time is meant. It is a matter of instinct, and a sense of general custom. Habit and usage have also fixed the places where particular events take place; it is another mark of the degree of socialization of an oral culture. For instance, it does not need to be expressly stated that the gathering of the clan takes place at the village square, and the gathering of the extended family in the home of the family head.

There are other ways of delimiting time, such as the use of market days to indicate the weekly cycle, and the lunar cycle to break the year and create a temporal framework for the major annual festivities. Historical time is determined by reference to landmarks in the life of the community and to contemporaneous events, or by recourse to a genealogical "chart" as with the Tiv of Nigeria. But the historical past is only relevant in terms of present necessity, and knowledge is retained of only those events which are pertinent to social relationship within the community, a process Goody and Watt call "the homoeostatic organization of the cultural tradition".[2]

In portraying the realities of West African traditional life, novelists constantly give the various ways in which the concepts of time and space are expressed, for example, the use of natural time indicators like the sun and the moon. In *The Concubine* "Ihuoma remembered vividly how when she was small her mother used to say to her after a day's work on the farm, 'Look at the sun, my child. We must hurry home before it gets to Chiolu'."[3] Chiolu is a village to the west of Omokachi. The sun's journey from east to west as regulator of the passage of time is felicitously recorded in *Danda*, where Nwankwo describes the rounding-off of a chieftain's funeral in the following way: "The sun had reached his home in Mbammili and was now about to sink into its waters. The chieftain, preceded by the emblems of his rank and followed by volleys of dane-guns, went home with the red deity. Aniocha rejoiced."[4] The moon too is an important measure of time, as in this conversation from *The Concubine*:

"Has the cock caught up with the moon yet?"
"I doubt it. I was up last night. The moon hid herself before the cock crew."
"In a day or two I suppose the cock will catch her."[5]

The two men, both musicians, are trying to decide the best time to "out" their new dance, and feel that the full moon would be best. By their calculation, the moon is fullest and therefore brightest when it stays effectively in the sky until morning, and morning is ushered in by the crowing of the cock. The confluence of the two events is mythopoeically expressed as a race between moon and cock. Achebe constantly uses these characteristic elements of daily experience as time-indicators among his rural characters. For example, Okonkwo, the good and efficient farmer, "worked daily on his farms from cock-crow until the chickens went to roost".[6] Nwankwo is even more emphatic in his definition of the length of a typical busy farming day: "In a few days the rain season would come and bring with it a ceaseless round of labour. And men would leave their homes with the first cry of the cock and would not return until the chicken came back to roost."[7]

More significantly, the writers use the seasons, the rhythm of agricultural work and the fixed festivals to demarcate the year by cycle. The seasons are clearly marked. In the main, there are two seasons, the rainy and the dry. The rainy is the season of agricultural work, planting, weeding and cultivation; the dry season is the period of harvest, rest and preparation for the next season, including the cutting down and burning of bushes and house-repairs. The fixed festivals and games are also part of the cycle, occurring mainly in the rest period, but a few taking place during the short break in the rains. The fixed nature of the seasons, the rhythm of agricultural work and the distribution of festivals give important temporal signposts. For example, Amadi finds the regular nature of shifting agricultural cultivation useful in plotting Ihuoma's age in *The Concubine*: "It was easy to reckon her age. Every farm land was used once in seven years. The piece of land on which her father farmed in the year of her birth was farmed for the fourth time last year. So she was just about twenty-two."[8] In *Things Fall Apart* and *Arrow of God*, the key events of the plot are given broad temporal dimension by this kind of seasonal or festive association. For example, the incorporation of the boy hostage Ikemefuna into Okonkwo's household takes place during the Sacred Week of Peace, which marks the period immediately before the new agricultural year:

> Ikemefuna came to Umuofia at the end of the carefree season between harvest and planting. In fact he recovered from his illness only a few days before the Week of Peace began. And that was also the year Okonkwo broke the peace, and was punished, as was the custom, by Ezeani, the priest of the earth goddess.[9]

Ikemefuna's execution, we are told, takes place exactly three years afterwards during another lax period, with the added excitement of a locust invasion.

This detailed temporal documentation advances narrative significantly. The consciousness of a series of events moving on through time and space is doggedly promoted; individual events are located in their appropriate temporal grids, so that the impression that forms in the end is of an assimilated action, full in all its realistic dimensions. Ikemefuna has thoroughly integrated himself into Okonkwo's household, participating in its domestic and agricultural life. "In this way," we are told, "the moons and the seasons passed. And then the locusts came . . . Okonkwo and the two boys were working on the red outer walls of the compound. This was one of the lighter tasks of the after-harvest season."[10] The choice of this season is significant in the overall scheme of the novel and in shaping its insight. For this is the season of rest from labour, the season of festivities and of peace. That Ikemefuna's fate should be sealed at this happiest of traditional seasons is an underlying irony. The events also throw light on the character of Okonkwo. Ikemefuna's coming is linked to the celebration of the Week of Peace, and this celebration to Okonkwo's impetuous beating of his wife which results in his punishment. Ikemefuna's killing three years later in the same season offers us an opportunity to see whether Okonkwo's character is mellowed by time. Three years before, Okonkwo had ignored the urgent entreaties of

125

others to stop beating his wife and desecrating the Week of Peace because he "was not the man to stop beating somebody half-way through, not even for fear of a goddess".[11] Now, after three years, he ignores the advice of an old man who asks him not to be a party to Ikemefuna's murder. " 'That boy calls you father. Do not bear a hand in his death.' "[12] But Okonkwo actually cuts Ikemefuna down when he runs to him for protection because "He was afraid of being thought weak."[13] Three years have passed but nothing has changed in the life of this simmering, volcanic, titled elder. And not even the beneficent influences of the season of peace and goodwill can mellow the man's ferocity. The remorselessness of the time-scheme seems related to the inflexibility of his nature: a tragic fact like the passing of time.

In *Arrow of God* these patterns of work and rest play an even more important part in the development of the plot. The Feast of the New Year is central to the scheme of the plot, because it is a focus of crucial aspects of the lives of the people in the novel. It is an occasion for ritual celebration in honour of the tutelary deity of the clan and his satellite gods, for ritual purification and religious communion, for census-taking and for ushering in the harvest season. Its significance is stressed throughout the novel, nowhere more emphatically than towards the end, on the eve of the great confrontation between the Chief Priest and the people of Umuaro. This passage is crucial:

> This feast was the end of the old year and the beginning of the new. Before it a man might dig up a few yams around his house to ward off hunger in his family but no one would begin the harvesting of the big farms. And, in any case, no man of title would taste new yam from whatever source before the festival. It reminded the six villages of their coming together in ancient times and of their continuing debt to Ulu who saved them from the ravages of the Abam. At every New Yam feast the coming together of the villages was re-enacted and every grown man in Umuaro took a good-sized seed-yam to the shrine of Ulu and placed it in the heap from his village after circling it round his head; then he took the lump of chalk lying beside the heap and marked his face. It was from these heaps that the elders knew the number of men in each village . . . It was also from these yams that Ezeulu selected thirteen with which to reckon the new year.[14]

The Chief Priest keeps the communal calendar by disposing of the thirteen yams that mark the thirteen lunar months of the year. He announces the appearance of each new moon and declares the Feast of the New Yam which is held on the thirteenth new moon. From this point in the novel to the end, the action is defined largely by the seasons. The Chief Priest is released from detention in "the heart of the wet season". The interlude between his return and his tragic confrontation with the clan is covered by "a spell of dry weather" in which are located "the minor feasts and festivals of the year"; the "daily rounds" of domestic chores, child-bearing, domestic rivalries, artistic pursuits, sacrifices to the gods and ancestors go on as if everything were normal. But the calm is deceptive; the festivals are like a comic interlude before the final and overwhelming tragic explosion. Below the surface of normality, threatening undercurrents are building up. The narrative flows gradually and undisturbed towards the tragic precipice. The next major event is again defined in terms of a public festival, a "minor feast which Ezeulu's village, Umuachala, celebrated towards the end of the wet season and before the big festival of the year – the New Yam feast. This minor celebration was called Akwu Nro . . . This year's Akwu Nro was to have an added interest because Obika's age group would present a new ancestral Mask to the village."[15] When the crisis impends the narrative is brought back to chronological particularity. The Chief Priest's attendants assemble to remind him of the approaching new year: " 'It is now four days since the new moon appeared in the sky; it is already grown big. And yet you have not called us together to tell us the day of the New Yam Feast – . . . By our reckoning . . . the present moon is the twelfth since the last feast.' "[16] It becomes clear that the Chief Priest has decided not to call the festival.

In *Danda* too the seasonal rhythm is felt to mark the periodic distribution of feasts and the patterns of work and rest. Most of the incidents described in the novel take place in the dry season, between the harvest and the first rains. This explains the predominantly festive and happy mood of the book. The major incidents of the novel are also defined by the seasons like the annual festival to celebrate the Founder's Day and the expiatory sacrifice in honour of Mgbafo Ezira, which both take place in the dry season, while Danda's estrangement from his father takes place in the rainy season – because he shirks farm work. Araba's illness and Danda's return to favour, his marriage and return to duty also take place in this season, and his reform is shown by his return to serious farming. The arrival of Danda's male child, which opens the final stage of the novel, again takes place in the dry season.

A radical change in seasonal rhythm is described in *Things Fall Apart*: "The year that Okonkwo took eight hundred seed-yams from Nwakibie was the worst year in living memory. Nothing happened at its proper time; it was either too early or too late. It seemed as if the world had gone mad. The first rains were late, and, when they came, lasted only a

127

brief moment."[17] While it records such abnormalities, the socialization process follows the well-established and normal lines of experience. Exceptions do not invalidate well-grounded natural observations. In any case, except in cases such as the Feast of the New Yam, which is based on a fixed phenomenon – the appearance of the new moon – most temporal and seasonal calculations are necessarily approximations. Pinpoint precision is neither desirable nor appropriate to the seasons. The individual event however can always be situated in time.

Temporal particularity and generalization both have their place in the rural novels, and tend to reinforce each other. An apt example is Obierika's story of the destruction of Abame. He tells the story to Okonkwo during one of his last visits to him in exile:

> "Abame has been wiped out," said Obierika. "It is a strange and terrible story. If I had not seen the few survivors with my own eyes and heard their story with my own ears, I would not have believed. Was it not on an Eke day that they fled into Umuofia?" he asked his two companions, and they nodded their heads.
>
> "Three moons ago," said Obierika, "on an Eke market-day a little band of fugitives came into our town. Most of them were sons of our land whose mothers had been buried with us . . . During the last planting season a white man had appeared in their clan . . . And he was riding an iron horse . . . The elders consulted their Oracle and it told them that the strange man would break their clan and spread destruction among them . . . And so they killed the white man and tied his iron horse to their sacred tree because it looked as if it would run away to call the man's friends."[18]

There are two time-schemes here, one particular and precise, the other generalized. Obierika is assuming a certain intimacy with events. He has seen the survivors, he says, "with my own eyes", and heard their tales "with my own ears". The phrases indicate the degree of his emphasis and his anxiety to be believed. The matter must therefore be precisely situated, even to the detail of an actual date; it cannot admit vagueness or generalization without losing part of its intrinsicality. Temporal precision in this instance is a way of creating circumstantial credibility. The generalizing of the time when the white man riding the iron horse was done to death necessarily means that the narrator is not under the same type of pressure to give temporal precision to the event. It is given a broad temporal scope: "during the last planting season" is a temporally conceived idea but much more diffuse and less precise than "three moons ago on an Eke market-day".

The novelists are always aware of the close connection of time and space; locating an action or experience in time, they find themselves instinctively driven to give it reality in space. And to do this convincingly, they fall back on the ways in which traditional people express space. The thing that strikes one in this regard is how the writers emphasize the closeness of places and things in the traditional setting, especially through the closeness of sounds, as in this passage from *Danda* which describes the universal musical activities in "the season of feasts":

> The people in the surrounding villages had also come out to bid farewell to one half of the year. From Eziakpaka up the hill the warrior song trickled down as if from the sky. But before it reached Aniocha it had to filter through the huge forest at the boundary and eventually arrived from the bowels of the earth.[19]

Or this description from *The Concubine*:

> She [Ihuoma] came out of the reception hall into the caressing warmth of the setting sun. She could hear the sound of oduma . . . coming from Omigwe, the next village. Omigwe was very close. The time to get to it was scarcely enough for a meal. So she could hear the individual notes of the oduma and she recognized the particular tune being played.[20]

Sound is one way of establishing spatial contiguity; for instance, it is easy to rouse an entire population by a town crier's night round, as in the announcement of the clan assembly in *Things Fall Apart*;[21] in the language of the drum announcing Ezeudu's death;[22] or in the Mother of the Spirits' weeping-fit after Enoch has "killed" a Mask, which heralded the final showdown between the antagonists.[23]

The actual spatial setting of each novel is pretty well defined. The limits of the traditional world are narrow and circumscribed: beyond lies the unknown, the nebulous, the conjectural world. In *Things Fall Apart*, for example, the opening sentence of the first paragraph defines the firmly established spatial certainties: "Okonkwo was well known throughout the nine villages and even beyond." The extension of the statement is a weak tail to the solid body. The clan context is the spatially realized context, the domestic context of intimate knowledge and association. Okonkwo's positive activities in the novel are defined in the spatial confines of the nine villages, and when he moves outside this domestic environment, as when he fights Umuofia's wars, exacts redress from Mbaino for the murdered Umuofia woman, or flees to Mbanta after his accidental homicide, he meets an outside world which he has little sympathy with. It is a confrontation, and costs him considerable effort and adjustment. But granted that the interaction between a domestic and

129

an external world is a realistic necessity, it remains that the traditional world of the novels is narrower than the modern world. In *Things Fall Apart,* the interaction is within a group of neighbouring villages which include Mbaino, Mbanta, Abame and, of course, Umuofia. In other novels the spatial limits of their traditional setting are also stressed. Thus, in *The Concubine,* Amadi carefully sets out the spatial dimensions of the action by a detailed geographical description:

> Omokachi was a small village comprising eleven family groups. Each family group occupied a cluster of compounds and every compound had a path bursting into the main path running across the village. The main path ran east towards Aliji, a village rather bigger than Omokachi, and west towards another village Chiolu.
>
> But the nearest village to Omokachi was Omigwe . . . Only the braves could go as far as Aliji. It was a whole day's journey from Omokachi. The path went through forests and swamps and there was no knowing when and where head-hunters would strike. When there was any message to be relayed to Aliji two strong men ran the errand. Emenike often went on these delegations.[24]

One may think the novelists have actually shrunk the compass of this world to a size smaller than it actually had. But they also often show that exceptional individuals, such as diviners and medicine men (and one should add enterprising traders and ironsmiths), like Anyika in *The Concubine,* were exceptionally mobile, and constituted link characters between different traditional societies. Certainly, the Awka blacksmiths and Aro traders were famous throughout traditional Igboland for their journeyings and trading. And the Nri priesthood, which was widely recognized and fulfilled ritual expiations, must have formed spatial and cultural bridges between the traditional communities. But the novelists are involved with those areas of social and individual experience in which spatial contiguity defines the precise assessment and elucidation of action. They deal with individuals mainly in the context of their intimate relatedness to the environment and show how their distinctive personalities work for good or ill. In this respect the area of concrete contact between the individual and his environment is the village and its neighbours. It is the area of interaction in everyday activities, including trade, working in neighbouring farmlands, sharing religious experiences, participating in festivities, funerals, title-celebrations, dances, marriages and so on.

Beyond this concrete spatial focus of individual and group experience all is vague and blurred, and belongs to the realm of the fanciful and the

130

speculative. Such, for example, is the tale surrounding the appearance and disappearance of locusts in *Things Fall Apart* in which "The elders said locusts came once in a generation, reappeared every year for seven years and then disappeared for another life-time. They went back to their caves in a distant land, where they were guarded by a race of stunted men. And then after another lifetime these men opened the caves again and the locusts came to Umuofia."[25] Similarly, in Amadi's *The Concubine*, the villagers attribute the "making" of the harmattan (the cold dry wind of the desert) to the Wakanchis, "a race of dwarfs skilled in medicine and other mysterious powers".[26] It is this kind of myth-making about life beyond the immediate neighbourhood which in the past made Igbo people imagine that white men emerged from holes in the ground, a fancy later conventionalized in the art of Mbari houses. Significantly, the diviners and oracles who had wider contact with the outside world and who acted as intellectuals in traditional society seemed to have more accurate knowledge and a better imaginative grasp of the unusual than the rest of the people. For example, when the people of Abame consulted their oracle about the lone white man on the iron horse, he told them among other things that other white men, like a swarm of locusts, were on their way, and that the lone white man was "their harbinger sent to explore the terrain".[27]

The traditional imagination can also exhibit unique versatility and an acuteness of perception beyond that of people who subsist only on modern realities. It is sensitive to the deeper layers of experience in a way that is no longer common in modern industrial societies. It perceives without difficulty the reality of the world of spirits, gods and ancestors and the mystical bonds that unite all beings. Whether in their folklore and mythology, in their symbolisms and figures of language, in their religious and magical beliefs, they have a total view of the universe as a continuum and a perpetual flow of being and experience comprehending the visible and invisible universe, the world of nature and the supernatural, and of the living and the dead.

Traditional characters are constantly plunging inward into this deep metaphysical region of the mind, especially in moments of crisis when surface realities have failed to provide the insights needed to resolve life's problems. Every novel set in the traditional environment attends to the movements of the characters' minds from empirically apprehended realities to the deep metaphysical dimension. Characters faced with serious problems attempt to resolve them by asking such questions as, what is the will of the gods in these matters? How did the ancestors handle these problems when they were confronted by them? Or how would they have handled them if they had had to? What forces are at

131

work here and how can they be harmonized, conciliated, diminished, increased for the benefit of man? Beyond the metaphysical perception lies the need for action, for restoring balances and assuaging ruffled feelings, so the people of Umuofia consult the Oracle of the Hills and the Caves about whether or not to go to war,[28] or Araba's family consult a diviner to discover the cause of his sudden illness,[29] or Madume placates the spirit of Emenike having indirectly contributed to his death.[30] Or outstanding or neglected ritual obligation is fulfilled, as when the Uwadiegwu umunna perform the annual sacrifice in honour of Mgbafo Ezira.[31]

Certain specific periods such as the new moon or the time just before cock-crow, and certain specific places such as cross-roads, are ideal for ritual and religious purposes. For example, Ezeulu (in *Arrow of God*) venerates his deity on every new moon, Madume is required to carry out his sacrifice at "any road junction"[32] and Okuata, Obika's wife, has her Sacrifice of Coverture performed near a junction "of their highway and another leading to the bride's village along which she had come that very day".[33] On the other hand, there are situations in which time and space lose all relevance, as when mystical power is magically unleashed against a predetermined target. Mystical force is not circumscribed by time and space; it annihilates both. This is often expressed in mythopoeic oratory. A classic example is Ezeulu's speech at the Feast of the Pumpkin Leaves when he tells how he combatted and overcame the four days of the week. The piece is so well done that it deserves to be quoted here. The Chief Priest is doing his ritual dance as he pronounces his oration and approaches the centre of the arena:

"At that time ... when lizards were still in ones and twos, the whole people assembled and chose me to carry their new deity. I said to them:

" 'Who am I to carry this fire on my bare head? A man who knows that his anus is small does not swallow an udala seed.'

"They said to me:

" 'Fear not. The man who sends a child to catch a shrew will also give him water to wash his hand.'

"I said: 'So be it.'

"And we set to work. That day was Eke; we worked into Oye and then into Afo. As day broke on Nkwo and the sun carried its sacrifice I carried my *Alusi* and, with all the people behind me, set out on the journey. A man sang with the flute on my right and another replied on my left. From behind the heavy tread of all the people gave me strength. And then all of a sudden something spread itself across my face. On one side it was raining, on the other side it was dry. I looked again and saw that it was Eke.

"I said to him: 'Is it you Eke?'

"He replied: 'It is I, Eke, the One that makes a strong man bite the earth with his teeth.'

"I took a hen's egg and gave him. He took it and ate and gave way to me. We went on, past streams and forests. Then a smoking thicket crossed my path, and two men were wrestling on their heads. My followers looked once and took to their heels. I looked again and saw that it was Oye.

"I said to him: 'Is it you Oye across my path?'

"He said 'It is I, Oye, the One that began cooking before Another and so has more broken pots.'

"I took a white cock and gave him. He took it and made way for me. I went on past farmlands and wilds and then I saw that my head was too heavy for me. I looked steadily and saw that it was Afo."[34]

The Chief Priest overcomes obstacles by a mixture of propitiatory sacrifices and magical power, but the lesson is quite explicit. He has overcome the four days of the traditional Igbo week; the inference is that not only magical power but also a strong man, that is, one who is mystically charged, can annihilate time and space.

Another aspect of traditional realism is the place history occupies in its consciousness. Since traditional practices are hallowed by time and established by ancestral charter, the past is never remote from the present but is frequently a backward extension as well as a reinforcement of the present, a manner of elucidating contemporaneous experience as well as a validation of such experience. There is a deep and abiding interest in history, not as a dead substance of remote antiquity, but as an accumulation of human achievement, a testimony of the triumph of human ingenuity and will reaching down to ancestral roots. The perception of time and space embodies the continuing influence of the past on the present, either by providing it with its charter, defining and determining its mores or creating its institutional framework.

The traditional people's sense of history is constantly reflected in the rural novels. Events are evaluated in terms of how seriously or decisively they affect people's lives, whether they carry historical weight or are only of a transient nature. Where they carry historical significance, they are worked into the more durable structures of traditional life and become part of the historical record. In the novels, almost every traditional society dealt with has a tradition of its origin, often linked to a founder-ancestor or a tutelary deity. This becomes a force for social cohesion and is woven into the rhythm of religious festivals as with Ulu in Umuaro in *Arrow of God*, or the feast in honour of Obunagu, the father of Aniocha in *Danda*. The re-enactment of the coming of Ulu occupies so central a position in the narrative scheme of *Arrow of God* because it emphasizes the continuing redemptive and protective role of this deity in the life of the community. When this historical expectation can no longer be fulfilled the historical unity of the community breaks up.

But history is not a closed concern, a permanent casting-back for a validating authority for present life and action. It is constantly being made. Traditional characters recognize the dynamic nature of history and are able to absorb its message. In *Arrow of God* and *Things Fall Apart*, for example, the coming of administration is seen as an event of historical significance by the people of Umuaro and Umuofia. In *Arrow of God*, its significance begins to impinge dramatically on the consciousness when Captain Winterbottom, the British Commissioner, intervenes in the war between Umuaro and Okperi and destroys the combatants' guns, thus impressing on the local people the reality of the arrival of a new order.

> The war was waged from one Afo to the next. On the day it began Umuaro killed two men of Okperi. The next day was Nkwo, and so there was no fighting. On the two following days, Eke and Oye, the fighting grew fierce. Umuaro killed four men and Okperi replied with three, one of the three being Akukalia's brother, Okoye. The next day, Afo, saw the war brought to a sudden close. The white man, Wintabota, brought soldiers to Umuaro and stopped it. The story of what these soldiers did in Abame was still told with fear, and so Umuaro made no effort to resist but laid down their arms . . . The white man was not satisfied that he had stopped the war. He gathered all the guns in Umuaro and asked the soldiers to break them in the face of all, except three or four which he carried away. Afterwards he sat in judgement over Umuaro and Okperi and gave the disputed land to Okperi.[35]

The breaking of the guns is a symbolic act indicating the passing of traditional independence and free action, and since history is documented mainly in terms of outstanding symbols, the people of Umuaro build this event into their historical repertoire by creating a new age-grade and calling it the Age Grade of the Breaking of the Guns. The British official responsible is immortalized in local lore as Wintabota, the Destroyer of Guns.[36] The creation of the age-grade becomes a mnemonic device as well as a means of giving concreteness to the specific historical episode.

Historical reference-points of this nature become temporal and histori-cal yardsticks for measuring related events in the life of the community. Thus, the conflict itself provides the first indication of the breach be-tween the clan and the Chief Priest, since he had to testify against the clan before the Commissioner at the hearing of the case. The shock-wave generated by such a sudden breakdown of old conventions and solidarities prepares the way for the final events. Even Ezeulu's trusted friend Akuebue sees the repercussions as boding ill for the Chief Priest since " 'Umuaro will always say that you [the Chief Priest] betrayed them before the white man.' "[37] The unhappy story of Abame mentioned both in *Arrow of God* and in *Things Fall Apart* is such an historical signpost. It is a reference-point that marks the finality and terror of the colonial power. The shooting up of the unsuspecting town has become a caution-ary tale to restrain all those who might be tempted to resist the new administration. It is related in *Things Fall Apart* with much circum-stantial detail. Ironically the moral of the tale is lost on Okonkwo, to whom the story is told, and to whom it ought to be a warning against the impetuosity that is later to drive him to disaster.

Time and space are apprehended as approximations made more con-crete by time-distance and space-distance, and socialized through cus-tomary usage and collective agreement. Time in the traditional con-sciousness is less significant than social institutions – ethics, religion and aesthetics. Since the traditional setting is largely an agrarian society and small in scale, time and space have less significance than in urban or industrial setting. So West African novelists show an awareness of this relative irrelevance.[38] Some of the novelists even draw attention to the peculiarity. According to Nkem Nwankwo, "Punctuality is not one of the virtues of the Aniocha man. He takes time over his snuff and his palm wine and if you attempted to hurry him from either he would excuse himself by reminding you of the proverb: where the runner reaches there the walker will reach eventually."[39]

There is no effort to describe minute-by-minute and day-to-day experiences, because this would be meaningless. The absence of a detailed functional time in these novels gives a leisurely tempo to life. Neither in the domestic lives of the characters nor in the community assemblies nor at weddings and funerals does one get the impression of eagerness to hurry through what is being done. The emphasis is always on the complete observance of the prescribed ritual or social function, the perfect exercise of the approved etiquette of speech and behaviour, the elaboration of points with flourish and oratory much reinforced by

135

repetition. There is much truth in Ruth Benedict's statement that the value traditional people place on time is low because to them "wisdom" is far more important than "efficiency".[40] The only instance in which a rigid time-scheme is established is in Achebe's *Arrow of God* where the priest of Ulu sacrifices to his god and eats his ritual yam every month. This adherence to a time-scheme is necessary to the plot, for the crisis of the story arises from the break in routine when the priest is removed from his home and imprisoned by the District Officer.

The different novels are nonetheless structured temporally, implicitly, by reference to incidents which the understanding reader can himself date. Thus Achebe's novels can be given a time-scheme from the internal evidence, and so can all the other novels. *Things Fall Apart* illustrates the point. Its action refers to the period of early missionary penetration of a cluster of villages east of the Niger, from the missionary base in Onitsha. The local British administration was settling conflicts arising from traditionalist resistance to this missionary effort. The "shooting" of Abame people by the administration has a historical basis in the murder of Dr Stewart in Ahiara in 1905 followed by a punitive military action against the culprits.[41] As in the case of Dr Stewart, the people of Abame tie up the murdered white man's iron horse on a sacred silk-cotton tree to prevent its running away and reporting the crime. The action of the novel could therefore be placed in the late eighteen-nineties or the first decade of the twentieth century.

In the urban environment, time acquires significance. Bureaucratic systems of administration in industry, commerce and the civil service, the need to have numbers of people drawn together from different parts of a large metropolis, require adherence to time schedules. People's lives are being increasingly controlled by the clock. The tempo of life in towns is strict because there are so many things making demands on the time of the townsmen; to attend to them all he has to be very mobile, physically and mentally. Life has become a nightmare rush to keep up with things – with one's profession, with social engagements, with trade union and political meetings, with funerals, marriages and outings, with football matches, with the theatre and the cinema, and even with one's sex and drink. Time is master and the townsman its slave.

Spatially, the world of the West African urban novel is different from that of the rural novel. In contrast to the relatively circumscribed, homogeneous world of the rural novel, modern urban West Africa is marked by spatial openness and extensiveness. A modern town is several times the size of a traditional village. But more important than physical size and population is the fact of heterogeneity. The great advances in modern communication and transport and the creation of new geopolitical structures drawing together huge areas and large numbers of previously isolated ethnic nationalities have made it possible for people who in the past would have been trapped in their traditional homelands to be attracted into the towns. Metalled roads, railways and waterways radiating from the towns into the villages become channels through which the villagers pour into the towns in search of work, trade, and new economic possibilities, and along which they return periodically to renew contact with their rural roots. A unique feature of urban life in West Africa is this tendency for most urban dwellers to develop a rhythm of life which swings between town and village. This means that a realistic perception of life among townsmen will recognize their dual loyalties – to the town in which they live and work, and the village from which most of them came originally, with which they are in constant contact throughout their working life, and to which they will retire from work. The town has to be seen in the context of its intimate connection with the country through its commuting inhabitants. In very few of the urban novels is all the action centred on the town. In Achebe's two urban novels, the action in *No Longer at Ease* moves between Lagos and Umuofia, and in *A Man of the People* between Bori (Lagos thinly disguised) and Anata. In Nzekwu's *Wand of Noble Wood*, the action moves between Lagos and Ado (the traditional name for Onitsha) and in *Blade Among the Boys* between Ado and northern Nigerian towns. Ekwensi's Lagos novels also concern a fair section of the countryside. Jagua in *Jagua Nana*, as well as being fully immersed in Lagos life, finds time to visit her home village of Ogabu and the Creek villages of Krinameh and Bagana, and in the end retires to Ogabu. In *Beautiful Feathers*, again set in Lagos, the chief characters spend some of their time in a Benin village. Even in *The Interpreters*, in which the action swings between Ibadan and Lagos, the main characters have time to travel to the creeks in the futile quest for Egbo's patrimony.

Lagos is a town of a million people. Its inhabitants have to cover large distances every day as they travel from their homes to their places of work, shopping centres and recreation grounds. The novels give a kaleidoscopic picture of its life, reflecting the immense variety of urban activities and the hectic pace at which the characters live. The consequence for characterization is far-reaching. The characters are like faces in a crowd that is ever breaking up and reforming. They move so quickly from one social situation to another, have such slight personal attachments, that we are hardly able to see anything of their inner lives or identify intimately with them. In contrast, in the rural novels where life flows smoothly in a kind of slow-motion we are able to follow the characters' gestures and attitudes so closely that we know them intimately and are able to grasp their predicaments, dreams, frustrations and aspirations.

Between the extremes of the slow-motion of the rural novels and the raciness of Ekwensi's novels come Armah's *The Beautyful Ones Are Not Yet Born*, Soyinka's *The Interpreters* and Achebe's *A Man of the People*, where the authors manipulate time and space as a way of advancing their narrative insights. The most common device is the technique of the spotlight, a way of concentrating the attention for a considerable time on a single scene or object, exploring it in all its details before moving on to another scene or object. They follow the spotlight until it alights on the scene or object of interest and then stop with the spotlight, taking in all the impressions before moving on again. Armah uses this technique to great effect, illuminating post-independence corruption. Achebe and Soyinka use the technique successfully, but in their works the tempo is faster, since the space to be covered is wider and more diverse than in Armah's novel. And Soyinka introduces complications in the use of time and space by dislocating the time-scheme and letting the spotlight travel forward, backward, and sometimes inward to focus on the characters' minds, reflecting their disjointed thoughts which may also plunge backwards, stand still, or lunge into the future. These complications are not merely a juggling of time sequences, but also spatial in that space is not entirely physical but also internalized in individual consciousness.

Thus the establishment of a structural relationship between the surface spatial realities in Egbo's life and the underlying movements of his mind gives rise to the see-saw narrative structure of *The Interpreters*. Egbo recognizes the burden of the past, and at a purely intellectual level abjures it because it does not hold anything for him. His world is the modern stage, his Foreign Office job, and his association with his friends, the modern young intellectuals of Lagos and Ibadan, and not with the Osa Descendants Union or his blind, ageing grandfather whom he is expected to succeed as chief. But emotionally, and so insidiously and persistently because unconsciously, he is very much a part of the past; or to put it differently, the past is still very much a part of him. Because Soyinka's spotlight travels now on the surface, or visible, plane of the interpreters' collective experiences and now on the submerged but crucial plane of Egbo's mind and its persistent emotional preoccupations, the temporal development of the narrative is very complex and often confusing.

It is fair to say that the urban novels rely more on space than on time for their development. The absence of a time-factor as a unifying element gives them loose structures of action in which two-dimensional characters float through space from one situation or incident to another.

This is particularly so of *People of the City* and *Jagua Nana* where there is a deliberate effort to describe the lives of individuals but to explore the life of the city. It is less true of the more integrated novels like Ekwensi's *Beautiful Feathers*, Achebe's *No Longer At Ease* and *A Man of the People*, Soyinka's *The Interpreters* and Armah's *The Beautyful Ones Are Not Yet Born*, where it is shown how events and incidents transpiring through time affect the lives and circumstances of the chief characters.

6

Setting

There is a distinctive local colour in West African novels, since the novelists describe an environment and situations which are characteristically West African. These situations affect character and action, and provide background to both. The treatment of setting both in the rural and the urban novels affects the domestication of the novel in West Africa. One can no more think of West African novels apart from traditional West African village environment and the new urban settlements than one could think of Hardy's novels or Fielding's prose fiction without thinking of the Wessex countryside and the eighteenth-century England of country estates, inn-keepers and post-boys.

In a sense the novels are largely preoccupied with the description of setting. This is mainly a result of the "engaged" attitude of the novelists. They attempt to portray village life in its entirety in order to stress its logicality and its autonomy and self-sufficiency. There is no extended effort to describe "scenery" as such, because nature is not apprehended as an independent reality or in its decorative aspect but as an integral part of the traditional world. Rather, the description of setting builds up atmosphere by concentrating on the physical, social, moral and intellectual environment.

The first thing we notice about the village novels is the small-scale, almost claustrophobic, nature of their physical environment. There are no vast open spaces but small clearings covered with closely set buildings, and hemmed in by dark, heavily wooded forests through which narrow tracks connect the village with its neighbours. The villages teem with people. The closeness of the houses makes for intimate social relationships. Everyone knows everyone else, their antecedents, family history, character traits, social stigmas and personal problems. Collective participation is the keynote of village activities. Whether in community games, singing and dancing, work on farms or building houses, or what has to do with birth, death, marriage or religious worship, the emphasis is

140

always on group participation. The community takes part actively in the working of social institutions, shares common beliefs, attitudes and values.

In *Things Fall Apart* and *Arrow of God* Achebe has done more than any other West African novelist to create the classic traditional village setting. He has a gift for atmospheric immediacy, as in the first few lines of *Things Fall Apart*, in which he establishes both the social and physical setting of the novel and its intellectual outlook:

> Okonkwo was well known throughout the nine villages and even beyond. His fame rested on solid personal achievements. As a young man of eighteen he had brought honour to his village by throwing Amalinze the Cat. Amalinze was the great wrestler who for seven years was unbeaten, from Umuofia to Mbaino. He was called the Cat because his back would never touch the earth. It was this man that Okonkwo threw in a fight which the old men agreed was one of the fiercest since the founder of their town engaged a spirit of the wild for seven days and seven nights.
>
> The drums beat and the flutes sang and the spectators held their breath. Amalinze was a wily craftsman, but Okonkwo was as slippery as a fish in water. Every nerve and every muscle stood out of their arms, on their backs and their thighs, and one almost heard them stretching to breaking point. In the end Okonkwo threw the Cat.[1]

Here is a small-scale society in which the impact of events has a limited spatial dimension. Okonkwo's fame as a wrestler may be great, but its impact is not felt much beyond the nine villages that compose the clan. The wrestling match itself tells us something about the intimate relationship between the individual and the group, as between Okonkwo and the people of Umuofia. The first two sentences strike the keynote to the social background of Okonkwo's life – "fame" and "personal achievement". This is a society that appreciates personal success and recognizes individuality. But the success of the individual is related to the well-being of the whole community. There is little room for fame for fame's sake and achievement for achievement's sake; there is little room for purely egoistic calculation as social philosophy. We are told about the community life of the village, its heartbeat punctuated by drums and flutes, its folk-mythological outlook touched on in the reference to the fight between its founder and a spirit of the wild, and its linguistic habits indicated in Amalinze's sobriquet "the Cat", and the conventional comparison between the growth of Okonkwo's fame and "a bush-fire in the harmattan". We feel how the links between individual, society and its ethos are conveyed in this brief passage. The integrative technique in which background and atmosphere are interlaced with the action of the narrative must be regarded as Achebe's greatest achievement in the rural novels. But he can also create an immediate and vivid picture of a single element of the environmental experience, as in this description of a tropical thunderstorm:

> At last the rain came. It was sudden and tremendous. For two or three moons the sun had been gathering strength till it seemed to breathe a breath of fire on the earth. All the grass had long been scorched brown, and the sands felt like live coals to the feet. Evergreen trees wore a dusty coat of brown. The birds were silenced in the forests, and the world lay panting under the live, vibrating heat. And then came the clap of thunder. It was an angry, metallic and thirsty clap, unlike the deep and liquid rumbling of the rainy season. A mighty wind arose and filled the air with dust. Palm trees swayed as the wind combed their leaves into flying crests like strange and fantastic coiffures.
>
> When the rain finally came, it was in large, solid drops of frozen water which the people called "the nuts of the water of heaven" [aku mmiri-igwe]. They were hard and painful on the body as they fell, yet young people ran about happily picking up the cold nuts and throwing them into their mouths to melt.
>
> The earth quickly came to life and the birds in the forests fluttered around and chirped merrily. A vague scent of life and green vegetation was diffused in the air. As the rain began to fall more soberly and in smaller liquid drops, children sought for shelter, and all were happy, refreshed and thankful.[2]

This is effective description, almost a set piece: but Achebe is not so much concerned with painting a particular natural scene as with the realistic relation of a natural phenomenon to the general rhythm of life, which gives *Things Fall Apart* its distinctive local colour. The picture of the thunderstorm is part of a strategy for indicating the significance of nature in determining summarily, sometimes brutally, the destiny of the people in the traditional agricultural societies of his rural novels. For these farming people rain and drought, sunshine and lack of sunshine, heat and cold can be a matter of life and death. The strong sense of fatality which pervades *Things Fall Apart* is fortified by this suggestion that the forces that destroy man and his well-being emanate from nature itself. In industrialized Western society, science and technology have provided means of reducing the destructive effects of natural forces. In

142

the less technologically developed parts of the world the effect of natural disasters is unquestionably more devastating.

A strong theme of Achebe's treatment of setting in his rural novels is the part which darkness and light play in the life of his villagers. The darkness of a moonless night is almost palpable, and its silence, rendered more profound and sinister by the occasional chirrup of the cricket or a solitary foot-fall, lies heavily on the minds of the villagers. The mysteriousness of night contrasts with and balances the universal laughter and social integration of daytime traditional life. Piercing the silent darkness, the voice of the "crier"[3] or the incantatory singing of the priestess of Agbala[4] or the cracked guttural voice of the spirit chorus[5] have a weird immediacy that makes people prick up their ears in subdued apprehension. Darkness also expresses the unravelling of a tumultuous or disorganized mind by way of dream or nightmare. This is so in *Arrow of God*, *One Man One Wife* and *Danda*. In each of these books, the novelist projects popular associations of night and darkness through the solitary and tortured mind of an individual who sees his own destiny entangled in these associations. Dreams and nightmares, because they are tacitly believed in, merge into reality in two of the three cases.

Here is an instance from *Things Fall Apart*:

> The night was very quiet. It was always quiet except on moonlight nights. Darkness held a vague terror for these people, even the bravest among them. Children were warned not to whistle at night for fear of evil spirits. Dangerous animals became even more sinister and uncanny in the dark. A snake was never called by its name at night, because it would hear. It was called a string. And so on this particular night as the crier's voice was gradually swallowed up in the distance, silence returned to the world, a vibrant silence made more intense by the universal trill of a million million forest insects.[6]

Or that other night on which the priestess of Agbala "abducted" Okonkwo's ailing daughter:

> The night was impenetrably dark. The moon had been rising later and later every night until now it was seen only at dawn. And whenever the moon forsook evening and rose at cock-crow the nights were as black as charcoal.[7]

In contrast, the village under moonlight, in its calm glow and radiance, makes the electric light of the town seem harsh and tawdry. It evokes pleasant associations of children playing and telling folk-tales in the village square or in open compound yards, or of young men paying dis-

143

creet court to their intended brides and of different age-groups performing their organized dances. In *Things Fall Apart* Achebe shows us how
a moonlight night is always different from a night of darkness: "The
happy voices of children playing in open fields would then be heard. And
perhaps those not so young would be playing in pairs in less open places,
and old men and women would remember their youth. As the Ibo say:
'When the moon is shining the cripple becomes hungry for a walk.' "[8]
Daylight, like moonlight, has no terror. All the fearful associations of
the night vanish with the first streaks of the light.

Achebe also describes particular aspects of the large environment. For
instance, his skilful description of the Ulu shrine – the damp chill of
the room, the grinning skulls of previous chief priests looking down from
the rafters, the acoustic weirdness of the room and the fact that the
Chief Priest has to enter the room walking backwards[9] – evokes not so
much a calculated macabre effect as the atmosphere of uncanny mysticism which pervades shrines and sacred groves.

In *The Concubine*, Elechi Amadi shows a comparable gift for reproducing the physical and atmospheric effect of village life. The world
of his novel is, like Achebe's, a small-scale, self-contained one, with a
few jungle paths offering the only outlet to the outside world of identical
villages located a few miles apart. The magical, the metaphysical and the
empirical are inextricably woven into a consistent world view, the gods
jostle men and women in their everyday lives and provide a background
to the events that take place among them. The medicine man and diviner
is an indispensable intermediary. The society is close-knit, with people
crossing and recrossing one another's paths several times a day, whether
at public events like funerals, marriages, births, festivals and games, or
in market places or on the way to and from the farms and streams. They
are constantly chatting, joking, quarrelling and sometimes fighting with
one another. Amadi's crisp sentences and staccato dialogue take the
place of narration, and this affects his handling of setting. Much of the
setting is implicit in the verbal exchanges continually taking place between the characters. Only occasionally, as in his description of the grove
of Amadioha referred to earlier,[10] does Amadi break away from the
integrative approach to paint a formal picture of some aspect of the
environment.

Life flows in an even tenor in *The Concubine*. The villagers live a
thoroughly integrated community life which, when it is disrupted at all,
is disrupted by forces beyond the control of man. Amadi conceives his
novel as an idyllic tale and paints a picture of a fully integrated, serene
and dignified community within which everyone feels a sense of belonging and an instinctive goodwill towards his neighbours. Everyone is

reasonably happy, reasonably supplied with the necessities of life; there is no hunger, hardly any sickness, no rudeness; the only serious quarrel is between the single bad man of the village and its best man, but the hand of the gods is in it, and the bad man hangs himself. There is a lot of singing and dancing, plenty of good-natured banter and little ill-humour. In other words, this is an ideal world but for the meddlesomeness and malevolence of the gods and the spirits. In one of his few authorial comments Amadi underlines the idyllic nature of his vision:

> Omokachi village life was noted for its tradition, propriety, and decorum. Excessive or fanatical feelings over anything were frowned upon and even described as crazy. Anyone who could not control his feelings was regarded as being unduly influenced by his *agwu*. Anyika often confirmed this, as in Ahurole's case.
>
> Even love and sex were put in their proper place. If a woman could not marry one man she could always marry another. A woman deliberately scheming to land a man was unheard of. True, she might encourage him, but this encouragement was a subtle reflex action, a legacy of her prehistoric ancestors. A mature man's love was sincere, deep and stable and therefore easy to reciprocate, difficult to turn down. That was why it was possible for a girl to marry a man without formal courtship. Love was love and never failed.[11]

Idyllic pictures are attractive because they offer a dream escape from the realities of the world one knows and lives in. But if Amadi has over-played the stability and the decorum, he has handled the intervention of the supernatural in traditional life most convincingly. It is not simply that the gods and spirits mingle freely with the people, shaping their destinies for good or ill; Amadi's tale conveys this effect with ease and conviction, as in the scene in which Madume consults Anyika the dibia after cutting his toe in Emenike's compound. Emenike had died after a fight with him, so the event is more than a coincidence:

> Anyika cast his cowries to and fro for some time. Then he chewed some alligator pepper and spat it out in a fine spray in front of his temple. Madume watching him keenly, wondering what pronouncements he had up his sleeve. He thought himself clever to have come to Anyika to know the true story behind what he thought of as his toe disaster. He had not been mistaken. The gods were behind it. It was certainly a premonition.
>
> "You were lucky," Anyika said slowly, "to have come out alive from Emenike's compound."

145

"Ojukwu forbid!" Madume stammered.

"Several spirits swore to kill you there and then."

"Emenike's spirit must have been among them."

"No, you are mistaken. He was not among them. Unknown spirits, some of them from the sea, teamed up to destroy you. Let me see, oh yes, Emenike's father was among them."

"What is to be done, dibia?"

"They don't want you to have anything to do with Ihuoma [Emenike's widow]. They have been on the lookout for you. So far they have been unable to enter your compound because of the talisman you buried at the entrance."

"What is their grievance?" Madume queried timidly.

"There will be several sacrifices to appease Emenike's father and his train."[12]

The sacrificial material proves a formidable list: "seven grains of alligator pepper, seven manillas, an old basket, three cowries, a bunch of unripe palm fruit, two cobs of maize, a small bunch of plantain, some dried fish, two cocks, one of which must be white, seven eggs, some camwood, chalk, a tortoise (or the shell) and a chameleon.[13] The matter-of-fact way in which the supernatural is presented and the total absence of scepticism help to reinforce the idyllic quality of life in *The Concubine*. Even when the gods intervene to strike a man down, there is no struggle; the blow is hardly audible; it is sudden, sharp and decisive, and life continues to flow on as if nothing had happened.

Nkem Nwankwo in *Danda* shows a masterly handling of setting, not so much in its physical aspect (though much is made of the scorching sunshine and the "akpaka" trees under which the villagers take shelter and drink their palm-wine) but in its social and human aspect. He captures the moods and attitudes of his villagers, as moved to ecstasy by the lyricism of Danda's fluting, or as bystanders watching a serious, tragic or comic drama acted out by their fellows. Here they perform the role of a chorus, making comments, airing sentiments, giving advice and passing judgement. This is well illustrated by the scene describing the arrival of the first motor car in Aniocha.[14]

Nzekwu's handling of setting is not as fully integral to the narrative as Achebe's or Nwankwo's. He approaches the setting mainly through customs and social habits. He describes them in a language often more suited to anthropology than to literature. He does not always succeed in satisfying the basic requirement of literary creativity described by Humphry House as "the process of imaginative transformation from original to fiction".[15] Occasionally however he can build up atmosphere by listing material items which together present a single vivid image. Such is the atmosphere surrounding the formidable god Iyi-ocha.[16] Nzekwu gradually adds one detail after another until we feel an inscrutable and vigilant power that has held its ground in spite of social change. The presence of Western articles like refrigerators, degree hoods and radiograms as expiatory offerings to the Iyi-ocha by its victims' kinsmen symbolizes the staying power of tradition over Western innovation and sophistication.

Aluko's particular form of satire is caricature. This leads inevitably to the distortion of social and environmental reality. For him there is no dignity in traditional life. The gods of the village of Isolo are a ragged and disreputable lot. The atmosphere of the village is one of confusion, vice and squalor. There are abductions and divorces, litigations, violence, disease, fear and hopelessness. There is little real community life either among the traditionalists or among the Christian converts.

Aluko suggests the traditional atmosphere through allusions to legend and cautionary folk-tales, but these ring hollow amid the prevailing purposelessness and futility. Thus, it is ironical that the tale of Niku, the girl who defies her parents over the choice of a husband and ends up marrying a boa in human form, is told by Toro, for she grows up to reject the husband to whom she has been betrothed since infancy by her parents. Aluko's anti-traditionalist outlook is also indicated by such touches as the dim light of the hurricane lantern on a peg on the wall of the Asolo's council chamber, throwing blurred and grotesque images of the elders on the opposite wall.

In Ekwensi's *Burning Grass*, the very opening lines set the atmosphere of aridity characteristic of the northern savannah. His realistic description of setting is indicated by the minutely worked-out topography of the action, and his close attention to the chronological sequence, so that we are able to follow the wanderings of Mai Sunsaye and Rikku from burning grass to fresh pastures and from one watering place to another. Ekwensi's description of landscape gives pictorial reality to the story.

Burning Grass differs from the novels set in the densely peopled villages of southern Nigeria. Here we are made aware of the vastness of wild nature dwarfing the Fulani and their cattle into insignificance. In southern Nigerian villages, man and his affairs crowd nature out of significance. *Burning Grass* reveals the enormous potential for an open-space literature in West Africa, which could be contrasted with the claustrophobic fiction of the crowded southern villages and Lagos.

The Voice is a parabolic novel and the setting is conveyed through symbolism and imagery. Okara cuts out all particularity of detail both in social relationship and physical environment, and description of the setting becomes a way of extending the moral insight. The natural environment is made to mediate the sense of evil which broods over the world of the novel, as in this, a sunset scene in the nightmare village of Amatu:

> It was the day's ending and Okolo by a window stood. Okolo stood looking at the sun behind the tree tops falling. The river was flowing, reflecting the finishing sun, like a dying away memory. It was like an idol's face, no one knowing what is behind. Okolo at the palm trees looked. They were like women with hair hanging down, dancing, possessed. Egrets, like white flower petals strung slackly across the river, swaying up and down, were returning home. And, on the river, canoes were crawling home with bent backs and tired hands, paddling.[17]

Here there is neither beauty nor magnificence. The dominant images are of death, loss of vitality, brooding and threatening mysteriousness and frenzied madness. It appears that nature is victim of the evil forces that dominate society. It is not surprising that Okara adopts this approach. Where the moral environment has been polluted, the natural and physical environment will not be expected to escape the corruption. The imagination that perceives moral corruption must notice also, because of the integrative nature of the world, that the physical and natural universe shares the depreciation and devitalization. The forces of dictatorship and social corruption are against spontaneity, creativity and individuality and therefore, indirectly, against the life principle and the light. The dominant symbol of the novel is darkness, a near-tactile darkness in which people grope about in moral blindness at the mercy of the dictators. Light appears intermittently and then only emphasizes the darkness. Okara uses animal images to represent his villagers, especially on the night of Okolo's arrest. He is being dragged from Tuere's hut to Izongo's palace:

> The people snapped at him like hungry dogs snapping at bones. They carried him in silence like the silence of ants carrying a crumb of yam or fish bone. Then they put him down and dragged him past thatch houses that in the dark looked like pigs with their snouts in the ground; pushed and dragged him past mud walls with pitying eyes; pushed and dragged him past concrete walls with concrete eyes; pushed and dragged him along the waterside like soldier ants with their prisoner. They pushed and dragged him in panting silence, shuffling silence, broken only by an owl hooting from the darkness of the orange tree in front of Chief Izongo's house.[18]

Dogs struggling for bones, pigs with their snouts in the ground in search of food, soldier ants carrying a crumb of yam or fish-bone across the kitchen, soldier ants dragging their victim, the owl hooting from a tree-top at night – these are familiar enough, but when used to describe human beings and human action, the effect is reductive: the humans emerge as less than human. Such images are part of Okara's way of showing that dictatorship reduces human dignity in the people who subscribe to it. The images are part of the moral determinism of the parabolic narrative and its physical world. The symbols of darkness together with the animal and insect imagery lead to the heart of the book.

Most of the urban novels except *The African* and *The Beautyful Ones Are Not Yet Born* are set in Lagos and try to capture the physical and social atmosphere of the city and to show the characters are influenced by it. We are made aware of the constant noise of traffic, the honking of cars, the loud-speakers blaring out "high life" tunes from record shops or advertising articles from commercial vans; of the hawkers crying their wares along the streets; of the unstable crowds massing wherever there is an incident, holding up traffic and adding to the hubbub; of the crowded slums side by side with ultra-modern office blocks; at night, of the radiant street lamps, the desperate gaiety of night-club life and the sordid activities in the dingy, ill-lit areas inhabited by the underworld, the pimps and the prostitutes. All these provide a background against which the characters play out the hectic game of survival.

Ekwensi is most successful is relating his Lagos characters to their physical and social environment. He knows the Lagos of the underworld and of the slums better than any other Nigerian writer. But his success in relating social situation to physical environment and at revealing character through setting is intermittent, giving rise to a panoramically rather than an organically developed narrative. This is particularly marked in *People of the City*, where Ekwensi takes the reader on a guided tour of Twenty Molomo Street with its community outlook, the smoke-filled and spirituous atmosphere of the All Language Club, the musty, hostile atmosphere of the office of the *West African Sensation*, and the slummy, congested home of Aina; and in *Jagua Nana*, of the "depraved surroundings" on the outskirts of Lagos inhabited by Rosa and the prostitutes. Ekwensi's descriptions are related to his sociological intention of stripping Lagos bare of its urban sophistication and revealing its corruption, degradation and sordidness. *Beautiful Feathers* shows a more organic narration, and setting is subordinated to psychological necessity.

Achebe's *No Longer at Ease* shows a different Lagos. It explores the Lagos of respectable middle-class civil servants and professionals who inhabit the secluded suburbia of Ikoyi and hail one another with the question "How is the car behaving?" Achebe's narrative technique is largely discursive, and the physical setting is often implied rather than described, as when, instead of describing Ikoyi, where Obi Okonkwo lives, he launches into a description of its "graveyard" atmosphere and class significance. His hero contrasts this genteel but "dead" Lagos with the other half of the "twin-kernel," the Lagos of open drains, of exposed food, meat-stalls and bucket latrines.[19]

Description in *A Man of the People* is fragmentary, creating a sociological background. There is little integration of setting with narrative and little use of it to further psychological insights, unlike the urban novels of Ekwensi where slums breed their own type of character. Interjected authorial comment is also used as when Odili contrasts the plush habitations of privileged politicians and the nouveaux riches with the slums:

> The surprises and contrasts in our great country were simply inexhaustible. Here was I in our capital city, reading about pails of excrement from the cosy comfort of a princely seven bathroom mansion with its seven gleaming, silent action, water-closets![20]

His failure to integrate setting with narrative in his Lagos novels (one of the finest achievements in his rural novels) indicates, one suspects, Achebe's own uneasiness in the Lagos setting. He had lived in Lagos, with only a few intermissions, between 1954 and 1966, during his career in the Nigerian Broadcasting Corporation, but it is likely that he never really got into the spirit and rhythm of life of that turbulent city. Lagos must have seemed to him, in his quiet, self-possessed, sober, introspective life, a threatening whirlpool round which it would be necessary to pick one's way cautiously to avoid being drawn in. A writer need not live through every experience and attach himself physically to every setting he deals with in his work. But the novel requires not so much personal contact as a passionate drive to approach and examine, if only imaginatively, each object that excites the writer. If he is, by reason of his own temperament, repelled by some aspect of his subject, a flagging of artistic vitality is bound to result. The Lagos of Chief Nanga and Obiajulu Okonkwo is without the infectious excitement of the Lagos of Amusa Sango and Jagua Nana and the vitality of the Lagos of Soyinka's "Bohemians" and "Lagoon" prophets. Ekwensi's outgoing temperament and Soyinka's dramatist's cosmopolitan temperament prepared them to explore the physical realities of Lagos in a way which Achebe's more retiring, introspective nature must have inhibited.

Achebe's temperament finds more congenial the even rhythm and controlled vitality of rural life. It is not accidental that in both *A Man of the People* and *No Longer at Ease* the setting comes suddenly alive in the rural passages. In *A Man of the People*, for example, the concreteness of setting and the ease with which Achebe creates it is unmistakable, from a simple description of greed-filled Odo's rope-making within his hut of red earth and thatched roof[21] to the scene in front of a local shop where the villagers demonstrate their disapproval of the theft of a blind man's walking-stick by a local rascal.[22] The weakness of setting in Achebe's Lagos novels, especially in *No Longer at Ease*, may also be due to adventitious characters subsisting in an artificial situation. The phenomenon of urban tribalism presents a problem for the writer: how can he give these people a full, integrated existence in an urban setting? Even though Obi Okonkwo's education, social status and job mark him out as middle class, the long shadow of rural Umuofia, materialized in Lagos as the Umuofia Progressive Union, falls over him and makes him partly middle class and partly a villager. His clansmen of the Progressive Union are even less urbanized, and their lives, divided between city and village, cannot easily be defined in terms of the urban setting. They are like exotic plants on a foreign soil, or, to stick to the original image, like unnaturalized plants that cannot put roots down in the soil on which they grow. The position is hard to handle, especially where characters need to be explored in their attachment to a physical, environmental and social setting.

Soyinka's urban characters are well integrated in their milieu, whether they be fastidious, falsely genteel academics, "Bohemian" activists, or Lagoon spiritualists; whether in their studios, working through art to bridge the gap of reality between experience and mythology, or in the clubs where the interpreters carry on their witty, verbal campaign against society and one another. As a master of particularity, Soyinka pursues each incident until he runs it to earth and nails it firmly to its physical ground. For example, when Egbo takes a canoe trip to his unclaimed chiefdom in the Creeks, the atmosphere is created by minutely detailed description:

> Two paddles clove the still water of the creek, and the canoe trailed behind it a silent groove, between gnarled tears of mangrove; it was dead air, and they came to a spot where an old rusted cannon showed above the water. It built a faded photo of the past with rotting canoe hulks along the bank, but the link was spurious. The paddlers slowed down and held the boat against the cannon. Egbo put his hand in the water and dropped his eyes down the brackish stillness, down the dark depths to its bed of mud. He looked reposed, wholly withdrawn.[23]

151

Soyinka's description suggests the movement of a cinema camera. The lens travels as the author directs, resting where he wills, and taking in the details he thinks relevant. The effect is to foster specific feelings or insights. Once the camera has travelled over the picture and established a strong visual impression, the image so formed can become a frame of reference for subsequent illumination and interpretation of other actions and impressions. Thus this canoe journey forms an imagistic framework for interpreting Egbo's subsequent experiences. He has an affinity with water, especially flowing water, which explains why during the thunderstorm which opens the novel he is deeply disturbed by the rising pool of water on the floor into which he pours his beer, why his mind runs to canoe-images in a moment of sexual ecstacy with Simi ("through hidden floods a sheath canoe parts tall reeds, not dies, God, not dies a rotting hulk . . . parting low mists in a dark canoe . . ."),[24] why in a moment of anguish caused by Sekoni's death, Egbo's instinct drives him to the bank of Ogun River, and why he goes back with Kola in search of the mystery of Lazarus' night ritual in the winding waters of Lagos lagoon.

Soyinka's camera technique is a key to the windings of the narrative movement in *The Interpreters*, especially the device of short cuts and no continuity. The oscillation between Ibadan and Lagos means that already there is a major fracturing of the setting. The story does not move entirely on the surface level but also in the submerged plane of the characters' minds, so that below the surface of fragmented experience there is a subconscious level of continuous relationship between past, present and future, and the detailed surface impression subserves that lower level. It is the level characteristically defined by Sekoni as "the dome of continuity", the dome of life, where we find religious ideas about gods and ancestral beliefs underlying the lives of men and women of modern culture and sensibility, whose present occupations and concerns anticipate a revolutionary future. That Soyinka's novel is conceived in terms of a historical and cultural continuity is no surprise, for he has already given proof of this interest in his plays, especially *A Dance of the Forests*. His choice of incidents and build-up of atmosphere is an attempt to do a similar thing in a novel. That explains his interest in creeks, rivers, lagoons, rocks, bridges and gods, which supply the archetypal and mythopoeic images in the exploration of the deeper levels of his characters' minds as well as the surface connections between past and present. The coexistence of these features with the man-made city and its artefacts indicates the unique physical basis of life in West African novels. The jungle is more than a submerged area of the modern consciousness; the creeks and swamps are also real in the surface sense, and part of daily life.

Soyinka derives his conception of life as a continuum from the African traditional world view, and more specifically from Yoruba metaphysics. He states the point explicitly in his article mentioned earlier:

> The past, the present and the future, being so pertinently con-
> ceived and woven into the Yoruba world view, the element of
> eternity which is the gods' prerogative does not have the same
> quality of remoteness or exclusiveness which it has in Christian or
> Buddhist culture. The belief of the Yoruba in the contempor-
> aneous existence within his daily experience of these aspects of
> time has been long recognized but again misinterpreted. It is no
> abstraction. The Yoruba is not, like the European man, concerned
> with the purely conceptual aspects of time – they are too concretely
> realized in his own life, religion, sensitivity to be mere tags for
> explaining the metaphysical order of his world. If we may put the
> same thing in fleshed-out cognitions, life, present life, contains
> within it manifestations of ancestor, the living and the unborn.
> All are vitally within the intimations and affectiveness of life, be-
> yond mere abstract comprehension.[25]

But this interest in life as a continuously flowing stream does not blind him to the pressures of contemporary reality. While he is prepared to set up this mystical scale of continuity for gauging the life and actions of his "new interpreters", he cannot help seeing the rest of the characters, especially those he criticizes, largely in terms of the contemporary setting. Side by side with the concern for a deeper apprehension of the eternal truths, there is the purely transient concern with a specific life which is convicted immediately and summarily for its materialism, lack of spiritual depth and spurious modernity. This second concern locates *The Interpreters* firmly among novels like *A Man of the People* and *The Beautyful Ones Are Not Yet Born*. The false gentility of an Oguazor can be implied in his artificial house decorations. Once the theme has been isolated, it takes only a few such touches to give it body. Social disparities are forcefully illustrated by paying a visit to a toilet belonging to the elite and a latrine among the common people.

The central theme of *The Beautyful Ones Are Not Yet Born* is social corruption; Armah approaches it through the tradition of parabolic narrative, and through well-chosen illustrative images. Like Soyinka, Armah employs a cinematographic technique, following his spotlight over well-chosen areas, dwelling on them long enough to build up impressions through which the moral state is expressed. He takes the reader on a guided tour illuminating the differences between the way in which

153

the common people live and that of the elite, the filth and squalor of the one and the grandeur, opulence and sanitary splendour of the different world inhabited by the other. The matter-of-fact way in which Armah builds his tenacious picture of filth and physical corruption recalls Swift; but success in this requires an eye that takes in minute details, a nose that smells fine distinctions and a nervous system that is sensitive to the smallest distinctions of texture. Only a man whose every sense is sharp could draw this picture of the invisible filth and accumulation on the floor of a communal bathroom in a working-class quarter of Accra where the Man lives:

> Under his feet the cement floor was covered with some sort of growth. It was not the usual slippery bathroom growth. In fact, it was not really visible at all, and yet to the soles it felt quite thick, almost comfortable if one forgot to think about it. The hole leading the water out was again partly blocked with everybody's sponge strands, so that the scum formed a kind of bar just before the hole and the water underneath went out very slowly, a little at a time, and there was a lot of it covering the floor when the shower had been running even a little while.[26]

Conton in *The African* also uses the setting to express particular themes in his novel. With its strong propagandist overtone, the novel sets out to deal with a number of issues which confront the African in the world today: how he sees himself and his own world as compared with the Western world and culture, his feelings about nationalism, pan-Africanism, apartheid. The hero-narrator describes, elaborates, opinionates, attitudinizes, raises points and rejects or defends them. For example, the opening pages describe in some detail the narrator's family background, including the patterns of agricultural labour, but it soon becomes clear that the intention is to refute the accusation that Africans are lazy. In most of the novel the setting is handled with his intention of vindicating the African personality and culture.

7
Language

The novelist's tool is words. His description of his characters' appearance, clothes, actions, habits and inner feelings and thoughts, his exposition of a particular moral or vision, the ordering of his incidents and events to convey that moral or vision are conveyed entirely by his manipulation of language. Reliance on the written word makes the novel very different from the prose literature produced in a traditional oral culture. In the folk-tale, the prose form par excellence of West African traditional society, language is often greatly reinforced by physical gestures, facial expressions, vocal inflexions and other arts of the performer.

The individuation of character implies that no two people in a novel speak exactly alike. This clearly distinguishes the novel's linguistic technique from that of the oral tradition which permits and in fact depends on the use of stock expressions and characteristic turns of phrase.

The introduction of the novel into a region in which an oral tradition is still integral to the functioning culture and exists side by side with a growing literate tradition means that the language of the novel may be modified by the language of the oral tradition. This has happened in West Africa in the rural novels. The writers attempt to recapture traditional speech by translating fairly literally from the vernacular to English (extending to the syntax in Okara's *The Voice*). They do this chiefly by rendering the proverbs and characteristic turns of phrase used in rural communities; this gives authenticity to the writing.

The use of proverbs in the novels needs special attention if only to answer the criticism of impercipient readers that the ubiquity of proverbs, especially in Achebe's novels, is an idiosyncrasy rather than a natural way of representing the linguistic reality of the world of the rural novels. Proverbs are a natural part of the speech of all traditional societies. Other prose writers dealing with characters whose consciousness is conditioned by an oral rather than a literary tradition have recorded this tendency to be sententious and steeped in proverbial lore. Kazantzakis' Zorba, Tolstoy's Platon Karataev, Cervantes' Sancho Panza and Mark Twain's vernacular characters all show this peculiarity. Tolstoy writes in *War and Peace* of the peasant Karataev: "[He] did not, and could not, understand the meaning of words apart from their context. Every word and every action of his was the manifestation of an activity unknown to him, which was his life. But his life, as he regarded it, had no meaning as a separate thing. It had a meaning only as part of a whole of which he was always conscious."[1] In other words, Karataev, like all non-literates, is immersed in a speech environment which articulates a collectively defined tradition of which a major characteristic is the existence of fixed expressions that constitute the linguistic core.

Proverbs are the kernels which contain the wisdom of the traditional people. They are philosophical and moral expositions shrunk to a few words, and they form a mnemonic device in societies in which everything worth knowing and relevant to day-to-day life has to be committed to memory. Of their nature, they perform an ideological function by making available the ideas and values encapsulated in these memorable and easily reproduced forms.

These proverbs derive from a detailed observation of the behaviour of human beings, animals, plants and natural phenomena, from folklore, beliefs, values, attitudes, perceptions, emotions and the entire system of thought and feeling which Durkheim called *"les représentations collectives"* of a society. They derive their effectiveness and force from the collective imagination which apprehends the underlying connection between a literal fact and its allusive amplification and which vivifies an experience by placing it beside another which bears the stamp of approval. The use of proverbs is one more way in which the individual expresses the primacy of society – even in this matter of language. The man who proverbializes is putting his individual speech in a traditional context, reinforcing his personal point of view by objectifying its validity, and indirectly paying tribute to himself as a possessor of traditional wisdom. So the use of proverbs, instead of individuating, both communalizes and traditionalizes a speaker. The effort of the traditional user of proverbial language is not to express his distinctiveness from the rest of the people but to indicate attachment to the community and its linguistic climate.

The proverbs are numerous enough and sufficiently broad in scope to cover adequately the kind of experience with which the novels deal in West Africa. There are proverbs for every occasion, proverbs to suit every situation and to light up every experience. Every significant affirmation can be strengthened with a proverb; every customary value, belief, attitude or outlook can be supported with proverbs; social problems and personal difficulties can be settled by an appeal to the sanctioning proverbs. Even contradictory views can be sustained by an appeal to different proverbs, and so, though in form the proverb constitutes a fossilized unit of linguistic expression, in actual communication there is much flexibility, since such different viewpoints can be maintained. This manipulability becomes an important functional asset to those novels which draw on proverbs for the development of their action and insight. As well as conveying linguistic reality, proverbs can become an artistic device for giving complexity to narrative, unity to form, coherence and pattern to action, and direction to moral and social insight. They can also indicate force and resourcefulness of character: the strong mind can manipulate the repertory of proverb to its own advantage.

Achebe more than any other African novelist has conveyed the importance of proverbs as a mode of expressing and exploring reality. In *Things Fall Apart* and *Arrow of God,* which are set entirely in the traditional village and, to a lesser extent, in *No Longer at Ease* and *A Man of the People*, in which people and events flow between town and country, his characters constantly speak in proverbs. In his grasp, proverbs yield easily to formal manipulation and convey insight into character and give pattern to narrative action.

One can even study the characters and themes of Achebe's rural novels through a number of key proverbial motifs. In *Things Fall Apart*, Okonkwo's character can be explained by analysis of power and personality motifs embodied in proverbs. As Okonkwo begins to rise after the disappointments and disaster of his early life, the prospects opening up for him are conveyed through a proverb: "If a child washed his hands he could eat with kings. Okonkwo had clearly washed his hands and so he ate with kings and elders."[2] When Okonkwo shows one of his weaknesses by grossly insulting a less successful kinsman, the people show their disapproval through another proverbial statement: "Those whose palm-kernels were cracked for them by a benevolent spirit should not forget to be humble."[3] Okonkwo's own prowess is admitted through the narrator's comment: "When a man says yes his *chi* says yes also. Okonkwo said yes very strongly; so his *chi* agreed."[4] But the hand of fate is seen even in personal success, and the fate that helps a man to rise can also thrust him to the ground. When this happens to Okonkwo later, the reversal is again proverbialized: "Clearly his personal god or *chi* was not made for great things. A man could not rise beyond the destiny of his *chi*. The saying of the elders was not true – that if a man said yea his *chi* also affirmed. Here was a man whose *chi* said nay despite his own affirmation."[5] It is not so much that the one saying of the elders is untrue as that in their manifold wisdom they have proverbs for all varieties of human aspirations, successes and failures.

157

These proverbs which complement and sometimes contradict one another form the ideological pivot round which the action of the novels revolves, or are the ideological matrix which holds the action together. "Proverbs" writes Achebe, "are the palm-oil with which words are eaten."[6] The moral lesson exemplified by the novels is contained in the clusters of proverbs which are the ethical indices of its action. In *A Man of the People* the cluster is formed by "eating" proverbs and in *Things Fall Apart* by the "chi" and "solidarity" proverbs. Achebe's flexibility in the use of proverbs can be illustrated in those incidents in which a number of proverb-clusters cohere to sustain a many-sided reality. The drama of conflict and change in *Arrow of God* is a good example. Here we have a cluster of proverbs which reflects the anxiety and fear of the local people confronted with threatening new experiences: "What a man does not know is greater than he,"[7] "an animal more powerful than *nté* was caught in *nté*'s trap"[8] (varied to "a thing greater than *nté* had been caught in *nté*'s trap"),[9] "a disease that has never been seen before cannot be cured with everyday herbs",[10] "a man who has nowhere else to put his hand for support puts it on his own knee",[11] "you must expect foreigners to talk through the nose",[12] "we are like the puppy in the proverb which attempted to answer two calls at once and broke its jaw".[13] The element of the unusual is conveyed in these proverbs; so is the element of danger. Another proverb-cluster indicates positive disapproval of change or compromise with the agents of change, as in "as soon as we shake hands with a leper he will want an embrace",[14] or "a man who brings ant-ridden faggots into his hut should expect the visit of lizards".[15] Then there are other proverbs in the cluster which reflect a pragmatic approach to change, to its inevitability and the need to come to terms with it, as in "a man must dance the dance prevalent in his time"[16] (repeated with variation as "a man must dance the dance prevailing in his time"),[17] "a man of sense does not go on hunting little bush rodents when his age mates are after big game",[18] "if the rat could not run fast enough it must make way for the tortoise"[19] (with the variant "if the rat cannot flee fast enough let him make way for the tortoise").[20]

Sometimes a proverb from one cluster may be repeated when it is strategic to the evolution of the action, as in some of the proverbs above. For instance, in the middle of the action, a character uses that last proverb to emphasize the need for people to adjust to change and make the best of its chance, but towards the end of the narrative, the same proverb is used to indicate that the dramatic breakdown in the traditional system has turned slow change into an avalanche. The proverb can be interpreted to reflect the new reality. The bursting of the dam of tradition releases a cataclysmic overflowing of the cultural bounds by the new forces of change. The old system is now something from which people are scampering away into the safety of the new order. Hence, the word in the second proverb has shifted from "run" to "flee".

For purely dramatic purposes, proverbs can become a defining-point of a novel's action and so serve the dual interest of aiding plot development and heightening emotional response to the action. A good example is the cluster of proverbs which issues from the Ogbazulobodo in the final ritual run that heralds the end to the action in *Arrow of God*:

> When a handshake passes the elbow it becomes another thing. The sleep that lasts from one market day to another has become death. The man who likes the meat of the funeral ram, why does he recover when sickness visits him? The mighty tree falls and the little birds scatter in the bush ... The little bird which hops off the ground and lands on an ant-hill may not know it but is still on the ground. ... A common snake which a man sees all alone may become a python in his eyes. ... The very Thing which kills Mother Rat is always there to make sure that its young ones never open their eyes. ... The boy who persists in asking what happened to his father before he has enough strength to avenge him is asking for his father's fate. ... The man who belittles the sickness which Monkey has suffered should ask to see the eyes which his nurse got from blowing the sick fire. ... When death wants to take a little dog it prevents it from smelling even excrement.[21]

The Ogbazulobodo is speaking these proverbs within the tradition of gnomic boasts proper to it as a fierce midnight spirit, and the effect of its language is to heighten the awe produced by the Ayaka in the population. The gnomic virtuosity is admired, as is the physical prowess of the run itself, but in the novel these elements are reinforced by using the run and the proverbs together to build up to the final tragedy. The tragic life of the Chief Priest, like the ritual run of the night-spirit, is about to end. The rounding-off of a drama in which gods, ancestors and men of huge stature have participated calls for a worthy coda, and this is fittingly supplied by the proverbial language of the Ogbazulobodo. The dominant images invoked in the proverbs are death and defeat; so a sense of finality and inevitability pervades them. Ezeulu's fate was sealed from the moment he squared up for battle against his people, but his defeat and destruction do not come home to him and to the reader until the death of his favourite son, who also runs the Ogbazulobodo. The proverbs are an ironic coda to the novel: they both prepare the way for the end and apply directly to the speaker. "When death wants to take a little dog it prevents it from smelling even excrement" is soon fulfilled, for, without knowing it, Obika is death's prize and fate's pawn. The effect of these numerous correspondences in language and structural development is to heighten the emotional impact of the tragic ending.

There are other traditional conventions of language used by West African writers. One of those most frequently represented is the fastidious art of conversation, raised into a ritual act of social communion. The elaborate attention given by speakers and audiences in the village setting to the formal conventions of address, to the minute courtesies and standard exchanges reflects the use of language not so much as a way of communicating meaning as a means of establishing a friendly rapport between speaker and listener, of reinforcing a sense of integration, community solidarity and sympathetic relatedness, the use of language referred to by Malinowski as "phatic communion".[22] This is highly developed in the village setting, for the ties of blood and community are very strong and social intercourse is largely face to face. The need for good and friendly relations is more strongly felt than in the urbanized, less personalized setting in which contact among people is selective and infrequent. A proper adherence to conversational conventions is a prudent way of oiling the wheels of intimate or social relationship.

A good deal of the ritual of "phatic communion" consists of the repetition of stock greetings followed by stock responses, the exchange of local gossip, accounts of happenings extraneous to this occasion, or even the expression of views which are either banal or so teasingly outrageous as to draw the listener into mock verbal combat. Western visitors to Africa always remark the disproportionately long spells spent on the exchange of greetings in homes, market and work places, or by the road, and infer the banality of "the native mind" which finds interest in the tiniest irrelevances of conversation. Those seeming irrelevances supply part of the emotional and social matrix that holds together more serious forms of relationship. To dispense with them in communication is often an indication of a breakdown in personal, social or inter-group relationship. This is well illustrated in *Arrow of God* when Ogbuefi Akukalia, the diplomatic emissary of Umuaro to Okperi, brusquely cuts off every conversational courtesy as he presents Umuaro's ultimatum to Okperi.[23] The establishment of a sympathetic setting for social relationship in the long run justifies the time and delicate handling devoted to conversation in small communities in which the working of institutions is based on the sharing of sympathy, goodwill and community of interests among the members of the participating group.

Ritualization of certain aspects of conversation is not peculiar to the traditional society but can also be seen in a modern, urban society in the stereotyped phrases of greeting and the use of small talk to break the ice of reserve as a prelude to more serious conversation. This is true; but the need to demonstrate social solidarity, or a sense of sympathy and union with others is much less pressing in the large, relatively impersonal, heterogeneous modern society than it is in the small, homogeneous, intimate traditional society; for relationship in the first is often well defined by contractual social practices, whereas relationship in the second draws elaborately from a general agreement which in turn is promoted by goodwill and sympathy.

Almost every situation in *Things Fall Apart* and *Arrow of God* is a practical illustration of the significance which Achebe allots to the proper conversational conventions. Elechi Amadi also gives a large place to this aspect of tradition in *The Concubine*. The most fine-grained examples of the traditional conversational art can be seen in chapter 11 of both *Arrow of God* and *The Concubine*. The openings of these two passages deserve to be quoted:

> The first time Ezeulu left his compound after the Pumpkin Festival was to visit his friend, Akuebue. He found him sitting on the floor of his *obi* preparing seed-yams. . . .
> The two men shook hands and Ezeulu took his rolled goatskin from under his arm, spread it on the floor and sat down. Akuebue asked him about his family and for a while continued to work on his yams.
> "They are well," replied Ezeulu. "And the people of your compound?"
> "They are quiet."
> "Those are very large and healthy seed-yams. Do they come from your own barn or from the market?"
> "Do you not know that my portion of the Anietiti land. . . ? Yes. They were harvested there."
> "It is a great land," said Ezeulu, nodding his head a few times. "Such a land makes lazy people look like master farmers."
> Akuebue smiled. "You want to draw me out, but you won't." He put down his knife and raised his voice to call his son, Obielue, who answered from the inner compound and soon came in, sweating.
> "Ezeulu!" he saluted.
> "My son."
> He turned to his father to take his message.
> "Tell your mother that Ezeulu is greeting her. If she has kolanut let her bring it." Obielue returned to the inner compound.

"Although I ate no kolanut the last time I went to the house of my friend." Akuebue said this as though he talked to himself.

This light bantering and joking goes on until the kolanut arrives, so ushering in the next stage, the usual mock contention around the breaking of the nut (kolanut is never broken without this ritual palaver). The young man takes the kolanut in a wooden bowl first to his father and then to his father's guest.

"Thank you," said Ezeulu. "Take it to your father to break."

"No," said Akuebue. "I ask you to break it."

"That cannot be. We do not by-pass a man and enter his compound."

"I know that," said Akuebue, "but you see that my hands are full and I am asking you to perform the office for me."

"A man cannot be too busy to break the first kolanut of the day in his own house. So put the yam down; it will not run away."

"But this is not the first kolanut of the day. I have broken several already."

"That may be so, but you did not break them in my presence. The time a man wakes up is his morning."

"All right," said Akuebue. "I shall break it if you say so."

"Indeed I say so. We do not apply an ear-pick to the eye."

Akuebue took the kolanut in his hand and said: "We shall both live," and broke it.[24]

Here is the opening passage from *The Concubine*:

Nnenda, Ihuoma's neighbour, entered Wigwe's compound feeling a little guilty. She had not been to see Adaku's wonder baby for so many markets. She had no excuse. She had passed the compound on her way to the market and to the dance arena.

"Nnenda, my daughter," Wigwe exclaimed, "I have not seen you for some time."

"Dede, the children have been sickly of late."

"Poor child. How is Owhoji, your husband?"

"He too has not stirred for three days now. He has a large painful boil on his thigh."

"Is it ripe with pus?"

"Not yet, dede."

"Relief will come as soon as the pus is expressed. I must go and see him, even though it is risky for me to do so."

"Why is that so, a boil is not contagious, is it?"

162

"It is not, but my body is peculiar. As soon as I see a case of boil, I develop one soon afterwards."

Adaku who had been bathing came out of the house still rubbing her arms with palm kernel oil.

"I see your eyes at last, Nnenda, my daughter."

"You must pardon me, Adaku. Please let me carry the baby. How fast he is growing. He will begin to walk any moment now."

"People say so, but really his growth does not appear remarkable to me." Adaku said, with pride and tenderness in her eyes.

"No mother ever notices her child's growth."

The child smiled and beat the air with his arms.

"He smiles like his father. Look at the dimple on the right cheek, so exact."

Wigwe smiled almost shyly. Then changing the subject:

"Her husband has a boil on the thigh," he said.

"Ewuuu!" Adaku exclaimed. "Then I should not blame you for not calling. Is it egbe-ohia?"

"Yes."

"That is terrible. He will be bed-ridden for a market or two. I wonder who shot him in the dream."[25]

And so this conversation flows on in its smooth, slow course, full of snippets of information with nothing really profound. Now and again, commiserating noises are added, fresh bonds of sympathy are tied and new feelings of group relatedness are forged. All of this bears out the comment which Achebe unobtrusively edges into *Things Fall Apart* that "among the Ibo the art of conversation is regarded very highly".[26] But the reproduction of the conversational realities of traditional life is, in the novels, aimed at the goal of plot-development. Reproducing conversation is not an end in itself. In a genre as fully developed as the novel, conversation-pieces need to forward the general, formal unity of the whole. So the first conversation contributes to the rounding-off of our view of the Chief Priest. We see him here in one of his rare relaxed moods. We find someone other than the harassed politician or the factious priest fighting for principles where personal pride is bound up with public and religious duty. The man revealed in this relaxed, bantering mood with his friend is an amiable, humane person with whom it is easy to identify. The tragic sense which the reader feels at the end of the novel arises partly from our perception of the humane, humorous side of the terrible man of the power struggle. The second passage, in addition to reinforcing the idyllic atmosphere of the novel, leads the plot forward by introducing a major complication in the narrative: leaving

Wigwe's compound, Nnenda is followed by Wigwe's son, Ekwueme, and is given his first love-message to Ihuoma. This ushers in the courtship that is to dominate the novel from this point to the end.

The points of highest conventionality in conversation are the initial stages of contact and the final phases marked by parting greetings and benedictions. In Igboland, for example, the formality of the opening stages of contact and conversation is ritualized in the presentation and sharing of the kolanut among guests and host, which anthropologists refer to as "kola" hospitality.[27] The expression of goodwill through conventionalized conversation is so important that it has had to be built into the ritual fabric of the culture. Every important social or religious group-enterprise is preceded by the presentation of the kolanut, accompanied by elaborate verbal exchanges. The propriety, order, status and stability which are cultivated in traditional society are well articulated during the mock contest to establish who is the right person to break the kolanut. In such contests, the art of refined conversation is at its height and is often diversified by witty sallies and light-hearted teasing, punctuated with murmurs of approbation or subdued catcalls.

The different forms of oral literature carry their own clear differentiation of language. The highly formalized language of court-poets and griots (praise-singers) differs from the lyrical flights of the common village satirist–commentator, as much as the latter's style differs from the studied rhetoric of the clan demagogue. So in the novel the verbal styles of village satirists and wags like Danda and Wodu Wakiri differ from that of Nwaka the demagogue and spell-binder. In a similar way, there is linguistic differentiation between different sections of the community. The language of clan elders is punctuated with proverbs, aphorisms and modes of expression which reflect traditional wisdom and familiarity with traditional lore. But women use these forms rarely and then mainly among themselves, and children hardly ever use them. In the passages quoted above, we notice that Ezeulu's talk is reinforced with proverbs, but in the second, in which a young woman is involved, there are no proverbs. Language is determined by the status of the speaker vis-à-vis the listener. It would be improper for a young man or a woman to speak to a male elder in proverbs, for speech types express the speaker's social status, and it is a mark of traditional discretion to express oneself in a manner befitting one's social position. We find Ezeulu in *Arrow of God* losing his temper with the young emissary of his rival, Ezidemili, when the latter affects the roundabout mode of speech appropriate to a more elderly person.[28]

So the use of proverbs and traditional lore gives the speech of male elders a dignified ponderousness which contrasts with the light, down-to-earth, rambling or bantering style of female speech and the jerky, elliptical syntax of children. A realistic reproduction of traditional speech therefore involves awareness of this linguistic differentiation. Achebe and Amadi especially, and sometimes Nzekwu and Nwankwo, show this awareness.

Ezeulu in *Arrow of God* is a full-fledged elder and as Chief Priest a pillar of the traditional system. We expect his speech to reflect this. Each of his appearances is a masterpiece of linguistic propriety. Let me take the example in which he calls together the elders to acquaint them with his sudden summons from the British Commissioner in Okperi. His short address illustrates most of the qualities of traditional linguistic decorum:

> The Chief Priest rose to his feet, adjusted his toga and gave the salutation which was at the same time a call to Umuaro to speak with one voice.
> "Umuaro kwenu!"
> "Hem!!"
> "Kwenu!"
> "Hem!!"
> "Kwezuenu!"
> "Hem!!"
> "I thank you all for leaving your different tasks at home to answer my call. Sometimes a man may call and no one answers him. Such a man is like one dreaming a bad dream. I thank you that you have not let me call in vain like one struggling in a bad dream." Somewhere near him someone was talking into his talk. He looked round and saw that it was Nwaka of Umunneora. Ezeulu stopped talking for a while, and then addressed the man.
> "Ogbuefi Nwaka, I salute you," he said.
> Nwaka cleared his throat and stopped whatever it was he had been saying to those near him. Ezeulu continued.
> "I was thanking you for what you have done. Our people say that if you thank a man for what he has done he will have strength to do more. But there is one great omission here for which I beg forgiveness. A man does not summon Umuaro and not set before them even a pot of palm wine. But I was taken by surprise and as you know the unexpected beats even a man of valour. . . ." Then he told them the story of the Court Messenger's visit to him. "My kinsmen," he said in conclusion, "that was what I woke up this morning and found. Ogbuefi Akuebue was there and saw it with me. I thought about it for a long time and decided that

165

Umuaro should join with me in seeing and hearing what I have seen and heard; for when a man sees a snake all by himself he may wonder whether it is an ordinary snake or the untouchable python. So I said to myself: 'Tomorrow I shall summon Umuaro and tell them.' Then one mind said to me: 'Do you know what may happen in the night or at dawn?' That is why, although I have no palm wine to place before you I still thought I should call you together. If we have life there will be time enough for palm wine. Unless the penis dies young it will surely eat bearded meat. When hunting day comes we shall hunt in the backyard of the grass-cutter. I salute you all."[29]

This passage illustrates a number of speech conventions. The information is not reported, but must have taken quite a part of the whole address. The rest of the time is given to creating the atmosphere, adhering to the courtesies and protocols of public address. The three sections of the address stand out clearly, the opening, the middle and the conclusion. The fact of the situation being of a formal nature calls for a formal manner of address, and part of this formality is the awareness of the conventional requirements of the different stages of a speech. The introduction calls people to attention, but it also has the nature of an appeal to their sense of social solidarity. The Chief Priest hails the assembly as a collectivity – "Umuaro kwenu!" means "People of Umuaro, respond to my greeting." But behind the call for attention is the appeal of one member to the whole group to hearken to his distressed cry with kinship and understanding ears. The call is from one whose destiny is integral with the group's. So the salutation is a call to Umuaro "to speak with one voice". This appeal to solidarity would normally smooth away opposition, except the most deeply rooted, like Nwaka's. Having called the assembly to attention, Ezeulu then moves on to the second stage, which is to cultivate its goodwill. First, he thanks the elders for hearkening to his call and proceeds to apologize for not presenting them with palm-wine as convention would have required him to do. Then having paved the way for a favourable reception he slides on to the core of the matter, which is to tell the people of the white man's order that he should come immediately to Okperi, the administrative headquarters. Then he rounds off with a further apology for summoning them at such short notice and without the full conventional arrangements. He ends with a salutation.

The style befits Ezeulu's social standing and ritual and religious role as Chief Priest. He speaks with dignity and in full possession of the values of the tradition. He understands all the conventional modes of address and observes the inner rhythms of speech expected of him, and as an elder he calls up the appropriate proverbs at each stage of his speech. He is quite aware that he is working within a rhetorical system, for he does not just round off his speech with one proverb but with two, a way of doubly reinforcing his apology and heightening the effect of his speech. His sense of decorum on such a formal occasion is also shown by the way he disposes of his enemy, Nwaka. In absolute breach of courtesy, Nwaka is still talking aside after Ezeulu has formally called for attention. Ezeulu pauses, to allow the assembly the opportunity to observe the breach also; then he addresses the barracker. He does not denounce or insult him. He "salutes" him, after calling him by his official title. It is not just an appeal for silence, it is also an appeal by one titled elder to another titled elder in the name of their status and the tradition from which they both draw their authority, to respect the established decorum of the society. It is no wonder that this silences Nwaka immediately.

In contrast to that dignified, decorous speech style, here is part of a conversation between two of his daughters and one of his wives at the end of the Feast of the Pumpkin Leaves:

> Akueke sought out her elder sister, Adeze, whom she had last seen running with the other women of Umuezeani. She did not search very far because Adeze stood out in any crowd. She was tall and bronze-skinned; if she had been a man she would have resembled her father even more than Obika.
>
> "I thought perhaps you had gone home," said Adeze. "I saw Matefi just now but she had not seen you at all."
>
> "How could she see me? I'm not big enough for her to see."
>
> "Are you two quarrelling again? I thought I saw it on her face. What have you done to her this time?"
>
> "My sister, leave Matefi and her trouble aside and let us talk about better things."
>
> At that point Ugoye joined them.
>
> "I have been looking for you two all over the market place," she said. She embraced Adeze whom she called Mother of my Husband.
>
> "How are the children?" asked Adeze. "Is it true you have been teaching them to eat python?"
>
> "You think it is something for making people laugh?" Ugoye sounded very hurt. "No wonder you are the only person in Umuaro who made no effort to come and ask what was happening."
>
> "Was anything happening? Nobody told me. Was it a fire or did someone die?"

167

"Do not mind Adeze, Ugoye," said her sister, "she is worse than her father."

"Did you expect what the leopard sired to be different from the leopard?"

No one replied.[30]

There is basic good feeling, and a good, easy relationship between the sisters and their father's wife; certainly the gentle teasing indicates this ease of relationship. There is also clear informality in their conversation, no dogged pursuit of subjects to their logical conclusions. In fact, the distinguishing feature of this conversation is its lack of structure. Subjects tumble in and out, are pounced upon and discarded with a few remarks. The important consideration is not the exchange of information but an exchange of goodwill, a sharing of fellow feeling and a sense of kinship. There are moments in which the friendly atmosphere comes dangerously near to being threatened, as for example when Adeze mentions a sore point – Ugoye's son's attempt to smother the sacred python – and when Ugoye, carried away by the sisters' teasing, joins in what could be an overt criticism of her husband. The sisters recognize the impropriety and are uneasy and silent. But the general mood is jovial, gentle, friendly and informal. The informality strongly contrasts with Ezeulu's formal address and less formal conversation with his friend Akuebue.

The lack of formalization is even more noticeable in the speech of children, as in this simple domestic scene in which Ezeulu's children are shown around a hearth telling folk-tales:

"Shall we go back to the beginning?" asked Nkechi.

"Yes," said Obiageli. "The big ukwa fruit has fallen on Nwaka Dimkpolo and killed him. I shall sing the story and you reply."

"But I was replying before," protested Nkechi, "it is now my turn to sing."

"You are going to spoil everything now. You know we did not complete the story before the crier came."

"Do not agree, Nkechi," said Nwafo. "She wants to cheat you because she is bigger than you are."

"Nobody has called your name in this, ant-hill nose."

"You are asking for a cry."

"Don't listen to him, Nkechi. After this it will be your turn to sing and I shall reply." Nkechi agreed and Obiageli began to sing again . . .

The singing is soon interrupted again.

"No, no, no," Nkechi broke in.

"What can happen to Earth, silly girl?" asked Nwafo.

"I said it on purpose to test Nkechi," said Obiageli.

"It is a lie, as old as you are you can't even tell a simple story."

"If it pains you, come and jump on my back, ant-hill nose."

"Mother, if Obiageli abuses me again I shall beat her."

"Touch her if you dare and I shall cure you of your madness this night."

Obiageli continued her song . . .[31]

The absence of structure is obvious. The subject of the conversation is there, of course: there is a story to be told and someone must tell it. The actual story is outlined, but who shall tell it causes a short, sharp conversational scuffle in which different attitudes are exposed, names called and threats made. There is no decorum in all this, no appeal to time-hallowed conventions or the values of the ancestors. Children are children.

These examples all come from one novel, but the same linguistic distinctions can be seen in other novels. For example, in *The Concubine* the cut-and-thrust of witty repartee between Ekwueme and his friend and age-mate, Wodu Wakiri, differs from the playful, gentle, confidential conversation of the village beauty Ihuoma, and her friend Nnenda, and this differs from the broader, less-well-controlled mutual teasing of the nubile Ahurole and Titi. The speech of each of them is in turn distinct from the dignified and measured utterances of the elderly characters like Wigwe, Wagbara, Nwenike and the medicine men Anyika and Agwo-turumbe.

Language habits are not inborn but a cultural fact learned by man in contact with other men. Speech styles and linguistic assumptions determine the verbal acquisitions and accomplishments of those born into a society. The art of conversation is, like all arts, something that has to be learned. Children are too far from the central operation of this art to be much influenced by it; young people are still sufficiently removed. Now and again, there may be a youth with exceptional verbal felicity, but he would be marked as a rising orator. Occasionally, a youth with such a gift may be given recognition and entrusted with missions requiring verbal skill. Such is the case of young Emenike in *The Concubine* of whom it is said, "He had won the old men's confidence and they always let him run errands that required intelligence and the extensive use of proverbs."[32] Women, because of the ritual inhibitions which keep them away from politics and religion, are somewhat outside the linguistic centre. Though there may be competent speakers among them, they never really have a public platform on which to perfect this art, except of course among their own sex. The result of status orientation in language is that male elders, in a largely patriarchal society, define the linguistic norms and conventions. And this is amply illustrated by the novelists.

Even though people are expected to speak in a particular way, some are better at it than others. They may be able to use proverbs more appropriately or forcefully than others. Proverbs are only a part of the entire body of expression: some speakers are bound to be more skilful in the manipulation of non-fixed expressions. This may mark them out as public spokesmen on important occasions. The traditional spokesman may be likened to a man writing within a literary convention, whose genius lifts his work above the plane of dull imitativeness. The use of fossilized expressions is important because beliefs and concepts of the universe and of life are collectively shared and transmitted by word of mouth. The free expressions characteristic of individual speech have no chance of survival or oral transmission, so in the final analysis fixed expressions form the main basis of the permanent linguistic tradition. These set expressions are the criterion of linguistic authenticity in novels set in the traditional rural communities.

The novelists do not try to reproduce more elaborate aspects of oral tradition such as tribal epics, panegyrical poetry or genealogical recitations; rather, they try to recapture everyday linguistic usage. This reveals one essential aspect of the traditional society, the absence of a dichotomy between the poetic and the prosaic, or of the literary and the vulgar. Ordinary speech uses metaphor, similes and other figures of speech which suggest an integrative world view. For example, the widespread use of sobriquets implies a comparison of human characteristics with those of animals and plants. When Achebe refers to Amalinze the wrestler as "the Cat", or to the clan as a lizard which if it loses its tail soon grows another, he is reproducing the traditional linguistic habit which concretizes meaning by a direct or implied comparison with a familiar object or phenomenon. When Nwankwo's Danda says that he fled to the land of the spirits on the wings of the eagle, he is conveying an ordinary experience in the language of folk-lore. Language is never simply a way of conveying direct and necessary meaning, for applying a single reference to a single object, but a means of expressing the underlying unity and association in nature which a speaker and his audience both apprehend between one set of realities and another.

When Lawrence or any other modern Western novelist uses language poetically, he is not reproducing a social linguistic reality but imposing a personal pattern of linguistic expression on life through his art. For the West African novelist writing about traditional society, the integration of prose and poetry is already there within the linguistic consciousness of the people, waiting to be exploited.

One West African novelist whose work has been misunderstood because many readers do not appreciate the linguistic impulse in his writing and his indebtedness to the oral tradition is Gabriel Okara. Some commentators on his short novel *The Voice* have tended to treat him as the wild man of the African novel, as Amos Tutuola was treated by less perceptive local critics. But if it is recognized how much of the linguistic reality of West Africa is conveyed in Okara's novel and how distorting it is to see his writing solely in the context of the Western novel, then we shall understand it better.

This passage describes Okolo's first arrest in his village. He is standing by his window watching the fading evening when a crowd of people led by the Chief's messengers arrive to arrest him:

> Okolo seeing the messengers, recognised them and questioned them. But the men, in spite of their grim faces, opened not their mouths. The remaining crowd hushed. The silence passed silence. The three messengers faced Okolo, opening not their mouths. A man from the back of the crowd pushed his way to the messengers. The four of them put their heads together while with their eyes they looked at Okolo. They put their heads together for awhile and walked towards Okolo, as if stalking an animal. And Okolo stood looking. They moved nearer. Okolo stood. They moved nearer and suddenly, pounced on Okolo. Okolo and the men fell to the ground. Hands clawed at him, a thousand hands, the hands of the world. Okolo twisted, struggled and kicked with all his shadow, with all his life and, to his astonishment, he saw himself standing free. He ran. Running feet followed. He ran. A million pursuing feet thundered after him. He ran past his house without knowing and ran into another. A woman giving suck to her baby screamed. Out Okolo sprang and ran. The running feet came nearer, the caring-nothing feet of the world. Okolo turned a corner and nearly ran into a boy and girl standing with hands holding each other. They did not look at him. He turned a corner. A dog barked at him. Okolo ran. He was now at the ending of the town. Only one hut was left and beyond it the mystery of the forest. Okolo ran and as he ran past, a voice held him. "Come in" it said, "Come in quickly." In Okolo went, instinctively and in the gloom, stood panting.[33]

And this is the description of Okolo's first night in Sologa of the Big One after he has been arrested and thrown into a dungeon:

Through the black black night Okolo walked, stumbled, walked. His inside was a room with chairs, cushions, papers scattered all over the floor by thieves. Okolo walked, stumbled, walked. His eyes shut and opened, shut and opened, expecting to see a light in each opening, but none he saw in the black black night.

At last the black black night like the back of a cooking pot entered his inside and grabbing his thoughts, threw them out into the blacker than black night. And Okolo walked, stumbled, walked with an inside empty of thoughts except the black black night.

When Okolo came to know himself, he was lying on a floor, on a cold cold floor lying. He opened his eyes to see but nothing he saw, nothing he saw. For the darkness was evil darkness and the outside night was black black night. Okolo lay still in the darkness enclosed by darkness, and he his thoughts picked in his inside. Then his picked thoughts his eyes opened but his vision only met a rock-like darkness. The picked thoughts then drew his legs but his legs did not come. They were as heavy as a canoe full of sand. His thoughts in his inside began to fly in his inside darkness like frightened birds hither, thither, homeless . . . Then the flying thoughts drew his hand but the hands did not belong to him, it seemed. So Okolo on the cold cold floor lay with his body as soft as an over-pounded foofoo. So Okolo lay with his eyes open wide in the rock-like darkness staring, staring.

Okolo for years and years lay on the cold cold floor at the rock-like darkness staring. Then suddenly he saw a light. He drew his feet with all his soul and his feet came. He drew his hands and his hands came. He stood up with his eyes on the light and walked towards the light. As he moved towards the light, the light also moved back. He moved faster and the light also moved faster back. Okolo ran and the light also ran. Okolo ran, the light ran. Okolo ran and hit a wall with his head. Okolo looked and the light was no more. He then stretched his hands forth and touched the wall. His fingers felt dents and holes. Okolo walked sideways like a crab with his fingers on the wall, feeling dents and holes, dents and holes in the rock-like darkness until his feet struck an object. As Okolo stopped and felt the object his body became cold. His heartbeat echoed in the rock-like darkness and his head expanded. Still, he felt along the object until his fingers went into two holes. As his fingers went into the holes he quickly withdrew them and ran. He ran and fell, ran and fell over other objects. He ran and knocked against the wall and fell. Still he ran, then suddenly stopped. He saw a light in front of him. He moved gently crouching forward like a hunter stalking game. Then when he nearly reached the light, he rushed forward.[34]

Those two passages illustrate the quality, range and variety of indebtedness of Okara's art to the oral tradition. What is most striking is the deliberate manner in which Okara works the different rhetorical devices into a sustained and singularly successful medium to convey the peculiar experience which we find in *The Voice*.

The most striking feature of Okara's art is the repetition of single words, phrases, sentences, images or symbols, a feature highly developed in traditional narrative, especially the folk-tale with its scope for dramatic pauses, facial contortions and gestures. Notice for example the effect suggested in the first passage by the repetition of "Okolo stood" and "They moved nearer." It is as if Okolo is fixed to the spot under a hypnotic spell while his sinister adversaries make their sharp, furtive moves, full of menace. The sense is carried in "as if stalking an animal". In the next lines the nightmarish quality of the episode is reinforced by vividly described physical activities. The assailants "pounce" on Okolo and a struggle ensues.

To Okolo, the hands of four men in that brief and silent struggle produce the sensation of "a thousand hands" – the reader feels this just as he feels the sensation of being pursued by a million "thundering" feet in the dark silent night.

The reiteration of short dramatic phrases like "Okolo ran", reinforced by clearly hyperbolic statements like "a million pursuing feet", gives the concrete physical sensation of wild and uncomprehending flight. Notice also Okara's way of rendering the single consciousness at bay in all its actions: "Okolo stood", "Okolo twisted", "Out Okolo sprang", "Okolo turned a corner", "Okolo ran".

This reiteration, giving concreteness of physical sensation in a single consciousness, is developed further in the second passage. The reiteration of "black" gives the darkness of the night an obsessive quality. The reiterated sense of darkness, implying obstruction, threat and fear, is particularly effective, especially as it is reinforced by Okara's invocation of the horrific in terms of human sensations – eyes trying to pierce an impenetrable darkness, hands and feet that refuse to move at one moment and then shoot out in a single automatic movement in the next, the groping of the fingers into dents and holes, the crab-like movement, the head knocking on the wall, the body becoming cold, the heart-beat echoing, the head expanding, the running and falling. All these physical actions assume a nightmarish quality because they take place in the dark.

Okara brings his poetic gifts to bear in his choice of images and

173

symbols. His metaphors, similes and other figures of speech give concreteness and body to the heavily oppressive atmosphere. In doing this, he draws on the vernacular tendency of language to concretize experience. By such devices even the most abstract notions are rendered as physical realities. Okara is in this sense a materialist, because he attempts to convey actions, feelings, and sensations through material or physical realities. This tendency could be called "reification", giving the quality of "thingness" to mental and abstract constructs. So Okara describes Okolo's confusion in the dark room by likening his mind to "a room with chairs, cushions, papers scattered all over the floor by thieves", Okolo's "thoughts in his inside began to fly in his inside darkness like frightened birds hither, thither, homeless". A related synecdoche gives concreteness to misery, hostility and squalor in the town of Sologa:

> So Okolo walked in Sologa of the Big One passing frustrated eyes, ground-looking eyes, harlots' eyes . . . despairing eyes, nothing-caring eyes, grabbing eyes, dust-filled eyes, aping eyes. . . .[35]

The process of reification in *The Voice* is increased by the rhythm of Okara's prose, the rhythm of words found under the immediate pressure of what is being done, felt or suffered. The power of the second passage comes from Okara's ability to capture the rhythm of action and of physical sensation through very simple words which acquire sensuous and sinister overtones – words like "dents", "holes", "the thing". When the hero's fingers enter "two holes" and he pulls them out in horror, we have a horrified suspicion that we are in a room where there are human skeletons; we share the horror and revulsion but we do not put it into words – we cannot bear to.

The main impulse in *The Voice* obviously derives from the oral tradition, especially the folk-tale. Okara's rhetoric, especially his deliberate repetitions, his metaphorical and hyperbolic elaborations and his colloquial rhythm, belong essentially to the oral tradition. The ghoulish and the nightmarish elements so well developed in *The Voice* are features of the folk-tale. Okara's interest in the Ijaw oral tradition goes further than any other novelist's interest in oral tradition, for Okara alone among these writers attempts to reproduce not only literal meanings from the vernacular (as in expressions like "Okolo had no chest", "he had no shadow", "all his inside", "with all his shadow"), but also actual syntactical forms, in sentences like: "Who are you people be?" "If you are coming-in people be, then come in." Even the process of reification is derived from the vernacular; it is a well-attested phenomenon of West African languages.

Language in the traditional setting also embodies the concept of the creativeness and force of the spoken word. In all magic the operation is never complete until the material dispositions have been accompanied by an appropriate verbal formula.[36] Language whose function in the conventional European novel would be "largely referential"[37] becomes in the traditional West African context largely allusive, symbolic, transformative. It creates a cosmos out of chaos through magical symbolism. Janheinz Jahn has noted this magical quality of the word in the poetry of Negritude. It has been called surrealism by European commentators but owes more to a sophisticated exploitation of the traditional belief in the omnipotence of the spoken word.[38] The spirit of surrealism is foreign to the traditional African experience. The surrealist image emerges out of the subconscious dreams of the private individual, but the traditional image derives from a collectively shared cultural experience. A similar point is made by the Latin American writer Alejo Carpentier in his novel *El Reino de Este Mundo* (*The Kingdom of This World*), a historical novel dealing with the overthrow of the tyrannical King Christophe of Haiti. In this story the leader of a revolt uses magical rituals to win over the populace against the tyrant. Carpentier, in the introduction to the novel, draws attention to the difference between the reality of magic in the folk-imagination of the Haitians and surrealism which reflects the fragmentation of the collective consciousness in Western society. The language of magic is often semi-specialized and reserved for important occasions and incidents in the life of the community, for it operates at a level in which social and psychological significance comes from the perceptions of the collective unconscious. One is dealing with "facts" and ways of knowing whose essence is not scientific but intuitive. The language of appropriate expression shifts from that of objective exposition to the language of emotive effect, structured in the gnomic tradition. It is language necessarily condensed to make its impact with the least waste of effort, by putting together words that conjure up a powerful association, an emotionally satisfying symbol or a gripping image. That is why language in magical or semi-magical situations, as in divination or religious ritual, is always exciting. To the uninitiated, it is mumbo-jumbo and verbal trickery, but to the initiated, the magical situation is an extension of the possibilities of language, accommodating the deeper levels of human experience. Indigenous African writers, recognizing the significance of this area of traditional experience, treat it extensively in their works. They do not necessarily share the magical view but they are able to recreate magical situations with assurance, especially in appropriate language.

Ezeulu's ritual language at the Festival of Pumpkin Leaves is a good illustration of the successful creation of the language of magic and

175

mythopoeic experience. The passage constitutes a journey into the traditional imagination, building out of its material an immensely convincing picture. The experience on which it is based is deeply significant for the people of Umuaro; the Chief Priest's recitation is an account of an event deeply embedded in the collective memory of the clan, the investment of the community's security in the tutelary deity. The event is pitched in a mythologically defined antiquity, at a time when lizards were "in ones and twos". The house lizard is one of the commonest creatures in every compound. The time when there were few of them must have been at the very beginning of things. The dangers and risks of the Chief Priest's office are elaborately dramatized in terms of the mythopoeic struggle with the four days of the week. The efficacy of sacrifice in smoothing the way and removing life's obstacles is stressed. The images and symbols evoked are deeply etched into the imagination: fire, water and earth, rain and sun, streams and rivers, forests, farmland – all intimately connected with agricultural life and rural survival. Familiar things such as the parts of the body are also drawn in, as also are domestic animals such as the white cock, hen's egg, horse and ram. Around these familiar things are woven everyday activities like washing the hands, carrying a sacrifice, singing with the flute, wrestling, cooking, running and dancing. Even the familiar mental habit of pairing experiences and objects is worked into the rhythm of the recitation. We have parallel constructions in "the sun carried its sacrifices I carried my *Alusi*", "A man sang with the flute on my right and another replied on my left", "on one side it was raining, on the other side it was dry", "the sun came down and beat me and the rain came down and drenched me", "I looked on his left . . . I looked to the right", "saw a horse and saw a ram", "streams and forests", "farmlands and wilds". This rhetorical device draws from the mental habit of dualization – of placing an object in proximity to another with which it is in contextual association – which is highly developed in traditional culture. The Chief Priest's journey is not a physical one but a movement into the collective imagination, made possible by the magical and mythopoeic potentiality of the language. At this level, there is no need for a suspension of disbelief; there is a natural descent, through common images, words and actions, into the deeper areas of the subconscious in which the consciously impossible becomes possible. The transformation is brought about by everyday words and images linked to incidents which belong to folklore and fable, such as the humanization of the days of the week, the rain falling on one side of the road while it is dry on the other, a smoking, moving thicket, men wrestling on their heads, an old woman dancing strange steps on the hills – each of these is a familiar motif in folk-tale. The appeal to wonder

176

in these references is very strong, and so are the awe-inspiring and fear-some associations. The gnomic structure of the recitation adds to the poetic effect. What Achebe has done is to build his language around traditional linguistic characteristics, and to fuse them, by applying the mental and verbal habits of traditional people, into a magico-mythopoeic medium. Ezeulu speaks his ritual piece in a language which all Umuaro will recognize and rouses emotions of strong religious fervour through verbal invocations which depend on their magical impact on participants at the ritual festival. And this makes the language realistic, in that realism is determined by what people apprehend as real and their mode of apprehending it.

The language of the urban novels reflects the atomistic nature of urban society. There is no unified linguistic outlook such as we find in the traditional society. And yet one can see signs of a beginning of linguistic stratification based on an incipient social stratification. These main linguistic categories are clearly discernible: the language of urban tribalism, the language of the formally educated middle classes, and the language of the poorly educated and the underprivileged working class and tradesmen.

Proverbs, proverbial sayings and sententious expressions and fixed expressions of all sorts still occur, reflecting the relatedness of life in the town to life in the village, the fact that urban-dwellers in West Africa carry with them residual traditional beliefs and attitudes, as well as linguistic peculiarities deriving from the oral tradition. Most of them never altogether abandon the tendency to speak in proverbs. That is why they easily become sententious or develop an irrepressible tendency to back up their personal views with quotations from illustrious writers and authoritative books like the Bible, as traditional speakers use proverbs to validate their views. This tendency is very noticeable in the writings of the Onitsha popular writers.[39] But the more sophisticated West African users of the English language also show this tendency to quote from authoritative texts.

There are significant differences between the use of proverbs in novels set in the traditional environment and those set in the urban environment. In the first place, the frequency of appearance of proverbs in the different urban novels indicates how much intimacy there is between town and village and how much individuals depend on the vernacular tradition for their linguistic effectiveness. Where there is close contact, as in *A Man of the People* in which politicians in the town depend for support on the villages and where the townspeople maintain a degree of ethnic cohesion, and in *No Longer at Ease*, the use of proverbs can be expected. On the other hand, where a novelist is concerned mainly with urbanized and detribalized characters, as in *The Interpreters* and *The Beautyful Ones Are Not Yet Born*, there are few proverbs, and those few are not structurally integrated into the plots but express a fragmentary traditionalism somewhat at odds with the general linguistic atmosphere. For example, it is difficult to envisage Soyinka's individualistic interpreters or Armah's egoists speaking in proverbs like the peasants of Umuofia or Umuaro or even the urban peasants of the Umuofia Progressive Union, Lagos Branch. Yet occasionally one of these individualistic urban characters develops an urge to speak in proverbs, which shows a sudden sloughing-off of the gloss of linguistic modernity to reveal the under-skin of linguistic traditionalism. A good example is Chief Winsala, the corrupt board-man out to extract a bribe from the applicant Sagoe at Hotel Excelsior. Having fed him the false hope that a bribe is forthcoming, Sagoe tiptoes off and abandons Winsala to the disrespectful treatment of a waiter who is called Greenbottle because of his green uniform. Winsala is thoroughly ridiculed and his self-respect is "rolled in manure". In his discomfiture, he utters a string of proverbs which express his self-pity:

> . . . it is no matter for rejoicing when a child sees his father naked, *l'ogolonto. Agba n't'ara.* The wise eunuch keeps from women; the hungry clerk dons coat over his narrow belt and who will say his belly is flat? But when *elegungun* is unmasked in the market, can he then ask *egbe* to snatch him into the safety of *igbale*? Won't they tell him the grove is meant only for keepers of mystery? *Agba n't'ara.* When the Bale borrows a horse-tail he sends a menial; so when the servant comes back empty-handed he can say, Did I send you? The adulterer who makes assignations in a room with one exit, is he not asking to feed his scrotum to the fishes of Ogun? Agba n't'ara . . .[40]

We are not told whether Chief Winsala is a real traditional chief or one of the opportunistic new men who want to be recognized in the modern as well as in the traditional sectors of national life by acquiring the key symbols of both worlds. An honorary chieftaincy is one way of having a foot in the traditional camp. These modern chiefs are no more traditional in background than non-chiefs in modern urban life. But proverbial language is available to most people, since urban-dwellers also have a background of traditional culture. Winsala's proverbs do not constitute a coherent verbal communication as they would in a traditional situation; they are still-born, like the string of proverbs poured out by the Ogbazulobodo in *Arrow of God*. They are a linguistic symptom, a means towards some self-knowledge, a recourse to traditional authenticity. Perhaps an expression like "self-knowledge" is too lofty for a character as flat as Chief Winsala, but it is significant that the rogue should mutter these proverbs to himself, as if he recognizes in them a way of telling himself some home truths: "To himself, for himself alone, a stream of belated saws came from his lips, muttered silently while his head shook in self-pity. . .".[41] It is in moments like this that the gloss on urban characters wears off to reveal an under-skin of traditionalism. Since urban characters have partaken at some time or other in the traditional life, at moments of stress they give tongue to their feeling in that language in which they are most intimately linked with their deepest cultural being and least connected with the urban environment. In the novels, this causes the phenomenon in which private feeling is expressed in the language of public response, within an environment whose dominant linguistic outlook is individualistic. The phenomenon spreads across all social and cultural experience, leading to such situations as those in which university graduates and professionals accept the magical interpretation of reality in moments of serious difficulty, when science seems to fail them.

Proverbs and fixed expressions are used in the urban novels for the purely pragmatic reason that many of the urban characters use them. But another use, different from traditional use, should be pointed out. There is an ambiguity in their uses, especially in situations which are dubious, confused or plainly misleading. The effect is not so much to enhance communication as to achieve some personal, individual advantage. The paradox is that individualism is promoted through a collectively defined medium. Commentators seeking to establish a moral pattern from the proverbs and wise saws coming out of the mouths of urban characters may be led astray. Whereas in the traditional setting proverbs can be reliably used as ethical and ideological indicators, in the urban situation they may be used opportunistically by a character to gain social advantage, to wheedle neighbours, to cover up evil-doing, validate felonies or justify perversities. In *The Interpreters,* for example, Chief Winsala uses proverbs to intimidate Sagoe into paying him a bribe for the newspaper job he has applied for: "My boy, it never does to try your elders," he warns. "When a cub yields right of way to an antelope, first look and see if Father Leopard himself is not a few trees behind."[42] The result is the abuse of proverbial language, or its bastardization. Cases abound in the urban novels, and are used by the novelists to show the fall in moral standards within the urban setting.

Bastardization of proverbs, or reducing them to near-parody, is well illustrated in the scene in *The Beautyful Ones Are Not Yet Born* in which

179

the fallen Partyman, Koomson, is bribing the boatman who had worked for him in his days of glory to ferry him away from danger:

> His voice [Koomson's] was subdued, and his tone was much softer than that of a straight bargainer, though it had not sunk all the way to pleading.
>
> "You know what has happened," Koomson said.
>
> "Yes." The boatman's eyes were growing harder, and he smiled a little. Koomson tried to look straight into his face.
>
> "You used to repeat a certain proverb," said Koomson. "When the bull grazes, the egret also eats. Do you remember?"
>
> The boatman replied with a surly "Yes," as if to indicate that time and change ought to modify the truth of all such proverbs.[43]

The misapplication of this proverb is deliberate. In a traditional context it means the need for equitable disposal of social resources, so that no one is altogether without the means for his own survival. The principle is fundamental to the social organization of labour and underlines the feeling of responsibility which society and individuals share reciprocally for each other. As originally conceived, the proverb has nothing to do with giving and taking bribes, or with hoarding ill-gotten gains acquired by plundering society. In this context, the abuse is multiple. The proverb is inappropriately put in Koomson's mouth, since even though he has fallen from grace and is a fugitive he still retains the economic initiative. He is still the owner of a boat which he uses as bargaining counter to get away from danger. His use of the proverb is opportunistic and merely a means of eliciting the desired response in the corrupt-minded boatman. The intrinsicality of meaning does not matter here; Koomson just wants to touch a well-known stimulus and get the response which is bound to follow. The boatman does not really have to wait for "time and change" to modify the truth of proverbs; they have already been modified by wholesale bastardization in modern urban contexts.

The authors of West African novels are often aware of contextual abuse of the language of fixed forms, even though they sometimes behave as if they are not. The bastardization is often implicit in the effort by modern speakers to plunder the ancient tree of proverbial wisdom, but the attempt to give new social and ethical content to proverbs evolved in different situations leads inevitably to distortion of the experience and bastardization of the language. In one particular circumstance, the writers are explicitly aware of this. Many of the proverbs which they put in the mouths of their townspeople are watered down. Proverbs are supposed to be terse; they depend on verbal economy for their effect, since they were originally meant to be easily memorizable. This quality is often lost in urban novels. There is a certain porousness, an urge to explain and elaborate in a way inadmissible in traditional contexts. For example, when Odili asks Mrs Nanga if she is going to America with her husband she answers: "My brother, when those standing have not got their share you are talking about those kneeling. Have you ever heard of a woman going to America when she doesn't know ABC?"[44] The flatulent nature of the proverb comes out when we compare it with Unoka's answer to the creditor who comes to ask for the repayment of his two hundred cowrie shells. "Look at those lines of chalk. . . . Each group there represents a debt to someone, and each stroke is one hundred cowries. You see, I owe that man a thousand cowries. But he has not come to wake me up in the morning for it. I shall pay you, but not today. Our elders say that the sun will shine on those who stand before it shines on those who kneel under them. I shall pay my big debts first."[45] The flabbiness of Mrs Nanga's use contrasts with the firmness and appropriateness of Unoka's use. Mrs Eleanor John's attempt at proverbializing is even more disastrous than Mrs Nanga's, as in this quotation: "My people get one proverb: they say that when poor man done see with him own eye how to make big man e go beg make e carry him poverty de go je-je."[46] This reaches the very limits of vulgarization of traditional speech. What Ayi Kwei Armah calls "the ancient dignity of formal speech" has been lost in this trivializing context.

Even village characters in the modern novels seem to have lost the verbal mastery so well demonstrated in *Things Fall Apart* and *Arrow of God*. For example, when Mr Samalu, Odili's father, says "A mad man may sometimes speak a true word, . . . but you watch him, he will soon add something to it that will tell you his mind is still spoilt,"[47] we know that there *is* something in this way of speaking which lacks the assurance and precision of the speech of elders in the novels set in the traditional villages. There is a fumbling after fullness of communication and a tacit assumption that the audience will not be well informed, so that every scrap of information must be thrown in. This fumbling after detail is neither indulged in nor required in the traditional village, where homogeneity of cultural experience makes even ellipsis accessible to the users of a language. The use of a diffuse speech indicates the degree of breakdown in linguistic homogeneity, just as this breakdown is symptomatic of the general fragmentation of cultural life. West African writers who write about the modern scene use proverbs and fixed speech-forms to depict the persistence of traditionalism in society and language. But they are also careful to record the fragmentary nature of such linguistic experience. Indeed they use these peculiarities of language to underscore the fragility of experience in the modern setting, the confusion of values and the collapse of the homogeneous world of the traditional society.

As for the educated middle class, the members of this class like Obiajulu Okonkwo, Wilson Iyari, Kisimi Kamara, Peter Obiesie, Soyinka's interpreters and those they interpret, and Armah's observers speak Queen's English like the authors, with whom they share a middle-class educational background.

The use of standard English in West Africa is as old as the establishment of formal, Western-oriented schools, since formal education was connected with the need to establish English as a medium of administration, business and commerce, mass-communication and literature. The outcome was the emergence of a linguistically competent non-native user of English who approximates the native user of the language. From the beginning, there was an intensive effort to teach English grammar and literature as effectively as possible to the non-English learner. There was emphasis on correctness, and an attempt to train students in rhetoric and ordered composition where precision went hand in hand with elegance. Skill was developed in the selection of the most fitting and elegant word and in handling word-order and clauses. For a long time this perfectionist approach to English language and literature persisted in West African schools and colleges. English-language studies became the domain of fastidious grammarians and gerund-grinders, a regular haunt of the linguistic purists. The result was rewarding. The products of this thorough linguistic training (backed up by the discipline of training in the classics) attained a level of proficiency beyond the dreams of later West Africans. But above all, the early education established a common linguistic tradition which West Africans shared from then onwards with the rest of the English-speaking world. There are good reasons why the standard of correctness and the common linguistic tradition in the English-speaking world have persisted in West Africa, even in these days when the overall falling off in linguistic efficiency is becoming a global phenomenon. First, the West African educational system was patterned on British education, and English grammar and literature textbooks recommended for English schools were, until recently, also recommended for West African schools. Secondly, many teachers of English were themselves English or were West Africans trained by Englishmen. Thirdly, West African students used until recently to take United Kingdom examinations and had therefore to pass strict language requirements. Fourthly, modern institutions and professions have been patterned on the British ones, so that the language of their operation has been patterned on that used in Britain. Until recently, also, most West African professionals obtained their training in Britain.

Changes in linguistic taste and usage in West Africa often followed much later than such changes in the metropolis. There are elements of eighteenth-century usage and style persisting far into late-nineteenth- and even early-twentieth-century West Africa; elements of Victorian literary taste only wore off in the 1940s and 50s under the impact of American-trained graduates and the influence of the universities of Ibadan and Legon. Especially among the older coastal intelligentsia, it is still possible to encounter residual Victorianism in language, attitudes and values. From the 1930s a marked change took place in the quality of formal language in West Africa. The ornate, elaborately woven prose style of the Victorians of the coast began to make room for a less formal, more mobile prose to which the present generation of West Africans is heir. The creative prose works being dealt with here are a product of this period of greater stylistic informality and spontaneity.

This is important for an understanding of the language in urban West African novels. In broad outline the linguistic expectations in these novels are those of the Western novel. Here language is used to express individual rather than collective experience, within a largely empirico-rationalistic social setting, and therefore could be said to individuate rather than communalize characters. Many of the characters are university graduates educated both in West Africa and Great Britain (occasionally in the United States of America also), the pattern being that the character goes through elementary school and grammar school in West Africa, and then has an overseas undergraduate training. Some of them have been educated exclusively in West Africa, but they have been educated in English for long enough to acquire a competent knowledge of standard English. But these characters are also, for the same reason, highly differentiated linguistically. Each of them, while conforming to the basic grammatical and syntactical necessities of standard English, uses language to express individual peculiarities. All the urban novelists dwell on this peculiarity, the power of every character to stand aside in his own right as an individual to reveal himself through the words he selects and the inner organization he gives to them. *The Interpreters* is the best example of this linguistic individuation. Most of its characters are drawn from the same social class but each speaks differently from the others. One can of course, in a general sense, distinguish the language of the interpreters from that of the interpreted. The former are communicative, witty and able to pour out words from exuberant, actively responsive heads and hearts, whereas their opponents appear to be people of few but calculated words. Within each group personal differences are clearly marked. We cannot mistake the verbal stance of one character for another. For example, only Dehinwa with her deep but unsentimental affection for Sagoe could say to him: "I can just see you in your old age. An impossible old grouch." None of the other female characters in the novel could have said it with any conviction, not the English girl with her dangerously tottering marriage, not Simi, the Queen Bee, whose voluptuousness seems to fill her being and to exclude such finely discriminating feeling of personal affection and the wit of the educated woman. The harsh sentence "Metal on concrete jars my drink lobes," which opens the novel, can only belong to Sagoe, who has evolved a gritty, half-poetical, half-facetious manner of speech that half-conceals the inner tensions that set him at odds with the corrupt and complacent members of the establishment. Again, Professor J. D. Oguazor is so distinctive that when we hear 'Cem en der, . . . we mesn't keep the ladies wetting" we have no doubt who is speaking. The same peculiarity is observable in the other novels. Dr Abadi, the stooge of the dictator in *The Voice*, speaks the language of political opportunism when he says: "But I, my very humble self, knew where my services were most required and returned to Amatu to fight under the august leadership of our most honourable leader." "August leadership of our most honourable leader" is an expression Okolo would never have used because the flattery is too palpable and it embodies a certain negation of moral concern which is totally alien to his nature. This strict verbal identification of the middle-class characters is possible because their habit of expression is in character and reflects a distinctive personality. Verbal peculiarities are a matter of self-revelation. There is no better way of knowing people than by their words. This distinctiveness of language – the personalization of expression and the saturation of words with the inner distinguishing characteristic of personality – is one of the essential marks of modernity in language. Whereas in the traditional setting there is a natural resort to ready-to-hand formulae of verbal usage, the tendency is pushed out altogether or to the peripheries of the linguistic environment in the modern situation. Every man has become his own maker of a structure of verbal principle adequate to his own interests. He can choose his words from an array which is lexically public property and can give them a peculiarity of organization along a personally determined principle.

The consequences of linguistic individuation are immense. Because of their liberation from the group-determined linguistic formulae, individuals speak with greater spontaneity and respond with greater alacrity to verbal stimuli. The result is immediacy and spontaneity of verbal flow among these modern, urbanized characters. *The Beautyful Ones*

Are Not Yet Born provides convenient examples. The Man and the Naked Man recognize an affinity of interests as outsiders and seek each other out in moments of crisis and distress as a means of escaping the tyranny of the collectivity. This passage deals with one of these situations. After one of his never-ending scenes with his wife, the Man tries to find solace in the company of his friend, who is lying naked on the bed reading a book.

"What is that?" asks the man on the desk, indicating the book.

"I saw it yesterday. It was the title that interested me. *He Who Must Die.* Greek writer."

"Is it good?"

"Very. There are so many good things we don't get a chance to see. They have to get translated first. And even then . . ."

The man on the desk said nothing for a while, then, "People can see you like this from your window."

"If they care to stop and look. It doesn't worry me." The man on the desk chuckled feebly.

"So." The man on the bed spoke again. Not a question, not a statement.

"I wanted to come and see you," the man said.

The listener shook his head reprovingly: "Running from family peace again."

"It's serious, this time."

"It's serious, every time."

"You can laugh," the man said.

"You really think so?" asked the naked man. "You really think I can afford to laugh?" He was smiling.

"Well," the man said, "you have not made the most serious mistake."

The naked man laughed out loud. "You wouldn't want my life, I tell you."

"Teacher, you reduce everything to a joke."

"I am sorry. That is not my intention." There was a note of real unhappiness in the voice now.[48]

The important thing about this dialogue is that it is between people who are using themselves as their sole frame of linguistic reference. Each word has an immediacy of relevance which does not go beyond the matter under discussion. A single word has a single referent, a single expression, a single layer of meaning. First, there is the book, a foreign book, a foreign book in translation. The visitor is curious about it, asks questions and receives answers centred on the book. The speaker's mind

185

wanders away to his own thought on the inaccessibility of foreign books not in translation, but it is all part of the same stream of immediate experience. Then the conversation drifts back to the present, why the Man is paying this visit. Then the two people begin to unburden themselves of their inner unhappiness. The essential thing is that each word used, each expression formulated, has a direct reference to the two people, their states of mind and the circumstances immediately present to them.

If we compare the passage with one taken from *Arrow of God*, we see how the group style of language affects the nature of dialogue. Here, Ezeulu has just been released from detention and wants to set out for home but John Nwodika, his clansman in the service of the administration, decides to travel with him because it would be dangerous for him to undertake the journey alone. The two men are discussing the matter.

> "It is not a journey which a man of your station can take alone," he said. "If you are bent on returning today I must come with you. Otherwise stay till tomorrow when Obika is due to visit."
>
> "I cannot stay another day," said Ezeulu. "I am the tortoise who was trapped in a pit of excrement for two whole markets; but when helpers came to haul him out on the eighth day he cried: Quick, quick: I cannot stand the stench."
>
> So they set out.[49]

Brief as this passage is, it makes the point. Here there is much matter of direct and immediate personal reference. The situation itself – Ezeulu's desire to set out late in the day for his home and Nwodika's intention either to dissuade him or himself accompany the Chief Priest. But there is also another level of linguistic reference. "I am the tortoise . . . the stench," spoken by Ezeulu to reinforce his desire to travel immediately, does not follow in the direct line of verbal communication with Nwodika, but casts back into the storehouse of the community's traditional wisdom for an apt reinforcement, which itself arises from Ezeulu's desire to put his personal view into a wider, verbal context of the group. The mind is thus called upon to move from the immediacy of the matter at issue into the broader field of corporate sensibilities, analogies and applications. The use of language transcends the purely referential to accommodate the largely allusive and figurative. There are three layers of meaning here. First, we have the literal, surface meaning of a man in too much of a hurry to be getting home after a long period of incarceration. Then there is the surface story of the tortoise's peevish haste to get away from a stink in which he has lain for too long. Then there is the third layer of meaning linking the first two and operating on the basis of analogies, in which the Chief Priest likens himself to the tortoise. The

Chief Priest is a tortoise only in the limited sense of his being in great haste when salvation is in sight, after having already spent a long time in confinement. The proverb is thus used self-deprecatingly, which adds a fourth dimension of significance to the Chief Priest's language. He is, as it were, anticipating Nwodika's criticism without actually answering it. He recognizes that he is becoming absurd, like the tortoise in the story, by wanting to travel at once, but he is determined to go through with it in spite of the seeming absurdity. This many-layeredness of meaning and significance gives an effect of concentration to the language and, because of this concentration, slows its movement. There cannot be an easy flow of dialogue in circumstances where the language used is interlaced with multiply derived and externally defined layers of meaning, as when language is used referentially, with single words and expressions having only the meaning conferred on them by their immediate context. That confirms the impression of slow-motion in action, thought and language in the rural novels, as against the speedy movement of the urban ones.

Another factor needs to be mentioned. In the rural novel one is constantly confronted with directly translated verbal situations in which vernacular characters have their words taken out of their original linguistic setting and rendered in the new context of the English language in which the novel is written. A translation by its very nature retards the pace of verbal flow. The transfer of meaning (and sometimes verbal peculiarities) from one language into another involves a slowing-down process, so that a speaker and the audience, and through them the reader, may absorb the full import of the meaning which is being transferred. Transition from one linguistic sensibility into another calls for the expenditure of perceptive effort which in turn takes time to achieve. The result is that all such transitions involve a delayed action of the mind, a slowing-down of verbal perception to allow the time to assimilate the old matter into the new perceptive form. Thus, an English-attuned ear hearing the dialogue in the passage above is bound to pause, hit by a sudden roadblock, the moment the eye encounters Ezeulu's illustrative proverb. Some time is needed before the co-ordination of eye and ear is achieved in the mind, and before the mind is attuned to this new method of verbalizing experience. In the urban novels, with middle-class characters who think in English and express themselves in that language, there is no need for this slowing-down. The verbal movement is one straight line, only occasionally distorted by the imposed pattern of linguistic variation caused by the writer himself in deference to some necessity of his art or the pressures of events and character differentiation.

There is another English-language variant spoken by vast numbers of urban people in West Africa, especially those with little formal education. This is pidgin English.[50] Its evolution is historically as interesting as standard English. It dates back before the local introduction of standard English, to at least four centuries ago, when the need for communication between West Africans and Europeans stimulated its rise. One of the earliest records of this form of English is the diary kept by Antera Dake, a leading Calabar trader, at the end of the eighteenth century.[51]

This form of English developed *in situ* as a utility language without any conscious formalization through education, and this explains the peculiarities of its grammar, syntax and vocabulary. It readily absorbs elements from the local languages as well as from English and other European languages. Its informality is of course relative to the greater formality of standard English, because it has over the years attained a fair degree of stabilization in grammar and syntax. Its dynamism and lack of formal propagation have led to the existence of dialectal variations, with the highest level of development in Sierra Leone and the Cameroons where Krio and the Cameroon pidgin have become more or less the lingua franca of the coastal inhabitants.

In most of West Africa pidgin is primarily the language of semi-literate people who could fairly be designated as "pidgin" personalities. They represent the transitional masses who have partially escaped the socializing influence of traditional society without having undergone full modernization. Among these are the hordes of urban drifters and lumpenproletariat who, having inadequate educational training and skills, find it hard to fit into the economic and social structure. Then there are others, the manual workers of all sorts, the domestic servants, and the artisans, as well as the millions of petty traders and tradesmen who minister to the needs of the towns. These urban masses represent at least 70 to 80 per cent of the urban dwellers in West Africa, and because they are already detached from the traditional language anchorage (many of them at any rate), they tend to communicate with one another in pidgin, a language which participates of the composite nature of the urban setting itself.

The significance of pidgin has been recognized in the creative literature of West Africa, in drama, poetry and fiction by virtually all the important writers. Even non-West African writers recognize its significance, though their attempt to reproduce it is often extremely awkward and comically inadequate. At any rate, in a gesture to this linguistic reality, Conrad manages to get as far as "Mr Kurtz he dead" while Joyce Cary carves out a babu-type English for Mr Johnson. In urban novels by indigenous writers, on the other hand, pidgin is given a significance in dialogue only next in importance to standard English. Pidgin characters are given supporting roles in the action of the urban novels, and certainly in one of them, Ekwensi's *Jagua Nana*, a pidgin character attains the ultimate stature of heroine. The best-developed use of pidgin in literature is to be found in popular writing like the pamphlets of Onitsha Market, many of whose major characters are drawn from the pidgin section of the urban population. The popularity of pidgin is in large measure a result of its spontaneous evolution, and especially the fact that it absorbs numerous peculiarities of the vernacular languages of West Africa. For example, its word-order from fairly early in its history was that of many local coastal languages, which meant that urban migrants from the countryside could slide easily into pidgin speech-habits. Then the fact that large numbers of vernacular words are absorbed into its vocabulary and that mispronounced standard English words soon become orthodox pidgin make it easy for those without formal training in English to adopt pidgin. Then the use of pidgin becomes a functional necessity among people drawn from different linguistic areas and thrown, higgledy-piggledy, into the urban melting pots. Pidgin becomes for these people the language of contact and communication. The vast, sprawling urban slums and working-class quarters become the linguistic spawning ground of pidgin. Characters from these quarters speak pidgin much of their lives. The two characteristics which mark them out are a low level of formal education and low economic and social status.

But use of pidgin is not entirely restricted to pidgin characters. Pidgin is sometimes used by well-educated West Africans, especially when they speak to pidgin characters, and when they talk to one another in certain contexts. Educated middle-class people also speak pidgin because of certain factors peculiar to West African social change and modernization. These include the lack of rigidity in class structure in West Africa and the inchoate nature of the classes themselves. While it would be false to argue that there are no social classes in Africa, it would be equally false to impose a rigid demarcation between the classes. There is contact between the classes to a degree unknown in the more industrially and technologically developed Europe and America. In the matter of pidgin, the blurring of the line is quite marked. The answer could also be sought in the novelty of the middle class in West Africa. Apart from some coastal families whose members have had three or more generations of university and grammar school education, the largest proportion of the present-day educated middle class in West Africa is of the first generation. Most have risen from peasant or working-class family backgrounds. This means that these people, at some stage or other in their early upbringing, have been exposed to life in a pidgin environment or been in very close contact with pidgin characters.

189

There are many other factors making for linguistic proletarianization in West Africa. For example, until recently Africans of all social positions were herded together in native quarters, away from the European quarters, so that, whether they desired it or not, they shared an identical linguistic orientation; and since pidgin is the language of the majority, the minority that was exposed to formal training in English did not escape the effect of pidgin. Middle-class families engage the services of pidgin speakers as house-servants, maids, baby-minders, gardeners, drivers, cooks and stewards, and a fair number of them in a household would make their presence felt by influencing the linguistic development of the highly imitative young children of the family. Even European officials and their wives and children made up their small store of pidgin vocabulary from their large contingent of domestic servants. Some of them, like Winterbottom in *Arrow of God*, like to patter pidgin with their African domestics.

Owing to status differentiation through language, pidgin has come to be identified mainly with low-income characters and standard English with the higher-income people. In bureaucratic and domestic settings, low-income characters demonstrate their status of inferiority by speaking pidgin, while the middle-class characters generally emphasize their superior social position by speaking in standard English. Examples abound in the novels of this linguistic differentiation on the basis of status, as between Sagoe the journalist and his office messenger Matthias (*The Interpreters*) and between Obi Okonkwo and his servant Zaccheus (*No Longer at Ease*). The educated middle class do also speak pidgin, especially in lighter, conversational situations and among their social equals with whom they are in intimate relationship; examples are Obi Okonkwo and Clara and those exquisite buffoons of the Nigerian political circus, Chief Nanga and Chief Koko (*A Man of the People*).

This quality of eclecticism gives the language of the urban novels colour and variety. It should be noted however that the use of pidgin and proverbial language in the urban novels is more highly developed in the novels set in Nigeria, like *No Longer at Ease*, *A Man of the People*, *The Interpreters*, *Jagua Nana*, and *People of the City*, than in *The Beautyful Ones Are Not Yet Born* and *The African*, set in Ghana and Sierra Leone. It is hard to explain this, except that Western influences have gone farther and lasted longer among the West Coast Ghanaians and Sierra Leoneans than among Nigerians. The middle class in Ghana and Sierra Leone is certainly older and much more entrenched than in Nigeria. It is the most thoroughly Westernized, retaining Victorian traits of language, including the love of linguistic elegance. For these Black Victorians and their descendants pidgin is downright vulgar and not to be easily admitted into serious writing, though a few "wild men" use Krio in satirical and generally comic writing. Not being integrated into the tribal culture either, these coastal elite have on the whole not preserved traditional language habits such as an attachment to the proverbial lore. They are much more likely, like William Conton's hero in *The African*, to quote from the English classics than from traditional proverbs.

The lives of the authors offer added insight. Ayi Kwei Armah and William Conton, whose novels show marked linguistic departures from the other novels, share a background. Armah's childhood in Takoradi, a centre of surviving Victorianism in Ghana, and his education in Achimota school and Harvard University go some way to explain a marked lack of contact with pidgin and traditional language. Even his subsequent professional roles as English teacher and magazine translator–editor in *Jeune Afrique* could not much have advanced contact with the village culture or that of the urban working class and pidgin characters. It is no surprise that he avoids the use of gnomic language and portrays characters generally associated with a pidgin culture speaking standard English. Here for example is a dialogue between a messenger and the chief character in *The Beautyful Ones Are Not Yet Born*. The messenger has just won money in a Ghanaian lottery but is worried that corruption might rob him of his prize:

> ". . . everybody says the Ghana lottery is more Ghanaian than Ghana."
>
> "You're afraid you won't get your money?"
>
> "I know people who won more than five hundred cedis last year. They still haven't got their money."
>
> "Have they been to the police?"
>
> "For what?"
>
> "To help them get their money."
>
> "You're joking," said the messenger with some bitterness. "It costs you more money if you go to the police, that's all."
>
> "What will you do?" the man asked.
>
> "I hope some official at the lottery place will take some of my hundred cedis as a bribe and allow me to have the rest." The messenger's smile was dead.[52]

This could easily be a dialogue between two people of equivalent educational status, like that between the Man and the Naked Man. Since there is no indication that Armah is translating the messenger's words from the vernacular into English, it must be taken that he is recording them originally in English. It is of course possible that messengers in Ghana speak in flawless standard English, but what about the women who sell foodstuff and cry their wares by the waysides of Accra – do they also have a good education? Here is an encounter between one of these and Koomson, the suited man, in which it is hard to see any difference between the quality of their standard English:

> The suit stops in front of the seller, and the voice that comes out of it is playful, patronizing.
> "Mammy, I can't eat all of that."
> "So buy for your wife," the seller sings back.
> "She has enough."
> "Your girl friends. Young, beautiful girls, no?"
> "I have no girl friends."
> "Ho, my white man, don't make me laugh. Have you ever seen a big man without girls? Even the old ones," the seller laughs, "even the old men."
> "Mammy, I am different."[53]

Armah is aware that there ought to be some kind of linguistic differentiation between the "mammy" trader and "the suited man" and that the absence of this differentiation reduces the realism of the scene. He tries to make up for this in other ways, especially through interposed authorial comments. For example, he tells us earlier that Koomson's voice, "a very Ghanaian voice" was artificially inflected to make him sound like a white man but that it sounded "like a fisherman's voice with the sand and the salt hoarsening it forcing itself into unaccustomed English rhythms", and later, that the same voice is "playful, patronizing". These comments are expected to do the work of linguistic differentiation. Koomson, speaking English with a simulated English accent, is out to impress the seller with his status and importance, and this attitude is reinforced by the word "patronizing", which is set off by a comma and accentuated in its final position. But it is doubtful whether the device is successful; it certainly shows up Koomson but does not explain why a "mammy" trader should talk like a university graduate. One suspects (though there is no proof of this) that Armah probably regards pidgin as unworthy of literary record. It is noteworthy that he finds a function for pidgin of a sort in the obscene scrawls on the lavatory walls.

William Conton is even more typical of the effect of a writer's background on his characters' language. Here, the triumph of residual Victorianism in language is unmistakable. Born in Bathurst of educated middle-class parents (his father was an Anglican pastor and his mother a schoolteacher), Conton was educated in Gambia, Conakry (Guinea) and Freetown (Sierra Leone) and had his high school and university education in England. This explains the essentially middle-class urbanity

and the lack of rural or traditional authenticity in his novel. He is one
of the most Westernized of West African writers. He tries at one stage to
make his blackmailing launch-driver, Kwaku, speak pidgin, but the
effort is very feeble and is soon abandoned through his hero cutting the
character short with "Stop speaking broken English. You know I don't
like it. Speak your own language."[54] Pidgin English is called "broken"
English by those who are prejudiced against it in favour of standard
English. Kisimi Kamara's words could quite easily have come out of the
mouth of an unimaginative or even a patronizing Englishman working in
West Africa who prefers to keep the well of English language undefiled.
But pidgin has established its own status and it demands attention just
like standard usage, particularly in creative contexts in which weight is
given to the actual words of characters who speak mainly pidgin. But
if a grudging recognition is extended to pidgin as the language of the
semi-educated, no such recognition is shown the language of the
vernacular characters who inhabit the villages, not because such characters do not appear in Conton's novel (indeed the hero's political success
over the old bourgeois elite of Freetown is said to be due to his successful
mobilization of the hinterland peasants) but because Conton is not
equipped to undertake the task of projecting them forcefully and
realistically. The chiefs, elders and people of the villages described in
The African hardly appear as real persons but as hundreds of bodies in
a hollow square "dancing by the silver light of the ubiquitous pressure
paraffin lamp. The throb of the drums, the clap of the hands, the shuffle
of the feet, the lilt of the voices; hips swaying, nippled breasts bouncing,
sweat streaming . . ."[55] All this is like a deliberate parody of a foreign
writer sensationalizing African peasants. What is most absent here is a
real human presence. These are hundreds of bodies without voices
and without a language, mere flailing limbs, shuffling feet, swaying hips,
hardly men and women, flesh and blood, whose existence is attested to
through participatory action, including the use of language. They are
here merged into a general rural backcloth to a novel whose linguistic
scope is urban and middle-class.

The imputation of residual Victorianism to writers in West Africa is
often regarded as overt criticism, but ought really to be taken as a
straightforward statement of a fact of West African literary history. The
Victorian peculiarity of old-world Western habits of linguistic usage and
attitudes, and a dogged adherence to them in the face of encroaching
tendencies towards change, is a fact of experience among many older
middle-class families of coastal Ghana, Sierra Leone, Gambia and, to a
limited extent, Nigeria. Among them there persists a style of English
with its roots in the eighteenth and nineteenth centuries, marked by a

dignified, urbane prose, expertly organized. This quality of cultivated prose, which has been lost in much of English-speaking West Africa, has managed to survive in these areas. Its movement in West African writing can be traced from the works of such West African prose stylists as Drs Horton and Blyden through those of John Casely Hayford, Mensah Sarbah and Thomas Horatio Jackson to those of later prominent intellectuals like Dr J. B. Danquah of Ghana, Abioseh Nicol of Sierra Leone and Conton himself. The significance of this form of prose is that it is dignified and expressive, but better fitted to the discussion of ideas than to the development of action. It is not surprising that with enough material for a number of action novels, Conton attained only discursive effectiveness in *The African*. There is very little dialogue and that little is handled in the same measured, dignified and balanced prose cadence. With neither the vernacular language to supply metaphorical energy nor modern English prose spontaneity to supply speed of movement, the language of *The African* flows placidly through the windings and turnings of the author's felicitous periods.

In contrast to Conton and Armah, Ekwensi has a positive attitude to pidgin as a language of the urban masses. He is himself a product of the pidgin environment. Son of a carpenter and born in the working-class urban settlement of Minna in northern Nigeria, he was educated in Jos Government School; Government College, Ibadan; Achimota College (Ghana), and Chelsea College of Pharmacy in England and has had a varied working life as forester, teacher, soldier, film-actor, chemist, scriptwriter, broadcaster and Director of Nigerian Information Service. Since the end of the Nigerian civil war, he has gone back to being a pharmacist. Ekwensi's early life in the mixed urban settlements of the North in which pidgin was a dominant language left him with an important asset for his creative career. He never lost his sympathy for and interest in the proletarian and pidgin section of the society. He writes mainly about such underprivileged urban dwellers as prostitutes, petty criminals, bandleaders and the anonymous little men and women who flock to the city to seek excitement and economic security, the people whom sociologists categorize as "transitional" between traditionalism and modernism, whose medium of general communication in West Africa is pidgin English. Ekwensi's interest in them implies his realistic intention to represent their linguistic habits, to see them through their common medium of expression and the language which best projects their transitional nature, their social volatility and energy and their social and economic vulnerability.

Earlier in the discussion, the dearth of creative prose works until the 1940s was attributed to various factors including the lack of intimate contact between the coastal, Westernized elite and the traditional culture which would have supplied linguistic stimulus as well as the creative myths and motifs. Looked at in the abstract, this might have seemed the least plausible explanation, but it becomes decisive when it is remembered that the most successful West African novelists have been those adequately exposed to this creative source of energy, the traditional African culture and its verbal environment. Achebe and Soyinka are cases in point.

In an interview given to **Mr Dennis Duerden** of the London Transcription Centre, Achebe stresses that his early upbringing took place in his home village, a largely traditional environment, and that much of his creative impulse is drawn from the traditional culture. His actual words deserve to be quoted because they focus the points being made here.

Duerden: Chinua, one has the feeling after reading your novel *Things Fall Apart* that the contemporary Nigerian society from which you spring must have preserved the patterns of African traditional life to a large degree, if not in the cities, at least in the villages. Is this true?

Achebe: Yes, I think it is true to a large extent; certainly it was true when I was growing up. I think it's not quite so true today because the change is sort of accelerating, but when I was growing up in my village, it was still possible to catch glimpses of what the complete traditional society must have looked like and one supplemented these impressions with accounts, stories told by old people – like my father. Now, my father, although he was a Christian convert, was very useful to me in this way because he told me how things were in the past. And I'd like to say, too, it's not only in the villages; even in the cities, if you look carefully enough, you can see patterns of the past too; it depends on how closely you look. If you take Lagos, for instance, today: you will find that many villages from the hinterland are presented here as units which you might call the improvement societies. Each village has its own meeting, perhaps the women have their dances and so on and the men hold some traditional celebrations and so on. So, the patterns although much paler today, the patterns are still there.

Duerden: Yes, when you wrote *Things Fall Apart* did you actually do it from a historical point of view, describing history, or was it from these experiences of yours when you were growing up?

Achebe: It was purely from the experience and of course a bit of imagination. I didn't have to do any research as such. The festivals were still there, most of them were still there, the whole attitude,

> really it's the attitude of the people; their philosophy of life was
> still there. I mean, you could see it; and the rest really was using
> your own imagination to create the details of the story.
> *Duerden*: What village actually did you live in?
> *Achebe*: A place called Ogidi, which is six miles from the Niger.
> *Duerden*: This was during the thirties, was it?
> *Achebe*: That's right.[56]

From an impressionable childhood spent in the village Achebe moved
on to become a university graduate and the first indigenous Director of
Nigeria's External Broadcasting Service and subsequently a university
professor, both pre-eminently high-middle-class appointments. But his
earlier contact with the village, like Ekwensi's upbringing in the urban
setting, has remained a dominant factor. His understanding of traditional
life is unrivalled. But more important has been his appreciation of its
verbal peculiarities and conventions which he recaptures with a degree of
verisimilitude unattained by any other African writer. His appreciation
of the significance of the gnomic and proverbial modes of communication as essential to the exploration of the more serious and tragic experiences of traditional characters is derived from contact with this form
of traditional speech and an understanding of its creative potential.

Wole Soyinka's background is broader, for he derives from a middle-
class family with strong peasant connections. He was born in Abeokuta
in 1934 and educated there and in Government College, Ibadan; University College, Ibadan, and the University of Leeds. His course at Leeds
plunged him into the very depth of European literary movements, especially its dramatic movements, under the great dramatic scholar G. Wilson
Knight. His work in the Royal Court Theatre in London also brought
close to him the full impact of the modernist trends in literature, especially in the dramatic works of playwrights like Synge, Brecht, Dürrenmatt
and Arden. But by far the most abiding influence of his creativity remains
the folk and traditional elements in Yoruba culture to which he has
been exposed in his infancy, a knowledge which he reinforced by his
study of Yoruba ritual drama with a Leverhulme fellowship. These
influences are expressed in his drama in which traditional themes, symbols and motifs are dominant and indigenous dramatic techniques –
spontaneous dialogue, folk music, simple stories, mime and dance – are
extensively used.[57] The African and the modern English elements are
dexterously assimilated. In *The Interpreters*, this fusion appears only
intermittently, compared with his plays, but it has to be taken into
account since the composite nature of his work is one of its peculiarities.
Soyinka reinforces normal English grammatical and syntactical forms

with traditionally derived images, symbols and idioms. He appropriates rhythmic patterns of traditional speech and builds them into the normal linguistic rhythms of English to produce a powerful synthesis. The best illustration of this complex style in *The Interpreters* is the opening paragraph of Part II which announces Sekoni's death.

> The rains of May become in July slit arteries of the sacrificial bull, a million bleeding punctures of the sky-bull hidden in convulsive cloud humps, black, overfed for this one event, nourished on horizon tops of endless choice grazing, distant beyond giraffe reach. Some competition there is below, as bridges yield right of way to lorries packed to the running-board, and the wet tar spins mirages of unspeed-limits to heroic cars and their cargoes find a haven below the precipice. The blood of earth-dwellers mingles with blanched streams of the mocking bull, and flows into currents eternally below earth. The Dome cracked above Sekoni's short-sighted head one messy night. Too late he saw the insanity of a lorry parked right in his path, a swerve turned into a skid and cruel arabesques of tyres. A futile heap of metal, and Sekoni's body lay surprised across the open door, showers of laminated glass around him, his beard one fastness of blood and wet earth.[58]

Here, Soyinka fuses poetic imagery with traditional nature myths and ritual suggestion to provide the background to a disaster. The reader ought to recognize the strands and above all to grasp the significance of the "Dome of Life" in the scheme of the novel. This fusion of variously derived elements produces strong effects, and sometimes difficulties and obscurities. But it is possible to disentangle the elements and to trace them to the tradition from which they were derived. For example, the traditional origin of the nature myth is clear enough, but the elaboration of this myth is the work of Soyinka's personal and poetic imagination. The linguistic organization belongs to the literary tradition. Even though the underlying myth belongs to the oral tradition, it has here been assimilated into the literary tradition. The length and the complexity of the sentences, the complexity of the inner movements and shifting nuances suggest that the author's organizational outlook is modern and literary. The philosophical element represented by the "Dome of Life" is one of the novel's major preoccupations. Ironically, it was introduced by the dead man early in the narrative and provides the conceptual basis of the action, linking the characters' present lives to their past and future, uniting the living with the dead. Here, traditional beliefs meet modern ideas and assumptions and scientific attitudes embrace ancestral mysticism.

The poet in Soyinka reveals himself in his choice of language in this novel, especially in the handling of situations which might appear coarse when rendered in realistic prose. Soyinka is an example of literary good breeding; he will not inflict linguistic vulgarity on the reader if he can help it. When he describes Egbo's sexual initiation at the hands of the experienced Simi, he prefers to do so through figurative language: "And a lone pod strode the baobab on the tapering thigh, leaf-shorn, and high mists swirl him, haze-splitting storms, but the stalk stayed him . . ."[59] This indicates the strength of Egbo's ecstacy without cheapening it. And why Soyinka should single out Egbo for this poetical treatment becomes clear when it is remembered that he is conceived in the personality of Ogun, the Yoruba patron of artistic creativity as well as, paradoxically, of war.

III THE CHANGING SCENE

8

Culture contact and culture conflict

For most Africans, life begins in the village, and wherever they go after that, they carry the village within them. There is often a certain ambivalence in their attitudes and behaviour when they enter modern urban culture. Most of the writers deal with these ambivalences of individual behaviour as well as conflicts and tensions in social relationships. But Achebe in *Things Fall Apart* and *Arrow of God* goes back in time to the earliest contact between the Western and the traditional cultures, revealing the great shock which followed the first impact.

I shall give considerable space to the theme of contact in *Things Fall Apart* and *Arrow of God* as Achebe's handling of it is profound and sustained. In the other novels the exploration of the theme is either fragmentary or marred by technical weakness. Moreover, because Achebe establishes a base-line of the "pure" traditional village culture we can identify the main values which sustained the traditional way of life and so can appreciate the other writers' treatment of the conflict of values in more recent times.

Things Fall Apart is set in Umuofia, a traditional village. Its action falls between the last ten years of the nineteenth century and the first ten of the twentieth, when Christian missions and the British administration first established their influence in the groups of villages north of Onitsha. Umuofia has a typical traditional village culture, handed down by word of mouth and intimate personal contact from one generation to another. The people of Umuofia are a community. On these two words, "tradition" and "community", depend our understanding of culture and human relationship as described by Achebe in *Things Fall Apart*.

In traditional society, the present life of the people, their norms of behaviour, customary beliefs, attitudes and values have come down to them with as little modification as possible from the immemorial past.[1] The institutions of society have evolved in such a way that fundamental changes do not take place; all important aspects of cultural life are protected by religious sentiment, and great store is set on social conformity. The existence of a traditional culture depends on the existence of a community, that is, the kind of society in which there is intimate face-to-face relationship and co-operation among people permanently resident in a single locality and who as a result experience what C. H. Cooley calls "a certain fusion of individualities in a common whole, so that one's very self, for many purposes at least, is the common life and purpose of the group".[2] Cooley's definition can be compared with MacIver's in *Society*: "Wherever the members of any group, small or large, live together in such a way that they share, not this or that particular interest, but the basic conditions of a common life, we call that group a community. The basic criterion of a community . . . is that all of one's relationships may be found within it."[3] Robert Redfield lists the attributes of a community in his book *The Little Community*: physical proximity of the members, smallness of the group, the enduring character of its social relationships, the relative similarity of activities and states of mind of the members, the relative self-sufficiency of the community and the self-perpetuating propensity of the groups forming the community.[4] For the German sociologist F. Tönnies, community (*Gemeinschaft*) is an "intimate, private and exclusive living together" as opposed to association (*Gesellschaft*) based on the "rational pursuit of individual self-interest".[5] Okonkwo's Umuofia has the attributes of a community, especially the fusion of interests and the relative similarity of activities and states of mind of the members.

The identification of the individual with the group of which he forms part, and with its social and cultural outlook, is the very essence of traditionalism. It finds expression in the individual's acquiescence in the beliefs and customs of the group and his sharing with the rest of the group a feeling of social unity. His individual self-interest is always subordinated to the overall interest of the group. This is an important traditional value which the novelists emphasize, contrasting it with the opposite value based on individual self-interest in the modern urban situation.

It would be wrong to interpret the concentration on common goals and the primacy of the common interest as a matter of suppression of the personality from the outside, of constraint on the part of an authority. Social conformity and the discouragement of deviation from the common norms of behaviour are not the same thing as the repressive curbing of individual freedom. Social freedom is in the final analysis related to legality, and this is commonly expressed as the principle of the greatest good of the greatest number. The traditional social philosophy is based

202

on this principle and, because it is fundamental to the very survival and general health of society, is given validity by being anchored in customary practice and protected by divine and ancestral authority.[6] Traditional society was not tyrannical because it was never remote from the people who composed it, and was not easily manipulated by ambitious or perverted individuals because of its corporate nature.

We are reminded of that very tense scene in *Arrow of God* in which the Chief Priest is locked in a conflict with his people that threatens them with imminent famine. One of the elders appeals to the highest value in society in order to break the priest's intransigence; he appeals to the common good and the solidarity of the group. He asks the priest simply, "Do you think there is another Umuaro outside this hut now?" to which the latter replies, "No, you are Umuaro."[7] The question and answer underline the central essence and ideological base of the traditional system. Society is not an abstraction detached from the people who inhabit the specific place in a particular time, it is the people themselves – Umuaro is no mere geographical location but people who know themselves (and are known by others) as Umuaro and identify one another by definite kinship relationships traceable to a common real or hypothetical ancestor and original father. This view is supported by ethnographical research, as in this passage taken from **M. M.** Green's *Igbo Village Affairs*:

> As of Agbaja itself, a number of different principles of social grouping enter into the make-up of this village group, as of most other Ibo social units of this kind. In the first place it is a local unit in the sense that its inhabitants occupy a common territory, the villagers being scattered through the bush over an area that is roughly speaking about three miles square. It is also a mythical kinship unit with relationship becoming genealogically traceable within, and often between, the kindreds that make up the villages. All the people born in Agbaja, with a few exceptions which do not invalidate the principle, claim descent from a mythical pair of ancestors, a man called Ngalaba and a woman called Okpu Ite.[8]

The term Umuaro is inclusive as well as exclusive – it distinguishes all those who belong from all those who do not belong. If you are Umuaro then you are tied to the rest of Umuaro by bonds of a common belonging and you have rights and obligations defined within the social structure and inviolable because they bear the stamp of custom and tradition and are sanctioned by ancestral authority. You are subject to the laws of the community because you have a stake in the peace and survival of society. You are subject to its taboos and prohibitions and are entitled to participate fully and actively in the life of the community. The protection of society from the whimsical and arbitrary intervention of individuals is the assurance of the freedom of individual members. This in itself is a satisfactory rationale of social homogeneity and traditional order.

How does Achebe perceive traditional life and how does he depict it before and during its confrontation with Western cultural influences? He uses the career of Okonkwo to explore the twin themes of individual and group tragedy which result from the break-up of the unity of this traditional life. Here I shall look more closely at Okonkwo and his Umuofia, in order to isolate the values which Achebe regards as having animated and sustained traditional life, and whose destruction has brought such dislocation to the individual African.

Okonkwo's life-history illustrates the working of the traditional system because he is a fully realized traditional character. This is not to say that Okonkwo is a representative of the Igbo race in particular or that his life is an illustration of the values which Igbo people admire (the view held by J. D. Killam, which I believe to be in error). All one can justifiably say is that Okonkwo is a fully realized traditional character who also has, as human beings must have, distinctly individual traits. Indeed he is atypical in some respects, and his extreme idiosyncrasies draw him into conflict with traditional practices. His friend Obierika, who is a flexible, pragmatic Igbo titled elder, is nearer the traditional ideal. But for all his personal weaknesses Okonkwo is a full-blooded traditional character and can be used to examine the relation between the individual and society under the traditional system. As a wily young wrestler, he brings victory and honour to his kinsmen by his successes at wrestling matches; as an adult, he takes part in his people's wars against outside aggressors and earns the gratitude, respect and affection of his clan; as a titled elder he helps to settle internal disputes between individuals and families. He follows the traditional occupation, which is farming, and in spite of having inherited nothing from his indolent father, he is able by hard work to achieve the three chief status symbols of his society – a large barn, wives and children, and titles. He is pious, for his material success does not lead him to think he is exempt from the laws of society sanctioned by the ancestors. He performs his religious and secular duties punctiliously.

But Okonkwo is also an individual with obvious personal weaknesses. Achebe balances Okonkwo's traditional virtues against these weaknesses as a person. Like most self-made men, and especially because his father's improvident and unsuccessful life hangs over his self-confidence like a permanent reproach, Okonkwo is impatient with weak unsuccessful men.

Fiery of temper and quicker with blows than with words, he sometimes breaks some of the serious taboos of his community, as for instance by beating his wife during the Week of Peace and so bringing down the rigour of communal disapproval on his head. His contempt for misfits, which he does nothing to conceal, often violates traditional politeness which, because of the face-to-face nature of the social relationship, avoids giving offence or hurting feelings wherever possible – a thing which distinguishes rural people from the tough, flippant residents of the city. Okonkwo's fear of appearing weak and sentimental is behind some of the apparently callous things he does, such as cutting down the boy Ikemefuna, who has been his ward for three years. It also explains his heavy-handed domination of his household. He makes himself appear an ogre, though this severe exterior hides his deep-seated affectionate nature. The individual in him finds expression in his many faults, but as a traditionalist he accepts without a murmur the punishment imposed on him by the community for his offences.

The operation of the traditional spirit does not therefore imply uniformity in individual characters and temperaments. And since individuals differ temperamentally, and in character, they were in pre-colonial traditional society, as now, liable to offend one another and fall short of the norms of behaviour acceptable to society. The idea of pre-colonial traditional society as a haven of peace, a state of egalitarian self-satisfaction, idyllic bliss and sweet reasonableness is a utopian myth as falsifying as the opposite view, which sees it as a state of chronic anarchy, a bloody battlefield in which the weak and the helpless were trodden down by the strong.

But the traditional did work towards the maintenance of internal social harmony and good external relations. Politics provided the framework for defining and delimiting social relations, individual rights and obligations, and the specific roles and statuses attaching to different offices, and law was directed towards reconciling the parties in every conflict and restoring a state of normality.[9] These things are central in *Things Fall Apart*. We are fully conscious of the traditional community spirit in the interplay of political and judicial forces in the life of Umuofia.

We find an Athenian-type democracy, a citizens' assembly, in operation in the Umuofia village-group on the occasion of the murder of a female member of the Umuofia community by someone from the neighbouring village-group of Mbaino. The assembly of ten thousand people massed in the village square has to determine how to meet this flagrant provocation. Obviously, there is a danger of conflict between the two communities. The case for war is put by Ogbuefi Ezeugo, a Demosthenean orator of the village square. Feelings of anger and desire for revenge are aroused in the assembled people, but in the end it is decided "to follow the normal course of action". According to this "normal course", an ultimatum is immediately despatched to the culprits asking them to choose between war and compensation. Not unexpectedly, they choose the second alternative.

Achebe's handling of this incident reveals his narrative gift. First, suspense and expectancy are created by the town-crier's summons to the male adult population of Umuofia to assemble at the village square in the morning:

> Okonkwo had just blown out the palm-oil lamp and stretched himself on his bamboo bed when he heard the *ogene* of the town-crier piercing the still night air. *Gome, gome, gome, gome,* boomed the hollow metal. Then the crier gave his message, and at the end of it beat his instrument again. And this was the message. Every man of Umuofia was asked to gather at the market-place tomorrow morning. Okonkwo wondered what was amiss. . . . He had discerned a clear overtone of tragedy in the crier's voice, and even now he could still hear it as it grew dimmer and dimmer in the distance.[10]

The suspense is deepened with the mystery of the night, but for a warrior and man of action like Okonkwo, the message holds no terror. At the Citizens' Assembly itself, the scene is given cinematographic effect:

> There must have been about ten thousand men there, all talking in low voices. At last Ogbuefi Ezeugo stood up in the midst of them and bellowed four times, "*Umuofia kwenu,*" and on each occasion he faced a different direction and seemed to push the air with a clenched fist. And ten thousand men answered "yaa!" each time. Then there was perfect silence. Ogbuefi Ezeugo was a powerful orator and was always chosen to speak on such occasions. He moved his hand over his white head and stroked his white beard. He then adjusted his cloth, which was passed under his right arm-pit and tied above his left shoulder.
>
> "*Umuofia kwenu,*" he bellowed a fifth time, and the crowd yelled in answer. And then suddenly like one possessed he shot out his left hand and pointed in the direction of Mbaino, and said through gleaming white teeth firmly clenched: "Those sons of wild animals have dared to murder a daughter of Umuofia." He threw his head down and gnashed his teeth, and allowed a murmur of suppressed anger to sweep the crowd. When he began again, the

anger on his face was gone and in its place a sort of smile hovered, more terrible and more sinister than the anger. And in a clear unemotional voice he told Umuofia how their daughter had gone to market at Mbaino and had been killed. That woman, said Ezeugo, was the wife of Ogbuefi Udo, and he pointed to a man who sat near him with a bowed head. The crowd then shouted with anger and thirst for blood.[11]

The build-up of effect is deliberate, systematic and sustained. Every gesture made by the orator, every expression on his face is directed towards rousing and holding the attention of ten thousand men in an open forum. The harangue to the assembly is a call to solidarity, an invitation to be attentive and to enter fully into the situation which is about to unfold. Even the modulation of the voice from the level of anger to that of emotionless objectivity is a deliberate effort to channel the response of the audience constructively, to impress the assembly with the seriousness of the event while preparing it for a rational response to a monstrous provocation. And as might be expected, anger in the assembly gives way to constructive deliberation:

> Many others spoke, and at the end it was decided to follow the normal course of action. An ultimatum was immediately dispatched to Mbaino asking them to choose between war on the one hand, and on the other the offer of a young man and a virgin as compensation.[12]

The people of Mbaino recognize the reasonableness of Umuofia's demand. They too know that this is the normal course when a serious breach of peaceful, good-neighbourly relationship has been committed. Otherwise, there would be so much insecurity that life would come to a halt, since there was no overall centralized authority to enforce security. Inter-village and inter-clan collaboration would become impossible if every woman who went from her village to a neighbouring village to trade were to lose her life, or go unavenged. Umuofia's culpable neighbour, recognizing the justice of the ultimatum, therefore makes reparation.

> And so when Okonkwo of Umuofia arrived at Mbaino as the proud and imperious emissary of war, he was treated with great honour and respect, and two days later he returned home with a lad of fifteen and a young virgin. The lad's name was Ikemefuna, whose sad story is still told in Umuofia unto this day.[13]

It is worth noting that when a similar situation necessitating the sending of an ultimatum develops in *Arrow of God* between Umuaro and Okperi over a contested piece of land, the traditional diplomatic procedure adopted here is not followed, so that at the time of *Arrow of God* the traditional system was already under pressure and was fast breaking down.

One element of traditionalism which deserves attention here is the central ideological relevance of the supernatural and the magical as a defining element in people's attitudes and beliefs. Even in the matter of declaring and prosecuting war, no people could move without the assurance that they are doing so with the support and active participation of their gods. Umuofia is no exception:

> Umuofia was feared by all its neighbours. It was powerful in war and in magic, and its priests and medicine-men were feared in all the surrounding country. Its most potent war-medicine was as old as the clan itself. Nobody knew how old. But on one point there was general agreement – the active principle in that medicine had been an old woman with one leg. In fact, the medicine itself was called *agadi-nwayi*, or old woman. It had its shrine in the centre of Umuofia, in a cleared spot. And if anybody was so foolhardy as to pass by the shrine after dusk he was sure to see the old woman hopping about.
>
> And so the neighbouring clans who naturally knew of these things feared Umuofia, and would not go to war against it without first trying a peaceful settlement. And in fairness to Umuofia it should be recorded that it never went to war unless its case was clear and just and was accepted as such by its Oracle – the Oracle of the Hills and the Caves. And there were indeed occasions when the Oracle had forbidden Umuofia to wage a war. If the clan had disobeyed the Oracle they would surely have been beaten, because their dreaded *agadi-nwayi* would never fight what the Ibo call *a fight of blame.*[14]

There is hardly any important area of human experience which is not linked to the supernatural and the people's sense of religion and religious piety. Achebe shows how these things are part and parcel of the ideological structure of traditional society, and so essential to a proper interpretation of experience in the traditional social context. By the time of *Arrow of God* a good deal of the traditional reverence for the gods as the ultimate arbiters of human affairs has been lost. Where it would be inconceivable for Umuofia to go to war against the orders of its Oracle and without the backing of its war-medicine, the people of Umuaro storm into a war of revenge against the people of Okperi, even against the advice of the Chief Priest whose god was evolved as protector of collective security.

208

The episode throws light both on the spirit in which the traditional system operated and on traditional community life. First of all, we notice the segmentary nature of group relationship. The individual has a meaningful identity only in terms of the social group to which he or she belongs. Umuofia reacts as a unit of solidarity to the murder of one of her daughters and exacts redress from Mbaino also as a unit of solidarity whose member or members committed the crime. There is a traditional mode of inter-clan relationship, which has been operated from time immemorial because it has been effective in averting the threat of internecine feuds or vendetta between people who have much in common, including ties of marriage and economic interdependence.[15] This is a case in which the threat of a feud is applied as a judicial process by people without centralized legal institutions. The conciliatory aspect is implicit (in spite of the hard feelings) in that the kinsmen of the homicide would rather pay compensation than "fight a fight of blame". So the people of Mbaino give a young virgin and a young boy to make good the reckless action of one of their members.

The spirit of traditionalism is shown again in even clearer relief in the adjudication of cases involving members of the same community. Its conciliatory rather than contractual and rigidly legalistic nature is best seen in the case which modern lawyers might call "Uzowulu versus Mgbafo". The case is again heard by the Citizens' Assembly, presided over by nine masked ancestral spirits (mmo) representing the nine villages of the Umuofia village group.

Uzowulu, the plaintiff, an irascible and incorrigible wife-beater, has again beaten his wife, Mgbafo, but this time her brothers invade his house and, having thoroughly belaboured him, take away their sister. Uzowulu, feeling aggrieved, takes recourse to the communal tribunal, hoping either to recover his wife or the bride-wealth he has paid for her. The ancestral spirits acting as jury, after deliberating over the deposition made by both plaintiff and defendant, decide that Uzowulu should apologize to his wife with a pot of palm-wine and that his wife should then be allowed to go back to him. The summing-up of the Senior Ancestral Spirit deserves to be cited in full for the light it throws on the traditional attitude to the resolution of disputes among members of the *in*-group:

> Evil Forest rose to his feet and order was immediately restored. A steady cloud of smoke rose from his head. He sat down again and called two witnesses. They were both Uzowulu's neighbours, and they agreed about the beating. Evil Forest then stood up, pulled out his staff and thrust it into the earth again. He ran a few steps in

209

the direction of the women; they all fled in terror, only to return to their places almost immediately. The nine *egwugwu* then went away to consult together in their house. They were silent for a long time. Then the metal gong sounded and the flute was blown. The *egwugwu* had emerged once again from their underground home. They saluted one another and then reappeared on the *ilo*.

"*Umuofia kwenu!*" roared Evil Forest, facing the elders and grandees of the clan.

"Yaa!" replied the thunderous crowd; then silence descended from the sky and swallowed the noise.

Evil Forest began to speak and all the while he spoke everyone was silent. The eight other *egwugwu* were as still as statues.

"We have heard both sides of the case," said Evil Forest. "Our duty is not to blame this man or to praise that, but to settle the dispute." He turned to Uzowulu's group and allowed a short pause.

"Uzowulu's body, I salute you," he said.

"Our father, my hand has touched the ground," replied Uzowulu, touching the earth.

"Uzowulu's body, do you know me?'

"How can I know you, father? You are beyond our knowledge," Uzowulu replied.

"I am Evil Forest. I kill a man on the day that his life is sweetest to him."

"That is true," replied Uzowulu.

"Go to your in-laws with a pot of wine and beg your wife to return to you. It is not bravery when a man fights with a woman." He turned to Odukwe, and allowed a brief pause.

"Odukwe's body, I greet you," he said.

"My hand is on the ground," replied Odukwe.

"Do you know me?"

"No man can know you," replied Odukwe.

"I am Evil Forest, I am Dry-meat-that-fills-the-mouth, I am Fire-that-burns-without-faggots. If your in-law brings wine to you, let your sister go with him. I salute you." He pulled his staff from the hard earth and thrust it back.

"*Umuofia kwenu!*" he roared, and the crowd answered.

"I don't know why such a trifle should come before the *egwugwu*," said one elder to another.

"Don't you know what kind of man Uzowulu is? He will not listen to any other decision," replied the other.

As they spoke the two other groups of people had replaced the first before the *egwugwu*, and a great land case began.[16]

We see here the importance of kinship groups in providing moral and other support for their members when in conflict with the members of other similar groups. Both defendant and plaintiff are surrounded by their nearest of kin while the tribunal sits – in fact, Mgbafo is answered for in the case by Odukwe, her eldest brother, partly because she cannot as a woman speak before the masked ancestral spirits and partly because her close kin represent her as of right.

We notice the representative nature of the political and judicial institutions. Though all Umuofia is assembled in the village square, the masked ancestors who represent the nine villages act as the executive judicial body and produce a unanimous verdict. Each of them represents the opinion of his own village; hence the decision, to command universal approval, has to be unanimous.

From the aside between the two elders, we learn that Uzowulu is a difficult clansman and not likely to respect a verdict from any tribunal other than the highest in the land. Among the Igbo and many other West African peoples, masked ancestral spirits are not just Misters so-and-so in funny clothes and masks, they are supposed to be real ancestors (at least to the uninitiated) coming from the underworld through an anthole to take part in the worldly deliberations of their posterity.[17] The real function of the masked spirits is to put the stamp of ancestral authority on the verdicts of the community tribunal, a function which both Hoebel and Busia have noted in the Ashanti judicial process.[18] The ancestors not only hand down the norms of behaviour, they intervene actively in the maintenance of public order and good relations among the living, a point emphasized by Forde and Jones in their study on Igbo ethnography. "The ancestors (*ndichie*), who are also under the control of *Ale*, act as her agents, as guardians of morality, of which any departure from custom may be regarded as a breach. The head (*Okpara*) of each sub-lineage ... owes his authority largely to his role as the representative and mouthpiece of the lineage ancestors, symbolized by the religious staff (*ofo*)."[19] The masked ancestral spirits are a further manifestation and dramatization of this continuing interest of the ancestors in the affairs of the living.

That Mgbafo's kinsmen beat her husband up before taking her away is an effective way of compelling him to take judicial action so that they can call attention to his habit of beating her and mobilize public opinion against his doing it again. This is a well-known method of provoking judicial action or precipitating an issue, much as the Ashanti profane the name of an ancestor to induce the hearing of a case, or a Tiv agegrade may use commando tactics to compel the elders to give justice to an aggrieved member.

Finally, the spirit of conciliation, of what the Tiv call "repairing the

211

tar", is implicit in the preliminary remark of the spokesman of the masked ancestors before pronouncing verdict: "We have heard both sides of the case. . . . Our duty is not to blame this man or to praise that, but to settle the dispute." The fine itself, a pot of palm-wine, is meant to be a way of smoothing ruffled feelings, for undoubtedly both sides in the case will drink it together, and nothing inspires a feeling of generosity and spontaneous charitableness towards erstwhile adversaries like palm-wine shared. In these details which go to form the essence of community life in pre-colonial African societies, Achebe reveals his insight into the workings of the traditional system.

The essence of traditionalism is manifest throughout *Things Fall Apart* in the group determination of individual actions and in the detailed ordering of social institutions to protect the life, property and psychological health of the individual. It is not only that immediate steps are taken to right any situation which threatens the relationship of individuals, and through individuals the segments of the community to which they belong, but all those sectors of social relationship and all the economic and political factors which fundamentally sustain the community are linked to the supernatural and so guarded against the disintegrative and capricious forces of uncontrolled individualism.

In this respect, the earth goddess is the essential centre around which the most serious prohibitions and sacred sanctions are woven. Professor Meyer Fortes gives space in *The Dynamics of Clanship Among the Tallensi* to the central position of the earth in the determination of individual life and security among the Tallensi people of northern Ghana.[20] Forde and Jones' assessment of the relevance of the earth to Igbo culture provides this more immediately relevant text:

> Ale (Ala or Ane), the earth spirit, is the most prominent deity and is regarded as the queen of the underworld and the "owner" of men whether dead or alive. The cult of the ancestors is closely associated with Ale. She is the source and judge of human morality and accordingly exercises the main ritual sanctions in disputes and offences. Homicide, kidnapping, poisoning, stealing farm products, adultery and giving birth to twins or abnormal children are all offences against Ale. Laws are made and oaths sworn in her name. Priests of Ale are guardians of public morality and the cult of Ale is one of the most powerful integrating forces in Ibo society.[21]

The all-embracing scope is understandable. The earth for an agricultural people is the primary source of sustenance and so holds the key to survival. Therefore its priest is easily the most important religious (and because religion permeates every facet of social life, social) personage in the community. If the earth goddess is angry and refuses to reward the agricultural effort of the people, crops fail and there is general misery. The man who propitiates her and acts generally as intermediary between her and the people is naturally a most powerful personage whose pronouncements in his official capacity cannot be easily set aside. With this in mind, it is easier to accept what may appear to the modern reader the traditional callousness and brutal cynicism of some of the actions in *Things Fall Apart*.

For example, Ikemefuna's murder at the instigation of the Oracle of the Hills and Caves (who is also the Oracle of the Earth Goddess) revolts the conscience of the reader who has followed his "innocent" and vivacious young life throughout the three years in which he has integrated himself into Okonkwo's household. "Innocent" is put advisedly in quotation marks because he is innocent only in the sense that he has done nothing wrong. Our feeling for him should not obscure the fact that as soon as his people hand him over to Umuofia as a recompense for their murdered kinswoman, Ikemefuna loses his innocence. He becomes the bearer of the guilt of his whole people and must be sacrificed to expiate their crime of homicide.[22] When he falls, he does so by the operation of the lex talionis, for many traditional Africans like the Jews of old believed in an eye for an eye and a life for a life, especially in their dealings with those outside their own corporate groups. No one is better suited to take the dreadful decision than the oracle of the goddess whose duty it is to see to the security of the community and its members and to demand expiation when one of her children has been murdered. The earth requires that justice should be done, and it is done.

Indeed, Achebe shows that Ikemefuna's life is forfeit the moment he is given as hostage, for when he is first introduced as Okonkwo's ward, he is referred to as "the doomed lad who was sacrificed to the village of Umuofia by their neighbours to avoid war and bloodshed" and as "the ill-fated lad".[23] And later still, "The elders of the clan had decided that Ikemefuna should be in Okonkwo's care for a while. But no one thought it would be as long as three years. They seemed to forget all about him as soon as they had taken the decision."[24] But not the ever-vigilant goddess and her oracle.

Achebe does not gloss over such aspects of traditional life as the killing of Ikemefuna. He shows through his portrayal of the character of Okonkwo that the traditional individual is not the saintly phantom, the *sauvage noble* of Rousseauist romanticism; and he demonstrates through a realistic portrayal of Umuofia that the traditional society has its grim aspect. He balances the positive values against them and he stresses that

213

traditional life must be taken as a whole, so that it is seen to have a pattern and a logic peculiar to itself.

Apart from the killing of Ikemefuna, there is also the case of the twins who are thrown into the bad bush because twins are regarded as lusus naturae and hateful to the earth. Such practices may have been painful to those who had to carry them out, but there was so much to gain from conformity that the irksome cases are accommodated. As Margaret Green says: "In considering the question of social stability one must recognize, in the first place, that there is a general acceptance of the existing form of society. There are many personal dissatisfactions and criticisms, but they do not lead to general criticism of the status quo or demands for a revolution or a new order."[25] So we find Obierika, Achebe's rustic philosopher, regretting but acquiescing to the loss of his twins, a loss which even to his traditionalist mind has proved hard to absorb. He rationalizes this by arguing that since the earth has decreed it, there is no way out but to obey. "If the clan did not exact punishment for an offence against the great goddess, her wrath was loosed on all the land and not just on the offender. As the elders said, if one finger brought oil it soiled the others."[26] Hoebel, discussing the Ashanti legal process, notes the same belief in collective retribution: "The ancestors will punish the group as a whole, if the group does not punish a sinner and atone for his misdeeds."[27] The belief is the basis of what Durkheim calls "the mechanical solidarity" of kinship-organized communities and what Tönnies calls a "community of fate". Obierika's assent and the views of the sociologists underline one of the main facts about the traditional culture, collective responsibility. Because of the closeness of human association within the community, the action of one individual affects, in a far-reaching and often profound way, the lives and well-being of the others. To ensure that individual responsibility to the group is accepted, it is built into the network of customary beliefs and social attitudes.

Against this background of the primacy of the group and its interests over the individual and his self-interest Achebe shows the predominance of the earth-mother goddess in the moral scheme of traditional society; it explains the apparent inhumanity of the destruction of twins and killing of Ikemefuna, and all other situations in which the balanced and peaceful relationship between man and god, the living and the dead, and the living among themselves is subverted or threatened.

On the three occasions on which Okonkwo offends the earth, severe penalties are exacted. When he beats his wife during the Sacred Week of Peace the priest of Ani orders peremptorily, "You will bring to the shrine of Ani tomorrow one she-goat, one hen, a length of cloth and a hundred cowries."[28] Secondly, when he accidentally kills Ezeudu's son, he is made to flee his fatherland, and early the next morning, a large crowd including his best friend, Obierika, "dressed in the garb of war", storms his compound, burns his house, flattens the walls and carries away all his belongings including his animals and his yams – his memory is ritually blotted out of his society.[29] Thirdly, when he hangs himself, he commits the supreme sin against the earth and, great man though he is, he is denied the comfort of his people's burial. His epitaph is realistically supplied by Obierika: "That man was one of the greatest men in Umuofia. You drove him to kill himself; and now he will be buried like a dog. . . ."[30] The traditional law is hard and no respecter of persons, but it justifies itself on the ground that social order must be maintained and the health of the community protected.

The quiet resignation with which traditional people acquiesce in the dictates of their ancestors, gods and goddesses, in order to preserve the good health of the community and its members was governed by their predominantly stoical outlook on life, especially in the face of afflictions imposed on them by fate or as a punishment for individual or group malefaction. It leads to the growth of the religious and philosophical attitudes associated by Professor Meyer Fortes with Oedipus and Job.[31]

Belief in fate and divine justice is strong in Okonkwo's Umuofia and produces a stoical resignation to, and placid acceptance of, such calamities as the death of children, sudden death, failure of crops and those forms of misfortune which in some societies are explained by witchcraft.[32] Nevertheless, we can distinguish a large area of individual action covered by personal responsibility. (The Igbo proverb says that "when a man says 'yes' his *chi* also says 'yes' ".)

This ambiguity of belief – that destiny, fate or the supernatural determine an individual's fortunes and misfortunes on the one hand, and that the individual is responsible for determining the course of an empirically directed action on the other – is clearly reflected in the ups and downs of Okonkwo's life. Okonkwo's rise to fame in Umuofia from the poverty and misfortunes of his boyhood days is attributed by himself and others to his personal prowess and the success of his personal genius (his *chi*). His accidental murder of a fellow clansman and his subsequent exile he regards as a result of the weakness of his *chi* alone. Here we have a situation in which a man ascribes his success and good fortune to himself and his personal spirit but blames the latter alone for his misfortunes and by implication exculpates himself. Meek sees in this the source of the fatalism of the Igbo, and Fortes has seen the same tendency in many West African peoples.[33]

This fatalistic outlook is of a piece with the idea of traditional piety which informs the actions and attitudes of traditional characters, and reconciles them to the day-to-day disasters of chance and mischance. Resignation to the intractable powers of destiny is not only inevitable in the absence of a rationalist explanation, but the proper pious attitude to take. It is only thus that the individual's good relationship with the gods and ancestors can be reconciled with the misfortunes which beset life in spite of this good relationship.

This is also an element in the classical concept of tragedy; the individual, for all his personal efforts, and despite the secular and sacred institutions which he could take recourse to in extremity, is still the victim of blind anonymous forces which he can neither combat by self-will nor counteract by personal ingenuity.[34] Thus, Okonkwo's fall begins with his accidental killing of Ezeudu's son, which necessitates his seven years' exile from Umuofia. This in turn checks his rise to fame and the realization of his life-long ambition to become "one of the lords of the clan". The disappointment of his aspiration by his temporary exile disintegrates his self-control, and culminates in his rash murder of the insolent chief messenger and his subsequent suicide.

Okonkwo's example suggests that traditional society did not provide complete security to the traditional individual against the irrational and inhuman forces that threatened his well-being, especially if the individual had, like Okonkwo, some overpowering personal weakness. When such an individual was struck down, he was struck down alone, but the tragic experience was lived through vicariously by the other members of the community with whom his life was linked. The community rallied to ease his fall or to help him to rise again. In such cases, a man's kinship group, because it was the nearest and the most intimately involved in his life, partook most actively in his misfortune.

So Okonkwo's personal misfortune is alleviated by his being given a second home during his exile by his mother's people. He is given a plot of ground, helped to build a compound, and given land on which to farm his crops and a contribution of yams – these were the basic economic securities. He also enjoys the peculiar privileges appertaining to "sister's son". Okonkwo's uncle sums the position up when he says: "A man belongs to his fatherland when things are good and life is sweet. But when there is sorrow and bitterness he finds refuge in his motherland."[35] Understanding the real spirit of traditionalism involves an awareness of the economic, political and religious significance of the network of rights and obligations existing among those who are related by blood or through marriage. As Radcliffe-Brown puts it, "Reference to duties and rights are different ways of referring to a social relation and the rules of behaviour connected therewith."[36]

216

Okonkwo exemplifies the functional nature of kinship ties and their rights and obligations as well as the norms of behaviour expected in the particular case. Only one aspect of this question need be discussed here. As father to the children of his three wives he exercises patriarchal authority over them, exacting absolute submission from them (as well as from their mothers). As absolute leader of his family he shows a firmness that sometimes borders on callousness. He eschews all show of feeling though he has powerful feelings, especially for his daughter Ezinma.

> Okonkwo ruled his household with a heavy hand. His wives, especially the youngest, lived in perpetual fear of his fiery temper, and so did his little children. Perhaps down in his heart Okonkwo was not a cruel man. But his whole life was dominated by fear, the fear of failure and of weakness.[37]

His relationship with his children is based on inequality, with the children dependent on him for protection, care and guidance. He is deeply affronted when his son Nwoye, in defiance of his will and his efforts to bring him up in the way of the clan, transfers his allegiance to the Christians. The relationship between father and son (even in the traditional setting) always has elements of conflict. We are not told what Okonkwo's actual relationship with his own father was but we are sure in retrospect that he must have despised his indolence, improvidence and the general lackadaisical outlook which prevented him from providing for his son's future like most responsible and painstaking parents. Okonkwo's irreverence to his father's memory is unnatural (that is, untraditional, but the circumstances of his father's life and death explain and extenuate the untraditional attitude of a most traditional character). But Nwoye's deviation from filial duty is a kind of perversity (encouraged by the missionaries who take over the provision of the basic material needs for which he might have been beholden to his father). Implicit in the relationship between a father and his children, especially the male children, was the reciprocity of interests by which the father provided the material needs of the children and the children deferred to the father's judgements, respected his feelings and susceptibilities and accepted his leadership.

This premise of inequality which was assiduously cultivated, because the authority of the father must be unquestioned if he was to guide the lives of his children along traditional lines, is brought out by Achebe because it was the main basis of cultural continuity. For example, we find Ezeulu, in many of his turbulent encounters with his sons, emphasizing the old dictum that "A man does not speak a lie to his son." and that to swear by what a man has been told by his father is to swear the

217

greatest oath. The father, by example and by precept, brought his children up (the father concentrated more on the male children and the mother on the female) in the way of the clan.[38]

The father–son relationship was solidly based in religious belief, especially the cult of the ancestors. A man was reverent and obedient to his father, who, when he died and joined the rest of the ancestral dead, would continue to exercise a benevolent tutelary influence over him and his family. A father brought up his son in the best tradition of clan customs and usages, and worked hard to provide him with basic necessities, because when he died his spirit would draw sustenance from the sacrificial offerings which his living son would make him. More important still, the performance of the proper funeral rites which would smooth the father's way into the spirit world might to some extent depend on a living son's sense of obligation and indebtedness to his dead father. This is the basis of what Fortes calls "the ritualization of filial piety". He writes of Tallensi kinship and ancestor cult: "Tale social life is almost wholly organized by reference to relations of descent and kinship. Precise genealogical knowledge is necessary in order to define a person's place in society and his rights, duties, capabilities and privileges. This is one reason why the cult of the ancestors is so elaborate among them. . . . It is the religious counterpart of social order, hallowing it, investing it with a value that transcends mundane interests and providing for them the categories of thought and belief by means of which they direct and interpret their lives and actions."[39]

This is certainly true of most traditional African societies, almost universally so in West Africa except in the fully Islamized area. The religious implication of kinship is so fundamental that Achebe's persistent harping on it shows his grasp of the inner dynamics of the traditional system. He makes Okonkwo's distraught misapprehension of his eldest son's defection to the Christians assume "the prospect of annihilation":

> Suppose when he died all his male children decided to follow Nwoye's steps and abandon their ancestors? Okonkwo felt a cold shudder run through him at the terrible prospect, like the prospect of annihilation. He saw himself and his fathers crowding round their ancestral shrine waiting in vain for worship and sacrifice and finding nothing but ashes of bygone days, and his children the while praying to the white man's god.[40]

The relationship between father and sons was crucial to the traditional system because it is the foundation of the ancestral authority upon which the continuity of the institutions, common values, attitudes and sentiments of the traditional culture depended.

Traditional life in pre-colonial Africa subsisted on the collective solidarity of people who shared common customs and beliefs and an identical world view, were linked by blood or marriage ties and were, by the close-knit nature of their social relationships, deeply involved in one another's personal lives. We find that the value which sustains the society is collective responsibility, the responsibility of the group for the lives and well-being of the members. In both personal and social relationships, everything which disrupts the orderly life of individuals must be removed or set right. There is tremendous respect for customs and tradition. The group and its interests always take precedence over the individual and his self-interest. The individual values most admired are sociability, prowess, courage, integrity, piety and industry. Some allowances are made for temperament. Okonkwo's weaknesses are deplored but his greatness is recognized in spite of them. (His friend Obierika is much less temperamental, almost a foil to him, but not a greater man or more appreciated by the community.)

The first impact of change undermined collective solidarity and tradition and therefore the ideological matrix that held the pre-colonial traditional society together. The introduction of Christianity, for instance, alienated the converts from their traditional loyalty to the ancestors and with that went, for them at any rate, the strongest sanction for individual action, social attitudes and behaviour. The collective conscience was split and the community could no longer speak with one voice.

The early Christian converts neither appealed to clan solidarity nor responded to its appeal. As neophytes, they were obsessed with their own importance and contemptuous of all non-initiates. They called themselves "people of the Church" and the non-Christians "the people of nothing" or (when they felt more generous, as Achebe humorously observes) "the people of the world" (in Igbo, "ndi-nkiti" and "ndi-uwa").[41]

Achebe handles the conflict between traditionalists and the Christians with skill and fair-mindedness. He does not see it as a question of black versus white or of evil-minded foreigners subverting a perfect native way of life. That must have been a temptation in a time of militant nationalism, but it would also have been too simple, indeed unrealistic. He adopts the more difficult and complex but realistic procedure of probing his subject at the deep social and psychological levels, showing characters who are sincere in their convictions and who, because of their commitment to a creed or a way of life, cannot easily understand why things should be different from the way they want them to be. Over and

219

above the conflict of systems and values, there is also the more fundamental and more intractable conflict of personalities.

On the surface at least, no two religious systems can be more different
in their assumptions than Christianity and the traditional religion. For
example, Christianity with its insistence on the existence of only one God
is very different from the traditional religion with its multiplicity of gods.
The claim of Christianity to universality, especially to the belief (at least
in theory) that its one God is the father of all mankind, is again totally
different from the ethnocentricity of the gods who govern the lives of
traditional peoples. In recent years, Christian theologians and scholars
like Geoffrey Parrinder, B. O. Idown and Archbishop Arinze of Onitsha
have sought to establish common ground between the African religion
and Christianity, and the prevailing spirit of ecumenism is driving
Christians towards finding greater accommodation for African cultural
practices in their religious rites. But at the time to which *Things Fall
Apart* refers, the meeting of the two religious systems was a confrontation.

Conflict takes time to develop. The first contacts are no more than
skirmishes, to test the opponents' nerves and survey their intentions.
The traditionalists are sufficiently secure – perhaps too secure – in their
cultural life to feel unduly disturbed by the sudden appearance of a
small group of people preaching what must have seemed to them a mad
religion. Achebe handles the matter through verbal exchanges between
the local people and the missionaries:

> The arrival of the missionaries had caused considerable stir in the
> village of Mbanta. There were six of them and one was a white
> man. . . . Stories about these strange men had grown since one of
> them had been killed in Abame and his iron horse tied to the
> sacred silk-cotton tree. And so everybody came to see the white
> man. It was the time of the year when everybody was at home. The
> harvest was over.[42]

An audience being so easily made available, the white man and his
evangelists lose no time in opening their campaign:

> "We have been sent by [the] great God to ask you to leave your
> wicked ways and false gods and turn to Him so that you may be
> saved when you die."

The white man speaks and one of the evangelists interprets to the crowd.
The interpreter's dialect contains absurdities which cause much laughter
and comment among the people. Instead of saying "myself" in the local
dialect he always uses a word in his dialect which means "my buttocks"

in the local dialect. And so when the preacher breaks off, a wag in the audience tosses in a comic comment: "Your buttocks understand our language," while another asks the white man where he has left his own iron horse, in remembrance of that other unlucky white man whose iron horse was tied to a tree. Completely misunderstanding these frivolous sallies the white missionary gives an answer which for the first time rouses the people's suspicion and close attention. "Tell them," he said, "that I shall bring many iron horses when we have settled down among them. Some of them will even ride the iron horse themselves." The first part of his statement when interpreted to the audience gives rise to concern. The people had not imagined that the missionaries were intending to settle. For the missionaries to entertain and amuse the local people in the lax, holiday season in the village square is one thing, for them to want to live in the community is another, and this places a different complexion on the whole situation. The people thenceforth begin to question the newcomers more closely.

> At that point, an old man said he had a question. "Which is this god of yours," he asked, "the goddess of the earth, the god of the sky, Amadiora of the thunderbolt, or what?"
>
> The interpreter spoke to the white man and he immediately gave his answer. "All the gods you have named are not gods at all. They are gods of deceit who tell you to kill your fellows and destroy innocent children. There is only one true God and He has the earth, the sky, you and me and all of us."
>
> "If we leave our gods and follow your god," asked another man, "who will protect us from the anger of our neglected gods and ancestors?"
>
> "Your gods are not alive and cannot do you any harm," replied the white man. "They are pieces of wood and stone."
>
> When this was interpreted to the men of Mbanta they broke into derisive laughter. These men must be mad, they said to themselves. How else could they say that Ani and Amadiora were harmless? And Idemili and Ogwugwu too? And some of them began to go away.
>
> Then the missionaries burst into song. It was one of those gay and rollicking tunes of evangelism which had the power of plucking at silent and dusty chords in the heart of an Ibo man.[43]

From this brief passage, certain facts about this first encounter stand out. The traditionalists do not immediately recognize the extent of the threat posed to their religion and culture by the Christians. That explains why they treat the intruders with light-hearted buffoonery. The thought that there might be danger in these people who are also intending to settle brings a note of greater urgency and critical attention into the questions. But even then, there is no hysteria in the attitude of the traditionalists, and no note of exasperation in their voices. The traditional culture has reached that level of self-confidence and stability at which fear of subversion ceases to be an instinctive response. Moreover, it is usual under the traditional system for foreigners to be assimilated into the local population, as was the medicine man Anyika in *The Concubine*.[44] The crisis represented for the traditional community by the Christian strangers is the result of their appearing to be inassimilable: they no sooner come to a place than they begin actively to destroy the religious, and therefore ideological, foundation of society. In spite of the people's general tolerance, it is only a matter of time before serious conflicts develop. The people of Mbanta allow the missionaries to set up their shrine-house in the local evil forest, where it "stood on a circular clearing that looked like the open mouth of the Evil Forest".[45] The new religion makes little progress initially, but gradually begins to attract those who have not fared well under the traditional system – the caste slave, the mother of twins, and the possessor of a tender conscience who finds the traditional order too harsh. For such people, the new religion's profession of basic human equality, the universal fatherhood of God and the universal brotherhood of man, constitutes an awakening of submerged hopes, the resurrection of a sense of human worth long buried under the grave-mound of custom. One of those who recognize the new faith as a liberation is Nwoye, Okonkwo's eldest son, who has long suffered under his father's patriarchal harshness and has also been terrified by the severity of the traditional system. The appeal of the new faith is mainly emotional:

> It was not the mad logic of the Trinity that captivated him. He did not understand it. It was the poetry of the new religion, something felt in the marrow. The hymn about brothers who sat in darkness and in fear seemed to answer a vague and persistent question that haunted his young soul – the question of the twins crying in the bush and the question of Ikemefuna who was killed. He felt a relief within as the hymn poured into his parched soul. The words of the hymn were like the drops of frozen rain melting on the dry palate of the panting earth.[46]

But the promoters of the new faith evolve a still more effective strategy for drawing away followers from the traditionalists than this largely emotional and psychological appeal. Mr Brown, who set up the Umuofia mission, gradually recognizes the wisdom of combining material seduction with spiritual appeal, of combining straightforward proselytizing with provision of modern, literate education and such modern amenities as dispensaries. Various factors make this strategy a fruitful one. First, the basis of a local administration has already been established in Umuofia in which a number of semi-literate Africans are employed in supporting roles as court-messengers and interpreters; and these, because they can read and write and speak English, become a reference group for the missionaries when they wish to point out the blessings of a literary education. Indeed the astute Mr Brown does exactly that. "If Umuofia failed to send her children to the school," he argues, "strangers would come from other places to rule them. They could already see that happening in the Native Court, where the D.C. was surrounded by strangers who spoke his tongue. Most of these strangers came from the distant town of Umuru on the bank of the Great River where the white man first went."[47] This is a telling argument, though Umuofia's suspicion of the new faith and its material promises does not altogether vanish. By way of compromise, they send their slaves and indolent children, their expendable hands, to the mission school.

The co-penetration of Igboland by the British administration and Christian missionaries is a historical fact now documented in J. F. Ajayi's *Christian Missions in Nigeria, 1841–1891*, J. F. Ekechi's *Missionary Enterprise and Rivalry in Igboland, 1857–1914* and E. Ayandele's *The Missionary Impact on Modern Nigeria, 1842–1919*. The missionaries, trading companies and British administration did first set up a base in Onitsha; that town did supply the first African staff to be used by the missions, the trading companies and the British administration in the penetration of Igboland, east of the River Niger. So Achebe is thus historically correct when he sees the forces operating against the traditional system as tripartite: the Christian missions, the British administration and the introduction of European-type trading stores combined to overthrow the traditional way of life. "The new religion and government and the trading stores were very much in the people's eyes and minds."[48]

In *Things Fall Apart*, these radical changes are shown to have made serious inroads during the years of Okonkwo's exile. The report is as usual taken to him by his friend Obierika: "They [the missionaries] had built their church there, won a handful of converts and were already sending evangelists to the surrounding towns and villages. That was a source of great sorrow to the leaders of the clan; but many of them believed that the strange faith and the white man's god would not last. None of his converts was a man whose word was heeded in the assembly of the people. None of them was a man of title. They were mostly the kind of people that were called *efulefu*, worthless, empty men."[49] It is conceivable that the change might have gone on without serious confrontation, with the elders and leaders gradually accommodating to it in the spirit of stoicism in which they have always accommodated unforeseen disasters. But the presence of fanatics and zealots on both sides meant that the danger of somebody stirring things up could not be eliminated.

In the final drama the positions held by the various protagonists are clearly defined. On the side of the traditionalists, there are both hawks and doves. Okonkwo is the leader of the hawks, the militants who want the missionaries ejected, if necessary by force. The doves, who include Obierika, counsel caution, pointing out that the opportunity for drastic action has passed, since a fair number of clansmen have already thrown in their lot with the enemy. To attempt to eject the Christians would not only bring down repressive force from the administration but would cause a civil war. One of the most memorable passages in the whole book is that in which Obierika explains to Okonkwo why Umuofia can no longer make war on the new forces that are choking to death the old society that he loved. When Okonkwo says to his friend, "We must fight these men and drive them from the land," Obierika replies sadly:

> "It is already too late. . . . Our own men and our sons have joined the ranks of the stranger. They have joined his religion and they help to uphold his government. If we should try to drive out the white men in Umuofia we should find it easy. There are only two of them. But what of our own people who are following their way and have been given power? They would go to Umuru and bring the soldiers, and we would be like Abame. . . . How do you think we can fight when our own brothers have turned against us? The white man is very clever. He came quietly and peaceably with his religion. We were amused at his foolishness and allowed him to stay. Now he has won our brothers, and our clan can no longer act like one. He has put a knife on the things that held us together and we have fallen apart."[50]

Okonkwo's opposition to the missionaries is entirely in character. He is a warrior, a man of action rather than of thought, an impetuous man, impatient of failure and contemptuous of diplomatic restraint. But even stronger than his character and temperamental drives is the instinctive but well-founded fear that the new system will turn the world upside down and hurt the entire people whose lives are rooted in the traditional culture. He had already seen in his days of exile in Mbanta the abomination that came in the wake of the new religion when an overzealous convert killed and ate a sacred python. He had also seen his eldest son turn

224

renegade and join the Christians, a situation which threatens the ontological order of his tradition-oriented world. He has no doubt that the
new forces must be rooted out or they will destroy the structure of traditional life. The other elders of the community also recognize the threat,
but with greater discretion and power of analysis they are prepared to co-
operate with what they cannot avoid, or, at least, to play for time and
hope that the new forces will work themselves out and then disappear.

But this is not to be. On the Christian side, there are also fanatics and
hawks whose impetuosity soon leads to head-on collision with the traditionalists. Paradoxically, many of the die-hards are the people who until
recently were hardly regarded as effective human beings by their traditionalist neighbours. Having suddenly recovered their human dignity,
their first act of human will is to take revenge, with a remorseless
determination to tear down the system that had oppressed them in the
past. Their militant anti-traditionalism is perfectly understandable, though
the ethical basis of their action is entirely at odds with the new faith they
have just embraced. The new converts are singularly lacking in charity.

Under the wise restraining influence of Mr Brown, the Christian
fanatics are kept in check. Mr Brown opens a dialogue with the
traditionalists, learning as much from them as he is eager to teach them,
creating mutual respect which in turn creates goodwill and confidence.
Mr Brown's removal by illness brings on the final crisis. His successor,
the Reverend James Smith, is the kind of man who exasperates existing
difficulties; he is intolerant, dogmatic and tactless. His style is wryly
described in a memorable passage which sets the scene for the final
disaster:

> He condemned openly Mr. Brown's policy of compromise and
> accommodation. He saw things as black and white. And black was
> evil. He saw the world as a battlefield in which the children of
> light were locked in mortal conflict with the sons of darkness. He
> spoke in his sermons about sheep and goats and about wheat and
> tares. He believed in slaying the prophets of Baal.[51]

Mr Smith is exactly the wrong kind of man for this delicate and difficult time, a time needing tact, good sense, patience and sensitivity to the
feelings and susceptibilities of the members of a society mortally
wounded and in terrible agony. A hawk leading other hawks, a fanatic
at the head of fanatics, the Reverend Mr Smith's truculence and dog-
matism embolden his followers to provoke the traditionalists beyond
endurance. Enoch, the irrepressible, pint-sized die-hard, who was reputed to have killed and eaten a sacred, totemic python even during the
time of Mr Brown, now goes a step further, and unmasks an ancestral

225

spirit. This is the very limit of provocation because it strikes at the heart of traditional authority, ritual and religion. The traditionalists react immediately and with the usual assurance, the kind of assurance which has been fast seeping away under the pressures of the British administrative presence.

> That night the Mother of the Spirits walked the length and breadth of the clan, weeping for her murdered son. It was a terrible night. Not even the oldest man in Umuofia had ever heard such a strange and fearful sound, and it was never to be heard again. It seemed as if the very soul of the tribe wept for a great evil that was coming – its own death.[52]

The spirits assemble and move "like a furious whirlwind to Enoch's compound and with matchet and fire [reduce] it to a desolate heap".[53] Then they move against the church compound. In front of the compound, they come face to face with the pastor and his interpreter. What happens here is important. The concourse of ancestral spirits is still borne on the high wave of justified anger and would have knocked down both the missionaries and their church. But the voice of traditional authority intervenes, restores order and turns what would have been a chaotic act of vengeance into a judicial decision. Ajofia (Evil Forest) the spokesman of the nine executive ancestors of Umuofia, having restored peace among "the agitated spirits" addresses the white missionary:

> "The body of the white man, I salute you," he said, using the language in which immortals spoke to men.
> "The body of the white man, do you know me?" he asked.
> Mr. Smith looked at his interpreter, but Okeke, who was a native of distant Umuru, was also at a loss.
> Ajofia laughed in his guttural voice. It was like the laugh of rusty metal. "They are strangers," he said, "and they are ignorant. But let that pass." He turned round to his comrades and saluted them, calling them the fathers of Umuofia. He dug his rattling spear into the ground and it shook with metallic life. Then he turned once more to the missionary and his interpreter.
> "Tell the white man that we will not do him any harm," he said to the interpreter. "Tell him to go back to his house and leave us alone. We liked his brother who was with us before. He was foolish, but we liked him, and for his sake we shall not harm his brother. But this shrine which he built must be destroyed. We shall no longer allow it in our midst. It has bred untold abominations and we have come to put an end to it." He turned to his comrades.

"Fathers of Umuofia, I salute you"; and they replied with one guttural voice. He turned again to the missionary. "You can stay with us if you like our ways. You can worship your own god. It is good that a man should worship the gods and the spirits of his fathers. Go back to your house so that you may not be hurt. Our anger is great but we have held it down so that we can talk to you.[54]

The church building is levelled, a symbolic act which to the traditionalists means an end to the evil that has threatened the community. But the matter does not end there. The District Commissioner lures the elders of Umuofia into the court-house for a parley, surprises them and has them handcuffed and put in guardrooms until a collective fine of 250 bags of cowries has been paid. Then he makes them a pretty speech on the blessings of British imperial rule. "We shall not do you any harm," he begins, "if only you agree to co-operate with us. We have brought a peaceful administration to you and your people so that you may be happy. If any man ill-treats you we shall come to your rescue. But we will not allow you to ill-treat others. We have a court of law where we judge cases and administer justice just as it is done in my own country under a great queen."[55]

The coda to the tragic episode is supplied by Okonkwo's single-handed defiance of British authority, followed by his despair and suicide. At the meeting called to decide how to contain the imperialist threat in the clan, Okonkwo is at last hopeful that the time for action has arrived, the time to take up arms and expel the evil threatening the traditional order. How wrong he is is soon brought home to him when the court-messengers arrive to break up the assembly. He draws his knife and cuts off the head of the chief court-messenger. The incident is poignantly dramatic.

In that brief moment the world seemed to stand still, waiting. There was utter silence. The men of Umuofia were merged into the mute backcloth of trees and giant creepers, waiting.

The spell was broken by the head messenger. "Let me pass!" he ordered.

"What do you want here?"

"The white man whose power you know too well has ordered this meeting to stop."

In a flash Okonkwo drew his matchet. The messenger crouched to avoid the blow. It was useless. Okonkwo's matchet descended twice and the man's head lay beside his uniformed body.

The waiting backcloth jumped into tumultuous life and the

> meeting was stopped. Okonkwo stood looking at the dead man. He knew that Umuofia would not go to war. He knew because they had let the other messengers escape. They had broken into tumult instead of action. He discerned fright in that tumult. He heard voices asking: "Why did he do it?"
>
> He wiped his matchet on the sand and went away.[56]

Okonkwo recognizes the defeat of the traditional system which he is committed to. With its overthrow, he cannot envisage any other kind of life, and so he goes to the back of his house and hangs himself.

Achebe's use of religion as the central focus of his exploration of the theme of culture-contact and change shows that Umuofia belongs to the type of society designated "sacred" by social scientists. According to Howard Becker, "sacred" societies are those "which impress upon their members modes of conduct making for a high degree of resistance to change".[57] Religion and ritual provide the resistant matrix which holds together the elements of social action in such a society, defining at the same time its limits of permitted change.

There was scope for change in traditional society, but it had to be in areas outside those made sacrosanct by the religious and ritual order. In *Arrow of God*, for example, there are references to such marginal changes. Ezeulu is proud that his grandfather abolished the painful custom which made any child born to a widow a slave.[58] Nwaka of Umunneora points out that the people of Aninta even burnt their deity when he failed them.[59] But none of these changes affects the core of the belief-system and the values of the people. To burn a deity who has failed is not to repudiate belief in the gods. The deity is replaced by another who promises satisfaction; in the same way, an Igbo man can discard an Ikenga which has brought him consistent ill-fortune, and fashion himself a new one. The founding of Ulu as a god of security and solidarity for the whole Umuaro people is a master-stroke of innovative expediency within the general limits of cultural prescription; far from altering the structure of cultural experience, it reinforces it.

Christianity, on the other hand, confronted the traditional people with a radical alternative. It was a blow at the heart of the traditional system – the religious order which sanctioned and protected its ideological assumptions. By concentrating on this part of traditional life, Achebe reveals his grasp of the dynamics of social and cultural change. After the earliest stages of contact and change, economic, social and other factors become dominant, but, initially, the attack of the Christians on the traditional religion opened the flood-gates to the overwhelming changes that were to follow.

The impact of the new religion was devastating, for it affected the most fundamental and therefore most cohesive factors in the traditional system. When, in *Things Fall Apart*, the catechist, Kiaga, welcoming Nwoye to the church, says, quoting the Bible, "Blessed is he who forsakes his father and mother for my sake," he is pronouncing the doom of filial piety, the cornerstone of the stability and ordered continuity of the traditional way of life.

Even more significantly, the traditional social framework became inadequate to regulate the conflicts and stresses which arose from the culture-contact. Traditional customary laws became ineffective, not only because their religious basis was undermined by Christianity but because the colonial administration monopolized the use of coercion, and so weakened the capacity of traditional societies to exact conformity from their eccentric members, or to settle inter-communal strife by the threat of action or by action itself. We find the local British administration intervening decisively to terminate the feud between Umuaro and Okperi in *Arrow of God*. The sacking of the village-group of Abame as a reprisal for the murder of the white man "riding an iron horse" is a terrible demonstration of the power of the new administration and a lesson to the adjoining villages that neither political nor judicial initiative any longer rests with them. The conflicts between converts and traditionalists in *Things Fall Apart* show that the ultimate judicial sanction lies with the new administration, for the clan is not allowed to defend itself against the misguidedly zealous onslaughts of Christian converts. Yet two of the most heinous crimes committed by the converts, the killing of the sacred python ("the emanation of the god of water" and a tutelary deity of the clan) and the unmasking of an ancestral spirit (a central influence in judicial execution, as we have seen) strike at the heart of the traditional system, its religion and the ancestors, and would have called forth the fullest rigour of communal repression in pre-colonial days. Now, however, a salutary gesture of protest like the burning down of the local mission-house provokes the intervention of the local British administration on behalf of the culprits.

In *Things Fall Apart*, insensible of the tragedy unfolding before his eyes, the white administrator blissfully goes about his business of spreading Pax Britannica with the sense of duty and detachment to be expected of one whose disciplined unemotionalism had more likely than not been nurtured in a British public school and Oxbridge. It would be unreasonable to expect him to be sentimentally concerned with the lives of the local people or the death throes of their cherished way of life, which he sees from the outside, and as a curiosity. The drama of pacification which from the point of view of the Africans is a matter of profound social and personal anguish, is from his point of view comic, and with the lightness with which we apprehend comedy he, as an amateur anthropologist and "student of primitive customs" blithely records Okonkwo's tragedy as another episode in his projected book, *The Pacification of the Primitive Tribes of the Lower Niger.*[60]

It is possible to argue that Achebe is not entirely fair to his commissioner, but he can hardly be expected to do full justice to a character whose function is merely catalytic. On the few occasions when he appears, occasions which are decisive in the development of the story, his words and actions are almost unimpeachable, and his lecture to the arrested elders of Umuofia about the blessings of the British peace, if a little complacent, is not unworthy of one who finds himself in the capacity of a colonial father. It must have struck him as a quixotic folly for a handful of villagers to attempt to stay the tide of imperial expansion sweeping across the continent.

In *Arrow of God* Achebe attempts to enter more deeply into the administrative officers so as to see things from their point of view. This is a bold thing to do; a less gifted novelist could have created mere cardboard Europeans with stock attitudes and responses. His administrative officers are intensely real. His handling of the relationship between Captain Winterbottom and Mr Clarke, between the experienced but disgruntled administrator obsessed with his sense of personal merit and knowledge of local life and the zealous "new boy" who irritates his superior by his over-enthusiasm, is done with gentle humour and irony. The European characters are not however explored in any great detail. The novels are not about them, except in so far as they are one of the forces operating on the traditional culture and on Africans, as agents of change, in which role their ignorance of local customs becomes a functional part of the development of plot.

Malinowski explained why the colonial administrator, in spite of his good intentions, cannot really enter fully into traditional life or understand its workings. He writes:

> The average British official tries to administer justice and to be a father of his wards. But is he from his point of view an integral part of the tribe? No. He was neither born nor bred to it, nor is he very conversant with any of its ideas; he is, in fact, a servant of the British Empire, temporarily working in such and such a colony, a public schoolboy, an Englishman, or a Scotsman. He has to safeguard the interest of the empire first and foremost. He has to watch over European interests in the colony, as well as to maintain the balance of these interests as against native claims. To con-

ceive of the part played by European political agents in Africa in terms of a fictitious well-integrated community would blind us to the very definition of the tasks, nature, and implications of colonial administration.[61]

Achebe assumes this ignorance in his British administrators. Their physical and social distance from the local people is considerable. Winterbottom's official residence in Okperi, for instance, is called "Government Hill" and is set up far away from where "the natives" live. One of the most stringent colonial taboos is that which forbids serving officers "undue familiarity" with colonial subjects. In *Arrow of God*, Captain Winterbottom, who conceives it as part of his duty to keep the administrative staff in line (like "a school prefect"), takes steps to stop one of his men from socializing with the local people and thus lowering himself "in the eyes of the natives".[62] The degree of his detachment from the lives of his subjects is shown by the fact that the paroxysms that shake one of his nearby districts make no impression whatever. Achebe tells us that "He did not ever hear of Ezeulu again. The only man who might have carried the story to Government Hill was John Nwodika, his steward. But John had since left Winterbottom's service to set up a small trade in tobacco."[63] Of course, some sources are still open in spite of the official distance, but most of them are not reliable. For instance, the D.C. as magistrate can learn something from such incidents as Okonkwo's murder of the court-messenger and subsequent suicide. George Allen, the British Commissioner, promises to use this "knowledge" in his projected book on Nigeria. He could use information from local people working in Government House – clerks, interpreters, court-messengers, cooks and stewards – but this source may be misleading since some of these people may be alienated from the culture and likely to distort it, or they may not be local people at all, in which case they may be as ignorant of the local customs as the D.C. Some colonial administrators did manage to surmount the difficulties and crash the barriers, but for every one who succeeded, there were scores who could not. The administrators represented in *Things Fall Apart* and *Arrow of God* are, in this respect, conventional types. They maintain their imperial distance and see their "natives" from a proper official distance. It is no wonder that when George Allen, the D.C. of *Things Fall Apart*, produces his promised book, *The Pacification of the Primitive Tribes of the Lower Niger*, it is full of Kiplingesque rhapsodies about "those in search of a strenuous life . . . who can deal with men as others deal with material, who can grasp great situations, coax events, shape destinies . . . ride on the crest of the wave of time . . . [and] lead the backward races into line".[64] It is not surprising that Captain Winterbottom's understanding of local life is a mixture of stereotyped colonial prejudices and ethnographic fallacies, such as that the "*ikenga* is the most important fetish in the Ibo man's arsenal, so to speak", that "One thing you must remember in dealing with natives is that like children they are great liars" and that "the Ibos in the distant past assimilated a small non-negroid tribe of the same complexion as the Red Indians".[65] Achebe does not set out to damage the administrative officers particularly, except by poking fun at their ignorance which is only matched by their conceit. He does not portray them as evil-intentioned or bloody-minded, but as earnest, conscientious, ignorant officials whose very innocence brings unintentional suffering and tragedy to their traditional subjects.

By standing above the traditional institutions, and especially by setting up a court (where he judges cases "in ignorance") and so being the ultimate authority in the determination and punishment of evil-doing assessed largely by European common law, the District Commissioner becomes the innocent instrument of the disintegration of the traditional social order. By appointing non-traditional officials such as the irresponsible and corrupt court-messengers (the ashy-buttocks), and unrepresentative and pompous little tyrants like His Highness Obi Ikedi the First of Okperi, he unwittingly exacerbates the pains of transition from the traditional to the modern order. In the end, social change operates through individuals and if these are evilly disposed or crassly stupid, then the suffering involved in fundamental social and culture change is greatly increased. Okonkwo's tragic end, for instance, is certainly hastened by the provocations of the court-messengers.

So culture change, in its earliest form as described by Achebe in *Things Fall Apart*, involves the decay of collective tradition caused by the arrival of "hostile" strangers within the relatively homogeneous local community, strangers who like Tutuola's heroes are not assimilable into the local population and who (unlike the heroes of Tutuola's tales) disseminate foreign ideas, introduce foreign laws which they are able to enforce, and propagate a new religion which is agressively evangelistic and subverts the traditional religion. The beginnings of commerce, also introduced by strangers, have appeared but this is of less immediate consequence as a fact of cultural change. (After all, a man might change his hat and still retain his beliefs and his manners.) The new religion, by providing a set of moral values alternative to those offered by traditional religion, and a solidarity alternative to the solidarity of the clan, undermines traditional social life. The new administration, having at its disposal the military strength to enforce its will, deprives the traditional community of the power and the will to defend its interests. The result is the breakdown of social homogeneity and the collective outlook, which are the two distinguishing features of life in Umuofia before the new cultural forces began to attack it.

By tracing the course of this breakdown with such attention to detail, and especially by giving the reader a deep psychological insight into the characters involved directly in the drama of change, Achebe's *Things Fall Apart* has become a classic. Its importance will increase the further we move away in time from pre-colonial Africa.

The forces working against tradition seem already entrenched in the Umuaro of *Arrow of God*. The local school and mission station, irreverent strangers like the catechist Goodcountry, and the inarticulate though palpable reality of the white man's administrative presence, all these have undermined traditional confidence and shaken the sense of common purpose and solidarity which in the past constituted the spirit of traditionalism. The natives of Umuaro bear witness to these changes in matter-of-fact remarks which show that they are realistic enough to recognize that these things are there to stay. A character, for example, sees Mr Wright's new road connecting Umuaro to the administrative town of Okperi as a part of the new forces that are transforming the old society. "Yes, we are talking about the white man's road," he reminds his audience. "But when the roof and walls of a house fall in, the ceiling is not left standing. The white man, the new religion, the soldiers, the new road – they are all part of the same thing. The white man has a gun, a matchet, a bow and carries fire in his mouth. He does not fight with one weapon alone."[66] The theme of contact and change is not carried by such overt statements but rather by the human drama, in which those deeply entrenched in the past attempt to adapt to the present.

The conflicts in *Arrow of God* develop around the person of the Chief Priest of Ulu, who is the ritual and religious leader of Umuaro. On the one hand, there is the conflict between the local British administration represented by the old-fashioned administrator, Winterbottom, and the native authority represented by the Chief Priest. On the other hand, there are the internal politics of Umuaro and the conflict between the supporters of the Chief Priest and those of his rival, Idemili. On yet another level belongs the conflict taking place within the Chief Priest himself, a conflict between personal power, the temptation to constitute himself into an "arrow" of God, and the exigencies of public responsibility. All these are handled in the main plot. A subsidiary plot deals with the domestic tensions and crises in Ezeulu's own house, the tensions and stresses between the father and his grown-up sons and between the children of different mothers in his polygamous household.

Not all these conflicts are a result of culture-contact. Personality

233

deficiencies and mistaken judgements have something to do with some of them. The intervention of fate and chance also plays a part. But the contact situation exacerbates the conflicts and radicalizes the incipient oppositions and contradictions within the native tradition. Where this shows most emphatically is in the breakdown of the sense of solidarity among the traditionalists. Ezeulu, the Chief Priest and a man whose role marks him out as keeper of collective security, is the person who feels most keenly this breakdown, and he never tires of attributing the change, deprecatingly, to "the new age". At a critical stage in the narrative, after he has seen his advice set aside by the community, not once but twice in quick succession, Ezeulu reviews the situation, using the opportunity to reiterate the historical and ritual charter of his role as first among the leaders of the clan:

> In the very distant past, when lizards were still few and far between, the six villages – Umuachala, Umunneora, Umuagu, Umuezeani, Umuogwugwu and Umuisiuzo – lived as different people, and each worshipped its own deity. Then the hired soldiers of Abam used to strike in the dead of night, set fire to houses and carry men, women and children into slavery. Things were so bad for the six villages that their leaders came together to save themselves. They hired a strong team of medicine-men to install a common deity for them. This deity which the fathers of the six villages made was called Ulu. Half of the medicine was buried at a place which became the Nkwo market and the other half thrown into the stream which became Mili Ulu. The six villages then took the name of Umuaro, and the priest of Ulu became their Chief Priest. From that day they were never again beaten by an enemy.[67]

But all that seems to have suddenly changed. When the story opens, the authority of the Chief Priest is under active attack from the Priest of Idemili who uses his kinsman, the wealthy, volatile and demagogic titled elder Nwaka of Umunneora. Idemili is one of the old gods relegated to subordinate status by the coming of Ulu. Its priest had never altogether forgotten this setback and had been in latent opposition to the priest of Ulu from time immemorial. Ezeulu himself is aware of this: "He knew that the priests of Idemili and Ogwugwu and Eru and Udo had never been happy with their secondary role since the villages got together and made Ulu and put him over the older deities."[68] But the resentment was played down as long as the threat to collective security continued, since group solidarity is necessary to meet external threat and since only a deity evolved in the spirit of collective solidarity could be an adequate unifying symbol to ensure this solidarity. The presence of the colonial administration has the effect of increasing the need for collective security, since the colonial authority has taken away from the traditional authority and peoples their right to exercise judicial or even non-legal violence. The exercise of judicial coercion and violence belongs solely to the colonial regime from now onwards, as the people of Umuaro are to learn when they wage war on the people of Okperi. But the worst forms of local insecurity such as those caused by the Abam slave-raiders are certainly over. It is not surprising that institutions evolved to ensure collective security begin to weaken when the threats which gave rise to them are no longer felt. And the effect of the superimposition of a higher authority with a greater power of coercive violence is to create a ferment in the structure of traditional authority itself. Specifically, the older gods of Umuaro accepted the dominance of Ulu as long as the old power structure remained. But now, with the imposition of a higher authority over Ulu, the minor gods see the situation as an opportunity to shake off an irksome hegemony. The resentment that lay dormant in pre-colonial days becomes active again. The speech in which Nwaka repudiates the right of Ulu to lead the clan expresses all this. The speech is made at a secret rally attended only by Nwaka's partisans:

> Nwaka began by telling the assembly that Umuaro must not allow itself to be led by the Chief Priest of Ulu. "My father did not tell me that before Umuaro went to war it took leave from the priest of Ulu," he said. "The man who carries a deity is not a king. He is there to perform its ritual and to carry sacrifice to it. But I have been watching this Ezeulu for many years. He is a man of ambition; he wants to be king, priest, diviner, all. His father, they said, was like that. But Umuaro showed him that Igbo people knew no kings.
>
> "We have no quarrel with Ulu. He is still our protector, even though we no longer fear Abam warriors at night. But I will not see with these eyes of mine his priest making himself lord over us. My father told me many things, but he did not tell me that Ezeulu was king in Umuaro. Who is he, anyway? Does anybody here enter his compound through the man's gate? If Umuaro decided to have a king we know where he would come from. Since when did Umuachala become head of the six villages? We all know that it was jealousy among the big villages that made them give the priesthood to the weakest. We shall fight for our farmland and for the contempt Okperi has poured on us. Let us not listen to anyone trying to frighten us with the name of Ulu. If a man says yes his *chi* also says yes. And we have all heard how the people of

> Aninta dealt with their deity when he failed them. Did they not carry him to the boundary between them and their neighbours and set fire on him?"[69]

This is a piece of dangerous demagogy, to be treated with reserve. For instance, it is difficult to credit the view that the Chief Priest whose deity leads the people to war and protects them from external and internal insecurities did not have a strong voice in determining war policy. After all, if he refused to perfom the ritual functions of his priesthood, it is hard to see how his deity could be involved in action at all. The incitement against the authority of the Chief Priest is possible because the threat that made the founding of Ulu necessary has receded. Nwaka says as much. But traditional people are not so foolish as to base their institutions so narrowly. Indeed Ulu's power is not tied only to the provision of security. He is also the guardian of social well-being and keeper of the calendar. His priest keeps the agricultural calendar and calls the biggest feast of the year, the Feast of the New Yam which ushers in the harvest season. So his protection of security is not only religious, political, military and ethical, but also economic, and extends to such things as keeping the communal census. Nwaka's uncompromising attack is therefore a serious schismatic move indicative of the falling apart of the old collective ideology. His charge of ambition is exaggerated, though there is no doubt that Ezeulu's conception of his power is exorbitant. A peacetime Chief Priest has less scope for extending his power. Ezeulu is unaware of the limitation of his power and of the precise nature of his priesthood as the expression of corporate rather than personal will. This is shown in his own soliloquy:

> Whenever Ezeulu considered the immensity of his power over the year and the crops and, therefore, over the people he wondered if it was real. It was true he named the day for the feast of the Pumpkin Leaves and for the New Yam feast; but he did not choose the day. He was merely a watchman. His power was no more than the power of a child over a goat that was said to be his. As long as the goat was alive it was his; he would find it food and take care of it. But the day it was slaughtered he would know who the real owner was. No! the Chief Priest of Ulu was more than that, must be more than that. If he should refuse to name the day there would be no festival – no planting and no reaping. But could he refuse? No Chief Priest had ever refused. So it could not be done. He would not dare.
>
> Ezeulu was stung to anger by this as though his enemy had spoken it.

236

"Take away that word dare," he replied to this enemy. "Yes I say take it away. No man in all Umuaro can stand up and say that I dare not. The woman who will bear the man who will say it has not yet been born."[70]

This is a dangerous speculation – as dangerous as Nwaka's demagogic incitement. Even though until he refuses to call the feast of the New Yam the Chief Priest acts within his ritual rights and authority, in his mind he has already begun to assume for himself vast illegal powers that justify Nwaka's accusation. His thought is to prove father to his subsequent act. Though no overt act of his justifies the accusation of ambition, he has within him undoubted authoritarian urges at odds with the republican outlook of the people. So Nwaka's accusation cannot be dismissed out of hand, but is borne in mind, and lights up the subsequent action. The authoritarian streak in the Chief Priest contributes to the final crisis when a greater flexibility and devotion to the common weal would have eased the situation. Nwaka's appeal to republican sentiment is an astute move, calculated to carry weight with an egalitarian people, as the people of Umuaro appear to be. But this egalitarianism is itself overplayed. "That Igbo people knew no kings" is only true as a figure of speech; some Igbo communities do have kings, and certainly they recognize certain specific roles which are defined in the social structure[71] and they also recognize personal achievement. In addition, there are prescribed roles pertaining to those successful members of different families who have taken titles (ozọ and nidichie in the area of Igboland in which *Things Fall Apart* and *Arrow of God* are set) and who perform ritual functions in their family segments and have political and judicial roles in the clan. An elder who fails to take a title, like Unoka in *Things Fall Apart*, is an unfulfilled elder. It is fair to say that personal achievement is recognized in Igbo society within the framework of a hierarchy of titles, and a certain degree of ascription also obtains, since the process of title investiture takes place through elaborate ritual ceremonies which vest title-holders with semi-sacred attributes. Nwaka is aware of the mobile nature of the society, as well as its hierarchical features, but he chooses to emphasize the one and to ignore the other.

Nwaka and Ezeulu as types of character and temperament have always been a part of the traditional society. Since they differ so widely, they always repel each other and become a focus of inter-communal rivalry, factiousness and disagreement. But where the overall security of the community is paramount, personal rivalries and temperamental oppositions would not be allowed to undermine collective security. Nwaka would not be able openly to challenge the leadership of the Chief Priest in a matter of security in which his deity has a dominant influence. One finds confirming evidence for this in *Things Fall Apart* where we are told that Umuofia "never went to war unless its case was clear and just and was accepted as such by its Oracle – the Oracle of the Hills and the Caves. And there were indeed occasions when the Oracle had forbidden Umuofia to wage a war."[72] The oracle is the interpreter of the will of the earth goddess, the deity in charge of security. In *Arrow of God*, the god of security is Ulu, and his will is interpreted by the Chief Priest, who is thus in the position of the Oracle of the Hills and the Caves. The open attack on Ezeulu's authority, which would have been unthinkable in Okonkwo's Umuofia, becomes possible in Umuaro because under the combined pressure of the new colonial administration, the Christian church and the new economic forces, the oracles and the priests are beginning to lose their hold on the people. Nwaka's subversion of the Chief Priest's power succeeds because of the encroaching changes which are working towards a realignment of relationships and a readjustment of attitudes.

Ulu's dominance in the structure of traditional power is itself a result of social change. It represents a certain centralizing trend somewhat at odds with the federalizing, segmentary political relationships of earlier times. The centralization has not been consolidated or it would have led to a priest-kingship such as that of Umunri in Igboland and probably like the obaship among the Yoruba. This lack of consolidation is exploited by Ezidemili. He is always harking back to the golden age of the people's history "in the days before Ulu" when "the true leaders of each village had been men of high title like Nwaka".[73] This near-enactment of the Cassius–Brutus–Caesar syndrome is interesting because it supports the point that a feeling of greater security is behind the attack on Ulu's authority; the "security" role of Ulu is completely left out of Ezidemili's tirade. His conspiracy could only work at a time of increased security. The presence of the colonial administration and the end of the trans-Atlantic slave trade explain this feeling. But it should not be forgotten that the colonial presence generated its own insecurities, since the "pacification" involved the use of force. But the new threat to security differs from the sudden, unpredictable predations of marauding slave raiders.

Achebe here departs from the narrative strategy of *Things Fall Apart*. In *Arrow of God*, he starts the narrative in medias res, dipping back from time to time into the past for the historical material with which he impregnates the narrative present. From these brief but significant flashes back into the past, we build up a picture of the pre-colonial society with which the colonial present is contrasted.

His treatment is full of ironies. For example, the Chief Priest who, as a symbolic head, should be the rallying point of resistance to the colonial authority is unwittingly an instrument for subversion of the traditional system. At Winterbottom's prompting, he sends his young son Oduche to join the Christian sect and attend the village school. Oduche is to become Ezeulu's "eye" in the new situation. His reason is perfectly rational: one must change with the changing times. Several times this pragmatism finds outlet in a recurrent proverb: "A man must dance the dance prevalent in his time" and more poignantly in the extended metaphor of the elusive bird. "I am like the bird Eneke-nti-ọba," he asserts. "When his friends asked him why he was always on the wing he replied: 'Men of today have learnt to shoot without missing and so I have learnt to fly without perching.' "[74] In other words, the Chief Priest sees the strength of the new forces and is attempting in his own way to come to terms with them. With Oduche as a look-out in the enemy camp and himself in full control of the situation in the traditionalists' camp, the Chief Priest feels more secure. The rest of the story shows how this feeling proves illusory and the Chief Priest is smashed by the forces he had imagined to be under his control.

Oduche, the sacrificial offering to the new forces, precipitates the first of Ezeulu's crises. He becomes a Christian diehard, tries to suffocate a royal python, the totemic animal sacred to Idemili, and is found out. This heightens the ill-will between the priest of Idemili and Ezeulu, their families, villages and partisans in the clan. Ezeulu's enemies cite the incident as proof of his ambition to destroy every other source of authority in the clan in order to promote his own. It is argued also that his sending his son to school is part of his strategy for reinforcing his personal power by ingratiating himself with the British administration. Earlier, the good opinion of the white District Commissioner, won by testifying against the clan in the land dispute with Okperi, had been chalked up by his enemies as Ezeulu's first open act of betrayal, and proof of his ambition. His son's sacrilege five years later revives the memory and bitterness of that betrayal. Taken together, the two events look like an attempt by the Chief Priest to reach a personal accommodation with the forces threatening the old social order. And this renders his motives suspicious and dishonourable to his enemies and disturbing to his friends. Even his best friend and kinsman, Akuebue, finds it hard to reconcile the Chief Priest's traditional role as protector of communal tradition with his implied attack on this heritage by sending his son to join the Christians. He expresses his doubts:

"When you spoke against the war with Okperi you were not alone. I too was against it and so were many others. But if you send your son to join strangers in desecrating the land you will be alone. You may go and mark it on that wall to remind you that I said so."[75]

But the shattering blow is yet to fall. Captain Winterbottom, having received a directive to introduce Indirect Rule in his area of authority, decides to make Ezeulu a warrant chief for the Umuaro district. But the choice could not have been made at a less auspicious time than when the Chief Priest is taunted by his enemies as the creature of the British administration. Ezeulu at first refuses to leave his home immediately to go to Okperi as ordered by the white man. Instead, he summons an assembly of the leaders for advice and support. Nwaka and his partisans see this as an opportunity to accuse the Chief Priest openly of his deals with the white man. Nwaka makes a long speech full of taunts and innuendoes implying that Ezeulu should be cast out to face the music alone. His gibes are skilfully reinforced with his usual rhetoric and proverbs:

> "The white man is Ezeulu's friend and has sent for him. What is so strange about that? He did not send for me. He did not send for Udeozo; he did not send for the priest of Idemili; he did not send for the priest of Eru; he did not send for the priest of Udo nor did he ask the priest of Ogwugwu to come and see him. He has asked Ezeulu. Why? Because they are friends. Or does Ezeulu think that their friendship should stop short of entering each other's houses? Does he want the white man to be his friend only by word of mouth? Did not our elders tell us that as soon as we shake hands with a leper he will want an embrace? It seems to me that Ezeulu has shaken hands with a man of white body."[76]

The pun on "white man" and "leper" is Nwaka's indirect indictment of the Chief Priest and is calculated to wound most deeply. Ezeulu abandons the effort to mobilize support within his clan and sallies out to face his fate single-handed. His isolation is complete at a time when collective solidarity is a man's greatest strength. Totally embittered, he is in an uncompromising mood which is made no better by his being detained for not answering the summons promptly enough. Tony Clarke has taken over from Winterbottom, who has been suddenly taken ill, and finds the priest intransigent and baffling. Where he expects gratitude for the imperial favour of being raised to a paramount chief, he is confronted with haughty rejection. After two months, Ezeulu is released from detention to go back, still embittered against those who cast him out. The rest is a quick plunge into the molten centre of disaster. His two months' detention upset the agricultural calendar because he could not eat his ritual yams while in detention. He refuses to call the Feast of the New Yam until he has eaten all the remaining yams. The delay in harvesting the yams begins to hurt the people and threaten famine. Desperate and confounded, the people turn to the Christian religion for salvation. They send their sons with yam offerings to the Christian harvest festival and thereafter harvest their crops in the name of these sons. A tailpiece to the drama is provided by the sudden death of Obika, Ezeulu's favourite son. The Chief Priest goes mad and the people draw their own moral from his tragedy: "To them the issue was simple. Their god had taken sides with them against his headstrong and ambitious priest and thus upheld the wisdom of their ancestors – that no man however great was greater than his people; that no man ever won judgement against his clan."[77] But the people of Umuaro do not have the last word. This belongs to the novelist who sees the story in its total historical and cultural context.

> "If this was so [he argues] then Ulu had chosen a dangerous time to uphold this wisdom. In destroying his priest he had also brought disaster on himself, like the lizard in the fable who ruined his mother's funeral by his own hand. For a deity who chose a time such as this to destroy his priest or abandon him to his enemies was inciting people to take liberties; and Umuaro was just ripe to do so."[78]

The mass defection to the Christians which follows must be seen as the result of the failure of the old dispensation to provide security, and the availability of an alternative source of security.

The historical basis of the story is well known. It was one of the major setbacks to the British colonial administration in Nigeria. The attempt to set up warrant chiefs in the predominantly republican Igbo-land came to grief in the late 1920s, and led to widespread turmoil and rioting by women, since known as the Igbo Women's Riot (1927). The failure of the experiment in Indirect Rule is recorded by Dr P. C. Lloyd in *Africa in Social Change*. He writes:

> In attempts to "find a chief", men were often selected whose traditional roles had little to do with political authority. They were ritual experts or merely presided over councils of elders with equal status. Indeed the introduction of Indirect Rule on the Northern Nigerian pattern to the Ibo peoples and their similarly organized neighbours of Eastern Nigeria proved impossible. From the beginning of the century, administrative officers had created "warrant chiefs" – men who often had no traditional authority but who seemed powerful enough to act as British agents in recruiting

241

labour. Then when direct taxation was introduced in 1927, wide-spread rioting, led by Ibo women, disclosed the extent of hostility to these warrant chiefs. In the 1930s, therefore, councils were instituted which were based upon traditional political units and their representation.[79]

A good deal of the historical outline survives in *Arrow of God*, but Achebe's handling of the subject exposes the human realities, the dilemmas facing men and women who are caught up in the historical drama. He draws out of history the human dimension; by concentrating on the Chief Priest, a fully realized individual character, he brings the action out of the area of public gestures and abstract formulations to that of the emotions and attitudes of living people.

In *Arrow of God*, the cracks which had tragically developed in the traditional system in *Things Fall Apart* grow into chasms. But a good deal of the action is concerned with the attempt by the chief character to build a bridge over the widening chasm. Ezeulu fails because his grasp of the situation is inadequate and so he is constantly surprised. In the novels written about later periods greater objective knowledge of the new institutions can be assumed and it is easier for people to accommo-date themselves to them. The bridges are more firmly built, and sustain cooperation between Christians and the traditionalists. Individual dilemmas are no longer so largely due to inadequate understanding of the forces at work. The choices are more open and their consequences more readily predictable. The other rural novels show this.

In the Aniocha of 1949, internal dissensions occur and the old ancestral sanctions are often ignored, leading to incipient tendencies towards self-seeking individualism. For instance, Araba, even though he poses as a defender of traditional interests, is inclined not to respect customary usages that do not enhance his ego; this is particularly obvious in his hanging on to the family *ozala* even after the family leadership has passed to his rival, Nwokeke. In Aniocha also the initiative has passed to the Christian community which takes stringent action to keep its mem-bers within the fold and prevent back-sliding while the traditionalists are in utter disarray.

As soon as traditional society loses its collective outlook and the social forces which held it together, social non-conformism and rebels begin to appear. Thus Aniocha produces Danda, who, for all his poetic imagination and apparent light-hearted attitude, is at heart a rebel. Notice, for instance, how he flouts the establishment by donning the regalia of title without being himself titled, and by seducing the village chief's sluttish young wife. Here the traditional institutions are shown as external pomposities with much reduced internal significance. No one will blame Danda for showing disrespect for a bunch of bickering elders whose lack of dignity has discredited a way of life of which they are supposed to be protectors.

Danda is of considerable interest in the study of culture contact and social change because it illustrates that stage of social ordering in which the major elements which in the past had caused division have attained a fair degree of accommodation in a stable juxtaposition. The modern sector is fully established, especially the new patterns of economy based mainly in the towns and cities. There is increased appreciation for the new consumer goods, greater recognition of the utility of modern education and the need for technical and commercial skills. A good deal of traditional village life persists but influences from the towns are continually finding their way into the village and co-existing with traditional village life.

The hard edges of traditionalist–Christian opposition have now worn down. All families have mixed components of traditionalists and Christians. In Araba's household, for example, the dominant outlook is still traditional since he and his wives remain committed to the old way, but already two of his sons have been to school and have left home to find new life in the town. Danda, who has remained behind and outside the school influence, enjoys a brief but unsuccessful flirtation with the church, when he narrowly escapes being given "the water of God" (as the people called the sacrament of baptism) with the wildly improbable name "Robinson". But his two brothers, especially Onuma, are firmly Christian. Onuma even aspires to the Christian ministry. It stands to reason, therefore, that with the close links still existing between the two religious communities, finding a mutual accommodation is important for the survival of individuals. The Christians, in their moments of enthusiasm and sectarian exclusiveness, ask their members to forsake hearth and home and kin "for Christ's sake", but in times of sober reflection, their members recognize that no such drastic action is needed. Moreover, they realize how much they would be losing if they took the biblical injunction too literally. The areas of cooperation and those of uncompromising non-cooperation are gradually defined.

One example of the latter will serve as an illustration. There is a long-standing annual ceremony among the Uwadiegwu umunna – a ceremony concerning Mgbafo Ezira, a refugee widow in the family whom some members in a very remote antiquity had murdered, selling her seven sons to slavery. As an act of expiation, the kindred offer up an annual sacrifice of a cow to the spirit of the injured woman. In Danda's Aniocha,

243

the question is not whether this time-hallowed ceremony will continue but whether the whole body of the kindred group can still go on performing it, since collective expiation, like collective communion, is a manner of reinforcing collective solidarity. More specifically, are the Christians who have carved out a parallel solidarity for themselves going to cooperate in this traditional ceremony which is based on the traditional religion from which they have dissociated themselves? In the event, they do not cooperate. But the handling of the incident is a useful lesson in how far the two communities have adapted to the situation by exercising tolerance and understanding. The passage begins with a kinsman appealing to others to pay their contributions towards the ceremony and ends by his picking on the Christians:

> "And see here, let there be no question of churchman or non-churchman. The people who killed Mgbafo Ezira may have been the fathers of those who go to church today. Their descendants cannot hope to escape their own part of the shame by joining the white man."
>
> The church wouldn't contest the point. they had argued about it many times and it seemed futile to go on. So one of the members accordingly said that if they had known what the subject for the meeting would be they would not have come. As it was they couldn't stay. And with that he strode out followed by all the Christians.
>
> "We will deal with them," said Nwora. But this threat obviously was futile, it had no head. Three people out of ten cannot deal with seven, and the Christians outnumbered the pagans by an even greater proportion.
>
> "Things have spoilt," said Idengeli. And this note of resignation was echoed in the snuff sighs of the umunna.[80]

Nwora Otankpa's broadside swipe at the Christians notwithstanding, it is clear by implication that a measure of cooperation now exists between the Christians and the traditionalists; after all, the Christians attend the assembly as a matter of course, at least until the nature of the topic for discussion becomes clear. This cooperation therefore stops short of religious matters and ritual in which each community is expected to attend to its own affairs without interference from the other side. The same kind of collaboration in things pertaining to the welfare of the community as a whole is also observable in *One Man One Wife*, when the Christian and traditionalist elders assemble at the palace of the Asolo to find an answer to the epidemic of smallpox ravaging their community.[81] It is true that the two groups talk at cross-purposes, each seeking a

244

solution conforming to its own religious beliefs and assumptions, but the desire to deliberate together for the common good exists. A certain residual solidarity remains, in spite of the forces that have nearly torn the people apart. It would be fair to say that by the time in which the other rural novels are set, a fair degree of stability has been reached by these societies, with the rivalries between Christians and traditionalists reduced to manageable proportions. On the festive occasions of either group, all but the most hardened fanatics tend to be drawn into the celebrations.

One may feel some doubt about Nwankwo's observation that the Christians among the Uwadiegwu kindred outnumbered the traditionalists. This assumption is certainly not borne out by statistical evidence. Contrary to what many people believe, Christians remain a minority in rural Igboland, where *Danda* is set. According to Professor A. L. Mabogunje, "In Eastern Nigeria the large towns are predominantly Christian while almost all other classes of towns are predominantly Animist."[82] The statement is based on the 1952–3 Nigerian census taken only three years after the year in which the incidents in *Danda* are supposed to have taken place. Nwankwo has himself given cogent reasons why those who embrace Christianity gradually drift back to traditional religion:

> The chief source of grievance . . . was the stiffness and lack of colour of the church. Spirit worship was a colourful drama with masquerading and fluting and singing and dancing. Furthermore the festivals were well spaced out through the year and integrated with the rhythms of the seasons. On these occasions relatives from the other villages visited their kindred, rejoiced with them and strengthened that bond of affection which bound them and sustained their lives.
>
> The church on the other hand had no festivals. They had feasts of the saints referred to as "unexpected Sunday" but one didn't feast then, one attended church and sang the monotonous church songs and came home again no more refreshed than if there had been nothing uncommon. There was "kelesmes" too, if you could properly call that Christian. It seemed to have become more or less a day of rejoicing for everybody, Christians and spirit worshippers. And even at this period the church tried to curb the joy of its members. They forbade them to masquerade, for the masquerade, they said, was a pagan institution.[83]

Shrewd though this is, it does not take into account the important factor of cultural inertia, the staying power of cultures against the corrosion from new ideas, institutions and styles of life. No matter how attractive the new ideas and institutions, there are always built-in responses to the old ways which pull those exposed to the lure of change back in the direction of the old ways, often because of the fear of the unknown implicit in the encounter with the new, but more probably because the old has been found to answer the needs of man in the particular environment. This is very important in explaining backsliding from Christianity. If all backsliders were simply refugees from the liturgical drabness of Christianity to the carnival revelries of the spirit worshippers then the phenomenon would have ceased before now. The Christian sects have come to recognize that rigid adherence to received ceremonial purity, in utter disregard of the cultural realities of the African environment, is the easiest way to lose relevance and attraction. The African spiritualist churches like the one described by Soyinka in *The Interpreters* were quick to recognize the need to liven up their liturgies with African drums and percussion. The more orthodox sects, like the Anglican and Roman Catholic churches, were slow to Africanize their services. But even these have had to follow the examples of the spiritualist churches, the latter after Pope John XXIII's liberating ecumenism. The result is that a casual visitor to some of the Roman Catholic church services today is as likely to be greeted with rollicking native rhythms as he would have been by "monotonous church songs" in the past.

In spite of the effort of the Christian sects to meet traditionalism halfway as a strategy of survival, it is clear that traditional religion has never really been in danger of obliteration, for the simple reason that many of those who in their youth found their way into the church, often via the elementary school, tend in middle age to drift back, either in order to take the much-coveted traditional titles or to marry additional wives, an action likely to put them outside the orthodox Christian communion anyway. Even those who remain in the Christian fold try to have their cake and eat it: they profess Christian virtues but consort with traditionalist agents –medicine men, diviners and priests – especially during major crises when the Christian God has failed to provide remedies and respite. West African novels are full of examples of this. Elder Joshua, "one of the pillars" of the infant church of Isolo, not only alienates himself from the religion by aspiring to polygamy but advocates a traditionalist solution to the smallpox epidemic. "We must go back to the way of our fathers," he harangues the assembled elders. "As for this new faith, this new religion of 'one-man-one-wife,'...men of Isolo, it is the White Man's design to make women and slaves of the whole lot of us."[84] John Ikenga, the father of Patrick, the hero of *Blade Among the Boys,* is another example. He worships in the Christian manner but never loses faith in magic and charms. Of his Christianity, Nzekwu comments wryly:

> Had the priests gone behind the scenes they would have discovered that neither John Ikenga's brand of Christianity, nor those of many others he knew, was the model they preached each Sunday from the altar. They could have discovered for themselves the numerous charms John Ikenga hid behind photographs hanging on the walls of their parlour. His was quite a different brand of Christianity – a Christianity that allowed for the limitations of his upbringing in traditional surroundings, a Christianity that accommodated some principles and practices of his tribal religion. For one thing, he never could drop the primary aim of tribal worship: to reinforce life by means of prayers, sacrifices and sympathetic magic.[85]

Patrick himself is no less a two-timer than his father. His inclination is not so much towards magic and the "reinforcing" of life with tribal medicine as towards masquerades and revels (he is a fanatic in these things); his attempted escape from the traditional headship of his lineage group by trying to become a Roman Catholic priest is defeated by a young woman who seduces him with a love-potion, a fitting finale to a gerrymandering religious career.

Obi Okonkwo's parents in *No Longer at Ease* jettison one of the central ideological props of their Christian faith, human equality, when they unequivocally oppose their son's intention to marry Clara, the osu girl. Yet Isaac Okonkwo is the same man who as Nwoye Okonkwo (before his baptism) broke the heart of his father by deserting the traditional religion for Christianity because of what he felt were the harsh realities of the system. His lack of sensitivity in this matter of discrimination against innocent people shows how little his life has been permeated by the new religion. Ironically, he justifies his position by citing the Old Testament, the most traditional section of the Bible. "Naaman, captain of the host of Syria, was a great man and honourable," he intones, "he was also a mighty man of valour, but he was a leper."[86] Isaac Okonkwo may have abjured traditional religion in its disturbing aspects, but when the principles of his new faith are put to the test he fails because at bottom he is still guided by many of the traditionalist susceptibilities he is most eager to disavow.

I have given so much attention to the question of religion in rural social change because of the key position religion occupied, and still does, in the life of the rural communities and the consequent prominence given to it by the novelists themselves. Nevertheless, it is only one aspect of life and experience in the villages. Working for a living, for example, is also important in these novels. I have earlier suggested that the pre-colonial traditional life was a well-regulated one in which clearly distributed seasonal rhythms determined the patterns of work which in turn underlined the patterns of power, wealth and status. The changes which have taken place in that part of social life are also important for a full understanding of African life and experience, especially as they are projected in creative literature.

In the dense rain-forests of the south, agriculture is the mainstay of the economy, while in the sparsely covered thorn scrubs and savannah of the interior of West Africa cattle-rearing is the major occupation. Most of the novels dealt with here are set in the rain-forest region, especially in Igboland, while only one short novel, Ekwensi's *Burning Grass*, is set in the savannah region. I shall concentrate on the southern novels and make reference to *Burning Grass* whenever necessary.

The pre-colonial rural economy was marked by a near self-sufficiency. The main source of economic production was land, and this was available to every male member of a family by virtue of his membership. No free man was without employment because his entitlement to land made available to him something to farm. The ideological basis of the system of land tenure is, once again, the ancestral concept. Land, it was assumed, belonged to the ancestors, especially the founding fathers of the community. The living, as descendants of the ancestors, are entitled to full use of the land while here on earth, but purely as custodians holding it in trust for the ancestors. Part of the communal ancestral heritage, therefore, was this entitlement to land, the living holding it by right of their being an extension of the mystical continuity of the group.

The consequences are far-reaching in the novels. Everyone works on the land. Farming is the main occupation, though fishing, hunting, trapping and keeping of livestock are also undertaken. The major crop is yam, a tuberous plant with a green, climbing stem and clinging tendrils. The patterns of power, wealth and status are linked closely to success in farming because even though land is available to everyone, not everyone takes full advantage of his possession. The characters who are regarded as successful are those who have made a success of agriculture. In *Things Fall Apart*, which consciously explores the traditional ideas of success and power, individuals are weighed by how good and successful they are as farmers, and this in turn is linked to their standing in the community. Thus, Okonkwo's agricultural success and his high standing in Umuofia are clearly linked, and are established very early in *Things Fall Apart*: "He was a wealthy farmer and had two barns full of yams, and had just

248

married his third wife. To crown it all he had taken two titles. . . . And so although Okonkwo was still young, he was already one of the greatest men of his time."[87] The successful man from whom Okonkwo obtains his share-cropping yams is also defined by success at farming: "There was a wealthy man in Okonkwo's village who had three huge barns, nine wives and thirty children. His name was Nwakibie and he had taken the highest but one title which a man could take in the clan. It was for this man that Okonkwo worked to earn his first seed yams."[88] Okonkwo's father's failure is confirmed by his failure as a farmer. It was said of him that "his wife and children had barely enough to eat"[89] – a major indictment in the traditional society. Even the priestess of Agbala scolds him for his laziness and lack of application to his work: "When a man is at peace with his gods and his ancestors, his harvest will be good or bad according to the strength of his arm. You, Unoka, are known in all the clan for the weakness of your matchet and your hoe."[90]

In *The Concubine*, which is set in a pre-colonial Igbo village, everyone is a farmer. The villagers are constantly going to or returning from the farm, especially during the peak farming season. As in *Things Fall Apart*, the main crop is yams, and there is the same measure of success or failure. For example, Madume's failure is broadly hinted at by its being shown that he is an unsuccessful farmer: "Madume's yams were few. It was a lucky thing that barns were normally constructed in the farms so that it was not easy to know exactly how many ekwes or columns of yams a man had. Still he had to sell his yams at the waterside market during the harvest season and that gave him away."[91]

By the time of *Arrow of God*, new economic interests had arrived with the Europeans. But farming remained the main way of life. When the Chief Priest asks what the church bell he hears every Sunday morning says, and is told that it asks people to leave their yam and cocoyam and come to church he answers with prophetic discernment, "It tells them to leave their yam and their cocoyam, does it? Then it is singing a song of extermination."[92] The crisis which engulfs the people of Umuaro and the Chief Priest arises when the Chief Priest threatens the entire economic security of the people, even their lives, by refusing to call the Feast of the New Yam which ushers in the harvest. If the year's yam harvest perishes in the ground the people inevitably perish with it or at best become dangerously near to being destroyed, since the economic system is non-accumulating, depending on year-to-year cultivation and consumption of crops.

In addition to the yam crop there were other crops such as cocoyam, cassava, maize and a variety of vegetables and legumes which complemented yam. But the primacy of yam is emphasized in the social structure and underlined in the religious scheme. The dominance of yam was signalled by the fact that it is a man's crop. In the sexual definition of economic roles, yam had been institutionalized as the man's crop, while cocoyam and cassava were the woman's crops. It may be that the qualitative superiority of yam over other crops earmarked it for appropriation by the dominant male. Under the right conditions and with proper handling it could reward the farmer with amazing plenitude. (A good successful yam tuber can be the size of a human adult.) And it is a beautiful and delicate plant, climbing ever so gently with its tender stem and even tenderer tendrils, exhibiting an admirable tenacity and resilience that carry it to the top of a very high supporting stake. The degree of expertise required for the proper handling of the crop, from preparing the seed-yams for planting to the staking and fixing of the stems, raises yam cultivation into an art. The care and solicitude lavished on it by the farmer is not necessary for the cassava, which is a tree-crop, even though it has tubers like the yam. It is not a beautiful plant; it spreads its thin branches about and its body is covered with bumps. It is also a mediocre plant, neither large and imposing like most trees in the tropics, nor small and delicate like a shrub.

Achebe naturally concentrates on the yam as a focus for the exploration of traditional economy because it is the cornerstone of the economy and provides the staple diet. He stresses its relatedness to the male principle in the whole culture in a number of oriki-like references: "Yam, the king of crops, was a man's crop," he writes on page 19 of *Things Fall Apart*, and on page 29, "Yam, the king of crops, was a very exacting king," and yet elsewhere, "Yam stood for manliness, and he who could feed his family on yams from one harvest to another was a very great man indeed."[93] But more important, it was a crop sacred to the earth goddess. In the past, stealing yam was about the worst crime anyone could commit and was visited with the direst consequences, including death. The sacred nature of the crop is stressed in *Things Fall Apart* and other rural novels by its being associated with the most important festivals of the year, the minor festivals being fixed in relation to the various stages of yam cultivation.

Yam cultivation also illustrates the main elements of the traditional rural economy. In the first place, it demonstrates that the family was the normal economic social unit. Every grown member of the family, father, mother (or mothers) and children, participated in some stage or other of the process of yam cultivation, whether by cutting down, burning and clearing the bush; preparing seed-yams for planting; carrying seed-yams from the barn to the farmland; making yam-mounds; planting seed-yams; or weeding, harvesting and carrying the yam-crop from the farm to barn for storage. All the rural novels show the democratic nature of the traditional economy. The best detailed description is given by Achebe in *Things Fall Apart* in which every stage of agricultural labour is described as well as the persons involved.[94] The democratic approach to work in the traditional society is borne out in the autobiography of the eighteenth-century Igbo ex-slave and abolitionist, Olaudah Equiano, called *The Interesting Narrative of the Life of Olaudah Equiano, or Gustavus Vassa, the African.* Of the Igboland of his infancy he writes: "Our land is uncommonly rich and fruitful, and produces all kinds of vegetables in great abundance. . . . Agriculture is our chief employment, and everyone, even the children and women, are engaged in it. Thus we are all habituated to labour from our earliest years. Everyone contributes something to the common stock, and as we are unacquainted with idleness we have no beggars."[95]

What Equiano calls a "habituation" to labour was not a haphazard process but was carried out along the principle of the sexual division of labour. Certain types of agricultural labour and certain kinds of skills were reserved for men and others for women. Children were inducted into them by watching the adults at work and learning from them, as for instance when Okonkwo takes Ikemefuna and Nwoye through the art of preparing seed-yams.[96] On the whole, work requiring much strength, such as cutting down the bush and clearing the land after the burning, was done by men, and so also "the difficult art of preparing seed-yams", sowing them, staking them and placing the tendrils. Women took care of weeding, as well as planting ancillary crops, such as maize, melons and beans, between the yam mounds.[97] A woman could of course cultivate yam in her own right and certainly was always given a portion of the family land for her own crops, including the dominantly female crops, cocoyam and cassava. If she became a widow, she might be expected to take over full responsibility for maintaining her husband's yam stock, though in the circumstances she would draw on the labour support of the male members of the community and would be expected to scale down the family holding to manageable proportions. Such, for instance, is the case with Ihuoma after she has lost her husband. We are told that "Ihuoma's farm was in good shape, but it was much smaller than it had been. She had sold off a good proportion of her husband's stocks. A woman was not expected to grow yams as extensively as a man."[98]

The traditional economy also defined the pattern of parent–child relationship. The father was the captain of the domestic economic unit. As paterfamilias and controller of the agricultural produce, he had considerable power over his offspring. He could exact obedience from them and exercise authority over them by withholding food, or at least

251

threatening to do so. When in *Danda* Araba hounds Danda out of his *obi* for refusing to accompany him to the farm, he decrees to Danda's mother that henceforth no food shall be given him. He does so on the understandable ground that "he who will not work shall not eat".

Even the grown-up members of a man's family did not escape the labour tribute due the paterfamilias. As long as he remained alive, the head of the family continued to receive this tribute from his sons. This was both a way for the children to express their filial loyalty and for the family to maintain its inner cohesion and solidarity. It was also a practical demonstration of the ancestral basis of society, since the paterfamilias was the chief link between his family and the ancestral tradition. All those subscribing to the traditional system had to accept and respect the authority of the father over his sons. We notice, for example, that Ezeulu's children allot one day in the four-day week to working for their father. On the eve of this day they assemble at his *obi* and the eldest son, acting as chief spokesman for the other sons, asks for the work assignment for the next day. Ezeulu's eldest son is already married and has set up a sub-family of his own, but the concept of the family as an economic unit keeps the link between its members alive. And this link is expressed positively in collaborative manual labour.

The nature of agriculture and the very active part played in it by men explains one of the most persistent traditional characteristics – the desirability of male children. It is true that male children are desirable because the ancestral tradition is maintained along male lines, but the economic consideration is of immense practical significance. The more sons one has, the more hands one has available in a manually orientated economic system. The whole thing operates in a cyclical manner. The more hands one has, the better the prospects of agricultural success; and the better the produce, the greater the likelihood of the surplus being diverted to marrying new wives and of increasing the labour force even more. A great compound, as we have seen, is one with a large barn and many children, in which the father has achieved high status through taking titles, as in the case of Okonkwo's benefactor with "three huge barns, nine wives and thirty children".

The economic basis of the relationship between a man and his sons is explicit. It is not based on exploitation but hangs on clearly defined obligations on the part of the father. The sons of a man worked for him to sustain the family stock. In return the man fed, housed, and generally took care of their material needs until they set up a sub-family of their own. Then the man had to discharge more stringent obligations to them. First, he allotted them portions of the family land and quantities of yams on which they would lay their economic foundation. Then he built

252

houses for them within the large family compound and finally paid bride-wealth for their wives. Sometimes, "if his hand was sufficiently strong", he could even purchase titles for some of his sons.

The rural novels show the reciprocal nature of the father–son economic relationship in the traditional society. A number of the patriarchs in the novels shoulder responsibility for setting up their sons. Ezeulu marries a wife for Obika and gets the sons to use one of his tribute labour days to finish Obika's barn before the arrival of his bride. Araba sells some of his yams to get money to pay for the little "girl from Mbammili" for Danda. He even tries to make Danda a man of title, except that Danda runs away in the middle of the face-cutting that would have qualified him for the title. In *The Concubine* Wigwe uses his resources to marry Ahurole for his son, Ekwueme. In *Burning Grass*, Mai Sunsaye, the Fulani cattle-man, is also the patriarchal head of his family. His three sons mind the family cattle and in return he takes care of their material needs, including making available the cattle for paying their bride-wealth. Okonkwo's bitterness in *Things Fall Apart* arises partly from the fact that he has had to struggle single-handed from the very beginning, his father not being able to meet any of the traditional obligations a father owed his son. As Achebe says, "With a father like Unoka, Okonkwo did not have the start in life which many young men had. He neither inherited a barn nor a title, nor even a young wife."[99]

The ease with which the economic system worked and with which attendant expressions of rights and obligations were met is explained by the direct relationship between demand and supply. Most of the things needed for the satisfaction of material needs were available in the immediate environment or could be procured from within easy reach. Food, shelter and clothes, for instance, were immediately available to people in their daily encounter with the environment, by drawing on the resources of the land, the streams and the forest. From these resources surpluses accrued which were then diverted towards meeting such needs as marriage, title-taking and so on. Other needs not immediately supplied were procured in a market through exchanging what was on hand with what was required, by direct article-for-article exchange or through the mediation of some unit of exchange. In *The Concubine*, for example, the people of Omokachi who are farmers exchange their yam and cocoyam for fish which is brought in by the Rikwos, who are fishermen. They mediate this transaction by coins called manillas. We find Ihuoma and Ekwueme complaining about the imbalance in the exchange, because the Rikwos offer a low price for yams and demand a high price for the fish.[100] In *Things Fall Apart*, the standard currency is the cowrie shell. Cowries were in wide use in the Igbo hinterland, while manillas, which came in with the sixteenth-century contact between Portuguese and the deltaic peoples of the Lower Niger, were used in the southern part of Igboland adjoining the Niger delta.

By the late 1920s the time of *Arrow of God*, the British administration had introduced its own metropolitan currency. This began the era of a modern economy governed by the cash nexus. The story of West African cultural change became largely the study of this shift from peasant self-sufficiency, marked by a kinship-oriented agricultural economy, share-cropping and the limited use of currency and exchange by barter, towards a modern economy dominated almost entirely by the cash nexus.

The first evidence of divergence from the typical traditional economy occurs in *Arrow of God*. Even though one hears in *Things Fall Apart* that the "trading stores" have already arrived and even though the missionaries are busy holding out some vague material (monetary) inducements to lure children to school, one's perception of the economic life is still almost entirely in terms of limited needs which are easily met in the old, rural ways. In *Arrow of God*, on the other hand, the new attachment to "money" for the procuring of wildly proliferating new consumer goods is a palpable reality. And so also are the rapidly changing economic activities. Thus, the policeman sent to arrest Ezeulu is placated with "this small 'kola'" of two live cocks and two shillings.[101] John Nwodika, Winterbottom's steward, saves enough money from his work in Government Hill to set up "a small trade in tobacco".[102] Again, we find what appears like the first stimulus towards wage labour as the Otakagu age-group argue bitterly in support of a wage claim for the road they are building from Umuaro to Okperi. One of them, speaking for the rest, says: "I have heard that throughout Olu and Igbo, wherever people do this kind of work the white man pays them. Why should our own be different?"[103] And as for the new officials propped up by the colonial administration, from the warrant chiefs (like the one of Okperi) through the police officers to the prison warders, they are all absorbed in wage labour and are, in addition, making a little extra by twisting the arms of their victims.

From the twenties the new economic forces of change began seriously to erode the traditional order, and by the forties and fifties, in which novels like *Danda*, *One Man One Wife*, and *Blade Among the Boys* are set, the tempo of change in the villages had accelerated from the arithmetical progression of the earlier period to a geometrical progression. One important indication of the degree of this change is the swinging of the economic centre from the village to the town. Young people left the villages in large numbers to go to the towns in search of work and then later came back to the villages laden with the new consumer goods of the towns and introduced them to the villagers. The effect, of course, was to stimulate further exodus from the villages. The new consumer goods had to be paid for with money, and since rural agriculture was as yet of low cash yield, except where cash crops had also been developed, the tendency was for young people to look to wage labour and trade as the best ways to make money and satisfy the growing taste for new material goods.

All the novels dealing with rural life about this time feature the two-way movement between town and village, a movement in which the economic attraction of the town is constantly drawing people away from the village and, in reverse, the deep emotional attachments of those very people to the village are always pulling them back to their rural roots. Thus, most of those who leave the village to go in search of work in the town tend to come back.

Here, for example, is the homecoming of one of the travelled sons of the village. The incident is taken from *Danda*:

Araba's son was back home. The news formed the chief fare of local gossip for some days. Relatives from the surrounding towns came to the obi, rejoiced with the family, prayed for the newcomer and went home again. Then it was the turn of the umunna. Each of them had had a cup and as usual declared a moral on it.

"Yes, I must tell you the truth, son," said Idengeli. "The man who makes money makes it not for himself alone, but for the umunna. . . . If the road proves good it becomes the property of all. . . . Some men I know make money and give none of it to their people. That type of money is useless. It is like food which one eats alone, never sweet."

"True word," agreed Akumma Nwego, stretching his hand for a cup of wine.

The calabash was empty and Onuma filled it again from a huge pot at one corner of the room. He was a younger copy of his father, short with the same disproportionately large head but lacking the ferocity of expression.

"Welcome again, son," said Okelekwu. "Uwadiegwu will have its share of the white man's good things. You are our share."

"He is our share," said Nwafo Ugo, belching.

Araba said nothing, merely snuffed and listened. His heart was full. Often he would gaze fixedly at his son and then from him to the bright things that had been bought in the city. . . . A new bicycle as sparkling as they made them stood by the old ikenga.

255

> Finely worked glasses received the protection of the ofo. But the instrument to which most attention was paid was an iron box which talked and sang.[104]

Nwankwo's sharp eye for the incongruous and the ludicrous has not missed the comic juxtaposition – traditional spirits standing guard over precious modern possessions! The passage shows the general admiration for the village boy who has made good, who has left the village for the town, worked hard, accumulated savings and used them to buy goods which can later be displayed as a measure of this success. A bicycle, sparkling glasses and a gramophone, these are goods which originally belonged to the city but have made their way into the village among the personal possession of its homing sons. The same kind of feeling of admiration and wonderment surrounds the return of Joshua to the village of Isolo with a bicycle. Admittedly, his is not a new bicycle but one which "had belonged to many owners before" and been acquired "after a shady transaction between him and the cook of a railway official who owed him forty-five shillings".[105] But these rather unattractive sidelights do not appear to diminish the admiration with which the villagers greet the newcomer: "They all, men, women and children, agreed that he was wonderful."[106]

That economic life changed profoundly is shown by the way people in the village look increasingly to relations working in the city for help to sustain their aspiration to modernity. For example, they receive help with the payment of their children's school fees and sometimes for personal commitments, including the building of concrete houses roofed with corrugated iron for durability. More significantly, parents were now either less willing to or less capable of meeting their traditional obligations to their children working in the town, especially the obligation to pay their marriage expenses. Most of the young men find the money for their own bride-price. In *Danda*, for example, Onuma Araba sends thirty pounds *to* his father as the bridal money with which he is to find him a wife. Araba, who has met his traditional obligation to Danda by marrying a wife for him, is quite prepared to accept the changed situation in which his second son has to take the responsibility from him. He is even heard murmuring that the money is not enough. "Wives cost more of course but it is a beginning," he says.[107] Joshua in *One Man One Wife* is a notable exception. For all his Christianity, he insists on following the traditional practice to the letter. His son, Jacob, wishes to save for his marriage but Joshua will not hear of this. His reason for insisting on doing the traditional thing is clearly put. "[He] resolved that he was going to do his duty by his son, Jacob. He was going to provide Jacob with a wife, and pay the dowry and all other expenses connected with it. Why, his own father had done that for him while Jacob's mother was still a girl, and he had always revered the memory of his father for it. He must leave nothing but the best memory for his own son."[108] This high-minded traditionalism is of a piece with Joshua's patriarchal frame of mind, in spite of his Christianity. Most villagers with sons working in town would now expect them to earn the money with which to pay their own bride-price. The villagers of Isolo are of course somewhat different, being farmers of the commercially profitable cocoa. It is not surprising that a wealthy rural farmer can continue the old practice where less favoured villagers have adjusted their attitude to the shifting realities of the patterns of economy and wealth.

Where parents no longer meet their traditional obligations, their traditional authority tends to diminish. They can no longer impose their will with the force of economic sanction behind them; rather they try other ploys that may prove just as effective, including persuasion, the appeal to corporate well-being, mobilization of public opinion or outright blackmail. Thus, for example, Obiajulu Okonkwo's parents muster strong opposition against his desire to marry the girl of his choice, even though as a senior civil servant he has a high degree of economic independence and is indeed supporting his parents financially.

In the discussion of rural social change as reflected in West African novels, *The Voice* stands apart, because of its parabolic nature. The outlines of these questions are there, but they are not given the kind of deployment that would relate them to the other works. More than any other novel discussed here, it shows the complete death of the traditional spirit. The externals of traditional life are still there – the chief, the councillors, the villagers, the community gatherings and so on. But in place of the primacy of society there is the egoism of a dictator. Everything seems dead in the nightmare village of Amatu except the oppressive presence of Chief Izongo. There are no longer any of those values that give solidarity and dignity to the traditional way of life. What we have is an all-pervading materialism side by side with an inordinately corrupt and ruthlessly autocratic power. Here as in *Danda*, the result is the emergence of a rebel, not an anarchistic rebel like Danda but a Christ-like figure, who denounces the values of the corrupt society and advocates change.

Half a century separates the world of *Things Fall Apart* from the late colonial and post-colonial period to which most of the novels apply: half a century during which stupendous changes have already taken place in the social structure and also in the intellectual, moral and behavioural outlook of West Africans. In spite of these changes, the traditional cul-

257

ture (itself considerably affected by "modern" influences) has continued to exist side by side with the modern culture; its values and the sentiments deriving from it exist in uneasy juxtaposition with those of the modern urban culture. The conflicts and confusions which sometimes arise from the individual's appeal to one set of values in the wrong social context provide the novelists with one of their themes.

I should however draw attention to the basic difference between the kinds of conflicts and oppositions which exist in modern West African society and in the purely traditional society such as that represented by Okonkwo's Umuofia at the turn of the century. There it was a matter of the radical head-on collision of two autonomous systems of law, logic and convention.[109] We saw from the discussion of Okonkwo's Umuofia that the ancestral religion affects every facet of life within the traditional society and underlines not only the structure of social relationships but also the patterns of economic, political and kinship relationship, the system of rights and obligations, the moral outlook of individuals and the general attitudes prevailing within society. Christianity on the other hand brought with it an authority rival to the authority of the ancestors and an appeal to the universal brotherhood of man which contradicts the narrow appeal of the traditional system to the brotherhood of those bound by common ancestry and marriage. The immediate result of the pulls of the two systems was to undermine the sense of tradition and collective solidarity in the traditional society. With time however the hard points of conflict wore off and the hostility between Christian converts and their traditionalist kinsmen was eased if not removed altogether. All the rural novels apart from *Things Fall Apart* and *Arrow of God*, it has been observed, show some harmony and cooperation between Christians and traditionalists. The situation has passed from the stage of radical opposition to that of ordinary opposition and adjustment.

To take just one clinching example, when Obi Okonkwo returns to his native Umuofia after four years' study in England, his kinsmen assemble to greet him in his father's house. When kola nut is brought for the people there is a brief moment of embarrassment, for kola is a ritual object used in traditional prayer and the relatives are a mixture of Christians and traditionalists. The oldest man, whose duty traditionally it is to pray for the group and break the nut, picks it up and says, "Bless this kola nut so that when we eat it it will be good in our body in the name of Jesu Kristi. As it was in the beginning it will be at the end. Amen." Everyone echoes "Amen."[110] Now the elder is not a Christian but a titled traditionalist. This rapprochement would have been impossible in Okonkwo's day.

The cultural problems with which we are concerned here are of the nature of accommodation, synthesis or selection. In Obi Okonkwo's Umuofia, unlike the Umuofia of his grandfather, you either pray as a Christian or as a traditionalist; but good sense dictates that you pray the Christian way when you are in a Christian home and like a traditionalist in a traditionalist's home. There are alternatives, and one needs to take account of the context of each action to avoid muddle. And this is the problem of modern West Africans which the novelists deal with.

9

Conclusion

In *An Introduction to the English Novel*, Arnold Kettle argues that the novel originated when it did because of the changes which transformed England from a feudal and traditionally oriented to an industrially oriented society. This is a view which my own investigation supports. Social and cultural change has both given rise to the cultivation of the novel form in West Africa and largely determined the novel's form as well as its social and psychological content.

For us, social and cultural change in West Africa has not involved merely a transition from an old agrarian situation, in which oral tradition is the predominant mode of cultural expression, to a modern industrial one in which writing is the predominant mode, as was the case in Europe. The West African phenomenon is of the nature of a superimposition rather than a transition, so that we have a composite rather than a unified picture; elements of the old traditional culture exist side by side with those of the modern industrial culture, the oral tradition with the literary, and the traditional village with the modern town.

The two essential realities which condition human experience, cultural tradition and environment, have this composite nature in West Africa and thus affect decisively the subject and form of the West African novel. I do not suggest that the West African novel is fundamentally different from the novel as developed elsewhere. What has been stressed is that the cultural and environmental situation in West Africa has greatly influenced the representation of life and experience in the West African novel and given a distinctive local colour and texture to it.

In the first place, the introduction of literacy, the growth of mass media of communication and the substantial increase in the number of middle-class educated West Africans, all things which result from social and cultural change in West Africa, have all been factors in the emergence of the West African novel. They are important because they have encouraged the movement towards greater individuation and individual self-awareness, increased psychic, physical and social mobility, and a new confidence in the individual self and also in the historical and cultural self. The novel, a non-indigenous form and the most individualistic of literary forms, can be said to have emerged in West Africa at a time when society became sufficiently individualized and heterogeneous to produce potential authors with adequate literary training, imaginative complexity and a firm empathetic power, wanting to explore diverse characters and situations within a complex narrative medium, and to enter vicariously into the characters and situations thus explored.

The emergence of the West African novel is also an expression of the cultural confidence and self-assurance of modern West Africans. They are impelled to analyse and examine themselves in terms of their past cultural life and their present cultural situation, and this because of the recovery of creative confidence formerly emasculated by colonialism and foreign domination.

So the African has, in the West African novel, become an object of serious literary study. In much of the creative writing on West Africa by foreigners (Joyce Cary, Margaret Field and a few European novelists are the exceptions) the African is hardly seen as an autonomous human being with a rational way of life. Either he is merged into the general backcloth of barbarism, violence, exotic dances, witchcraft and magic, ritual murder and cannibalism (what the French call *l'Afrique de l'esprit* of the European writer, but what some of these foreign writers represent as *l'Afrique naturelle*); or he is portrayed as a mere servant, an inconsequential, silent, often anonymous and sometimes sinister figure, passing round a tray of sundowners among European guests. With the emergence of the West African novel by indigenous West African writers, the African, whether he is a peasant farmer like Okonkwo, a prostitute like Jagua, a social misfit like Danda or a university graduate like Obiajulu Okonkwo, achieves the dignity of a human being and his predicament is made a matter of interest to readers of creative fiction. His oral tradition, an essential aspect of his indigenous culture, is given attention by the writers who also partake of this tradition. The white foreigner, when he is present at all, is treated with tolerance, though he in his turn is now often merged into the background among the factors affecting the destiny of the African, or he is simply shown as an invited guest or an interested observer.

The content of the West African novel is also largely determined by social and cultural change. There are two aspects to this. The first aspect relates to the formal development of the West African novel and the social and cultural reality reflected in it. The second aspect deals with the problems arising from social and cultural change as they affect

261

the behaviour of individuals or groups of individuals, a situation reflecting what Mannoni calls "the painful apprenticeship to individualism".[1]

The formal development of the West African novel has been vaguely referred to as a domestication. This is the core of this study and involves the means adopted by the writers to accommodate the novel, a distinctly literary art form, to West African reality, in which two distinct traditions, oral and literary, and their peculiar modes of apprehending reality, have been interwoven. The interplay of elements peculiar to both traditions has given a distinctive local colour and flavour to the West African novel. While in broad outline remaining faithful to the formal requirements of the novel in the matter of characterization, time and space, setting and language, the West African novelists have necessarily had to represent traditional as well as modern beliefs, attitudes and modes of expression which combine to inform and define the West African concept of reality.

Thus, we find the scientific outlook existing side by side in these novels with belief in magic and mystical causality, particularity with generality of time and space, a high degree of socialization of personality with extreme individualism, linguistic particularity with the use of fixed expressions like proverbs, and rural traditionalism with urban modernity. All this follows because social and cultural change in West Africa involves the superimposition of a modern literary and technological culture upon a traditional, oral and predominantly agrarian one.

Cultural and social change provides the novelists with their themes and subject matter. Different stages of cultural and social change are represented in the novels, from the early contact between the classical traditional culture and modern industrial culture to the present time of considerable adjustment and synthesis. The novelists see the situation in terms of traditional–modern or rural–urban differentiation and consequent clash of values. They show that the behaviour of characters has been largely conditioned by the social, economic and political environment, which in turn has been very much affected by social and cultural change. They show their perception of this change by dramatizing the tensions and conflicts which result from it and which are reflected in the structure of social relationships. They portray characters and their personal behaviour, idiosyncrasies and predicaments, as a reflection of the conflicts and lack of full integration in the changing social scene. In this particular, because their novels tend to internalize external situations, they differ from Western novels which tend to externalize internal situations.

When we come to the actual themes of the novels, we find not only common ground but also close identity of views and attitudes between the writers. We notice, for example, that the novels, especially those of them appearing before 1965, are most concerned with the problems of cultural and social change, and especially with the conflict of values arising from the impact of the literate industrial culture of the West on the traditional agrarian culture of Africa, and the way these conflicts tend to be expressed in individual behaviour and social relationships. The conflicts tend to centre on the opposition of traditional to modern values and on the values of the village to those of the town.

This choice is natural, and involves a principle which in some situations is publicly shared. This is the awareness that the values of society are changing rapidly, that the old way of life is breaking up and being replaced by a new one. This change is most obvious in specific areas of personal and social relations. Awareness that these things are changing is one thing; acceptance or rejection of change is another. Novelists writing about these changes in life and society reflect a publicly recognized reality; their attitudes to these changes on the other hand will be determined by their perception of their mission as intellectuals in the changing society. In selecting and treating the specific themes, they show that they are aware of the areas in which change registers most emphatically in the public consciousness.

It is not surprising that novelists are interested in the problems of social and cultural change in Africa, their effects on individual behaviour, and the values which condition such behaviour. As intellectuals, one of the roles which distinguish them from the rest of people in society is their capability of taking an objective view of society as a whole. They are able to perceive with greater lucidity the real nature of the changes which are taking place in society. Edward Shils puts the case in the essay referred to earlier when he writes: "However modern the intellectual culture of most of the intellectuals of the societies of Africa and Asia, most of them live their lives in a vital domestic culture of kinship, tribe and religious outlook which makes them aware of their past and of the difference of that past from the modern intellectual culture which they espouse."[2] It is the overwhelming awareness that the old traditional culture with its attendant values is breaking up and is being replaced by a new culture with emergent values which has made culture-change the all-pervasive theme in the West African novel. Because the novelists share the background of the generality of the people they write about, they feel with them that culture-change is the most important reality of modern West Africa; but because they are intellectuals who of their nature are directly concerned with the state of society, and because their medium is well suited to the exploration of the problems of society, they are naturally drawn to write about the theme.

West African novelists are sometimes criticized by European readers for giving so much attention to the social and cultural background and public life of their characters and too little to their individuality and inner life. This is to ask the West African writer to escape the reality of his society by writing like a twentieth-century European, the break-up of whose "public background of belief" induces him to concentrate on the individual. The shared background of belief is crucial to the West African novelist's choice of theme and accounts for the social-documentary nature of West African prose fiction.

The case is well put by Achebe in the article entitled "The Role of the Writer in a New Nation", in which he defends the African writer's interest in the cultural question, particularly his interest in the past, in the context of a rapidly evolving present. In one of the most quoted statements on African writing, he says:

> This is my answer to those who say that a writer should be writing about contemporary issues – about politics in 1964, about city life, about the last *coup d'état*. Of course these are legitimate themes for the writer but as far as I am concerned the fundamental theme must first be disposed of. This theme – put quite simply – is that the African peoples did not hear of culture for the first time from Europeans; that their societies were not mindless but frequently had a philosophy of great depth and value and beauty, that they had poetry and above all, they had dignity. It is this dignity that many African peoples all but lost in the colonial period, and it is this that they must now regain. The worst thing that can happen to any people is the loss of their dignity and self-respect. The writer's duty is to help them regain it by showing them in human terms what happened to them, what they lost.[3]

In his opinion, to attempt to explore the present while ignoring the past, especially when the past is still so much alive in the present, is to "take off before we have repaired our foundations". Ideally, therefore, "we must first set the scene which is authentically African; then what follows will be meaningful and deep." At the Commonwealth literature conference in Leeds in the same year, Achebe attempted a much more elaborate defence of this view in a paper called "The Novelist as Teacher". Here is a relevant part of his exposition:

> Here, then, is an adequate revolution for me to espouse – to help my society regain its belief in itself and put away the complexes of the years of denigration and self-denigration. And it is essentially a question of education in the best sense of that word. Here, I think, my aims and the deepest aspirations of my society meet. For no

thinking African can escape the pain of the wound in our soul. You have all heard of the African personality, of African democracy, of the African way of socialism, of négritude, and so on. They are all props we have fashioned at different times to help us get on our feet again. Once we are up we shall not need any of them any more. But for the moment it is in the nature of things that we need to counter racism with what Jean-Paul Sartre has called an anti-racist racism, to announce not just that we are as good as the next man but that we are better. . . . I for one would not wish to be excused. I would be quite satisfied if my novels (especially the ones I set in the past) did no more than teach my readers that their past – with all its imperfections – was not one long night of savagery from which the first Europeans acting on God's behalf delivered them. Perhaps what I write is applied art as distinct from pure. But who cares? Art is important but so is education of the kind I have in mind. And I don't see that the two need be mutually exclusive.[4]

These are views with which most West African novelists would agree. The cultural question is as much a matter of concern as the more publicly dramatized interest in nationalist politics. In some respects, there is a blurring of lines between politics and cultural nationalism in a movement like Négritude. In practice, as soon as it becomes a clear choice between political discourse and literary exposition, especially where the novel is concerned, significant differences become apparent. Political propaganda is too simple to serve a form as complex and intricate in its inner demands as the novel. The novel deals with man in society and has to be attentive to surface social realities, to be faithful to the truth of human nature. The imperfections of human nature are mirrored in the imperfections of society. That is why it is difficult to write a satisfactory novel glorifying a social system or idealizing characters. This is probably one reason why French African writers of the Négritude movement idealize the African way of life in poetry, while African writers of fiction have, by and large, been constrained to handle the cultural question with greater realism.

This study has deliberately concentrated on the cultural and environmental background of the West African novel, on the general theme of the traditional culture, the contact with Western culture and their expression in the West African novel as a useful preparation for a fuller appreciation of the themes of politics and the problems of adjustment to modern social change with which the novels deal. The latter themes are in themselves important and constitute a vast, promising area of their own, but it seems sound sense, first and foremost, to survey the terrain, to observe the physical features, locate the signposts and generally create an outline map as aid to more realistic purposeful exploration of the literature.

The West African novel in English has established itself as a vital and flourishing phenomenon. It is slightly under two decades old but it has shown a remarkable growth and development. One can say with some justification that even though the coming of Europe caused problems of social, cultural and psychological adjustment, it has at least brought some positive gains, chief of which is the liberation of the African from ethnic isolation; one result is the emergence of the novel, the art-form best fitted to represent his new life and experience. The insights provided by the West African novelists into the cultural and environmental situation of the African can but prove a valuable addition to the human record embodied in the literatures of the world, by establishing what French Africans have elegantly referred to as "the African authenticity".

Notes and references

Chapter 1. Background to the West African novel

1 E. N. Obiechina, "Growth of Written Literature in English-Speaking West Africa", *Présence Africaine* (Paris, 1968), pp. 58–78.
2 E. M. Forster, *Aspects of the Novel*, p. 9; H. I. Chaytor, *From Script to Print*, p. 4.
3 See especially pp. 87–94.
4 Daniel Lerner, *The Passing of Traditional Society*, pp. 52–3.
5 *The Rise of the Novel*, p. 59.
6 See Helen Kitchen (ed.), *The Educated African*; A. I. Porter, "The Formation of Elites in West Africa" in W. von Fröhlich (ed.), *Africa im Wandel seiner Gesellschaftsformen*; J. F. A. Ajayi, *Christian Missions in Nigeria*; Sir Eric Ashby, *African Universities and Western Tradition* and Nduka Okafor, *The Development of Universities in Nigeria*.
7 *The Lagos Observer*, 18 January 1883.
8 *The Lagos Observer*, 22 June 1889.
9 "Mr. Courifer", a short story by Adelaide Casely Hayford, in Langston Hughes (ed.), *An African Treasury*, p. 135.
10 *Report on the Press in West Africa*, pp. 73–133.
11 E. N. Obiechina: *Onitsha Market Literature* and *An African Popular Literature*.
12 H. N. Weiler, *Education and Politics in Nigeria* (Freiburg, 1964), pp. 262–72.
13 H. I. P. Hogbin, *Social Change*, pp. 230ff.
14 In *Liberté I: Négritude et humanisme*.
15 Pp. 42–3.
16 E. W. Blyden, *Letters with Pope-Hennessy on the West African University*, Freetown, 1873.
17 *The Problem of Style*, p. 48.
18 *Nigerian Magazine*, no. 81, June 1964, p. 157.
19 *Nigerian Magazine*, no. 78, September 1963, pp. 217–19.
20 "The Headline Novels of Africa", *West Africa*, 28 July 1962.
21 Jahn, J. and J. Ramsaran (eds.), *Approaches to African Literature* (Ibadan, 1959).
22 M. M. Mahood, *Joyce Cary's Africa*, pp. 3–62.
23 Prefatory essay to the Carfax edition of *The African Witch*, p. 12.
24 Ibid., pp. 10–11.

25 *Stormy Dawn*, p. 49.
26 "African Twilight: Folktale and Myth in Nigerian Literature", *Ibadan*, no. 15 (March 1963), pp. 17–19.
27 *The Long Revolution*, pp. 64ff.
28 Dennis Duerden (ed.), *Cultural Events in Africa*, no. 6 (May 1965), p. 335.

Chapter 2. Oral and literary traditions in West Africa

1 *English Literature and Society in the 18th Century*, pp. 92–3.
2 See G. S. Kirk, *The Homeric Poems as History*, pp. 4–5.
3 *Selected Prose*, p. 20.
4 "Consequences of Literacy", p. 335.
5 See Fr James O'Connell's article of this title in *Ibadan*, no. 14 (October 1962), pp. 3–11.
6 "The Intellectual between Tradition and Modernity, pp. 60–1.
7 See *Bantu Philosophy*, p. 35. See also G. Parrinder, *African Traditional Religion*, pp. 20–4.

Chapter 3. Nature, music and art

1 *English Literature*, p. 129.
2 *Arrow of God*, p. 50.
3 *Things Fall Apart*, p. 142.
4 *The Concubine*, p. 11.
5 *One Man One Wife*, pp. 118–19.
6 *The Concubine*, p. 19.
7 *Things Fall Apart*, p. 13.
8 Ibid.
9 Ibid., p. 123.
10 Ibid., p. 40.
11 Ibid.
12 *Arrow of God*, p. 245.
13 *The Concubine*, p. 21.
14 *Danda*, p. 153.
15 *Things Fall Apart*, p. 133.
16 Ibid., p. 51.
17 *The Concubine*, p. 21.
18 *Arrow of God*, p. 2.
19 *Things Fall Apart*, p. 19.
20 Ibid., p. 75.
21 *The Concubine*, p. 269.
22 *The African*, pp. 60–1.
23 *Jagua Nana*, p. 180.
24 *The Beautyful Ones Are Not Yet Born*, p. 169.
25 *The Interpreters*, p. 110.
26 Ibid., p. 111.
27 *No Longer at Ease*, p. 18.
28 *The Interpreters*, p. 112.

29 Ibid., p. 63.
30 Ibid., p. 140.
31 Ibid., p. 125.
32 Ibid.
33 Ibid., p. 126.
34 Ibid., p. 127.
35 *Things Fall Apart*, p. 2.
36 Ibid., p. 4.
37 Ibid., p. 37.
38 Ibid., p. 51.
39 *Danda*, p. 132.
40 *The Concubine*, p. 260.
41 *One Man One Wife*, p. 78.
42 *The Voice*, p. 137.
43 *Danda*, p. 81.
44 *Blade Among the Boys*, p. 54.
45 *The Concubine*, pp. 56–7.
46 Ibid., pp. 16–17.
47 Ibid., p. 111.
48 *Danda*, p. 15.
49 *The Concubine*, pp. 35–6.
50 *Danda*, p. 83.
51 *Things Fall Apart*, p. 4.
52 In Echeruo and Obiechina (eds.), "Igbo Traditional Life", p. 105.
53 *Danda*, pp. 24–5.
54 *Things Fall Apart*, p. 38.
55 In D. W. Jefferson (ed.), *The Morality of Art*, p. 130.
56 See Professor Nketia's article "The Role of the Drummer in Akan Society", *Report of the Third Annual Conference of W.A.I.S.E.R.* (1963), p. 73.
57 *Arrow of God*, p. 85.
58 *The African Child*, tr. James Kirkup (London, 1955), p. 23.
59 *Danda*, pp. 43–4.
60 Ibid., pp. 190–1.
61 *The Concubine*, p. 33.
62 Ibid., p. 104.
63 Ibid., pp. 166–7.
64 M. W. Smith (ed.), *The Artist in Tribal Society*, p. 117.
65 See further: Ulli Beier, *African Mud Sculpture* (Cambridge, 1963); G. I. Jones, "Mbari Homes", *Nigerian Field*, vol. VI, no. 2 (April 1937), pp. 77–9.
66 *Arrow of God*, pp. 143–4.
67 *Things Fall Apart*, p. 62.
68 *The Concubine*, p. 161.
69 *Things Fall Apart*, p. 32.
70 Echeruo and Obiechina (eds.), "Igbo Traditional Life", p. 94.
71 M. W. Smith (ed.), *The Artist in Tribal Society*, p. 117.
72 *Arrow of God*, p. 86.
73 *The Concubine*, p. 22.
74 *Things Fall Apart*, pp. 11–12.
75 *Arrow of God*, p. 29.
76 *Danda*, p. 146.
77 Echeruo and Obiechina (eds.), "Igbo Traditional Life", p. 90.

78   *Arrow of God*, p. 45.
79   *Danda*, p. 20.
80   *Arrow of God*, p. 249.
81   Ibid., p. 62.
82   *Danda*, p. 22.
83   *Arrow of God*, p. 246.
84   *Danda*, pp. 22–3.
85   See Ian Watt, *The Rise of the Novel*, p. 31, and Arnold Kettle, *Introduction to the English Novel*, p. 37.
86   See Uche Okeke's *Drawings*, an Mbari publication (Ibadan, October 1961), in which the artist draws from Igbo folklore.
87   Introduction in *Nigerian Tribal Art* (London, 1960), p. 1.
88   *A Dream of Africa*, tr. James Kirkup (London, 1968), pp. 106–7.
89   *Blade Among the Boys*, pp. 54–5.
90   *A Man of the People*, pp. 108–9.
91   *The Interpreters*, pp. 99–100.
92   Ibid., p. 102.
93   Ibid., p. 243.
94   Ibid., pp. 244–5.
95   Ibid., p. 245.
96   Ibid., p. 245.
97   Ibid., p. 243.
98   *The Voice*, pp. 96–7.
99   See K. A. Busia, *The Challenge of Africa* (London, 1962), p. 137.
100 *No Longer at Ease*, p. 112.

Chapter 4. Characterization

1   E. Cassirer, *Language and Myth*, p. 3.
2   *No Longer at Ease*, p. 62.
3   *Things Fall Apart*, p. 36.
4   Illustrated by Joseph Bram in *Language and Society*, pp. 40–1.
5   *The Voice*, pp. 115–17.
6   *Arrow of God*, p. 253.
7   See William Bascom's essay, "Social Status, Wealth and Individual Differences Among the Yoruba", *American Anthropologist*, vol. 53 (1953), pp. 490–505.
8   See for instance the discussion of slave status in Hausaland in *Baba of Karo* by Mary Smith; M. M. Green's description of "osu" and "ohu" in Igboland in *Igbo Village Affairs*, pp. 23–4; J. V. Clinton's "Untouchability in Nigeria", *Contemporary Review*, vol. 191, pp. 217–20; W. R. C. Horton's "The Ohu System of Slavery in a Northern Ibo Village-Group" in *Africa*, vol. 24, no. 4, pp. 311–36; and a precise description of "osu" and "ohu" systems in Igboland in Forde and Jones' *The Ibo and Ibibio-speaking Peoples of South-Eastern Nigeria*, p. 23.
9   *Patterns of Culture*, p. 183.
10 *Danda*, p. 6.
11 Ibid., p. 28.
12 Ibid., p. 119.
13 Ibid., p. 108.

14 Ibid., p. 60.
15 Ibid., pp. 15–16.
16 Ibid., p. 28.
17 *One Man One Wife*, p. 10.
18 Ibid., p. 84.
19 *The Concubine*, p. 2.
20 Ibid., p. 7.
21 Ibid., p. 10.
22 *Arrow of God*, p. 155.
23 *Things Fall Apart*, pp. 1–2.
24 Ibid., pp. 79–80.
25 Ibid., p. 10.
26 Ibid., p. 2.
27 Ibid., p. 4.
28 Ibid., p. 3.
29 *Ibadan*, no. 22 (1966), pp. 46–59.
30 *Danda*, p. 33.
31 *Things Fall Apart*, p. 15.
32 Ibid., p. 5.
33 *Arrow of God*, p. 45.
34 Ibid., p. 12.
35 Ibid., p. 113.
36 Ibid., p. 266.
37 Ibid., p. 33.
38 Ibid., p. 45.
39 Ibid., p. 164.
40 Ibid., p. 241.
41 Ibid., p. 47.
42 Ibid., p. 10.
43 Ibid., p. 47.
44 Ibid., p. 49.
45 Ibid., p. 18.
46 Ibid., p. 49.
47 Ibid., p. 47.
48 *The Concubine*, pp. 14–15.
49 Ibid., p. 99.
50 Ibid., pp. 15–16.
51 Ibid., p. 199.
52 Ibid., p. 249.
53 Ibid., p. 128.
54 *Danda*, p. 80.
55 Jacob Drachler (ed.), *African Heritage*, pp. 76–81.
56 *The Voice*, p. 53.
57 Ibid., p. 56.
58 *Nigeria Magazine*, no. 75 (December 1962), pp. 63–6.
59 *The Voice*, p. 9.
60 See Obiechina, *An African Popular Literature*, Chapter 9.
61 Dillistone, pp. 19–20.
62 *The Voice*, p. 110.
63 *The Interpreters*, p. 15.
64 Ibid., p. 16.

65 D. W. Jefferson (ed.), *Morality of Art*, p. 126.
66 Ibid., p. 128.
67 *The Interpreters*, p. 219.
68 Jefferson (ed.), *Morality of Art*, pp. 127–8.
69 *The Interpreters*, pp. 250–1.
70 Ibid., p. 52.
71 Ibid., p. 251.
72 *The Posthumous Papers of D. H. Lawrence*, pp. 223–31.
73 *Technique of the Novel*, pp. 248–50.
74 *Aspects of the Novel*, pp. 54–5.
75 *The Voice*, p. 96.

Chapter 5. Space and time

1 M. Allott, *Novelists on the Novel*, p. 181.
2 "Consequences of Literacy", pp. 307–8.
3 *The Concubine*, p. 19.
4 *Danda*, p. 42.
5 *The Concubine*, p. 110.
6 *Things Fall Apart*, p. 11.
7 *Danda*, p. 81.
8 *The Concubine*, p. 14.
9 *Things Fall Apart*, p. 24.
10 Ibid., p. 47.
11 Ibid., p. 25.
12 Ibid., p. 49.
13 Ibid., p. 53.
14 *Arrow of God*, p. 253.
15 Ibid., p. 243.
16 Ibid., p. 255.
17 *Things Fall Apart*, p. 19.
18 Ibid., pp. 122–3.
19 *Danda*, p. 82.
20 *The Concubine*, p. 16.
21 *Things Fall Apart*, p. 7.
22 Ibid., pp. 107–8.
23 Ibid., p. 166.
24 *The Concubine*, pp. 18–19.
25 *Things Fall Apart*, p. 47.
26 *The Concubine*, p. 131.
27 *Things Fall Apart*, p. 123.
28 Ibid., pp. 9–10.
29 *Danda*, pp. 149–51.
30 *The Concubine*, pp. 74–5.
31 *Danda*, pp. 54–5.
32 *The Concubine*, p. 75.
33 *Arrow of God*, p. 147.
34 Ibid., pp. 87–8.
35 Ibid., pp. 33–4.
36 Ibid., p. 44.

37 Ibid., p. 162.
38 See N. Uka's paper, *The Development of Time Concept in Afrcian Children of School Age*, p. 17, for comparison between time sense among children from literate homes and those from illiterate and poor homes.
39 *Danda*, p. 53.
40 In H. L. Shapiro (ed.), *Man, Culture and Society* (New York, 1960), p. 187.
41 C. K. Meek, *Law and Authority in a Nigerian Tribe*, p. 11.

Chapter 6. Setting

1   *Things Fall Apart*, p. 1.
2   Ibid., p. 116.
3   Ibid., pp. 7–8.
4   Ibid., pp. 89–95.
5   *Arrow of God*, pp. 280–3.
6   *Things Fall Apart*, p. 7.
7   Ibid., p. 84.
8   Ibid., p. 8.
9   *Arrow of God*, pp. 262–3.
10 *The Concubine*, pp. 21–3.
11 Ibid., pp. 165–6.
12 Ibid., p. 74.
13 Ibid., p. 75.
14 *Danda*, pp. 5–9.
15 *The Dickens World*, p. 11.
16 *Wand of Noble Wood*, pp. 143–4.
17 *The Voice*, p. 13.
18 Ibid., pp. 31–2.
19 *No Longer at Ease*, pp. 16–18.
20 *A Man of the People*, p. 46.
21 Ibid., p. 100.
22 Ibid., pp. 95–7.
23 *The Interpreters*, p. 8.
24 Ibid., p. 60.
25 In Jefferson (ed.), *Morality of Art*, pp. 121–2.
26 *The Beautyful Ones Are Not Yet Born*, p. 119.

Chapter 7. Language

1   Quoted in Goody and Watt, "Consequences of Literacy", p. 338.
2   *Things Fall Apart*, p. 6.
3   Ibid., p. 22.
4   Ibid., p. 23.
5   Ibid., p. 117.
6   Ibid., p. 4.
7   *Arrow of God*, p. 105.
8   Ibid., p. 174.
9   Ibid., p. 275.
10 Ibid., p. 165.

11   Ibid.
12   Ibid., p. 170.
13   Ibid., p. 232.
14   Ibid., p. 177.
15   Ibid., p. 178.
16   Ibid., p. 234.
17   Ibid., p. 266.
18   Ibid., p. 209.
19   Ibid.
20   Ibid., p. 286.
21   Ibid., p. 283.
22   See C. K. Ogden and I. A. Richards, *The Meaning of Meaning*, p. 315.
23   *Arrow of God*, pp. 26–7.
24   Ibid., pp. 136–8.
25   *The Concubine*, pp. 78–9.
26   *Things Fall Apart*, p. 4.
27   See Victor C. Uchendu, " 'Kola Hospitality' and Igbo Lineage Structure",
       Man, vol. 64, no. 53 (March–April 1964), pp. 47–50.
28   *Arrow of God*, p. 65.
29   Ibid., pp. 175–6.
30   Ibid., pp. 90–1.
31   Ibid., pp. 79–80.
32   *The Concubine*, p. 6.
33   *The Voice*, pp. 15–16.
34   Ibid., pp. 84–6.
35   Ibid., p. 90.
36   See Joseph Bram, *Language and Society*, p. 20.
37   Watt, *The Rise of the Novel*, p. 32.
38   J. Jahn, *Muntu*, p. 146.
39   See Obiechina, *An African Popular Literature*, esp. Chapter 7.
40   *The Interpreters*, pp. 91–2.
41   Ibid., p. 91.
42   Ibid., p. 85.
43   *The Beautyful Ones Are Not Yet Born*, p. 205.
44   *A Man of the People*, p. 98.
45   *Things Fall Apart*, p. 5.
46   *A Man of the People*, p. 16.
47   Ibid., p. 135.
48   *The Beautyful Ones Are Not Yet Born*, pp. 61–2.
49   *Arrow of God*, p. 224.
50   John Spencer (ed.), *The English Language in West Africa* (London, 1971),
       esp. Introduction and Chapter 5.
51   Contained in C. Daryll Forde (ed.), *Efik Traders of Old Calabar*.
52   *The Beautyful Ones Are Not Yet Born*, p. 22.
53   Ibid., pp. 43–4.
54   *The African*, p. 165.
55   Ibid., p. 123.
56   D. Duerden and C. Pieterse (eds.), *African Writers Talking*, pp. 9–10.
57   Ibid., pp. 169–71.
58   *The Interpreters*, p. 155.
59   Ibid., p. 60.

Chapter 8. Culture contact and culture conflict

1 See Talcott Parsons, *Structure of Social Action*, p. 646.
2 *Social Organization*, p. 23.
3 R. M. MacIver and C. H. Page, *Society*, pp. 8–9.
4 P. 4.
5 *Community and Association*, p. 35.
6 See Forde and Jones, *The Ibo and Ibibio-speaking Peoples*, p. 25.
7 *Arrow of God*, p. 260.
8 P. 11.
9 The following works will throw light on African traditional politics and law: M. Fortes and E. E. Evans-Pritchard (eds.), *African Political Systems*; K. A. Busia, *Position of the Chief in Ashanti*; J. Middleton and D. Tait (eds.), *Tribes Without Rulers* (London, 1958); J. Bohannan, *Justice and Judgement Among the Tiv*; M. Gluckman, *The Judicial Process Among the Barotse of Northern Rhodesia*; and C. K. Meek, *Law and Authority in a Nigerian Tribe*.
10 *Things Fall Apart*, p. 7.
11 Ibid., pp. 8–9.
12 Ibid., p. 9.
13 Ibid., p. 10.
14 Ibid., pp. 9–10.
15 See Green, *Igbo Village Affairs*, p. 151, for the importance of exogamy in inter-village relationships.
16 *Things Fall Apart*, pp. 82–3.
17 For discussion of the masked ancestors as a sacred sanction, see Meek, *Law and Authority*, pp. 66–79; Forde and Jones, *The Ibo and Ibibio-speaking Peoples*, p. 26; William Bascom, "The Sociological Role of the Yoruba Cult Group", *American Anthropologist*, XLVI, no. 1, part 2, memoir 63 (1944).
18 Busia, *Position of the Chief in Ashanti*, pp. 24–5.
19 *The Ibo and Ibibio-speaking Peoples*, pp. 25–6.
20 Pp. 175–7.
21 *The Ibo and Ibibio-speaking Peoples*, p. 25.
22 Soyinka explores this theme of vicarious expiation in *The Strong Breed* through the consciousness of a sensitive and "unsoftened" carrier.
23 *Things Fall Apart*, p. 6.
24 Ibid., p. 23.
25 *Igbo Village Affairs*, p. 78.
26 *Things Fall Apart*, p. 112.
27 See *The Law of the Primitive Man*, Postulate IV.
28 *Things Fall Apart*, p. 26.
29 Ibid., p. 111.
30 Ibid., p. 185.
31 *Oedipus and Job in West African Religion*, pp. 13–18.
32 See E. E. Evans-Pritchard, *Witchcraft, Oracle and Magic Among the Azande*.
33 See Meek, *Law and Authority*, pp. 55–60, and Forde and Jones, *The Ibo and Ibibio-speaking Peoples*, p. 26.
34 G. Steiner, *The Death of Tragedy*, pp. 6–8.
35 *Things Fall Apart*, p. 120.
36 *African Systems of Kinship and Marriage*, p. 11.
37 *Things Fall Apart* p. 10.

38 See Green, *Igbo Village Affairs*, pp. 79ff.
39 *Oedipus and Job in West African Religion*, pp. 29–30.
40 *Things Fall Apart*, p. 137.
41 *No Longer at Ease*, p. 58.
42 *Things Fall Apart*, p. 129.
43 Ibid., pp. 130–1.
44 *The Concubine*, p. 7.
45 *Things Fall Apart*, p. 135.
46 Ibid., p. 132.
47 Ibid., p. 162.
48 Ibid., p. 163.
49 Ibid., p. 128.
50 Ibid., pp. 157–8.
51 Ibid., p. 164.
52 Ibid., p. 166.
53 Ibid., p. 168.
54 Ibid., pp. 169–70.
55 Ibid., p. 173.
56 Ibid., p. 182.
57 *Through Values to Social Interpretation* (Durham, N.C., 1950), p. 44.
58 *Arrow of God*, p. 164.
59 Ibid., p. 33.
60 *Things Fall Apart*, p. 185.
61 *The Dynamics of Culture Change*, p. 16.
62 *Arrow of God*, p. 38.
63 Ibid., p. 287.
64 Ibid., pp. 38–40.
65 Ibid., pp. 45–6.
66 Ibid., p. 105.
67 Ibid., pp. 17–18.
68 Ibid., p. 49.
69 Ibid., p. 33.
70 Ibid., pp. 3–4.
71 See G. I. Jones, *The Trading States of the Oil Rivers*, p. 5; Ikenna Nzimiro, *Studies in Ibo Political Systems*; and Richard Henderson's *The King in Every Man: Evolutionary Trends in Onitsha Ibo Society and Culture*.
72 *Things Fall Apart*, p. 10.
73 *Arrow of God*, p. 49.
74 Ibid., p. 55.
75 Ibid., p. 166.
76 Ibid., p. 177.
77 Ibid., p. 287.
78 Ibid.
79 Pp. 65–6.
80 *Danda*, pp. 55–6.
81 *One Man One Wife*, pp. 112–20.
82 *Urbanization in Nigeria* (London, 1968), p. 131.
83 *Danda*, pp. 70–1.
84 *One Man One Wife*, pp. 116–17.
85 *Blade Among the Boys*, p. 29.
86 *No Longer at Ease*, p. 133

87 *Things Fall Apart*, pp. 5–6.
88 Ibid., p. 15.
89 Ibid., p. 3.
90 Ibid., p. 14.
91 *The Concubine*, p. 5.
92 *Arrow of God*, p. 52.
93 *Things Fall Apart*, p. 28.
94 Ibid., pp. 27–9.
95 Paul Edwards (ed.) (London, 1967), pp. 7–8.
96 *Things Fall Apart*, p. 28.
97 Ibid., p. 29.
98 *The Concubine*, p. 38.
99 *Things Fall Apart*, p. 15.
100 *The Concubine*, pp. 189–91.
101 *Arrow of God*, pp. 190–1.
102 Ibid., p. 287.
103 Ibid., p. 106.
104 *Danda*, pp. 102–3.
105 *One Man One Wife*, p. 72.
106 Ibid.
107 *Danda*, p. 92.
108 *One Man One Wife*, p. 34.
109 See: G. and M. Wilson, *Analysis of Social Change*, pp. 125ff.
110 *No Longer at Ease*, p. 52.

Chapter 9. Conclusion

1 O. Mannoni, *Prospero and Caliban, The Psychology of Colonization* (New York, 1964), p. 66.
2 "Intellectual Between Tradition and Modernity", p. 60.
3 *Nigeria Magazine*, no. 81 (June 1964), p. 160.
4 *New Statesman* (29 January 1965), p. 162.

Bibliography

NOVELS STUDIED

Achebe, Chinua. *Things Fall Apart*. London, 1958.
   No Longer at Ease. London, 1960.
   Arrow of God. London, 1964.
   A Man of the People. London, 1966.
Aluko, T. Mofolorunso. *One Man One Wife*. Lagos, 1959.
Amadi, Elechi. *The Concubine*. London, 1966.
Armah, Ayi Kwei. *The Beautyful Ones Are Not Yet Born*. London, 1969.
Conton, William. *The African*. London, 1960.
Ekwensi, Cyprian. *People of the City*. London, 1954.
   Jagua Nana. London, 1961.
   Burning Grass. London, 1962.
   Beautiful Feathers. London, 1963.
Nwankwo, Nkem. *Danda*. London, 1964.
Nzekwu, Onuorah. *Wand of Noble Wood*. London, 1961.
   Blade Among the Boys. London, 1962.
Okara, Gabriel. *The Voice*. London, 1964.
Soyinka, Wole. *The Interpreters*. London, 1965.

BOOKS CONSULTED

Novels by non-West Africans

Abrahams, Peter. *A Wreath for Udomo*. London, 1956.
Cary, Joyce. *The African Witch* (Carfax edition). London, 1951.
   Aissa Saved (Carfax edition). London, 1952.
   An American Visitor (Carfax edition). London, 1952.
   Mister Johnson (Carfax editon). London, 1952.
Conrad, Joseph. *Two Tales of the Congo*. London, 1952.
Defoe, Daniel. *The Life, Adventures and Piracies of the Famous Captain Singleton*.
   London, 1906.
Field, Margaret (pseud. Mark Freshfield). *Stormy Dawn*. London, 1946.
Greene, Graham. *The Heart of the Matter*. London, 1948.
   A Burnt-out Case. London, 1961.

Bibliography

Huxley, Elspeth. *The Walled City*. London, 1948.
Loader, William R. *No Joy of Africa*. London, 1955.
    The Guinea Stamp. London, 1956.
Obeng, E. E. *Eighteenpence*. Ilfracombe, 1943.
Stoll, Dennis Gray (pseud. Denys Craig). *Man in Ebony*. London, 1950.

Other Works

Abernathy, David. *The Political Dilemma of Popular Education,*
    An African Case. Stanford, Cal., 1969.
Abraham, W. E. *The Mind of Africa*. London, 1962.
Adams, John. *Remarks on the Country Extending from Cape Palmas to the River*
    Congo. London, 1823.
Ajayi, J. F. A. *Christian Missions in Nigeria, 1841–1891*. Cambridge, 1964.
Allen, Walter. *The English Novel*. London, 1958.
Allott, Miriam. *Novelists on the Novel,* 3rd imp. London, 1960.
Ashby, Sir Eric. *African Universities and Western Tradition*. Cambridge, Mass.,
    1964.
Auerbach, Eric. *Mimesis: The Representation of Reality in Western Literature*.
    New York, 1953.
Azikiwe, Nnamdi. *Zik: A Selection from Speeches of Nnamdi Azikiwe*. Cambridge,
    1961.
Bascom, W. and M. Herskovits. *Continuity and Change in African Cultures*.
    Chicago and London, 1959.
Beljame, Alexandre. *Men of Letters and the English Public in the Eighteenth*
    Century. London, 1948.
Bendix, R. *Max Weber, An Intellectual Portrait*. London, 1960.
Benedict, Ruth. *Patterns of Culture*. London, 1961.
Bloomfield, Leonard. *Language*. London, 1935.
Bohannan, P. *Justice and Judgement Among the Tiv*. London, 1957.
Bottomore, T. B. *Elites and Society*. London, 1964.
    Sociology. London, 1962.
Bram, Joseph. *Language and Society*. New York, 1955.
Burns, Sir Allan. *History of Nigeria,* 5th ed. London, 1955.
Busia, K. A. *Position of the Chief in the Modern Political System of the Ashanti*.
    London, 1951.
Cary, Joyce. *The Case for African Freedom and Other Writings on Africa*. Austin,
    Texas, 1962.
Cassirer, E. *Language and Myth*. New York, 1953.
Chadwick, H. M. and N. K. *The Growth of Literature,* 3 vols. Cambridge, 1932.
Chaytor, A. J. *From Script to Print*. Cambridge, 1945.
Chiari, Joseph. *Realism and Imagination*. London, 1960.
Chiney, E. *Sociological Perspectives, Basic Concepts and Their Application*.
    New York, 1954.
Church, Harrison. *Environment and Politics in West Africa*. London, 1963.
Clough, Shepherd B. *Basic Values of Western Civilization*. New York, 1960.
Coleman, James. *Nigeria: Background to Nationalism*. Los Angeles, 1958.
Cooley, C. H. *Social Organization*. New York, 1929.
Coombes, H. *Literature and Criticism*. London, 1963.
Coulthard, G. R. *Race and Culture in Caribbean Literature*. London, 1962.

Crowther, Michael. *Pagans and Politicians.* London, 1959.
Daiches, David. *The Novel and the Modern World.* Chicago and London, 1960.
Dalziel, Margaret. *Popular Fiction 100 Years Ago.* London, 1957.
Dike, K. O. *Trade and Politics in the Niger Delta.* Oxford, 1956.
Dillistone, F. W. *The Novelist and the Passion Story.* London, 1960.
Diringer, David. *The Alphabet.* London, 1947.
Drachler, Jacob (ed.). *African Heritage.* New York, 1964.
Durkheim, E. *The Division of Labour in Society,* tr. G. Simpson. New York, 1933.
Duerden, Denni sand Cosmo Pieterse (eds.). *African [2] Writers Talking.* London, 1972.
Echeruo, M. J. C. and E. N. Obiechina. "Igbo Traditional Life, Culture and Literature." *The Couch,* vol. II, no. 2 (September 1971).
Elias, T. O. *The Nature of African Customary Law.* Manchester, 1956.
Eliot, T. S. *Selected Prose,* ed. John Hayward. London, 1953.
Ethnographic Survey of Africa. West Africa, 1–6. London, 1950.
Evans-Pritchard, E. E. *Witchcraft, Oracle and Magic Among the Azande.* Oxford, 1937.
Fanon, Frantz. *The Wretched of the Earth.* Harmondsworth, 1969.
Toward the African Revolution. New York, 1969.
Forde, C. D. and G. I. Jones. *The Ibo and Ibibio-speaking Peoples of South-Eastern Nigeria.* London, 1950.
Forde, C. D. (ed.). *African Worlds: Studies in the Cosmological Ideas and Social Values of African Peoples.* London, 1954.
Efik Traders of Old Calabar. London, 1956.
Forster, E. M. *Aspects of the Novel.* London, 1949.
Forster, G. M. *Traditional Cultures and the Impact of Technological Change.* New York and Evanston, Ill., 1962.
Fortes, M. *The Dynamics of Clanship Among the Tallensi.* London, 1959.
Oedipus and Job in West African Religion. Cambridge, 1959.
Fortes, M. and E. E. Evans-Pritchard (eds.). *African Political Systems.* London, 1940.
Freemantle, Anne. *Mao Tse-Tung: An Anthology of His Writings.* London, 1971.
Frölich, H. von. *Africa im Wandel Seiner Gesellschaftsformen.* Leiden, 1964.
Frye, Northrop. *The Modern Century.* Oxford, 1967.
Geertz, Clifford (ed.). *Old Societies and New States.* London, 1963.
Gleason, Judith. *This Africa, Novels by West Africans in English and French.* Evanston, Ill., 1965.
Gluckman, Max. *Customs and Conflict in Africa.* Oxford, 1963.
The Judicial Process Among the Barotse of Northern Rhodesia. Manchester, 1955.
Goody, J. R. and I. Watt. "The Consequences of Literacy," *Comparative Studies in Society and History,* vol. V (3) (April 1963), pp. 305–45.
Green, M. M. *Igbo Village Affairs,* 2nd ed. London, 1964.
Griaule, Marcel. *Conversations with Ogotemmêli.* Oxford, 1965.
Haines, C. Groves (ed.). *Africa Today.* Baltimore, 1955.
Hauser, Arnold. *The Social History of Art,* 4 vols. London, 1951.
Henderson, Richard. *The King in Every Man: Evolutionary Trends in Onitsha Ibo Society and Culture.* New Haven, Conn., 1972.
Herskovits, M. *Man and His Works.* New York, 1948.
Hodgart, M. J. C. *The Ballad.* London, 1950.
Hodgkin, Thomas. *Nationalism in Colonial Africa.* London, 1956.
Hoebel, E. *The Law of the Primitive Man.* Cambridge, Mass., 1954.
Hogbin, H. I. P. *Social Change.* London, 1948.

House, Humphry. *The Dickens World*. London, 1942.

Howe, Irving. *Politics and the Novel*. London, 1961.

Hughes, Langston. *An African Treasury*. London, 1961.

Idowu, The Rev. B. *Olodumare, God in Yoruba Belief*. New York, 1963.

Jahn, Janheinz. *Muntu*. London, 1961.

Jefferson, D. W. (ed.). *The Morality of Art*. London, 1969.

Jones, G. I. *The Trading States of the Oil Rivers*. London, 1963.

Kesteloot, Lilyan. *Les Ecrivains noirs de la langue française*. Bruxelles, 1963.

Kettle, Arnold. *An Introduction to the English Novel*, vol. I. London, 1962.

Killam, G. D. *The Novels of Chinue Achebe*. London, 1969.

Kirk, G. S. *The Homeric Poems as History*. Cambridge, 1964.

Kitchen, Helen (ed.). *The Educated African*. New York, 1962.

Kneller, George F. *Educational Anthropology, An Introduction*. New York, 1965.

Kroeber, A. L. *Nature of Culture*. Chicago, 1952.

Laver, John and Sandy Hutcheson (eds.). *Communication in Face-to-Face Interaction*. Harmondsworth, 1972.

Lawrence, D. H. *The Posthumous Papers of D. H. Lawrence*, ed. E. D. McDonald. London, 1961.

Leavis, F. R. *The Great Tradition*. London, 1960.

Leavis, F. R. and D. Thompson. *Culture and Environment*. London, 1953.

Leavis, Q. D. *Fiction and the Reading Public*. London, 1932.

Le Page, H. E. *The National Language Question*. London, 1964.

Lerner, Daniel. *The Passing of Traditional Society*. Glencoe, Ill., 1958.

Lewis, W. Arthur. *Politics in West Africa*. London, 1965.

Lloyd, P. C. *Africa in Social Change*. Harmondsworth, 1972.

Lloyd, P. C. (ed.). *The New Elites of Tropical Africa*. Oxford, 1966.

Lord, Albert B. *The Singer of Tales*. London, 1960.

Lubbock, Percy. *The Craft of Fiction*. London, 1921.

Lugard, Lord F. *The Dual Mandate in British Tropical Africa*. Edinburgh, 1921.

Lynn, Kenneth. *Mark Twain and South-Western Humor*. Boston, 1959.

MacIver, R. M. and C. H. Page. *Society, An Introductory Analysis*. London, 1962.

McKillop, A. D. *The Early Masters of English Fiction*. Lawrence, Kans., 1956.

McLeod, A. L. (ed.). *The Commonwealth Pen*. Ithaca, N.Y., 1961.

Mahood, M. M. *Joyce Cary's Africa*. London, 1964.

Malinowski, B. *The Dynamics of Culture Change*. New Haven, Conn., 1961. *Myth in Primitive Society*. London, 1962.

Mannoni, D. O. *Prospero and Caliban: The Psychology of Colonization*. London, 1956.

Maquet, Jacques. *The Premise of Inequality in Ruanda*. London, 1961.

Meek, C. K. *Law and Authority in a Nigerian Tribe*. London, 1937.

Miner, Horace. *The Primitive City of Timbuctoo*. New York, 1953.

Moore, G. (ed.). *African Literature and the Universities*. Ibadan, 1965.

Moore, Gerald and Ulli Beier. *Modern Poetry from Africa*. London, 1963.

Moorhouse, A. C. *The Triumph of Alphabet: A History of Writing*. New York, 1953.

Moynihan, Daniel. *Beyond the Melting Pot*. Cambridge, Mass., 1963.

Mphahlele, E. *The African Image*. London, 1962.

Muir, Edwin. *The Structure of the Novel*. London, 1928.

Murry, J. Middleton. *The Problem of Style*. London, 1952.

Nadel, S. F. *A Black Byzantium: The Kingdom of the Nupe of Nigeria*. London, 1942.

Nicol, D. A. *Africa, A Subjective View.* London and Accra, 1964.

Nketia, Kwabena. *The Funeral Dirges of the Akan People.* Achimota, 1955.

Nzimiro, Ikenna. "Family and Kinship in Iboland." Ph.D. thesis, Cologne, 1962.
Studies in Ibo Political Systems. London, 1972.

Obiechina, E. N. *Onitsha Market Literature.* London, 1972.
An African Popular Literature. Cambridge, 1973.

Ogden, C. K. and I. A. Richards. *The Meaning of Meaning.* London, 1923.

Okafor, Nduka. *The Development of Universities in Nigeria.* London, 1971.

Oliver, Roland and J. D. Fage. *A Short History of Africa.* London, 1962.

Ottenberg, S. and P. Ottenberg (eds.). *Cultures and Societies of Africa.* New York, 1960.

Parrinder, G. *African Traditional Religion.* London, 1955.

Parsons, Talcott. *Structure of Social Action.* Glencoe, Ill., 1937.

Passin, H. and K. Jones-Quartey (eds.). *Africa: The Dynamics of Change.* Ibadan, 1963.

Perham, M. *Native Administration in Nigeria.* London, 1937.

Political Systems and the Distribution of Power. A.S.A. Monograph 2. London, 1965.

Press, John. *Commonwealth Literature.* London, 1965.

Radcliffe-Brown, A. R. and C. D. Forde (eds.). *African Systems of Kinship and Marriage.* London, 1950.

Redfield, Robert. *The Little Community.* Chicago, 1955.

Report on the Press in West Africa, ed. Committee on Inter-African Relations. Ibadan, 1960.

Riesman, David. *The Lonely Crowd.* London, 1964.

Rotberg, Robert I. and Ali A. Mazrui (eds.). *Protest and Power in Black Africa.* Oxford, 1970.

Sartre, Jean-Paul. "Orphée Noir" in Senghor, L.S. (ed.), *Anthologie de la nouvelle poésie nègre et Malagache.* Paris, 1948.

Saunders, J. and M. Dowuona (eds.). *The West African Intellectual Community.* Ibadan, 1962.

Senghor, L. S. *Liberté I. Négritude et humanisme.* Paris, 1964.

Shapiro, H. L. (ed.). *Man, Culture, and Society.* New York, 1960.

Shils, Edward. "The Intellectual Between Tradition and Modernity: The Indian Situation". *Comparative Studies in Society and History,* supplement. The Hague, 1961.

Smith, Marian W. (ed.). *The Artist in Tribal Society.* London, 1961.

Smith, Mary. *Baba of Karo. A Woman of the Muslim Hausa.* London, 1964.

Smith, N. H. *Mark Twain, The Development of a Writer.* Cambridge, Mass., 1962.

Smythe, H. H. and M. M. Smythe, *The New Nigerian Elite.* Stanford, Cal., 1960.

Southall, Aiden (ed.). *Social Change in Modern Africa.* London, 1961.

Steiner, George. *The Death of Tragedy.* London, 1961.

Stephen, Leslie. *English Literature and Society in the 18th Century.* London, 1904.

Sutherland, James. *English Satire.* Cambridge, 1958.

Taylor, The Rev. John. *The Primal Vision.* London, 1963.

Tempels, Fr Placide. *Bantu Philosophy.* Paris, 1959.

Tönnies, F. *Community and Association,* tr. C. P. Loomis. Ann Arbor, Mich., 1957.

Uka, N. *The Development of Time Concepts in African Children of School Age.* Ibadan, 1962.

Urbanization in African Social Change. Centre for African Studies, University of Edinburgh, 1963.

283

Bibliography

Uzzell, Thomas. *The Technique of the Novel.* New York, 1964.
Van der Post, Laurens. *Dark Eyes in Africa.* London, 1961.
Van Gennep, Arnold. *The Rites of Passage.* London, 1960.
Vansina, Jan. *Oral Tradition.* London, 1965.
Ward, A. W. and A. R. Waller (eds.). *Cambridge History of English Literature*, vol. II. Cambridge, 1909.
Watt, Ian. *The Rise of the Novel.* London, 1960.
Weber, Max. *The Protestant Ethic and the Spirit of Capitalism.* London, 1930.
Wellesley, Robert. *Kossoh Town Boy.* Cambridge, 1960.
White, Morton and Lucia White. *The Intellectual Versus the City.* New York, 1964.
Williams, Raymond. *Culture and Society, 1780–1950.* London, 1961.
   The Long Revolution. London, 1965.
Wilson, G. and Monica Wilson. *The Analysis of Social Change.* Cambridge, 1945.
Wilson, Henry S. (ed.). *Origins of West African Nationalism.* London, 1969.

Index

Abeokuta, 196
Abraham, W. E.
  Mind of Africa (The), 16
Abrahams, Peter, 21
  Wreath for Udomo (A), 21; theme
    of violence in, 23
Accra, 9, 106, 192
Achebe, Chinua, 26, 37, 39
  biography, 7, 150, 195–6
  characterization, 6, 82–8 *passim,*
    90–6, 115; compared to Joyce
    Cary's, 25–6
  culture contact, 201
  grasp of dynamics of social and
    cultural change, 228
  historical accuracy, 223
  imaginativeness, 6
  magical language, use of, 175–7
  narrative method, 206–7, 238–9
  portrait of British administrators,
    229–32
  proverbs, use of, 157–60
  religious conflict, 219–20
  setting, 141–4
  themes, 6, 16, 24, 143
  understanding of pre-colonial
    African community, 212
  urban novels, 137
  view of traditional society, 204, 205,
    213–14
  Arrow of God
    characterization in, 83, 85, 86, 90,
      93–6, 114
    conversation in, 160, 161–2, 164,
      165–9
    cultural change, scope for, 228
    dating, 254
    decorative art in, 66
    deity in, 44, 46, 94–5, 238
    drum speech in, 63
    Ezeulu and Nwaka: their conflict
      due to breakdown of traditional
      framework, 233–8

  Ezeulu's strategy in face of
    cultural conflict, 238–9; final
    tragic incidents, 239–41; Ulu as
    god of security, 238
  festivals in, 56, 94
  group style of language in, 186–7
  historical basis of, 241–2
  magic in, 70, 132–3
  magical language in, 175–7
  masquerade in, 69, 70
  narrative method in, 238–9
  proverbs in, 158, 159–60
  ritual art in, 67, 68
  sense of history in, 134–5
  theme of darkness in treatment of
    setting, 143
  time and space indicators in,
    126–7, 129, 136
  traditional framework, breakdown
    of, 229, 234–8
  traditional society: its essence
    and ideology in, 203; under
    pressure, 207–8
  quoted, 66, 67 *passim*, 93–5, 126–7,
    132–3, 134, 161–2, 165–6, 167–9,
    203, 231–3 *passim*, 234, 235–6,
    239, 240, 241
Man of the People (A)
  language (pidgin English), 190
  masquerades in, 73
  narrative method, 150–1
  setting, 150–1
  time and space concepts in,
    138–9
  urban–rural connections in, 137
No Longer at Ease, 6, 51
  backsliding from Christianity in,
    247
  characterization, 103
  naming of characters in, 82
  narrative method in, 150
  popular music in, 79–80
  setting, 149–50, 151

No Longer at Ease (cont.)
  status differentiation through
    language, 190
  time and space concepts in, 138–9
  traditionalist–Christian
    rapprochement, 258–9
  urban–rural connections in, 137
"Novelist as Teacher (The)", quoted,
  264
"Role of the Writer in a New
  Nation (The)", 17; quoted, 264–5
Things Fall Apart, 6
  as a classic, 233
  characterization in, 84–5, 86, 87,
    90–3, 125–6
  compared with Joyce Cary's
    Mister Johnson, 25
  conflict of Christianity and
    traditionalism in, 219–27
  dating of, 136, 201, 257
  decorative art in, 66
  drum speech in, 129
  festivals in, 56
  human relations in, 86, 201, 202
  legends in, 131
  music in, 54, 60, 62
  mystical association of natural
    objects in, 45–8
  naming of characters in, 82
  narrative method in, 141–2
  Okonkwo: achievements, 204;
    assessment as fully realized
    character, 204; family relation-
    ship, 217–18; fatalism, 215–16;
    hawkish character, 224–5;
    leader of opposition to
    missionary penetration, 224;
    offences and punishment,
    214–15; psychological factors
    influencing him, 92–3;
    weaknesses, 204–5
  politics and government in,
    205–6, 208
  proverbs in, 157, 158
  sense of history in, 134, 135
  setting, themes in the treatment
    of: collectivism, 141–2;
    darkness and light, 143;
    moonlight, 143–4; mysticism,
    144
  time and space concepts in, 124,
    125, 128, 129–30
  traditional diplomatic procedure
    in, 206–7
  traditional judicial process in,
    209–12
  traditional medicine in, 48–9

  wealth, success and power in,
    248–9
  quoted, 44–9 *passim*, 55, 62, 66,
    91, 92, 125, 128, 141–4 *passim*,
    206–7, 208, 209–10, 214, 215–16,
    217, 218, 219, 220, 224–7
Achimota College, 9, 191, 194
Africa: culture, 15, 22, 32; early
  European awareness of, 18;
  European colonization of, 15; *see
  also* West Africa *and specific African
  countries*
Agaba (masquerade), 69
Agbala (goddess), 45, 143, 249
Agbogho Mmonwu (masquerade), 69
age-grade, 134, 211, 254
agwu (mild insanity), 99–100, 114
Ahiara, 136
Ajayi, J. F., 223
Akan people, 16
Akiga, Benjamin, 100, 101
Ala (earth goddess), 43, 212–14, 238
Aluko, T. Mofolorunso, 37, 116
  One Man One Wife, 80
    backsliding from Christianity,
      246
    characterization in, 88–9
    cultural change, evidence of, 256
    dating, 254
    deity in, 44
    music in, 55
    theme of darkness in treatment of
      setting, 143
    traditionalist–Christian
      cooperation, 244–5
    quoted, 55, 88, 89
Amadi, Elechi, 8, 37
  Concubine (The)
    characterization, 89–90, 96–100,
      114, 116
    conversation in, 161, 162–3, 169
    decorative art in, 66
    deity in, 44, 46–7, 89, 90
    idyllic setting in, 144–6
    legends in, 131
    music in, 54–9 *passim*, 64
    ritual art in, 67
    role of magic in, 39
    time and space indicators in, 124,
      125, 129, 130
    traditional medicine in, 49, 96
    wealth, success and power in, 249
    quoted, 47, 49, 55, 56–9 *passim*,
      64, 66, 89, 96, 97, 98, 99, 124,
      129, 130, 145–6, 162
Amadioha (god of thunder), 43, 44, 47,
  89, 90, 144

America, 50, 106, 120, 183, 189; U.S.A., 80, 183
Ani (earth goddess), *see* Ala
Arab writers on West Africa, 18
Arden, John, 196
Arinze, F. (Archbishop of Onitsha), 220
Aristotle, 11
Armah, Ayi Kwei
  biography, 8, 191
  Beautyful Ones Are Not Yet Born (The)
    absence of linguistic differentiation in, 191–2
    characterization in, 104–8, 109, 116
    cultivated nature in, 51
    linguistic individuation in, 184–5
    narrative method, 153–4
    proverbs in, 179–80
    setting, 153–4
    theme, 153
    time and space concepts in, 138–9
    quoted, 154, 180, 191, 192
Arnold, Matthew, 19, 39
Aro traders, 130
art, decorative, in West African novels, 64–79
  individualism in, 73–4, 75, 77
  popular, 78–9
  ritual, 67–8
  shifting of values in, 74–7
  symbols, 65, 73, 77
Ashanti: belief in collective retribution, 214; oral tradition, 32
Awka blacksmiths, 130
Awoonor, Kofi
  This Earth, My Brother, 107
Ayandele, E., 223
Azikiwe, Nnamdi, 12

Bathurst, 9, 192
Becker, Howard, 228
Benedict, Ruth, 84, 136
Benin, 65, 114, 137
Bible, 108, 177
"Black Victorians", *see* Victorianism
Blyden, Edward Wilmot, as a pioneer of West Africa's cultural nationalism, 10; campaigned for a West African university, 16; his cultivated prose style, 194
Borgu emirate, 21
Brazil, 37; immigrants from, 10
Brecht, Bertolt, 196
  Good Woman of Setzwan (The), 103

British administration, 134, 136, 165, 201, 227, 229–32, 239–41 *passim*
British penetration into Igboland, 223
"broken English", *see* English language, pidgin
bronze sculpture, 65
Buddhism, 153
Busia, K. A., 211

Calabar trader's diary, 188
calendar (Igbo), 126–7, 236
Cameroon pidgin, 188
Cape Coast, 9
caricatures, 88, 89, 110, 116, 147
Carpentier, Alejo, 175
Carter Bridge, 51
Cary, Joyce, 261
  characterization compared to Achebe's, 25–6
  English language in, 188
  theme of violence, 22–3
  treatment of Christianity and indigenous religion compared, 24
  view of Nigeria, 22
  African Witch (The), 21
    preface quoted, 22, 23
    theme of dynastic violence, 23
  Aissa Saved, 21
    theme of religious violence, 23
  American Visitor (An), 21
    theme of inter-tribal violence, 23
  Britain and West Africa, 21
  Case for African Freedom (The), 21, 22
  Castle Corner, 21
  Mister Johnson, 21, 22
    compared to Achebe's *Things Fall Apart*, 25
Cassirer, E., quoted, 82
Cassius–Brutus–Caesar syndrome, 238
Catholicism, 117; in Nigeria, 246
Caves, as home of Oracle, 45, 208, 213
census-taking: Igbo, 126, 236; Nigerian, 245
Cervantes, 155
Césaire, Aimé, 15–16
characterization
  and mythology, 111–15
  approaches to, 115–16
  education of characters, 120
  as guide to social criticism, 119
  human relationships explored, 86
  humanization of mystic characters, 98
  in individual novelists: Achebe, 82–96 *passim*; Aluko, 88–9;

characterization (*cont.*)
    Amadi, 89–90, 96–100; Nwankwo,
      86, 87–8; Soyinka, 110–15
    linguistic individuation, 183–5
    link characters, 130
    neurotic characters, 99–101
    parabolic characters, 105–8
    psychological factor in, 91–4
    in rural novels, 82–101
    symbols in, 91, 95
    traditional factors in, 91–101 *passim*
    urban influences in, 137–8
    in urban novels, 102–21 *passim*
Chelsea College of Pharmacy, 194
chi (personal spirit), 99–101, 117
Christmas, 73
churches, 50, 111, 114
Clark, John Pepper, 26
cock-crow, as measure of time, 123,
    124
Coleman, James, 5
collectivism in rural novels, 140–2
colonialism, 15–19 *passim*, 22
    administration, 134, 201, 227,
      229–32, 235; police, 254
    Belgian, 21
    European colonies, 34
    pre-colonial administration, 205, 212,
      219
comic characters, 87–8
    in Aluko, 88
    in Nwankwo, 87–8
    in Soyinka, 110
communication,
    see mass communication
community concept, 201–2
Conakry, 192
Conference of Teachers of English,
    University of Ibadan, 1965, quoted
    on oral tradition, 28
Congo (Belgian), 21, 79; writing of
    Graham Greene based on visit, 20
Conrad, Joseph, 188
    themes, 22
    Heart of Darkness, 21–2
    Outpost of Progress (*An*), 21
Conton, William, 8, 16, 37, 116
    biography, 191, 192–3
    African (*The*), 50
      language, 194
      setting, 154
      theme, 154
conversation in West African novels
    in Achebe, 160–9
    as aid in plot development, 163–4
    in Amadi, 162–3, 169
    linguistic differentiation, 164–6

"phatic communion" concept, 160
    in rural novels, 160–1
    speech conventions, 166–9
    in urban novels, 160–1
Cooley, C. H., quoted, 202
"Couriferism", 11
Craig, Denys (pseud.), *see* Stoll,
    Dennis Gray
Creoles, 36; early elites, 10
crier, *see* town-crier
"crocodile writers", 20, 21, 25
cultural nationalism, 14–17 *passim*
culture
    African, 15, 17, 22, 32
    c. change, evidence of, 255–6; scope
      for, 228; *see also* traditionalism
    c. conflict, 219–27, 238–9, 258; and
      characterization, 85–6
    c. contact and social change, 201,
      242–4
    European, 20, 85
    Muslim, 20
    Western, 15
currency, traditional, 253–4

Dake, Antera, 188
dancing, 60, 73, 92; group, 58; solo, 59;
    to "high life" music, 79
Danquah, J. B., 13
Darwinism, 10, 15
Dathorne, O. R.
    The Scholar Man, 21
dating of novels, 136, 201, 254, 257
Defoe, Daniel, 8, 13
    *Life, Adventures and Piracies of the
      Famous Captain Singleton* (*The*),
      quoted, 18
    Moll Flanders, 103
democracy, village, 205–6
dialogue, *see* conversation
Dickens comedy, 88
Dillistone, F. W., 109; quoted, 108
divination, 97, 99
    diviners as link characters, 130; as
      intellectuals, 131
Dos Passos, John, 117
Drum magazine, 8
drum speech, 63, 129
Duerden, Dennis, 195
Durkheim, E., 156, 214
Dürrenmatt, F., 196

Easter, 73
Echeruo, M. J. C., 104
education
    early products of in West Africa,
      9–10

traditional, limitations of, 4–5
of West African novelists, 9, *and see
individual novelists*
Western, effect of, 5
Ekechi, J. F., 223
Ekwensi, Cyprian O., 37, 78
biography, 8, 194
characterization, 102–4, 116;
compared to Dos Passos', 118
narrative method, 149
urban setting for novels, 103, 115,
149
view on African writing, 17
Beautiful Feathers, 50–1
characterization in, 116
time and space concepts in, 138–9
urban–rural connections in, 137
Burning Grass
role of magic in, 39
setting reveals potential for open-
space literature, 147
*Ikolo the Wrestler and Other Igbo
Tales*, 13
Jagua Nana, 50–1
characterization, 103–4
time and space concepts in, 138–9
urban–rural connections in, 137
People of the City, 13
characterization, urban, 102, 103
time and space concepts in, 138–9
When Love Whispers, 13
Eliot, T. S., quoted on oral tradition,
31–2
Elizabethan humour, 87
England, 106, 140, 192, 194, 258, 260
English grammar, 182
English language, 83, 177
as a medium of instruction, 5
newspapers, 7
Nigerian literacy rate in, 27
pidgin, 187–94
as spoken by characters of Cary and
Achebe, 25–6
standard English in West Africa,
182–3, 188
English literature: allusions to Africa,
18
English people: attitude to nature, 42
Equiano, Olaudah: account of Igbo
traditional society, 251
Eru (god of wealth), 95–6
European artistic outlook, 71, 72
European characters, 230
European colonization of Africa, 15
European common law, 232
European concept of soul, 117
European view of nature, 42, 49, 50

European writers, 81, 174; on West
Africa, 17–25
Europeans, 79, 153; in Igbo legends,
131
exorcism, 99

Fagg, William, 65; quoted, 67, 72
Fagunwa, D. O., 39
festivals: Christian, 73; as time
indicators, 126–7; traditional, 56,
126–7, 132, 167
fiction, *see* novels
Field, Margaret
biography, 24
*Religion and Medicine of the Ga
People*, 21
Search for Security, 21
Stormy Dawn, 21, 24–5
Fielding, Henry, 140
flute (oja), 60–1, 64, 92
folk-tales, 86, 107, 115, 122, 174
Forde, C. D., 211; quoted, 212
forest as mystical object, 46–7
Forster, E. M., 45, 119
Fortes, Meyer, 212, 215; quoted, 218
Fourah Bay College, 9
Freetown, 192, 193; establishment of,
9; writing of Graham Greene based
on visit to, 20
French realism, 104
French-speaking African writers, 15–16
Freshfield, Mark (pseud.), *see* Field,
Margaret
Freud, Sigmund, 22, 101

Ga people, 24
Gambia, 21, 192, 193
Ghana, 16, 21, 105, 122, 190, 191, 193,
194, 212
Ghana University College, 14, 21
gods and goddesses, 38, 44, 45, 50, 55,
74, 123, 125, 126, 131, 145, 147,
152, 159, 215
and war, 208
belief in, 33
burning of, 228
of creativity, 112–15
of earth, 43, 212–14, 238
of fortune (ikenga), 67–8
as patrons of art, 65
personal (*chi*), 99, 117
primal deity, 113
of purity, 112–15
of smallpox, 88
of thunder, 43, 89, 90, 144
of water, 43, 94, 95
of wealth, 95–6

Gold Coast, 21
Goody, Jack, 32, 123
Greeks, 19, 99, 117
Green, M. M.
  Igbo Village Affairs, quoted, 203,
    214
Greene, Graham, 109
  themes, 20, 21, 22
  Burnt-out Case (A), 20
  Convoy to West Africa, 20
  Heart of the Matter (The), 20
  In Search of a Character, 20
  Journey without Maps, 20

Haggard, Rider
  She, 19
  King Solomon's Mines, 19
  Allan Quartermain, 19
Haiti contrasted with West Africa, 175
harmattan, legend about, 131
Harvard University, 191
Hayford, John Casely
  as a pioneer of West Africa's
    cultural nationalism, 10
  prose style, 194
  Ethiopia Unbound, 13
herbs, curative quality of, 49
"high life" music, 79–80, 149; as
  source of social history, 80
history, sense of in traditional societies,
  133–5
Hoebel, E., 211; quoted, 214
Hoggart, Richard, 3
Homer, 19, 31
Horton, Africanus, as a pioneer of
  West Africa's cultural nationalism,
  10; prose style, 194; and West
  African university, 16
House, Humphrey, 146
human relationships, 204, 209, 216,
  252–3
  in Achebe, 86, 93–4, 103
  in Ekwensi, 103–4
  father–son, 218, 252–3
humanization of mystic characters, 98
humorous characters, *see* comic
  characters
Huxley, Elspeth, 20
  Four Guineas, 20–1
  Walled City (The), 20
    themes of violence and ritual
      murder, 23

Ibadan, 137, 138, 152
Ibadan Government College, 9, 194,
  196
Ibadan University College, 14, 183, 196

Ibo, *see* Igbo
Idemili (god of water), 43, 94, 95, 232
Idowu, B. O., 220
Ife, 65
Igbo people, 48, 83, 94, 204
  art, 65, 66, 67–8, 92
  calendar, 126–7
  census, 126
  conversation in, 163–4
  fatalism, 215–16
  gods and goddesses, 43, 44, 67–8,
    99–100
  kings, 237
  legends, 131
  masquerade, 68–9, 211
  music, 54–64 *passim*
  mythology, 44, 46
  oral tradition, 32
  osu (cult slaves) among, 84
  relevance of earth to culture, 212–15
  weekdays, 133
Igbo Women's Riot, 241–2
Igboland
  currency, 253–4
  economy of traditional society,
    248–54
  land tenure system, 248
  missionary penetration in, 223
  traditionalist–Christian relation, 245
  wealth, success and power in, 248–9
Igbo-Ukwu, 65
Ijaw oral tradition, 174
Ijele (masquerade), 69
Ikenga (god of fortune), 67–8, 228, 231,
  255
Ikoyi, 51, 150
Iliad, 31
"Improvement" unions, 36, 118, 151,
  178, 195
indirect rule by the British, 240, 241
individualism, 81
  in art, 73–4, 75, 77
  in characterization, 84, 90, 102,
    103–4, 120–1
  in Ekwensi, 103–4
  in Soyinka, 115
Iyi-ocha (god), 147
Izaga (masquerade), 71

Jackson, Thomas Horatio, 194
Jahn, Janheinz, 175
John XXIII (Pope), 246
Johnson, Samuel, 13
Jones, G. I., 211; quoted, 212
Jos Government School, 194
judicial process,
  see under traditionalism

Kafanchan, 73
Kazantzakis, N.
  Christ Recrucified, 108
  Zorba the Greek, 155
Kenya, 20
Kettle, Arnold, 260
Killam, J. D., 204
kinship ties, 211, 216
Knight, G. Wilson, 196
kolanut, 161–2, 164, 258
Krio, 188, 191

Lagos, 9, 50, 51, 111, 147, 178, 195
  dramatic society in, 11
  as setting for urban novels, 103, 104,
    118, 137, 138, 149–52
  writing by Graham Greene based
    on visit, 20
land tenure, 248
language, 155
  and status differentiation, 190
  conversation, 160–9
  group style, 183–7
  habits, 169–74
  linguistic differentiation in urban
    novels, 190–2
  linguistic realism, 169–77
  magical, 175–7
  proverbs, 155–60
  in rural novels, 155ff
  see also English language
Latin America, 15, 79, 175
Lawrence, D. H., 117, 170
Laye, Camara
  Dream of Africa (A)
    traditional artistic values in, 72
    quoted, 72
  African Child (The), 70
    drum speech in, 63
Leavis, F. R.
  Culture and Environment, 19
Leavis, Q. D.
  Fiction and the Reading Public, 19
Leeds University, 196
legends, 65; Igbo l., 131
Legon University, 183
Leopard, 107
Lerner, Daniel, 3, 7
Leverhulme fellowship, 196
literacy, 8; in Achebe, 6; and West
  African novel, 3–6; role in colonial
  West Africa, 32–3; statistics for
  Nigeria, 14, 27
literary tradition, 33–4; defined, 32
lizards, 176, 234, 241
Lloyd, P. C.; quoted, 241–2
Loader, William

Guinea Stamp (The), 21
  theme of violence in, 23
No Joy of Africa, 21
locusts, legends about, 131
London, 21, 36, 42, 119
London Transcription Centre, 195
Lugard, Lord, 20

Mabogunje, A. L., quoted, 245
MacIver, R. M., quoted, 202
magic, 38, 49, 80, 208; in Achebe,
  132–3; belief in, 33; its place in
  West African novels, 39; in
  masquerade performance, 70–1
magical language, 175–7
Malinowski, B., 160; quoted, 230
Mammy-Watta, 115
manillas, 253
Mannoni, D. O., quoted, 262
Marxism, 101
Masai people, 19
mask, *see* masquerade
masquerade, 56, 58, 64, 65, 88, 91, 127,
  129
  in Igboland, 211
  magic in, 70–1
  rural and urban compared, 73
  significance of, 69–70
  types, 68–9, 95
mass communication, 8, 33; and the
  novel, 7; compared with the town-
  crier, 7; effect on old social order, 7
Mbari art houses, 65, 131
Mecca, 75
medicine, traditional, 48–9
Meek, C. K., 215
"Melo-Dramatic Society", 11
middle class, West African, 8–14
Milton, John, 11
Minna, 194
missionaries, Christian, 72, 201; and
  dating of novels, 136; and formal
  education, 9; conversion of
  vernaculars into writing, 11; writings
  on West Africa, 18
moon, as measure of time, 124, 127,
  128, 132; mystical association of,
  47–8
Morris, William, 19
Murry, John Middleton, quoted, 17
music, 76
  in Achebe, 91–2
  audience of, 59–60
  Christian, 55
  for masquerade, 69, 70, 71
  popular, 79–80
  radio, 80

music (*cont.*)
  its rhythmic structure, 59–60
  in West African novels, 53–64, 79–80
mythology, 44, 46

naming of characters
  in Achebe, 82
  in Nwankwo, 82
  in Okara, 82, 106
  praise names, 82–3
  significance of names, 82
nationalism, cultural, 14–17 *passim*
nature
  cultivated, 51–2
  its divine and metaphysical powers,
    48–9, 142–3
  as object of veneration, 43
  as refuge for urban characters, 52–3
  in urban West Africa, 49–50
Négritude, 15–16, 17, 175, 265
neurotic characters, 99–101
New York, 36, 118–19
newspapers, 7; use of by middle-class
  elite, 10
Nicol, Abioseh, 194
Niger River, 136, 196, 223
  delta, 254; as setting for Amadi's
    novel, 39
Nigeria, 21, 123, 190, 193, 231
  civil war, 194
  Eastern, 27, 102, 241
  External Broadcasting Service, 196
  literacy statistics, 14, 27
  Northern, 20, 21, 27, 32, 194
  as seen by Joyce Cary, 22
  as setting for Joyce Cary's novels, 21
  Western, 27, 241
Nigerian Information Service, 194
Nketia, Kwabena, 16
Norsemen, 19
novels: compared with pamphlet
  literature, 13; development in West
  Africa, 11; effects of early politics
  on, 14
Nri priesthood, 130, 238
Nwankwo, Nkem, 7, 37, 116
  biography, 8
  Danda
    backsliding from Christianity,
      245–6
    characterization in, 84, 85, 86,
      87–8, 92, 100
    cultural change, evidence of, 255–6
    culture contact and change in,
      242–4
    dancing, 59
    dating, 254

festivals in, 56
masquerade in, 69, 70–1
music in, 54–6, 57–8, 61–2, 64
mystical association of nature in,
  46
naming of characters in, 82
ritual art in, 67
sense of functional time in, 135
setting in, 146
theme of darkness in treatment of
  setting, 143
time and space indicators in, 124,
  127
traditionalist–Christian relation,
  244–5
quoted, 55, 57, 59, 61, 64, 69, 71,
  87, 124
Nzekwu, Onuorah, 24, 37, 116
  biography, 8
  Blade Among the Boys, 55–6
    backsliding from Christianity in,
      247
    dating of, 254
    festivals in, 56
    rural and urban masquerades
      compared, 73
    urban–rural connections in, 137
    quoted, 55–6, 73
  Wand of Noble Wood
    role of magic in, 39
    urban–rural connections in, 137

Obatala (god of purity), 112–15
Obeng, R. E.
  Eighteenpence, 13
Obiechina, E. N., 60–1
Obumselu, B. E., 92
O'Connell, Rev. Fr James, quoted, 32
Oedipus, 215
Ogbunike, 45
Ogidi, 196
Ogun (god of creativity), 112–15 *pas-
  sim*, 198
Ogun River, 52–3, 152
oja (flute), 60–1, 64, 92
Ojike, Mbonu, 12
Okara, Gabriel, 37, 115
  biography, 8
  and oral tradition, 171–4
  as a materialist, 174
  Voice (*The*)
    artistic individualism in, 77
    biblical symbols in, 108–10
    characterization, 82, 101, 104–10
    death of traditional spirit in, 257
    linguistic individuation in, 184
    linguistic realism in, 171–4

music in, 55
naming of characters in, 82
narrative method in, 148–9
setting conveyed in symbolism and
    imagery, 147
quoted, 77, 101, 109, 148, 171–2,
    174
Okigbo, Christopher, 26
Onitsha, 45, 50, 136, 137, 201, 220;
    and early missionary activities, 223
Onitsha Market literature,
    see under pamphlet literature
Oracle, 45, 128, 131, 132, 208, 213
oral tradition
    and characterization, 107, 118
    and West African culture, 26
    and West African writers, 25–8
    compared with literary tradition,
        33–4
    defined, 31–2
    Iliad as an example of, 31
    limitations of, 3, 4, 6
    mechanisms of, 33
    Okara's indebtedness to, 171–4
    recording of, 11, 16
oratory in village assembly, 205–6
Orisa-nla (the primal deity), 113
ostracism, 85, 86
osu (cult slaves), 84, 103; as early
    converts to Christianity, 222
Ottenberg, Simon, 4
Owu (god), 114
Oxbridge, 229
Ozo (title-cult), 83

palm-wine, 76, 135
pamphlet literature: of Grub Street,
    London, 13; of Onitsha Market, 12,
    13, 78, 108, 177, 189
Paris as home of French African
    writers, 16
Parrinder, Geoffrey, 220
patriotic societies,
    see "Improvement" unions
Perham, Margery, 20
"phatic communion", 160
pidgin English,
    see English language, pidgin
Pilot (*The*), 12
politics and government,
    see under traditionalism
Pope, Alexander, quoted, 31
Portuguese writers on West Africa, 18
praise-names, 83
press: and literary awakening, 12;
    effect on traditional way of life, 7
printing press, spread of, 12, 13

proverbs
    in Achebe, 157–60, 181
    as aid to character study, 157–8
    as aid to plot development, 159–60
    in Armah, 179–80
    bastardization of, 179–81
    derivation, 156
    in rural novels, 155–60
    rural-urban uses of compared, 181
    in Soyinka, 178–9
    in urban novels, 177–80
    value of, 155–6
publishers
    Tabansi Bookshop, 13
    Faber and Faber, 17

Radcliffe-Brown, A. R., 216
radio, 80
rainbow, 42
Ramsaran, John, quoted, 26
rats, curative quality of, 49
realism, 117
    French conception of, 104
    linguistic, 169–77; defined, 177
    in linguistic differentiation, 192
    in rural societies, 131
    in traditional sense of history, 133–5
realities, cultural, *see* traditionalism
realities, magical, 70–1, 179
Red Indians, 232
Redfield, Robert
    Little Community (*The*), quoted, 202
reification in West African novels, 174
religion (Christianity)
    and break-up of traditional
        solidarity, 219
    and characterization, 108
    and tradition, 24, 38, 41, 153
    converts, 147, 195, 219, 225;
        backsliding of, 245–6
    music, 58
Richardson, Samuel, 8
Riesman, David, 4
Rousseau, Jean-Jacques, 16, 213
Royal Court Theatre, London, 196
rural life, 36
    and characterization, 82–101
    and conflict of cultures, 84–6
    dominated by nature gods, 43, 44
    farming as main pursuit, 43
    individualism in traditional society,
        84–5
    love for praise-names, 83
    masquerades in, 69–71
    ostracism as penal sanction in, 85, 86
    as represented in novels, 37–41

rural novels
    collectivism in, 140–2
    language, 155–77; group style of,
        186–7; linguistic habits, 169–74;
        magical, 175–7; proverbs, 155–60
    setting, 140–9
    time and space concepts in, 122–36
rural–urban connections, 137

sacrifice, 76, 147
Sarbah, Mensah, 194
satire, 88, 89
Schapiro, Leonard, 18
schools, establishment of, 9
seasons as time indicators, 124–8
Senghor, Léopold Sédar, 16
setting
    idyllic, 144–6
    in individual novelists: Achebe,
        141–4; Aluko, 147; Amadi, 144–6;
        Armah, 153–4; Conton, 154;
        Ekwensi, 147, 149; Nwankwo, 146;
        Nzekwu, 146–7; Okara, 147–9;
        Soyinka, 151–2
    northern and southern Nigeria
        compared, 147
    in rural novels, 140–9
    themes in the treatment of: customs
        and social habits, 146–7; darkness
        and light, 143, 148–9; moonlight,
        143–4; mysticism, 144; rural
        collectivism, 140–2; Yoruba
        metaphysics, 153
    in urban novels, 149–54
Shango (god of thunder), 43, 44, 50, 52
Shaw, Thurstan, 65
Shelley, P. B., quoted, 75
Shils, Edward, quoted, 37, 263
Sierra Leone, 16
    development of education in, 9–10
    English language in, 188, 190, 192,
        193, 194
    as setting for foreign writers, 20, 21
slave trade, 18, 238, 243–4; Olaudah
    Equiano, ex-slave, 251
sound as measure of distance, 129
South Africa, immigrant, 21; music,
    80
Soyinka, Wole, 8, 26, 39, 62, 116
    biography, 196–7
    individualism in, 115
    use of Yoruba religion and
        mythology, 112–15
    Dance of the Forests (A), 112
    "Fourth Stage (The)", 112
    Interpreters (The), 80
        artistic values in, 74–7

characterization, 110–15
    cultivated nature in, 51–2
    as example of linguistic individua-
        tion, 183–4
    linguistic style, 196–8
    metaphysical basis of, 153
    narrative method, 151–2
    proverbs in, 178–9
    setting, 151–2
    status differentiation through
        language, 190
    time and space concepts in, 138–9
    urban–rural connections in, 137
    quoted, 51–3, 74–6, 113, 114, 151,
        178, 179
space concept in rural environment,
    see time and space concepts in rural
    novels
Stephen, Leslie, 31, 42
Stewart, Dr, 136
Stoll, Dennis Gray, 24
    Man in Ebony, 24
sun, as measure of time, 124;
    mystical association of, 47–8
superstitious beliefs, 33–4
surrealism, 175
Swift, Jonathan, 154
symbols
    in art, 65, 66, 68, 73, 77, 78
    biblical, 108
    in characterization, 91, 95, 104,
        108–10, 113
    historical, 134–5
    linguistic in Okara, 173–4
    magical, 175
    in Nzekwu, 146–7
    religious, 211
    in Soyinka, 113
Synge, J. M., 196

Tabansi Bookshop, 13
Tallensi people, earth and culture of,
    212; oral tradition, 32
Tempels, Fr Placide, 38
Tennyson, Alfred, Lord, 11
time and space concepts
    festive indicators, 126–7
    functional time in, 135–6
    historical indicators, 133–5
    market-day indicators of, 128
    natural indicators of, 123–4
    in Nwankwo, 124, 127
    in rural novels, 122–36
    seasonal indicators of, 124–8
    in urban novels, 136–9
Tiv people: age-grade, 211; historical
    time measure of, 2; oral tradition, 32

Tolstoy, L., quoted, 156
Tönnies, F., 214; quoted, 202
tortoise, 87, 100, 107
town-crier, 7, 129, 143, 168, 206
towns, *see* urban setting
tradition, oral, *see* oral tradition
traditional medicine, 48–9
traditionalism (traditional system)
  balanced picture of, 205, 213–14
  conflict with Christianity and foreign
    administration, 219–27, 258
  currency in, 253–4
  defeat of, 228–9
  diplomatic procedure in, 206–8
  economy, 248–54
  essence and ideological base of,
    202, 203, 233
  fatalism in, 215–16
  human relationship in, 204, 209,
    216, 218, 252–3
  judicial process in, 209–12
  kinship ties, 211, 216
  magic in, 33, 70–1, 132–3, 208
  offences and penalties in, 214–15
  politics and government, 205–12
  religion as source of culture conflict
    in, 228
  scope for culture change in, 228
  traditionalist–Christian co-operation,
    243–5
  war in, 205–8, 235–6
  wealth, success and power in, 248–9
  world-view, 37–41
tragic characters, 88, 90–101; in
  Achebe, 90–6
trees, 42; curative quality of, 49; as
  measure of distance, 123; mystical
  and sacred, 45–6
Tucker, Martin, 17
Tutuola, Amos, 16, 26, 39
  Palm-Wine Drinkard (The), 17, 27
Twain, Mark, 156

Ughelli Government College, 9
uli (decorative colour), 66, 69
Umuahia Government College, 9
United States of America,
  see America
universities, 50, 106
urban influence in characterization,
  137–8
urban novels
  language, 183
  linguistic individuation, 183–5
  narrative approaches, 150
  pidgin English in, 187–94
  proverbs in, 177–80

setting, 149–54
  time and space concepts in, 136–9
urban setting, 36
  beliefs, 40–1
  characterization, 102–21 *passim*
  culture, 81
  masquerades, 73
  West Africa: its uniqueness, 49–50;
    love of "high life" music, 79
urban–rural connections, 137
Uzzell, Thomas, 117, 118

Vassa, Gustavus,
  see Equiano, Olaudah
Verga, Giovanni
  Mastro don Gesualdo, 117
"vernacular characters", 155–6
Victorianism, 191, 192, 193
  "Black Victorians", 10, 11, 190;
    and creative writing, 11; literary
    taste, 183; use of English
    language, 190–1
village democracy, 205–6
village life, *see* rural life
village square, functions of, 122–3, 205

Wallace, Edgar, 19, 25
  Green Crocodile (The), 20
Watt, Ian, 8, 32, 123
Waugh, Evelyn, 19
wealth, success and power in
  traditional societies, 248–9
West Africa
  English and French, 15–16, 73, 79
  rural and urban contrasts, 36–7
  unique urban phenomenon, 49–50
  use of English in, 182–3
West African culture, 3, 34–6 *passim*
  cultural nationalism, 15–16
  oral tradition as part of, 26
  rural and urban responses to
    cultural change, 36–7
West African intellectuals, 72; and
  traditional cultures, 37; love for
  cultivated nature, 51–2
West African languages, 174
West African middle class, 8–14
West African *Pilot*, 12
West African writers (foreign), 17–25
West African writers (native), 3, 7, 17
  educational background, 9
  in English, 15–16, 17
  in French, 15–16
  influenced by foreign novelists on
    West Africa, 17, 18
West Indian writers in West Africa, 21
West Indies, 37; immigrants from, 10

295

Williams, Raymond, quoted, 27
Wilson, Godfrey, 33
Wilson, Monica, 33
witchcraft, belief in, 33, 100, 101
women, 83
  and decorative art, 66
  characters, 111
  crops, 250
  employment in traditional Igbo
    society, 251
  masquerade, 69
  riot, 241–2

yams and Igbo economy, 248–50
Yoruba people, 16, 55, 74, 238
  drama, 196
  gods, 43, 110, 112–15 *passim*
  metaphysics, 153
  mythology, 44, 111–15, 197–8
  oral tradition, 32
  tales, 39

Zola, Emile
  Nana, 104
Zulu people, 19